To STAND STILL, *to mark time on one spot, to be contented with the first goal it happens to reach, is never possible in revolution. And he who tries to apply the homemade wisdom derived from parliamentary battles between frogs and mice to the field of revolutionary tactics only shows thereby that the very psychology and laws of existence of revolution are alien to him and that all historical experience is to him a book sealed with seven seals.*

—ROSA LUXEMBURG

T0126208

PRELUDE TO REVOLUTION

PRELUDE TO REVOLUTION
FRANCE IN MAY 1968

Daniel Singer

Haymarket Books
Chicago, Illinois

This edition published in 2013 by
Haymarket Books
PO Box 180165
Chicago, IL 60618
773-583-7884
info@haymarketbooks.org
www.haymarketbooks.org

Trade distribution:
In the US, Consortium Book Sales and Distribution, www.cbsd.com
In Canada, Publishers Group Canada, www.pgcbooks.ca
In the UK, Turnaround Publisher Services, www.turnaround-uk.com
In Australia, Palgrave Macmillan, www.palgravemacmillan.com.au
All other countries, Publishers Group Worldwide, www.pgw.com

ISBN: 978-1-60846-273-5

Cover design and art by Josh On.

Published with the generous support of Lannan Foundation and the
Wallace Global Fund.

Library of Congress Cataloging-in-Publication data is available.

Entered into digital printing April, 2021.

Contents

Is history a succession of disconnected and incomprehensible happenings? Not just a Martian but a conscientious newspaper reader may well have drawn such a conclusion watching the strange French events of 1969. On April 27 by nearly 12 million votes to 10.5 million the French electorate said *Non* for the first time in a Gaullist referendum. The questions put and the bill thus thrown out were irrelevant. What mattered, and the French voters knew it, was that a negative answer would send General de Gaulle into a second retirement at Colombey-les-deux-Églises.

For years the great performer had defied the Americans, toyed with his European rivals, fascinated the Third World. For a decade the General's tall figure had so dominated the French political stage as to conceal the social divisions underneath. His departure, official prophets had warned, would spell crisis and chaos; after him the deluge. But when he duly went, nothing happened. The country did not stir. It barely noticed.

The presidential election that followed in June was as puzzling for our serious newspaper consumer. He had learned that the main threat to Gaullism came from the left. France had a strong Communist party that was being gradually integrated into a popular front coalition with other left-wing groups. There was a strong possibility that France would be the first western country since the cold war to include Communists in its government. But here, in the presidential stakes, instead of a single candidate representing the united left, like François Mitterrand against General de Gaulle back in 1965, were four of them running under their own colors. Their forces were so dispersed they could not even get through the heats, and none of them was present in the final race where the two top contenders run for the presidency of the Republic.

In the place of the expected leftist, he saw somebody completely unknown, a man ignored by the vast majority of Frenchmen only a few months earlier. Alain Poher, the recently appointed leader of the Senate, looked too innocuous, too much the average little middle-class Frenchman, to be true. He seemed to be one of those strange figures that suddenly pop up on the historical stage only to fall back into oblivion. This is exactly what he did, having fulfilled his function—which was to ensure a conservative succession.

Yet what must have floored our informed observer completely was the choice of the successor. It was none other than Georges Pompidou (I nearly wrote Caligula's Horse), the man who, in political terms, was a pure invention of General de Gaulle, the private secretary whom De Gaulle had imposed on the French nation as Prime Minister and who had served him in this new function for six years. Admittedly, in 1968, as Pompidou revealed he had acquired a political life of his own, he was dismissed. But did Frenchmen throw out their monarch to replace him by his discarded dauphin?

The rise and fall of Charles de Gaulle will figure prominently in all future serious discussions about the role of the hero in history, a perfect illustration both of the hero's significance and of the ultimate limitations of his importance. As to the seemingly incomprehensible antics that followed De Gaulle's departure, the story has not been told from its real beginning. Go back to May 1968, to the traumatic crisis that shook France then, and all the pieces will fall neatly into place. The reign of Charles the Tall did not end in April 1969. It ended the previous May. His power, prestige, and policies were shattered, and his apparent triumph at the polls could not put them together again. For the French ruling class he became dispensable there and then. He had been tolerated previously, despite misgivings about the risks of his foreign policy, because he alone was allegedly capable of preventing a social upheaval. This was no longer true. The General was not only dispensable. He was positively a nuisance. After ten years of the legendary hero, it was high time to switch to a more conventional form of conservative rule. Pompidou was perfectly suited for the transition, and the electoral risks were small since the left was shattered as well.

Formally, the funeral of the stillborn popular front was held during the presidential election of 1969. In practice, the popular front, too, was a victim of the previous year's crisis. Not that the Communists at the time had acted in such revolutionary fashion as to exclude themselves from the politics of consensus. On the contrary, they behaved so cautiously as to deserve a medal from the Gaullist, and the international, establishment. Yet even when exercising restraint, French Communists showed their power, while their potential social-democratic allies revealed their weakness. The idea of bringing the Communists into the government as junior partners was thus killed by social realities, and it is difficult to see how it can be revived.

There is a moral in the story briefly summed up above. It is no use trying to understand what happens in France now or what is likely to happen for some time to come without going back to the origins of the current crisis, to the student rising and general strike that took the world by surprise in the spring of 1968.

The lessons of the May crisis are not only true for France, but extend well beyond French frontiers. Take the explosions of protest erupting periodically from Tokyo to San Francisco. If protest movements express only student unrest, society can cope with them. True, education now plays a bigger role in the process of production than in the past, and even a partial disruption of the universities would have serious consequences. Yet a society should be able to live with a revolt limited to the years of apprenticeship. Matters become quite different if the students express discontent with their future jobs, if they foreshadow the revolt of teachers, technicians, scientists, members of what, for lack of a better appellation, must be called the new professional intelligentsia.

Political sociology cannot afford to stage mass upheavals in order to experiment. A crisis like the French one, with the general strike paralyzing the country, provides a unique opportunity for studying the behavior of various social groups. Tentative findings do not seem to confirm the extreme theories about the birth of a new revolutionary class taking the place traditionally attributed to the industrial workers, to the proletariat. Yet they do suggest something equally, if not more, dangerous for established society. They suggest new splits, new cleavages, and new alignments reflecting new social contradictions. The technological transformation started during the last war, and the changes in organization of production it brought about are beginning to have an impact on social forces. Politics is beginning to catch up with economics. When mighty productive forces clash with obsolete social relations, one must have the intellectual horizon of a policeman to explain the resulting unrest in terms of the subversive work of a handful of political agitators.

Such findings are of interest to the world at large, particularly

to the United States, where changes in the technology and organization of production have gone farther than anywhere else. For
Europe, the lessons of the French upheaval are more immediate,
because there the age of conflict has already begun.

If the French crisis had ended on May 13, with a mass celebration of the political victory of students defeated on the barricades, it would have simply been a dramatic highlight in the saga
of student revolt. But it did not end then. It precipitated the
biggest strike in the country's history. Though the nature of the
strike was ambiguous, it nevertheless provided a vital reminder
and a fascinating suggestion. It recalled the paralyzing power of
workers in action. It gave a hint that the modern industrial state
might not be so powerful as it looks. This was enough to inaugurate a new period of struggle. The outbursts of social unrest
throughout Italy since then, aptly described as "creeping May," [1]
the wildcat strikes multiplying throughout western Europe, are
but skirmishes in a new social battle.

The front runs across western Europe, yet it is in France and
Italy that a political breakthrough is most likely. Why? The very
fact that it all started in France raises some additional questions.
Was Gaullism the main cause of the French upheaval? What was
Gaullism's specific nature? In what way did it differ from the general pattern of modern nation-states? Why are French workers,
whose living standards and working conditions are roughly the
same, more liable to take political action than their British or
German counterparts? A few years ago the answers to most of
these questions would have seemed simple. France and Italy are
in the foreground because they have the largest Communist parties. After the French crisis, in which the Communist Party played
a nonrevolutionary, not to say a counter-revolutionary, role, the
conclusion must be more balanced. Communist parties give the
impression that they contributed to create a situation they are
incapable of exploiting.

New contradictions, new forces, new forms of action. The tra-

1. The expression was first used, to the best of my knowledge, by Luigi
Pintor.

ditional union and Party establishment of the labor movement looks as bewildered by the sweep and significance of the new conflicts as are the rulers themselves. Such a general bewilderment is not entirely unprecedented. It usually marks the twilight of a reign.

Could it be that a socialist revolution is beginning, that Marxism is returning to its home ground, to the advanced countries for which it was designed? Put in this way, the question dissociates Marxism from the revolutions carried out in its name in the undeveloped areas of the world—too easy a way out. One cannot hail the October Revolution of 1917 as an epoch-making event, which it undoubtedly was, and forget about its Stalinist and post-Stalinist consequences. One can do it least of all when studying the crises of 1968. Prague, after all, was a counterpoint to Paris.

The Russian invasion of Czechoslovakia, in turn, raises a series of problems transcending Czech frontiers. If the frightened bureaucrats in the Kremlin sent their tanks to crush an experiment threatening the foundations of their neo-Stalinist rule, no country in eastern Europe can run far ahead of Russia. The pace of change is to be dictated by the Soviet Union. But will not the same rulers strike at home if their position is threatened? More than a doubt is thus cast on the possibilities of a peaceful and gradual transition from Stalinism. The revolutionary burden of necessary change in the Soviet bloc is shifted onto the shoulders of the Russian people, the Soviet heirs of October.

This is a rambling preface to what may appear a wandering book. Starting with a study of the unexpected upheaval caused by French students and workers, one is driven to look at the contradictions explaining the sickness of capitalist society, at the clash between productive forces and social relations, at the new movement of protest without a model, at the stifling weight of the unwithering state, and so on. This structure is not due to the author's predilection for digressions; it has an inner logic, at least I hope so, in its development. If the French May crisis was more than a historical incident, its implications and repercussions are international. If May was but a beginning, it must unfold at least on a

European scale. The pace of historical change in Europe has already quickened. The question at the heart of this book is whether the crises of 1968 point to a consolidation of authoritarian rule or whether they herald a new age of European revolution.

This is the place usually reserved for acknowledgments. Unfortunately, the two men I would have liked to thank most—my father, Bernard Singer, and my friend, Isaac Deutscher—cannot read this expression of my gratitude. It is from my parents and Isaac that I first learned what socialism is and what has happened to it in the peculiar circumstances of eastern Europe. Readers familiar with Isaac Deutscher's works will see for themselves the extent of my intellectual debt, a debt that cannot be paid in footnotes. What they can only imagine is the value of a lifelong friendship with such a profound and stimulating mind. But I am not trying to hide behind anybody's authority or prestige. The two men mentioned died shortly before the events that precipitated this book and cannot in any way be held responsible for my conclusions.

All the others who have made this book possible—family, friends, colleagues, participants in the movement who filled gaps in my knowledge—are too numerous to be thanked individually. But the book, in a sense, is collectively theirs. They may disagree with some of its aspects or suggestions. They all share the spirit that inspired it and the purpose for which it was written. I should, therefore, like to make an exception for my friend and colleague, Wendy Hinde, who, while disagreeing with much of the substance and certainly the conclusions of the book, has nevertheless generously contributed to improve its form. Since liberal humbug is so often attacked in the following pages, I am glad here to draw a distinction between personal fairness and political hypocrisy.

I should like to thank Mr. Paul Schmidt and Hill and Wang for permission to use Mr. Schmidt's translations of a few lines from Rimbaud.

DANIEL SINGER

WITHOUT A GUIDING ORGANIZATION *the energy of the masses would dissipate like steam not enclosed in a piston box. But nevertheless what moves things is not the piston, or the box, but the steam.*

—LEON TROTSKY

PART ONE
The Meaning of May

THE SUN WAS SHINING over Montparnasse as, red flags flying, the demonstration got on the move. There were some thirty thousand marchers, most of them young, the students outnumbering the workers. They were chanting together in a fearless mood. Amid the slogans old and new, one was again predominant, the slogan forever associated with the French May Movement, the jerky, confident, infectious, "Ce n'est . . . qu'un début. . . . Continuons le . . . combat."

'Tis but a beginning. A skeptic listening in was entitled to doubt. It was June 1, 1968. The shaken Gaullists had regained their poise. General de Gaulle, "the royal captain of this ruin'd band," had just recovered his voice and authority to proclaim that he was soldiering on. Georges Séguy, the Communist leader of the biggest trade union, had just called on his troops to make an orderly retreat. The police, its confidence restored, was not going to put up with any more mass demonstrations. It looked like the turn of the tide, the beginning of the end.

And yet the young students and workers were in the right mood. This was no funeral procession. They had not come to mourn the past. They could proudly look toward the future. Beaten, betrayed, yet undefeated, they had just shown Europe the way. They had brought hope again, prefacing a new chapter in revolutionary history.

Not Always in Primitive Lands

The cobblestones in the Latin Quarter are now covered with asphalt. How convenient it would be for many if the memory of the four weeks that shook France could be similarly coated over with some artificial layer of oblivion. Gaullists might then forget those last days of May when they trembled, expecting to be swept away by the broom of history. Communist leaders could parade with greater ease in their revolutionary disguise. There would be a sigh of relief, and not only in France. In Washington,

3

London, and Moscow, politicians, analysts, editorial-writers, would be able to go back to conventional wisdom, to the comfortable realm of consensus, to the predictable world of coexistence only marginally disturbed by war in Vietnam.

But the revolutionaries did not dream, and their opponents did not go through a nightmare. The barricades, the general strike, the social and political upheaval, were no hallucination. Even the asphalt now concealing the cobblestones is simply a sign that the Gaullist regime fears it might all happen again. (Policemen, like generals, may always be getting ready for the previous war.)

There is no asphalt of oblivion. Yet, if you cannot forget a traumatic experience, you may at least try to distort its meaning and minimize its importance. Did it not all end well with a Gaullist victory at the polls? Are not all the levers of power still in safe Gaullist hands? The staunchest defenders of the established order find only crumbs of comfort in such rhetorical questions. However calm the surface may seem, they know that something dramatic, if unexpected, has really happened and that politics will never be the same again.

Why should establishments tremble? What is the ghost, released in Paris, that once again haunts Europe? It is the old specter of revolution. The main message of the May crisis is unmistakable: A revolutionary situation can occur in an advanced capitalist country. Not just a *putsch,* a change of rulers or of regime, but revolution. Not in backward Asia or explosive Latin America, but in the heart of allegedly affluent Europe. Students have rebelled on all continents from Berkeley to Tokyo. Only in France, so far, has their rebellion spread to industrial workers, precipitating the biggest general strike France has ever known and, by the same token, raising the question of power in the country.

That a socialist revolution can take place in an advanced capitalist country, it will be objected, is not at all a new proposition. It is an echo of the *Communist Manifesto,* a Marxist truism more than a hundred years old. Admittedly. Only as the years passed, the proposition lost a great deal of its credibility. It was dismissed as nonsense not only by the spokesmen for modern capitalism, by the apologists of the affluent society, by academic clowns performing on television; until the French crisis the proposition was also doubted, questioned, or flatly rejected by socialists, by left-wing critics of capitalist society. Some rejected the prospect explicitly, like Professor Herbert Marcuse, who, drawing on the American example, concluded that the working class could no longer fulfill its mission as "midwife of history." Others did it implicitly like Marshal Lin Piao, by extending to world scale the Chinese precedent of a revolutionary countryside surrounding the towns.[1] By the mid-sixties, the truism was reduced to the role of a relic, venerated by many, believed by very few. It had ceased to perform its proper function as a guide for a global strategy.

There was no lack of historical reasons for such basic skepticism. More than fifty years had elapsed since Lenin and the Bolsheviks showed mankind that workers could seize power and hold it. But the Russian leaders, bred on classical Marxism, were well aware that the tools at their disposal had been designed for a more modern soil. To lift Russia from its backwardness they were relying on the help of socialist western Europe. They were pinning their hopes on the spread of revolution. And when these hopes were not fulfilled, Russia had to modernize on its own, to carry out its own industrial revolution. The process Russia had to undergo was vividly described as "primitive socialist accumulation,"[2] while the method through which this was done, the political system that grew with it, bore the dreaded name of the ruthless ruler who presided over the transformation. Russia, its neighbors, and the labor movement at large are still paying a price

1. In fairness, it must also be added, first, that in the Preface to the French edition of *One Dimensional Man,* written before the May crisis, Marcuse foresaw a possible exception to the rule in the cases of France and Italy, and, second, the Chinese, unlike the Russians, hailed and welcomed the French May Movement from the very start.

2. An expression used by V. Smirnov, elaborated back in 1924 by E. Preobrazhensky in *The New Economics* (republished in English by Clarendon Press, Oxford, 1965).

for Stalinism. Or would it be more correct to say for the failure of the revolution to spread westward?

The Soviet Union survived. After a long pause, the revolution even spread, sometimes from below, often from above, but always in relatively primitive surroundings. Until the last war and during its immediate aftermath one could find plenty of valid explanations why revolutionary opportunities, which did arise in western Europe, were not seized. There was the Nazi danger, the subordination of Communist parties to Russia's interests—some would say to the interests of the only workers' state—and immediately after the war the massive presence of American troops on European soil. In the last two decades, however, years of relative stability and fairly rapid growth throughout the western world, the prospect of revolution seemed to be vanishing. The West, its prophets argued, was entering the age of consensus. In plain language this meant the age in which the main contesting parties would play the rules of the game, accept the established order, and differ only marginally over the management of capitalism. And there were signs that the big Communist parties of France and Italy could also be fitted into this pattern.

Glancing back over the last fifty years, one questions whether the western labor movement, having failed to come to Russia's rescue, was then paid back in its own coin. The problem is complex, and this is not the place to analyze it thoroughly. Stalin, after all, cannot be blamed for all western failures, while the impact of the Soviet Union on the international labor movement has been many-sided. On the one hand, the survival of the U.S.S.R., its transformation from a primitive country into the second industrial power in the world, in other words the road from the land of the muzhik to that of the Sputnik, inspired millions of workers throughout the world and spurred them to action. On the other, turning the more or less necessary evil into virtue, Russia's primitive accumulation, with its inequalities and injustices, its bureaucratic rule and reign of terror, was raised to the status of a socialist model. Professional anti-Communists, painting in black, and Soviet officials, using exclusively bright colors, were agreed on at least one thing—namely, that what they were painting was social-ism. In the circumstances, in wealthier countries, where workers enjoyed a better life, it was quite easy to make propaganda along the simple lines that if this was the Workers' Paradise, let us rather have the Capitalist Hell or Social-Democratic Purgatory. And such propaganda had a great deal of success.

Squeezed between these two conflicting lines, a genuine social-ist was in a strangely defensive position. He had to defend the Soviet Union against the distortions of western propaganda. Si-multaneously, he had to explain that public ownership of the means of production is a necessary but not a sufficient prerequi-site for socialism, by the same token denying to Russia the title of socialist and meeting, therefore, the wrath of Communist offi-cialdom. The double pressure lost some of its power after Stalin's death, with the end of the cold war and the dismantlement of the once monolithic Communist movement. Since the prospect of revolution, however, was simultaneously receding on the western horizon, the scope for action for a socialist seemed also to be shrinking. He could strive at home for more or less radical re-forms and combine this task with an auxiliary role in the revo-lutionary struggle apparently limited to the have-not nations of the world. In the spring of 1968 this is how the situation was viewed by most left-wingers in Rome or Paris, London or Bonn. It is this deceptive picture that France's abortive revolution has torn apart, offering an entirely new perspective.

It is not being suggested for a moment that aid for heroic Viet-nam or the defense of the besieged Cuban Republic has lost its importance. On the contrary, it is being suggested that progressive Europeans can now play a more significant part in world affairs by starting with action at home. From the little that has been said, one can draw the conclusion that the message of May—the very possibility of revolution in an advanced capitalist country—changes completely the whole international equation.

A revolution from below, a spontaneous upheaval in a country like France, with its level of industrialization, its general culture, the degree of development of its workers, and the political sym-

pathy of a highly skilled intelligentsia, would be quite different
from the pioneering effort of the Bolsheviks. France should not
be compared with Russia now, but rather with backward Mother
Russia, which left its imprint on subsequent Soviet development.
The task of a revolutionary movement in a country like France
would not be to seek a short-cut, "rifle-in-hand" toward industrialization. It would be to search, on the tangible basis of capitalist
achievement, for a new form of democracy, including industrial
democracy, that does not just rest on an occasional ballot; to look
for a system combining broad planning with effective workers'
control; to offer a new conception of labor and leisure, fighting
against the discontents of the so-called consumer society; and to
harness the enormous potential of modern science and technology, not for the perpetuation of society as it is but for the fulfillment of this new vision. It is in Paris rather than Prague that the
oft-mentioned marriage between socialism and freedom has a
chance of being crowned with success and of attracting the attention of the world.

An advance on the still uncharted road toward socialism could
not for very long be confined within French frontiers. The Italian
border might be the first to be crossed. A socialist France, as we
shall see, would be bound to influence its Common Market partners. Yet the influence would not stop there. Budapest, Prague,
and Warsaw could not remain indifferent to this new center of
attraction. And why not Moscow, Leningrad, and Kiev? After
all, this would be merely the old Bolshevik dream come true, admittedly after a delay of half a century. The Bolshevik dream
fulfilled does not mean that it would have the blessing of Messrs.
Brezhnev, Kosygin, and colleagues. Russia's bureaucratic leaders
know only too well that any revival of socialist democracy would
spell the doom of the post-Stalinist system.

Paradoxically, only a France seeking a socialist solution could
sustain the otherwise empty dream of Gaullist foreign policy,
turning nationalist gestures into a coherent policy. Stopping the
"American invasion"? Only a socialist France would be in a position to supply the planned means and a valid reason for resisting

the challenge of American capitalism; it could turn to the people of Europe and tell them why, in the name of which alternative, they should reject the "American way of life." Europe "from the Atlantic to the Urals"? Here again, only a France building socialism could hope through its infectious example gradually to whittle down the present great divide. Finally, a socialist France, showing the way to Europe, would exercise more than a verbal influence from Paraguay to Pnompenh. The potential fallout not from a nuclear but from a revolutionary *force de frappe* can hardly be exaggerated.

The Vanishing Vanguard

Let us not get carried away by what might have been or what might still be. At this stage it is necessary to explain why it has not happened, why the revolutionary beginnings fizzled out into an electoral farce. The revolutionary students dared to do what had seemed unthinkable. Bewildered, the government blundered. It hit first and surrendered afterward. The lesson of this surrender was not lost on the workers: Through direct action it was possible to force the impregnable state, and the employers, to yield. The workers, in turn, staged sit-down strikes and occupied factories all over the country. The spontaneous forces carried the movement as far as they could against the opposition of all official establishments. There was, however, no party, no body, no organization to take over and carry the movement to its logical conclusion—that is, the seizure of power.

Yet France has a big Communist party, which claims that its historical birthright is to fulfill this very function. For half a century it insisted that it was different from all other political parties, *"un parti pas comme les autres."* It justified its rigid discipline, its "democratic centralism"—or, if you prefer, the absence of inner democracy—by the Bolshevik heritage and the need to be ready when the hour of revolution should strike. And when it struck, the self-appointed "vanguard of the working class" found itself in the rear, dragging the French workers by their overalls along the road to electoral defeat. On this occasion, the party cannot produce any overriding external factor to justify its negative action. There was no Nazi threat, no apparent risk of American intervention at the time, and Stalin is dead. Waldeck Rochet, the party's secretary-general, and his colleagues must shoulder responsibility themselves.

The extraordinary conduct of the French Communist party is the second historical lesson of the May crisis. Its performance is so crucial to an understanding of the events as well as to an analysis of the prospects that it will figure prominently in this story. Already here, however, one objection must be tackled— the inevitable Communist argument that the party behaved in such an orderly electoral fashion because the situation was not revolutionary. Naturally, history does not allow for experiments, and there are no laboratories in which a situation could be analyzed, then scientifically labelled "quasi-revolutionary," "prerevolutionary," or whatnot. The examination must, therefore, stick to established facts. The Communist party does admit that the strike was "unprecedented," the situation "exceptional." The only question, therefore, is whether the Communist leaders did everything in their power to exploit this exceptional situation to the full and, if a successful revolution was impossible, to turn the May crisis into a dress rehearsal. Even the party-liners, deep in their hearts, know that there is only one answer. As the story unfolds, we shall see that all attempts to change the nature of the strike, to create a power parallel to that of the government, that all efforts to set up revolutionary action committees or let the strikers run the factories themselves—that all this had to be done against the opposition of the Communist-dominated union, the Confédération Générale du Travail (General Confederation of Labor), or CGT. The party was not the driving force in this movement. It was the permanent brake.

In the authorized versions of what happened produced since then by Communist writers the party, naturally enough, assumes a more heroic posture. But the elaborate constructions can hardly conceal one awkward fact, namely the spectacular failure of the attempt to bring the strike to end in the middle of the crisis. The unions, the government, and the employers reached a draft compromise in the early hours of Monday, May 27. That very same morning the car workers of Renault rejected the compromise, and their resounding *Non* spread throughout the country, showing that the mood of the workers was more militant, more radical, than that of their spokesmen and thereby undermining the whole Communist thesis. Yet it would be equally distorting and inaccurate to suggest that the ten million strikers refusing to go back to work were all full-fledged revolutionaries determined to bring down the Gaullist regime, nay, to abolish capitalism. If they had been so politically conscious no party apparatus could have stopped them, but there is no precedent for such political consciousness of the masses.

Anyone who during those crucial May days mingled with the workers and listened carefully to exchanges outside factory gates emerged with a more complex impression. The French workers had just recovered their collective strength. They, too, were somewhat surprised and bewildered by the discovery. They felt rather dimly that no wage increase, no material concession, could be really big enough to match their new political power. They were half-consciously aware that fatter pay envelopes would be more or less rapidly cut down to size by rising prices, that to consolidate their gains, to alter their condition, they had to bring down the whole system. All this, however, was diffuse, semiconscious, barely articulate. The famous definition of Sieyès for the third estate fitted perfectly the mood of the French working class: It had been nothing, it could be everything, it wanted to be something. But to turn such a loose aspiration into a decisive political force required guidance and strategy. The Communist party was either unwilling or unable to provide them. There was no time to improvise a substitute in the heat of battle.

Absence of a revolutionary strategy is probably the chief among the many reasons put forward to explain the Fabian tactics of the Communist party. Undoubtedly there were many other considerations. Thus, Gaullist foreign policy, with the advantages it holds for the Soviet Union, cannot be left entirely out of account, though it mattered only marginally: Western Communist parties are no longer so obedient to Moscow's orders. Fear of Gaullist repression may genuinely have been a factor. A more important one was the reaction of a bureaucracy faced with a movement it had not initiated, a spontaneous movement spurred by ultra-leftists, which threatened to overwhelm the traditional left-wing establishment. On the other hand, fear of competition may have driven the Communists to more radical moves. On balance, the mainspring of their action may well have been the absence of a vision, the gradual conversion to an exclusively parliamentary line.

During the Gaullist Republic the Communists had ceased to be the untouchables of French politics. For several years before the crisis they had been working with relative success for the formation of a new popular front, an electoral alliance with the socialists and the radicals then regrouped within the Fédération de la Gauche Démocrate et Socialiste (Federation of the Democratic and Socialist Left), or FGDS. It was in this frame of mind that the Communist leaders faced an entirely unexpected situation. With their eyes glued to the electoral horizon, they tried to fit a revolutionary development into a parliamentary pattern. Their somewhat childish hope was that in some magic way the movement would speed up the formation of a popular-front government with Communist ministers. It is difficult to believe that this hope was genuine. The Gaullists were in power and could only be thrown out by popular pressure. As for the unlimited general strike, the main instrument of such pressure, it had never been an electoral weapon. And so the Communist leaders, the new standard-bearers of law and order, which under the circumstances meant capitalist law and order, were leading their troops to certain defeat.

If the western Communists have now traveled quite a long way along the social-democratic road—that is, if they have implicitly accepted a share in the management of capitalist society—they have not traveled far enough to be lumped together with Mr. Wilson's Labour party, Herr Brandt's Social-Democrats, or Signor Nenni's United Socialists. The difference does not lie simply in slogans, banners, or party statutes. After all, it was only in 1958 that the German Social-Democrats officially repudiated their Marxist charter. The Labour party waited till 1960 to emasculate its famous clause four, with its provision for "the common ownership of means of production, distribution, and exchange." As to the French socialist party, it is still bound in principle to eliminate the exploitation of man by man. Yet nobody in his senses would seriously suggest that Wilson, Brandt, or Guy Mollet are a menace to private property. Dusty statutes simply survive long after they have ceased to bear any relation to the practical performance of a movement. For Communist parties, however, the problem is still more complex. If they drop their revolutionary program, they lose their *raison d'être* and run the risk of finding a competitor, of being overtaken on their left.

A dual pressure forces them into a contradictory posture. Their wish for a popular front, for an alliance with parties well within the capitalist system, drives them to accept a minimum program of reforms that must exclude any measures clashing with the inner logic of that system. At the same time, they must proclaim that their real objective is the destruction of capitalism. The devoted party member who, come rain or come shine, sells *L'Humanité* at street corners on Sunday morning must have the feeling that his action, however humble, is a contribution to the ultimate transformation of man's estate. The party gives increasing signs of a split personality. In its everyday clothes, it looks like the others and practices the same narrow reformism. In its Sunday best, it preaches to the faithful the doctrine of revolution in the Marxist sense of the term—that is, the seizure of power by one class from another, implying a radical change in all property and other social relations.

Gradually the Sunday preaching is becoming only a routine. But in times of normal stress the contradiction between theory and practice can be concealed. The militant can maintain his conviction that the Day will come. It is when something like dawn appears on the horizon that real trouble starts. The passion with which the party press abused the revolutionary students during the crisis, outbidding in its wrath official Gaullist propaganda, the insults directed since then against all ultra-leftists, must be recorded now because they will be disbelieved in the future. Yet all these violent attacks make sense. An individual vituperates in this way when he has an uneasy conscience. A party does it when it feels that it is failing to fulfill its historical mission. And woe to the heretic who dares to remind it of its political conscience. If he is not outshouted, he may be believed.

The very ambiguity of the Communist party is both a significant symptom and a political factor in itself. The French party cannot openly reveal a change of color. Waldeck Rochet must still proclaim that it is "truly revolutionary" because of the members, because of the rank and file. Intellectuals now feel ill at ease within its ranks, and its hold on the French intelligentsia is incomparably looser than in the years after the war. The party has also lost much of its influence among the young in general and students in particular. Nevertheless, up to now a radical French workman would feel that his natural home was the party or the CGT. This explains why during the crisis it was difficult to improvise a revolutionary organization and why it may still not be easy to set in motion a new movement. At the same time, it shows that the temper of the French workers is more militant than in most neighboring countries. The Communist parties of France and Italy have plenty of differences. But the two countries have something in common. They have the two biggest Communist parties in western Europe. And this is one reason why, in spite of all that has been said, France and Italy should figure at the top of Europe's revolutionary agenda.

In politics, as in war, an able commander takes advantage of the weaknesses of his opponents. When General de Gaulle, the main crisis over, frightened the French people with the dangers of "totalitarian communism," it may have sounded ironical in retrospect and certainly ungrateful. Ungrateful, but tactically clever. The Communists in this crisis got the worst of both worlds. They were not daring enough to exploit an exceptional situation. But they had a sufficiently revolutionary reputation to be used to scare political innocents. The General, once he knew that the Communists would not act, had no reason to spare their feelings. The coexistence between Gaullism and Communism in France is as complicated and full of contradictions as the coexistence between the two superpowers on a world scale. Occasional common interests do not mean that there is any love lost. Whatever their motives on this occasion, the Communists enabled General de Gaulle to recover and to survive with their tacit blessing. The unexpected tide receded. France, this time, had no revolution.

When History Quickens Its Pace

No revolution, yet many of the symptoms of one. Whoever, living through those days in France, dared to stick his neck outside the safety of his room had plenty to see and to learn. It was not just a question of barricades, of tear gas in the eyes, or of the noise of concussion grenades. Peering through the yellowish atmosphere left by the gas, he could perceive what happens to a society when history quickens its pace, when the levers of power do not seem to respond to their masters, when factories stand idle while many minds begin to work on their own; in short, when the seemingly passive masses suddenly occupy the center of the political stage. Students of political science learned more about the nature of society in a few weeks in the street than they had learned in years in lecture halls. In a sense they learned all sorts of things that a conventional university is designed not to teach them. And they were not alone. A whole nation had a refresher course on The State and Revolution.

To start with revolution itself: A subtle propaganda, aided by the image of Stalinism, had managed to create the legend that revolutions are not only bloody and useless, but that they are also gray, dreary, regimented, and of course inspired, directed, and paid for from abroad. True, the most recent one to succeed, the Cuban, hardly fitted the pattern, but this could be put down to the "Latin-American temperament." Now a movement springing up in the very heart of Europe showed something quite different. It showed that, at least in its initial stages, a socialist revolution is carried out with spontaneity, freedom, and egalitarianism. Spontaneity and improvisation were probably the main features of the May Movement. Its slogans were full of popular wit, but also, since they were inspired by students, they had a surrealist tone, symbolized in the assertion that "imagination has seized power." Freedom of speech could be observed not only in the interminable debates at the Sorbonne. It was also strangely present in the heat of action. In the early days, when the Latin Quarter was barred by the police, students used to gather for demonstrations nearby, in the Place Denfert-Rochereau. It was moving to watch their spokesmen up on the statue of the lion in the middle of the square, debating among themselves and then with the mass of demonstrators about the direction to take: Shall we march on Broadcasting House or the prison or the Ministry of Justice? The decision somehow emerged from this collective dialogue.

New situations produce new men. This is not to deny the role of active minorities, without which the student explosion might have taken quite a different shape, nor the role of the individual in history. The fact that the Union Nationale des Étudiants de France (National Union of French Students), or UNEF, had at its head a young man, Jacques Sauvageot, with a sense of the occasion and an ear for the mood of the crowd, was important in shaping the course of events. The fact that a lecturers' union, the Syndicat National de l'Enseignement Supérieur (National Union of Higher Education), or SNESup, had as its secretary a dynamic young scientist, Alain Geismar, who proved a man of action, was equally important. Yet the third name that springs to mind—that of Daniel Cohn-Bendit—raises immediately the whole question of leadership. Not that this gifted student of sociology did not possess the talents of a born leader of men. He clearly did. But the group to which he belonged—the March 22 Movement—denied the need for leaders and considered its more prominent members as simply spokesmen for the rank and file, and interchangeable ones at that.

Indeed, "Danny the Red" was in part built up by the press, which needed to have idols or bogeys, and which found in him a marvelously eloquent counterpart to Germany's "Rudi the Red." For once the sensational press, unwittingly, performed a major service. Because Danny was Jewish and legally a German citizen, because the French government thought it clever not to allow him back to France, some fifty thousand young Frenchmen, standing within sight of the Bastille, shouted at the top of their voice: "We are all German Jews." It was an unforgettable scene that at once became part of revolutionary lore.

It will be argued later that the May Movement was exceptionally spontaneous, probably too exclusively spontaneous to last. At first, it improvised its action step by step with an extraordinary skill, guided by some collective instinct. Then it met the bureaucratic machine and after some sturdy efforts failed to overcome this resistance, to drive upward. Since the revolutionary engine cannot stop halfway up the hill, it had to back down. How much organization a revolution needs to succeed, and what kind of an organization—these, as we shall see, are among the most crucial and controversial problems of our time. What the French experience, however, confirms unmistakably is that no revolution can be the work of clever manipulators or foreign agents. To gather momentum a movement must release pent-up discontents. It must, therefore, correspond to the mood of the people. Revolution, after all, as Trotsky put it, is "the forcible entrance of the masses into the realm of rulership over their own destiny."

Our wide-eyed student of politics learned also a great deal about the state, or rather about its seamy side. The task of academic wisdom is to deny that the state is the expression of a class, that it corresponds to a system of production and property; to insist on the variety of mediating functions performed by the state; to present it as something abstract, expressing if not the whole nation at least the general will; to conceal the springs of its

repressive action. Then, suddenly, when their colleagues are arrested, the students refuse to follow the routine. They do not go
home to sign a petition. They fight back. The state, then, takes
its elaborate mask off and assumes the shape of the gendarme
with a truncheon. When the workers join the students and things
get really serious, tanks appear in the background as the ultimate
source of power or legitimacy. It is to Baden-Baden that General
de Gaulle went to seek his real investiture among the army commanders. May was undeniably a month for learning. To take just
one other example, judges sentencing students to jail and then
releasing them a few days after to suit the government's whims
taught the student more about separation of powers than a hundred lectures on the principles of Montesquieu.

The lessons were absorbed the more easily since the prevailing
ideology was crumbling. Its purpose, somebody wittily noticed,
is to drive the flock in the desired direction while allowing space
between the sheep so that each can preserve its illusion of independence, initiative, and individualism. Wits by definition over-
simplify. Ideological conditioning does not prevent movement in
more than one direction. Democracy, however formal, differs
from dictatorship, and France under Gaullism is not a totalitarian
state. But the amount of freedom allowed is inversely propor-
tional to the strength of the pressures building up within society.
The time for democratic niceties is not when pressures have
reached the bursting point. Yet this is also the moment when the
complex conditioning machine gets out of order. It gets bogged
down because though the buttons are still being pressed, individuals for once fail to respond.

Not all those who rebel are heroes, pioneers fighting for a new
age. A revolution that seems to be succeeding also attracts a number of timeservers who climb on the bandwagon when it seems to
be driving toward victory. Above all, however, a revolutionary
situation awakens those who are slumbering; it attracts into the
movement those who yesterday seemed passive. The reason is
quite human. Risks that looked excessive when only marginal
gains were at stake are suddenly worthwhile for the sake of real,

radical change, and one result of such a social upheaval is that everything seems possible. In France that May the great surprise was the strike of state television. The small screen was General de Gaulle's favorite instrument for propaganda, his chosen weapon. But in the second half of the crisis even the hand-picked television stars refused to be their master's voice. Journalists joined the producers and technicians in a nationwide stoppage.

Even before that, reporters on France's commercial radio stations, by giving vivid live broadcasts of clashes between the police and the students, had been serving truth rather than the interests of the advertisers on whom their stations depend. In view of what was at stake, the press itself did not entirely fulfill its conditioning function. The political vacuum precipitated an ideological void, and this in turn was filled by posters and pamphlets, by leaflets and a spate of new journals. Some of the magazines had actually existed before, but the crisis provided them for the first time with a mass public. Meanwhile, the traditional molders of public opinion, the prophets of the dominating ideology, were either silent or on the defensive. They recovered their full voice when the state recovered its levers of command, and even then panic drove them to unguarded statements. Nothing is more revealing in this respect than the *cri de coeur* of Professor Raymond Aron, France's most subtle and sophisticated defender of the western establishment, who bluntly asked his imaginary opponents: "Do you expect a bourgeois state to finance a Cuban university?" [3] Beneath the free world, behind the classless industrial or postindustrial affluent society, the bourgeois state rears its ugly head in the hour of crisis. Is the moment of angry fear also the moment of truth?

Revision of values is an infectious phenomenon. When the productive machine grinds to a halt, the cogs themselves begin wondering about their function. When there is no gasoline, when public transport has come to a halt, when there is no smoke com-

3. *Le Figaro,* June 14, 1968. And the day after: "It remains to be seen whether the bourgeois state will keep a school for revolutionaries. . . ." *Ibid.*

ing out of the factory's chimney, no normal work in the office, when the usual rhythm of social life has broken down, can the human mind alone stick to the routine? Do you remember those rare sleepless nights when, lying uncomfortably awake, you vividly recollect the hopes or illusions of youth and set this promise against the fulfillment, when with painful lucidity you ponder the meaning of your life? Something of that kind all at once happens to thousands, and it happens during the day. Only this collective blues is coupled with collective hope, is really inspired by it. The prospect of change releases the inner censorship. It prompts one to confess that the present is intolerable, to admit it to oneself but also to others. In factories, in offices, groups gather to discuss what can be done. Hackneyed words like "man's hope" or "man's dignity" acquire a fresh meaning.

There is also man's loneliness. Better than poems and novels, an exceptional situation expresses the deep longings of our atomized society: solitude combined with a life that precludes individualism, isolation coupled with an urge to communicate, to belong. In France that spring, industrial workers occupying their factories, all sorts of men and women busy reforming in committees and commissions, got to know their mates, their fellows, their companions, and this contributed to create an atmosphere of brotherhood. In the second half of May, when the police had gone, the Latin Quarter was a vast Hyde Park Corner, with groups talking and talking well into the night.

It would be childish to suggest that everybody was involved. There were those who spent the crisis, metaphorically, under their beds, very often trembling for imaginary privileges. There were others with clenched teeth and clenched fists, waiting for the day of revenge, when they could come out into the streets shouting "Open our factories." Finally, there was the mass of waverers, taken by surprise by a movement that sprang up almost unheralded: not just the typical lower middle classes, the proverbial shopkeepers, torn between their desire for and their fear of change, but millions of people in various social groups, hesitant, bewildered, uncertain about their choice. When history quickens its pace and normal standards are shattered, the mood changes from hour to hour. Incidentally, this shows how absurd, or dishonest, it is to measure the temper of May by the votes cast at the end of June.

The foundations of French society were even more shaken by the upheaval because, at least at the intellectual level, it was a total rebellion questioning not just one aspect of the existing society but both its ends and means. It was a mental revolt against the existing industrial state, both against its capitalist structure and the kind of consumer society it has created. It was coupled with a striking revulsion against anything coming from above, against centralism, authority, the hierarchical order. Reacting against technocratic mumbo jumbo, against a political system providing mystery and pomp but no effective means of exercising influence, many people felt that everything had to be changed starting, for once, from the bottom. As the existing opposition parties and the trade unions were unwilling, and probably unable, to come to terms with such a movement, they in turn came under suspicion.

Indeed, enthusiasm in May was mingled with mistrust. The great fear of the young revolutionaries was that they and the movement would be somehow "recouped," reclaimed for merely reformist ends; hence the general climate of suspicion of established parties and leaders, of orders from above, of prefabricated programs and slogans. In a country usually highly respectful of titles, medals, and ribbons, a country particularly conscious of the hierarchical ladder, the bout of disrespect took an acute form. The attack on inherited privilege gradually extended to cover privilege acquired through past performance. No veteran, no mandarin, could any longer rely on his reputation for preeminence. The professor's gown ceased to be by itself a symbol of knowledge. A glorious record in the Resistance to the Germans no longer justified its holder in laying down the law now. Nobody was to be taken on trust. Ideally, in this mood a man had to go on proving himself all the time—a man as well as any institution.

Contestation was the fashionable word. "To contest" has in

French a stronger sense than in English. It means to call into question the validity of a fact, a position, a situation; but it has also preserved from its Latin origin the connotation of an appeal against this validity to some superior—in the past, to natural law or God; in modern usage, to public opinion.[4] Politically conscious students set the tone for this radical criticism. They refused to be reduced to the obvious alternative, to the choice between an old-fashioned university, which might produce misfits, and a modern or technocratic university, which could fit them only too well into the existing capitalist system. They did not wish to fit. They decided to change at one and the same time the university and its environment, and since they were socialists, they turned to the workers as their only effective allies in this battle. Indeed, by agreeing to fight it out in the streets, by building barricades, they symbolically borrowed the traditional methods of the revolutionary working class. Symbolism on this occasion was coupled with success. It was then the turn of the workers to contest. They had much greater social power but less clarity of purpose. In a vague way their general strike questioned both the employers and the absurdity of their own life. It was the job of the trade unions to turn such a rebellion into dollars and cents.

Inspired by the vision of the students, encouraged by the power of the workers, the questioning mood invaded various professions. Teachers, lecturers, even professors, began to criticize the "uncritical" university and their own roles in a system that perpetuated privilege or conditioned the intellectuals of tomorrow. Scientists sat on commissions discussing not only the best method of organizing research, but also the part played by profits, by financially effective demand in determining the framework of their projects. Architects did not simply argue about their corporate interests. They emphasized the conflict between an economy based on profits and the vital needs of town planning. Writers, painters, actors, attended assemblies and joined in heated debates about their own functions in the life of the country. The

4. See Annette de Bergevin, "Note sur la Contestation," *Esprit*, June–July 1968.

youngest, though not the least active in the movement, were the schoolboys and girls in the highest forms, the students of tomorrow, questioning the world they were about to enter and, by the same token, contesting in many cases the authority of their parents.

Attempts have been made to describe the whole phenomenon in psychoanalytical terms as the rejection of the father figure, and to reduce its importance to the level of a conflict of generations. Yet it cannot be reduced in this way any more than the desire of millions to shape their own destiny can be satisfied by a sham formula of participation. If age was a factor in May, it was in the historical sense of a struggle between an old world and a new. If the young were more prominent on one side of the fence, it was because the young have more daring, are less integrated, less corrupted by the existing system. They are the dynamic element in their social group. Young workers acted as a link with students. But the students themselves from the very start put forward socialist objectives, and it was only when they obtained some response from the workers that the crisis became serious, the country paralyzed, society shaken. If the politically conscious students provided the vision, rebellion was changed into potential revolution when the workers intervened. It is in this conjunction, it can never be sufficiently emphasized, that the originality of the French movement lies. It is this conjunction, too, that enabled the contesting spirit to permeate most unexpected quarters.

Such apparent pillars of the consumer society as market research institutes, whose normal job is to help to sell any product, were also swayed by the wind of revolt. Their employees organized special meetings to discover how they, too, could perform a socially useful function. Civil servants were also on strike. Those in the Ministry of Equipment and Housing, for instance, held a permanent assembly and discussed among other subjects how they could serve a different policy. Even the holy of holies, the Ministry of Finance, was affected by the spirit of unrest. More important than that, in striking factories the traditional division between wage and salary earners, between manual and white-collar workers, was much less rigid than in the past. In several cases scientific workers and graduate engineers joined the strike and declined pay increases so that the increment could be more equally divided; and they spent hours debating problems of management and self-management.

Technological change is gradually altering the structure of the labor force. The number of university graduates, clerical workers, and highly skilled technicians is inevitably rising. This is an international trend, and French trade unions could not afford to ignore it. They therefore set up special sections for these so-called *cadres*. (In French, the scientific, technical, and managerial staffs are lumped together in the loose concept of *cadres*.) To interest these precious newcomers no effort was spared. It was made plain that the left had no intention of reducing their status or their privileged position. The Communist-dominated CGT emphasized the fact that it always fights for proportionate wage increases, that is to say for the maintenance of a wide range of differentials. All this wooing did not meet with very great success. For the defense of their narrow material interests the men involved had already a corporate union—the Confédération Générale des Cadres (General Confederation of Scientific, Technical, and Managerial Workers), or CGC—which could perfectly well compete on this ground.

Yet man does not live simply by stereotyped leisure or as a user of durable consumer goods. Work is a crucial part of his life and the French spring of discontent revealed how much dissatisfaction there was with the organization of work in the apparently privileged sections of society. Admittedly, a movement of social protest originating with students was bound to affect their older colleagues, the graduates working in various branches of the economy. Equally, dissatisfaction with the way in which the boss was running things, technocratic ambitions, were mixed with social discontent. Finally, even frequent exceptions cannot be turned into a rule. Nevertheless, the blurring of the line in factories between those who have nothing to sell but their brawn and the rest is a fact, and a significant one at that. Here again, the message of May is that what prompts men into action more than the prospect of narrow immediate gain is the perspective of radical change.

It will be necessary subsequently to proceed with a more detailed analysis, distinguishing in particular differences in conduct during the strike between those *cadres* who are directly involved in the productive process and those who have an executive function, carrying out orders from the top. Such a distinction is instructive. More important, however, is the trend itself, foreshadowing a potential widening of the revolutionary base. Such a development has two vital consequences. The first can be seen through a contrast with the past, a comparison with the Russian experience. When the Bolsheviks took over, scientists, engineers, economists, statisticians, technicians, were terribly scarce in Russia—scarce and often allergic to the new order of things. The expert, the so-called *spets,* was hard to get and then had to be supervised by a trustworthy though uninitiated workman. Obviously no country, and certainly not France today, has enough technical and intellectual skill. The spread of education, as well as radical changes in its contents and methods, are indispensable means for progress. Yet France has a sufficient pool to draw upon not to be paralyzed by individual desertions. The willing collaboration of the bulk of the professional intelligentsia would render the years of transition to socialism easier. It would also facilitate the search for industrial democracy.

The second consequence is more fundamental. A shift in manpower from brawn to skill and knowledge is a natural corollary of technological progress. It may be assumed that, whatever the crises, material production will go on rising, and increasingly skilled labor will get a portion of this increment. One could make the further assumption that a bigger supply of consumer goods is a guarantee of social peace and that the new beneficiaries will thus be absorbed into the system. This is the crude, unwritten premise of many more or less sophisticated theories that are now fashionable. Projecting the American model into the future—in its present social shape without any qualitative changes—and taking for granted that western Europe at least will follow the American road, the more or less critical apologists of the capitalist system have rather rapidly concluded that the West has entered definitely into the age of gradualism, that revolutionary change may remain the privilege, or rather the curse, of the undeveloped.

But the premise does not stand the test of facts. Relying implicitly on the omnipotence of capitalist conditioning, it ignores the fact of political consciousness. In one and the same country the better-off workers are not necessarily less militant or more integrated. Countries with comparable standards of living, like Britain, France, or Germany, have a working class and a labor movement that are not at all similarly integrated. And the French events have shown how widespread beneath the calm surface is the discontent among those who were believed to be the darlings of consumer society. In foreshadowing joint action between the old working class and the new, backed by an alliance on a broader intellectual front, the French may well have outlined an alternative model for the future.

"You Are All Concerned"

In this introductory chapter, which tries to recapture the mood, to sketch the essential, one is invariably forced to throw up ideas, to put forward hypotheses, to generalize. These generalizations will have to be backed by facts and figures in the rest of the book. Yet, already at this stage, the reader must be warned against jumping to conclusions. The makings of a revolution should not be confused with revolution itself, the potential with the real, the portents with the future. The May Movement, as we saw, did not involve everybody. Nor could it last for long without gaining ground. It is during the short spell of apparent interregnum that power had to change hands, allowing a new era to begin. But power did not change hands. Gaullism and capitalism survived. France witnessed, at the most, the prelude to a revolution.

When gasoline got flowing anew, when trains began to run, when engines in most factories started up again, conditioned reflexes also came back. A break of a few weeks was not sufficient to alter habits acquired over years. After the short disintoxication cure, the nation seemed to be back on its usual drugs. Triumphantly returned to office, the Gaullists still had to decide how to digest the concessions granted in a moment of panic, how to absorb the shock, how to divert the nation's discontent and harness it if possible. But they also covered the cobblestones with asphalt, not knowing what might hit them next. How to trust a people that if only for a spell perceived the possibility of real change? By sowing doubt in the established order, by sowing hope in the future, the May Movement may well have planted the seeds of Europe's revolution.

An attentive reader will not allow the author to get away with such an unexplained substitution of Europe for France. While they were watching with fascination the unexpected and therefore strange convulsions of Gaullist France, most outsiders were repeating—many with relief, a few in sorrow—this can't happen here. These were Europeans as well as Americans. Indeed, during the very early phase one could detect a note of *schadenfreude* in many western chanceries. Here was a lesson for General de Gaulle, for the troublemaker within NATO, for the man who kept Britain out of the Common Market, a lesson for the haughty, self-satisfied General who never missed an opportunity to preach to others.

The glee, however, did not last. It rapidly turned to anxious watchfulness. Western rulers—and in a different way their Soviet counterparts—quickly grasped that they had nothing to gain from the change, that the movement in a sense was directed against them all. The conflict with Gaullism appeared as what it really is—painful, acute, yet still a family quarrel. It was amusing to observe in the middle of the crisis General de Gaulle's cordial talk with the new American ambassador and, at the end of the crisis, to witness the relief in Washington over the Gaullist victory. (For superficial observers what an eye opener!)

The French ruling class was, thus, not the only one to feel threatened. The reader's objection remains valid nevertheless. Each situation is, after all, a product of its own environment, and France had many special features conducive to an explosion. Its administration is more dependent on a central authority than any other in the West (some even see here an analogy with the Soviet bloc). This is the heritage of Louis XIV, of Jacobin centralism, of Napoleon. In political terms, Gaullism, the modern variant of Bonapartism, had eliminated intermediaries, weakened parliamentary and other safety valves. Stronger than the parliamentary republic, it was also more vulnerable or rather more likely to provoke an explosion.

The French economy also presents some peculiarities. The original industrial revolution did not proceed in France as far as in Britain or even in Germany. Its second phase, since the war, is for that very reason creating a bigger social upheaval. Before the war France was a semirural country. Since then it has had to absorb a rapid migration from country to town. Not so long ago France was sheltered by a high tariff wall. Now its frontiers are open, and not only to its Common Market partners. The opening of frontiers, the growing dependence on foreign trade, have in turn speeded up industrial concentration, brought the level of unemployment more in line with other western standards, made France more sensitive to the vagaries of the trade cycle.

All these political strains and economic stresses will have to be scrutinized to see how much they each helped to bring the situation to a breaking point. Nevertheless, the French experience, for all its peculiarities, is relevant for the world at large, and not merely because the example is contagious in this age of interdependence. Even this factor should not be underestimated. American students rebel. Their German colleagues are inspired by this action. The Germans and the Italians, in turn, influence the French. Or to take another instance, the Tet offensive in Vietnam at the beginning of 1968 threw French students into action. It was directly responsible for the creation of the March 22 Movement, which was to be the driving force of the student revolt. And the examples can be multiplied. But the French precedent is relevant not only because it may give others the idea of acting. It contains lessons at least for countries at roughly the same stage of development, in other words, for the whole of western Europe.

Each country, after all, has its own background. Some have stronger parliamentary traditions, a greater degree of social discipline, than others. Radical changes may, therefore, take a more or less violent form, be concentrated in a longer or shorter period, come sooner or later. But if there are peculiarities, there are also points in common, general trends sweeping across frontiers. Basically France is not very different from its neighbors in the level and organization of production, the distribution of ownership, its civilization and way of life. The Parisian explosion came almost without warning. The extent and virulence of pent-up discontent were almost unsuspected, and not all the roots of that discontent are national or Gaullist. If anything crucial differentiates the immediate French prospects from those of, say, Germany or Britain, it is a subjective factor, the potentially more militant posture of its working class. And this is why France or Italy may be showing Europe the way.

International comparisons are rendered even more difficult by the fact that the French crisis was probably transitional in two ways. It reflected the transition of French society mentioned above, and it also heralded a transition in the revolutionary movement itself. During its brief life the French movement contained, naturally in miniature and in a mild form, elements of revolutions old and new. Maybe each revolution, and even each revolutionary attempt, borrows heavily from the past, partly because all situations have a point in common—the transfer of politics into the streets—and, to a lesser extent, because the actors are consciously or unconsciously influenced by past experience. Watching the revolutionary stirrings in France, this witness at least was always being reminded of things he had learned about all modern revolutions.

In its spontaneity, fervor, a kind of gaiety amid drama, in its mixture of anger and hope, of barricades and an atmosphere of popular *fête*, it was reminiscent of the Spring of the People in 1848, but also of Cuba. The Cuban model was more consciously present in the minds of many young revolutionaries who were relying on the shock effect of the daring deed. The barricades themselves were a symbolic reminder of the Paris Commune of 1871. The action committees, the embryo of parallel power, were a faint echo of Russia's soviets, while the emergence of youth, the scribblings on the walls—and not just at the Sorbonne—provided a link with China's cultural revolution.

Some of the similarities were only superficial. All borrowings were quickly naturalized, and no previous script, for obvious reasons, was played to the full. Yet this unfulfilled revolution also contained elements of the future. Its violent verbal attacks against the all-pervading consumer society, its emphasis on democracy as something springing from below, its still timid attempt to forge an alliance between the manual and all nonmanual workers, are sketchy outlines of the shape of things to come. A successful synthesis of all such ingredients would be really explosive, and this is why the famous ghost has jumped out of the pages of the *Communist Manifesto* and is once again haunting Europe.

By a curious coincidence the first student demonstrations in Paris occurred just at the time when the one-hundred-fiftieth anniversary of the birth of Karl Marx was being celebrated. In the elegant, modern building of UNESCO, nearly next-door to the provisional headquarters where the North Vietnamese delegates were giving their press conferences, distinguished academicians from all over the world had gathered for the occasion. There are many ways of crippling living thought, though few are more efficient than to embalm the thinker, put him in a mausoleum and cover him with wreaths. With a few notable exceptions the distinguished visitors had come here to bury Marx with faint or fulsome praise. Western academic dignitaries were willing to treat Marxism with respect as a contribution to science now overtaken by subsequent developments, as something innocuous and no longer social dynamite. Soviet academicians did better still. They reduced a critical doctrine into a sacred book, which was then elaborated and codified as "Marxism-Leninism" so as to provide apt quotations to justify anything from a method of milking cows to the invasion of Czechoslovakia.

But just as learned speakers were burying him in the UNESCO building under heavy wreaths, one can imagine the bearded iconoclast, who hated such solemn and pompous occasions, slipping out to roam around the city he knew so well. If he picked up the second issue of the new revolutionary journal *Action,* he would read there that the young rebels were being described as the "grandchildren of Marx and the Commune." If he was not expelled as a dangerous "German anarchist" and was able to observe French developments for a while, he would be bound to notice that some of his basic tenets—about the crucial social weight of the working class or its power of attraction—were being confirmed. Returning to the officiating assembly, he could have retorted: Not so dead, after all. . . .

The French crisis was in a sense a vindication of Marxism, though not of any kind of Marxism; certainly not a vindication of the academic bromide or the Soviet holy book. What is once again in demand is a doctrine that combines a call to action with dialectical tools to help in that action, tools so critical that they must be permanently applied to their own assumptions. Such Marxism must still explain in its own terms why it has had more success in primitive countries than in the industrialized West for which it was originally conceived. The search for this explanation may also help to eliminate this basic contradiction and do so sooner than many people think. The May crisis may well be the first sign of Marxism returning triumphantly to its birthplace, to western Europe. The May Movement may well be the first sign of Europe's socialist revival. Resurrection might be a more appropriate word, because the once inspiring doctrine has been so hideously distorted that it now needs to be reborn.

And so we have stuck our neck out at the very opening of the book. To speak of socialism in Europe, to prophesy revolution at a time when hopes have been dashed in Prague and capitalism seems to have recovered its poise in Paris, is to invite at worst angry derision, at best a benevolent shrug. No matter. The prediction, however, must be defined so as to show that it is based neither on wishful thinking nor on a Utopian dream. No attempt is being made here to be precise about the date or the place, to say exactly where and when. The tide may return in France. Opportunity may knock next in Italy. It may be in a few months' or in a few years' time. And there is no guarantee that when new opportunities occur they will be seized. The only proposition that is really ventured is that western Europe has now entered a new phase; that, say, the next decade will be a period of tension, of growing conflict between revolutionary forces and increasingly authoritarian rule.

The underlying assumption in this argument is that history is not determined by the length of Cleopatra's nose, that mankind does not advance from quirk to quirk. Even incidents, to be historical incidents, usually have a cause and an effect. The French May crisis was no mere incident. It was a warning and an important historical fact. A warning can be heeded or not. A historical fact can be interpreted, studied, exploited, and acted upon—or it can be ignored. To a large extent the outcome of the next clash depends on the seriousness and skill with which the contesting parties have profited from the lessons of the previous experience.

To forecast a decade of conflict between revolution and authoritarianism is to remind people of the 1930's and revive the nightmarish vision of Nazism. The analogy is much too gloomy. There are many degrees of authoritarian rule, and even a police state is not necessarily totalitarian. Fascism is by far the most extreme form of antisocialist struggle and one that is resorted to in very exceptional circumstances. The rise of Nazism was preceded by galloping inflation, mass unemployment, an economic catastrophe that had prepared the uprooted and angry middle classes for a totalitarian regime. Nothing so dramatic now looms on the European horizon, at least not yet.

If the inner conflict between Europe's financial and industrial giants, and their more contradictory battle with America's super-giants, can be fought for a few more years within the existing framework and in a climate of relative growth, each capitalist establishment is likely to defend its domestic fortress in a comparatively "civilized" fashion. Should the scramble for markets and profits bring the international economic and financial system down and result in mass unemployment and terrible social turmoil, then anything could happen. Yet this is in no way a justification for passive, cowardly tactics. Nobody has ever prevented a storm by hiding his head in the sand. Hitler did not come to power because the socialist and Communist parties were too strong. He managed to seize power because they did not use their full strength in time. Thus, whatever the circumstances, the strategic duty of the opponents of the established order is the same: to prepare the trial of strength and to prepare for it.

It is the other side that now faces a dilemma over policy, and post-Gaullist France, still in the front line, illustrates perfectly this predicament, wavering constantly between two temptations. On the one hand, it provides additional space in its jails, calls up more policemen, improves their wages and weapons. On the other hand, aware that repression alone is not enough, the regime tries to find a new equilibrium, in which even the enforced concessions could be turned into new assets.

Wages had to be raised? This, by squeezing marginal firms, could have helped in the process of concentration. Employees want a bigger share in running things? This could be used in some way to increase the efficiency of the firm. Even the student rebellion, carefully handled, could provide the drive for the desired technocratic reform of the university. The snag is that the two conflicting policies cannot easily be combined. While one minister is giving the carrot and another wielding the truncheon, the regime must determine the most effective proportion of the two.

The tactics of the revolutionary opposition depend, therefore, on the mixture administered by the government. All or nothing is not always a revolutionary maxim. If in the moment of climax,

at the time of crisis, a compromise may spell treason, in between
crises it may be an indispensable instrument of struggle. It remains to be seen what compromise. The object of the reforms
proposed by the government is to consolidate the regime. The
object of the opposition is to blow it up. Hence, each reform must
contain the thin edge of the wedge in order to precipitate its successor, so that the government is rapidly compelled to veto it,
showing thereby that the government's inner logic is incompatible
with the desired change. This, as we shall see, was the method
applied by the student rebels of Nanterre. But to be successful in
the long run such tactics require a strategy.

Questioned at the height of the crisis about their concrete proposals for such and such a precise problem, the students used to
reply that a movement finds its bearings while advancing (*"un
mouvement se prouve en marchant"*). It was a perfectly legitimate reply. Nobody climbs barricades with an insurance policy
in one pocket and a blueprint guaranteeing a sectional advantage
in the other. People climb real or metaphorical barricades because they find their situation unbearable—which is a relative
feeling—and see more than a glimmer of hope. A detailed blueprint for a very distant future may often be simply an excuse for
inaction. This is not to say that a revolution is just a mechanical
addition of objective circumstances and determined men. To
be popular, to attract, and thus to fulfill its mission, a movement
requires a conception of the world, a sense of direction, and
therefore a strategy. This is a problem not for Frenchmen alone.

If history is not shaped by the length of Cleopatra's nose,
neither is it an indulgent grandmother partial to grandchildren
who can afford to miss one opportunity after another. If the next
opportunities are missed, we shall all pay the price. Daring
French students brought hope and its companion, danger. The
French are still in the front line. But they could echo beyond
France's frontiers one of the better-known slogans of the May
days, namely "You are all concerned." Their message should
find a response among those who refuse to be the playthings of
events, all those who are not resigned to the alleged alternative

between a milder form of Stalinism and a more state-controlled version of modern capitalism, or at best a queer mixture of both. If this book helps in any way to encourage the indispensable international debate, it will have fulfilled its purpose.

To discuss the consequences, it is necessary to know the facts. To determine what should be done, it is important to grasp what really happened in May. And since nothing, however surprising, comes entirely out of the blue, let us start with the origins.

IT IS TRULY WITH CONFIDENCE *that I envisage, for the next twelve months, the existence of our country . . . in the midst of so many lands shaken by so many jolts, ours will continue to give the example of efficiency in the conduct of its affairs.*

—CHARLES DE GAULLE,
New Year's broadcast, December 31, 1967

PART TWO
The Hidden Powder Keg

THE STAGE WAS SET *for a great anniversary celebration. True, the Fifth Republic does not like to be reminded of the original sin of its inception. May 13, 1958, with its* putsch *by colonial colonels backed by settlers in Algeria, was a shabby beginning for the men now parading as the keepers of law and order. Gaullists do not like to recall how they had to plot to bring down the tottering Fourth Republic. General de Gaulle himself preferred to forget how he had to maneuver to get out of the enforced retirement at Colombey-les-deux-Églises. Legitimacy personified, he did not want to be reminded of the military barons who had made him king. But this could be easily avoided. By shifting the date from May 13 to June 1, from the* putsch *to its successful legal conclusion, it was possible to dismiss the regime's doubtful origins and produce a glittering story of ten years of progress and stability, peace and national grandeur.*

The script was actually ready. A splendid saga was to be staged by the official propaganda machine, describing how the General came back and the miracles began. In one decade the national product rose by sixty-three per cent, foreign trade tripled despite the shift from colonial to more competitive markets, and six billion dollars worth of gold and foreign currency was piled up in the formerly empty coffers of the Bank of France. Overseas, the Algerian war was brought to an end and France was really at peace for the first time since 1939. Crusader of national independence and grandeur, General de Gaulle managed to challenge America's supremacy, to open the way for détente in Europe, and to gain applause throughout the tiers monde. *Yesterday's Sick Man of Europe was now the envy of the entire world. All this, the story ran, had been made possible by political stability, resting on solid institutions set up by an exceptional man. After years of the governmental merry-go-round France had only two Prime Ministers in nearly a decade, and in effect only one government, since both Michel Debré and Georges Pompidou were no more than the General's lieutenants.*

Inevitably the official story was so one-sided that opposition critics had no difficulty picking holes in it. The rate of growth was no faster under the Fifth Republic than under its predecessor. France, far from being a pacesetter within the Common Market, was rather a laggard. The pile of gold was a high price to pay for unemployment, and it was small consolation for poor Frenchmen that their country was "rich." Peace in Algeria, the counterargument ran, was fine, but the Gaullist Republic had had to have another four years of war before it could bring about a settlement, and useless delays did not improve the final solution. As for foreign policy, opposition critics asked ironical questions about which of the many Gaullist policies should be taken into account, since the wooing of Adenauer's Germany, for example, was not a logical prelude to the search for a détente with Russia. What was described by the faithful as elaborations on the main theme was dismissed by opponents as acrobatics caused by shortsightedness.

For the opposition, even stability could not be put squarely on the credit side of the regime. Stability for what? Ten years in office to carry out what structural reforms? Besides, the electoral base of Gaullism was shrinking. The General's spell was broken. In 1958 he had captured eighty per cent of the votes cast in his first referendum. In December 1965, he could not get an absolute majority on the first ballot of the presidential election, and had to defeat Mitterrand, the candidate of the left, in the second round, on points. By March 1967, the Gaullists, as usual disguising themselves under new initials, could only scrape through in a general election and captured a parliamentary majority with that modern equivalent of rotten boroughs—the overseas or colonial seats.

Whatever his friends and opponents might say, General de Gaulle himself was not unduly perturbed by his reduced majority in the Chamber. Contemptuous of Parliament, he could rely on a constitution tailored to his measure and reshaped to suit his whims. To tame a reluctant Assembly, he forced it from the start to grant the government special powers to carry out unpopular measures by decree. Thus, he could return in peace to his favorite game of international politics.

Everybody admitted, at least implicitly, that only age or illness could remove the General. It was not only the foreign diplomats who were speculating about what would happen to France after the General's departure. French politicians, too, were mainly preoccupied with the fashionable sport of après-Gaullisme. All of them were gambling on the succession stakes. On the Gaullist side, the race for the leadership of a conservative coalition was between Georges Pompidou, then the orthodox favorite, and the younger former Minister of Finance Valéry Giscard d'Estaing. On the left, Mitterrand, wearing the colors of the popular front, was being groomed for his second presidential race. Everybody's eyes were already fixed on 1972, the year when—ceteris paribus—both a presidential and a parliamentary election were to be held.

But things refused to be the same. While General de Gaulle was dreaming of foreign triumphs, while politicians were busy calculating shifts in marginal constituencies, nobody bothered to look beneath the electoral surface at the movement of real social forces. No wonder that the explosion came as a surprise. It often happens that way, and not only in France.

Oisive jeunesse
À tout asservie,
Par délicatesse
J'ai perdu ma vie
Ah! Que le temps vienne
Où les coeurs s'éprennent*

—ARTHUR RIMBAUD

University in Turmoil

Progress in science, in general knowledge and skill, seems as indispensable to the growth of a modern economy as freedom of movement; that is to say, it is as indispensable as the abolition

*Dreaming children
Held in thrall,
Lack of heart
Has cost me all.
Oh, will the day come
When all hearts are one?

of serfdom was to the development of manufacturing and the industrial revolution. If it is to advance rapidly, a modern economy requires scientific research, both pure and applied, in order to stimulate technological change. It also needs an increasingly flexible and educated labor force capable of adapting itself to such change. The rate of growth is, thus, to a large extent dependent on the spread of general education.

The principle would be entirely true and the maximum extension of permanent and polyvalent education would be imperative if the purpose of modern society were to turn man from the servant into the master of the machine; to reduce routine work to a minimum and gradually to eliminate the difference between manual and intellectual labor; to provide the community of producers with sufficient knowledge of their environment to allow them to evolve the most satisfying mixture of labor and leisure, progressively obliterating the frontier between the two. But this is not the purpose of our system of commodity production for a market, that is, for effective demand backed by purchasing power. Capitalism, while through increased productivity reducing the hours of work required, must simultaneously go on creating profitable jobs. For its own survival it must stimulate and invent needs so that it can keep on producing more marketable goods and services.

All this complicates the problem of the role of education. Experts are divided about the part actually played in industrial expansion by research and development, a part that inevitably varies according to a country's ability and willingness to live on borrowed technology. Yet it is the very concept of growth that must now be questioned; not so much the rate or measure of growth as its very purpose. It is increasingly difficult to distinguish how much the spread of education adds to the productive forces of a country and how much it is designed to perpetuate a system of social relations.

But the demand for learning was never prompted by exclusively economic reasons. Now that greater knowledge and skill are taken as an indispensable passport to any form of betterment, the pressure for more and higher education is stronger than ever and governments have to take it into account. The educational drive, fed by distorted economic demand and growing social pressure, in turn presents a challenge to the establishment, nay to all establishments.

The mass spread of education is usually coupled with the development of the critical spirit, a state of mind that is dangerous for any political system that does not correspond to the basic interests of the majority of the people. For the rulers, therefore, the ideal educational method would provide narrow specialists not unduly concerned with anything outside their jobs. Such an ideal, however, is not easy to achieve. In western countries, traditions of academic freedom compel the authorities to put up with a "tolerable" amount of "subversive" teaching. The assumption is that it will be drowned in the prevailing orthodoxy, submerged by social pressure, and may in fact be reduced to a useful antidote. There is no guarantee, however, that heretical thought can always be contained within tolerable limits. In the Soviet Union, on the other hand, heresy is outlawed. Yet, paradoxically, there are massive doses of it within the venerated orthodoxy, in the Marxist classics and in the work of Russian revolutionary writers. How long will the party establishment manage to prevent its rapidly growing intelligentsia from applying the critical tools at their disposal to their own environment and not just to the czarist past or the outside world?

Specialization, which looked for a time like a political answer, contains its own contradictions. The rapid changes in scientific knowledge are a handicap for the repetitive, narrow specialist. The graduate emerging from college now will have to go on learning and may well have to change the nature of his job in, say, twenty years' time. If only for reasons of efficiency the functions of the university should be increasingly to teach its students to learn, to encourage intellectual initiative, independent thought. Herein lies the threat to both eastern and western establishments. How the two systems will manage to cope with this inner contradiction remains to be seen as the balance of population is gradually tilted in favor of these new educated generations, but the spread of higher education has already gone far enough to affect the structure of modern society. If one concentrates on the western world, the scientific revolution, the mass production of graduates, the part played by scientists and technicians in the process of production, by economists, sociologists, and the like in management and social integration—all this has created an entirely new context. It is within this different framework that student unrest appears as neither transient nor local nor marginal. The United States, so far ahead in its development, is also a warning to Europe that these are not just teething troubles.

France was no exception to this general trend. Indeed, in terms of student populations it figures fairly high in the west European league, though the data on which such tables are based must be treated with caution since they often rest on different sets of statistics. In France, even more than elsewhere, the educational trend was reinforced by a radical change in the demographic curve. After a century of near stagnation French population suddenly expanded as a result of the baby boom at the end of the last war. This bulge had to work its way up progressively through primary and secondary education until it reached the university level in the mid-sixties. The wave inevitably lost a great deal of its force on the way, as only a small proportion of children entering elementary schools had a chance of reaching the stage of higher education. In 1966, for example, all French boys and girls up to the age of fourteen were attending school, at least in theory. But only half of the sixteen-year-olds were still within the educational system, and of the twenty-year-olds only one in ten was still studying. The university is still a place for a privileged minority.

But however much its force was spent, the demographic wave was still powerful enough to damage an academic edifice. The centralized foundations of this edifice go back to the Napoleonic era, but they had been entirely reshaped by "republican reformers" roughly toward the end of the last century, when the bourgeois Republic finally triumphed over its monarchist opposition. The edifice began to crumble under the weight of sheer numbers. The figures speak for themselves. Before the last war, France had about 60,000 students in a population of 42 million. The student body was only slightly larger immediately after the war. But by 1958, France had 175,000 students, and by the time of the May explosion in 1968, 500,000 were registered at universities out of a total population of 50 million.[1] Under the combined influence of population pressure and a somewhat more democratic intake, the number of students had nearly tripled within a decade.

At some point quantitative growth brings about qualitative changes. The French university system was in a state of crisis not only because it was bursting asunder—because the buildings, the amenities, the teaching staff, could not keep pace with rising numbers. It was, and is, also in a state of crisis because its nature and function are altering as a result of the increased number of students. When students were a tiny elite, it was possible to maintain a leisurely, "gentlemanly" academic atmosphere in which experts were being produced at the same time as skeptical, cultured amateurs whose counterparts are known in Britain as the products of Oxbridge and in the United States as the Ivy League type.

It did not matter unduly if these children of the upper and middle classes rebelled against their own privileges, if they were occasionally tempted by the red flag, like the Oxbridge students in the 1930's. Youth must have its fling. . . . The fatalistic shrug could be the more relaxed since most of the rebels, including the "upstarts," were bound to be absorbed into a comfortable niche more or less near the top of the establishment. And if a few decided to stay on the other side of the fence, this could not be helped. Intellectuals "betraying their class" have always provided the ideas and often the leaders for revolutionary movements.

An important and growing minority is quite different from a

1. All the figures refer to students registered in a faculty and are, therefore, comparable. The actual number of students is higher. Thus, in 1968, to the half million mentioned above, one must add: 34,000 students in special state institutes of higher education (*grandes écoles*); 56,000 young people preparing to take competitive examinations for such schools within the state system; and 24,000 students in private institutions. All these are students, though not registered in a faculty. One thus obtains a total of more than 600,000 students, a figure that was used by most commentators during the May crisis, but which may involve some double accounting.

tiny elite. Higher education is now a vital element in the economic machine. Self-perpetuation is not its only task. University education is not just for boys who will take over from daddy or for future lawyers who will go into politics or business. It does not just provide the high priests of the administration and the captains of industry. It also supplies the lieutenants and, increasingly, the noncommissioned officers for the huge social organization. If the supply does not fit the demand, or if the students rebel, the social disruption and its political consequences are incomparably more serious than in the past. This is why the university has to be at one and the same time more flexible, more diversified, and more stratified than it used to be.

It must both produce the old Oxbridge or Ivy League types and achieve the mass output of less academic products. It has to try to include within the same system studies of various length and different kinds. Such a transformation is usually described in rather loose terms as the transition from Europe's liberal nineteenth-century model to America's technocratic pattern of the second half of the twentieth century. In this context, "liberal" is not a very accurate concept. American universities can afford to be more liberal in many respects than their European counterparts. The evolution may be more aptly defined as a drive toward the functional, if that adjective be taken to mean designed to fit into a social pattern without any approving judgment of value about the given society.

Gaullism, too, made some haphazard efforts to adapt the inevitable growth in the student population to the needs of French capitalism. The latest, in 1965–1966, was the crude and clumsy plan known as the Fouchet reform, from the name of the then Minister of Education.[2] The gist of the project was the division of higher studies into several cycles. There would still be four-year

2. Since the same Christian Fouchet was Minister of the Interior—that is, boss of the police—during the May crisis, it was easy for the student spokesmen to argue that education and the police are only two sides of one and the same repression, that the truncheon intervenes when the gown can no longer perform its function.

degrees for people completing their university education and in some cases going on to postgraduate work. But the university would also provide second-rate degrees, after two years of study, preparing students for junior jobs in teaching, government, or industry. Similarly, each new technological institute (Institut Universitaire de Technologie, or IUT) would supply practical engineering graduates with a less academic background.

The idea of a cheapened degree provoked such protests that it had to be dropped, at least temporarily. Another aspect of the reform, the proposal to abolish free university admission, raised real pandemonium. A young Frenchman who manages to clear the hurdle of the *baccalauréat*—that is, the stiff examination sanctioning the end of secondary studies—is thereby entitled to go to the university. If the *bachelier* wants to enter one of the small and very reputable institutes of higher education, or *grandes écoles*,[3] he is forced to take highly competitive exams. On the other hand, he had the right to a place in the normal faculties, such as arts or science. It is this right that the Fouchet reform proposed to take away. Unwilling or unable to preserve free admission, the Gaullist government decided to follow the British example of limiting the number of new students to what the authorities thought the system could bear. The proposed switch to this principle of selective admission incensed students, divided professors into conflicting factions, and precipitated a passionate debate. This verbal war over selection or no selection foreshadowed in many ways the explosion to come.

On the face of it, this was a phony war about a mythical problem. France is not the first country in the world to offer a university education to all its young people. We just saw that at twenty-one only one Frenchman in ten goes on studying. The *baccalauréat* is a wholesale slaughter which usually eliminates about half the candidates. The Gaullist reformers were, thus, only trying

3. The most famous are: the École Normale Supérieure for arts and science; the École Polytechnique for technology; and, since the war, the École Nationale d'Administration for top civil servants.

to add a final hurdle to an educational steeplechase that really starts with childhood.

Is not some form of selection inevitable? The fashionable advocates of rule by a meritocracy might be tempted to take France as a model. On paper, it has a perfectly democratic system. Its primary education—the proud achievement of the bourgeois Third Republic—is compulsory, equal, and free for all. Its best secondary schools are the state-run *lycées* and not, as in Britain, the public (that is, private) schools. Everywhere admission is based on results of competitive tests and is apparently independent of wealth. A young man with a gift for examinations, who manages to squeeze into one of the *grandes écoles* and to emerge from it toward the top of the examination list, has a brilliant career assured, whatever his background or accent.

But the admirers of a new aristocracy should beware before jumping to conclusions. Judged by results, the French method, too, is one of social selection, in which privilege is perpetuated. A workman's son has an incomparably smaller chance of getting to the university than the son of a manufacturer, a don, or a high official. And it is clearly not a case of genetic inequality, unless one is ready to assume that God distributed genes in such a fashion as to render children from privileged backgrounds particularly gifted for longer and materially more rewarding studies like medicine. Indeed, social discrimination in learning is even greater in France, the land of equality, than in snobbery-ridden Britain with its two nations ostensibly separated by an accent.

A book eloquently called *The Heirs* [4] attempted to analyze the roots of this discrimination. Its authors claimed that the problem was not essentially financial, that even a massive supply of grants and scholarships—which in France are the exception—would not radically alter the social origins of the student population. The heart of the matter lies in the very conception of education, in the methods of teaching and the manner of selection. In France even

4. P. Bourdieu and J.-C. Passeron, *Les Héritiers* (Paris, Les Éditions de Minuit, 1964).

more than elsewhere, success at school is largely based on the pupil's veneer of general culture, on his elegance of expression and skill in writing.

A boy or girl coming from an upper-class home, where books are lying around, where the language and vocabulary are those of the system, has a built-in advantage. The children of intellectuals have as a rule the best opportunities, though well-off parents in industry or trade can compensate through private tuition, foreign travel, and so on. The son of the workman or the agricultural laborer must be exceptionally gifted to break through the barrier. The authors of the book argued that short of a revolutionary transformation of the purposes of education, of syllabuses, tests, and methods of assessment, equality of opportunity would remain a legend, the social structure of the university would only be altered slowly, and the change could never be completed. The recent rapid rise in the number of students has altered the figures on which this argument was based without radically affecting its gloomy conclusions.

When a whole structure rests on class distinction, you cannot crown it with a top layer that shows no social bias. For this reason the passionate quarrel over selectivity at the university level sounded rather strange to the outsider. And yet it was not a phony conflict. It was a portent of things to come. The cleavage it revealed was not so much between the advocates of stability and the advocates of change within the university. The deep split it foreshadowed was between those who think of possible change within the existing social system and those who, striving for the desirable, are only too glad to smash the established order in the process; it is the classical split between reformers and revolutionaries.

Sticking to what is immediately possible, the defenders of a selective system could put up quite a strong case. They could argue that it had been possible to pack many more students than was bearable into the universities because France had no strong tradition of seminars or tutorials and many of its students never attended the overcrowded lectures. In the end, however, the students themselves were the victims of the liberal admission system. In the French university many are called, but few are chosen. It is estimated that out of every three students entering the university, only one will stay the course; the other two will fall by the wayside. In most cases, such seemingly reasonable pleas were based on a series of assumptions that could be summed up in the ultimate proposition that only marginal change is possible. Differences in skill and knowledge are inevitable and must therefore be rewarded. Social discrimination is regrettable but cannot be uprooted too fast. The government could and possibly should shift some resources, say, from defense to education, yet this would hardly change the problem. When you scratched highly sophisticated arguments, you found at the bottom bourgeois wisdom parading as common sense, with its basically simple premises: Men are unequal, things are what they are, and (the Wellsian ironic precept for Homo Tewler) "You can't be too careful with them ideers." [5]

At the other extreme, amid the most radical opponents of selective admission, the mood was exactly the opposite. They were perfectly well aware that the university was part of a whole that had to be overhauled from top to bottom; the battle over free admission was also part of a general struggle. Society owed it to itself and to its citizens to spread knowledge, to provide permanent education for all. Privileges had to be uprooted. Genuine differences in ability did not have to be sanctioned by inequalities in status and income. The government could not afford to spend so much on the university? So much the worse for the government, and so much the better. The university would fail to fulfill its social function? Splendid. The overcrowded university would become the center of political ferment. Instead of cementing existing society. it would help to tear apart an order triply damned as Gaullist, bureaucratic, and capitalist. The budding slogan of

5. This sentence roughly sums up the advice Edward Albert Tewler gave his son at the opening of the book. H. G. Wells, *You Can't Be Too Careful* (London, Secker and Warburg, 1942).

permanent education contained the prospect of permanent revolution.

Naturally the division between revolutionaries and reformers was not so logical and rigid even at the height of the May crisis. In the preceding period it was quite blurred. The Communists, for instance, who were soon to appear as sweetly reasonable and highly orderly, were then still on the side of the opponents of selectivity. But they were already perturbed by the action and the vision of some elements on their side of the fence. Already, then, they were beginning to use the same vocabulary as the Gaullist government to condemn the wild ones, the mad ones, the *enragés*.[6] But whereas the Gaullists mocked the spoiled children or the pampered rebels, the Communists emphasized their background in order to explain that ultra-leftism was a bourgeois deviation. The accent of the prosecutor was clearly on the social origin of the culprits.

Telling their leftist leaders that students were still part of a privileged minority was simply preaching to the converted. They were the last to deny a truth spelled out plainly in the official statistics summed up in the table on the next page.

The bias in favor of students coming from an academic background, from the liberal professions and top management, is striking. The advantages enjoyed by the sons of manufacturers and wealthy tradesmen are partly concealed because big and small shopkeepers are lumped together. The lower middle classes come out rather well in the table, because they include elementary schoolteachers, who tend to push their children toward higher education. Farmers, like the workers, are visibly handicapped.

Averages can be misleading. A rich farmer or a wealthy tradesman should not be confused with a poor peasant or shopkeeper.

6. The nickname goes back to the Great Revolution. It was applied, in 1793, to the followers of Jacques Roux and, a year later, after their elimination, more loosely to the Hébertists. That the Gaullists should use the term with contempt is understandable. That the Communists, who admire Robespierre, should condemn his opponents, still makes sense. But that they should consider the name given to the most plebeian faction in a bourgeois revolution as the supreme insult is curious. Or is it?

TABLE 1. Social Origin of French University Students, 1967

Profession of Parents	Percentage Attending University of Total University-Age Youth in Social Group	Percentage of Total University Student Population
Farmers (including laborers)	4.6	6.6
Employers in industry and trade	17.1	14.9
Top management and liberal professions	57.0	29.3
Middle management and teachers	30.0	15.8
Employees (shop and clerical)	14.1	8.5
Workers	3.4	9.9
Total (including miscellaneous)	12.7 *	100.0

* Percentage attending universities of total university-age population.

Whenever a closer analysis is possible, it reveals new layers of discrimination. For instance, the children of laborers have an even smaller chance of ever getting to the university than the sons of skilled workmen. Or to take another example, the longer and the more arduous the studies, the smaller the proportion of students from working-class homes. But the real difficulty is not in finding statistics but in using them properly. In putting the accent exclusively on discrimination, which remains an undeniable fact, one runs the risk of concealing changes in the social makeup of the student body, which are also a relevant factor. The mass entry of young people into the various faculties was bound to have some democratic influence. The share of the lower middle classes has risen; even the proportion of the working class has grown. Before the war, a workman's son was an oddity at college, barely more than one in a hundred. By now, he is nearly one in ten, that is to say, he is more than an exception to the rule.

And, finally, there is the abuse of statistics for purposes for which they are not properly designed. The social origin of students tells something about the inequalities, the bias, of a given society. It does not necessarily prove much about the political outlook of the students. As the conflict grew more and more acute, Communist spokesmen tended to treat a bourgeois background as a kind of original sin beyond any possible redemption.[7] To quiet this Calvinist zeal, one of the party's chief intellectuals, the no longer orthodox Roger Garaudy, had to remind his colleagues that they were using a concept evolved by the bourgeois Henri Taine and not at all a tool of Marxist analysis. For Marx, political consciousness was determined not so much by social origin as by the part performed in the process of production. Students are here an exceptional social group, since their productive function is still to come. Their political behavior is thus at least to some extent determined by their prospects, and this perspective is much more cloudy for the big academic battalions of the 1960's than it used to be for the small companies of prewar days.

Socially, students are in a strangely suspended state. Tomorrow they will be absorbed by the productive machine, conditioned by their class interest, more or less integrated into the system. Today, not quite torn from the domestic background but not yet prisoners of their future jobs, they are in an intermediate stage, when they are more likely to question their environment. Intellectuals more than any other social group can break with their class. Students are more likely to do so than graduates thrown onto the market. For some the choice will be lasting, for others

7. The highest pitch of the ridiculous was reached at the time not in France but in Italy by Pier Paolo Pasolini, better known outside his country as a film-maker, who in June 1968 expressed his hatred for students of bourgeois origin: ". . . When you were fighting with the cops, my sympathy was with the cops. Because cops are the sons of poor people." He went on to explain that "a bourgeois redeemed . . . should banish forever from his soul the idea of power." This splendid piece of reasoning should have driven poor Pasolini to side with fascist thugs against the followers of Marx, Engels, Lenin, Gramsci, or Togliatti, all doomed by their social origins and who dared not only to think but to write about power. Stupid sympathizers perform a useful role. They carry the argument to its logical conclusion and reveal its full absurdity.

just the last rebellion of youth, but for the student body as a whole the mood will be more influenced by prospects than by memories of childhood. The student revolt is, therefore, a concentrated and exaggerated reflection—but a reflection nevertheless—of a more general malaise of graduates in the modern economy. It is the acute symptom of a deeper, though more diffuse, sickness affecting all our societies, and not just a bout of French flu.

Naturally French students had plenty of reasons of their own for unrest. Some of these causes were pretty old, though even these were exacerbated by the growing numbers of students. The rigid centralism, leaving the university chancellor very little scope for improvisation; the rigid division of faculties, leaving the student little chance to switch; the ruthless guillotine of examinations; the absence of contacts between professors and students; the total lack of guidance; the routine of set lectures—these are only some of the traditional causes of discontent, aggravated each year by the mass invasion of the universities by a new and bigger contingent of students. And by the mid-sixties, the spread of unemployment, affecting particularly the young and the middle-aged graduates, provided two more reasons for worry: the fear of not finding a job and the fear of being a squeezed lemon at forty. When two thirds of an institution's members are doomed to failure, it is a perfect hunting ground for political activists, and the university was beginning to be described as a school for misfits.

The result of it all was a piling up of grievances, a mixture of discontents. Students disappointed with the existing system because it did not function adequately according to its own rules mingled with others who rejected capitalist society as such. Young men who were frustrated because they felt they would not be members of a tiny elite sided with colleagues who wished to abolish privileged positions. With their narrow interests thwarted, and with their illusions about the university as a temple of knowledge dashed, many were ready to listen to talk of a radical transformation. For the government, the temptation was great to try to split the potential reformers from the would-be revolutionaries. But it misjudged the mood of the students, the extent of their discontent and its cumulative effect. The Gaullists, like the Communists, thought that the revolutionary students, because they were a minority, just a few "grouplets," could be isolated and crushed. Both were to learn through bitter experience that in the troubled academic aquarium the revolutionaries, in keeping with Mao's dictum, were like "fish in the water."

Politics in the Latin Quarter had been swinging sharply to the left, and the government did not really know how to cope with this new situation. Before the war, if anyone had the upper hand in the student district, it was probably the right, the aristocratic roughnecks known as the King's Hawkers or Camelots du Roy. From the mid-fifties onward, the UNEF has been in the hands of an increasingly radical left. The heyday of the UNEF was during the Algerian war, when it spurred on the labor unions and opposition parties to anticolonial struggle. The end of the war brought an anticlimax. For a while the leading group attempted to forge a syndicalist line, starting with an analysis of the role of the university in bourgeois society and moving on to a critical assessment of the contents and methods of education. It failed to hold the ebbing tide.

The Gaullist government tried to revenge itself by sponsoring a nonpolitical union, which never managed to strike roots, and by depriving the UNEF of its subsidy. Without money with which to carry out its welfare and corporate functions, the students' union, it was hoped, would lose influence. Although the scheme did not really fail, it proved counterproductive. The UNEF, though weakened, became even more political. It was turned into a battleground between various groups, the most conservative of which was the orthodox Communist faction. Their conflicts led to successive crises. The latest occurred in April 1968 and led to the resignation of the chairman. This is how his deputy, the twenty-five-year-old bachelor in law and history of art Jacques Sauvageot, was thrust onto the center of the stage. He soon showed that he could act his part, and he was helped by activists from yesterday's warring factions both within and outside the students' union.

At this point one should look at the *enragés,* the revolutionary "grouplets" despised by some, overemphasized by others. The first point to make is that they were filling the void left by the orthodox Communist party. Radical workers were still flocking to the CGT; voters still considered that the Parti Communiste Français (French Communist Party), the PCF, was on the extreme left of the electoral spectrum, but the students had already changed their mind. The party had appeared to its young supporters too lukewarm during the Algerian insurrection. More recently it was clinging to "Peace in Vietnam," when their slogan was already "FNL will win." In domestic politics, its alliance with Mitterrand's FGDS was taken as a proof, a confirmation of its departure from the revolutionary road.

Altogether, too coexistentialist in foreign policy and too reformist at home, the PCF was dismissed by the most radical students as a new member of His Gaullist Majesty's opposition and treated as part of the capitalist consensus. Indeed, the party had to purge, ban, dissolve its student organizations, as did the Labour party in Britain and the Sozialdemokratische Partei Deutschlands (Social-Democratic Party of Germany), or SPD.[8] Since the various revolutionary movements were filling the void left by the Communist party, it is not surprising that they can be roughly listed under the headings of the main heresies: Maoism, Trotskyism, anarchism, and other, looser forms of revolutionary socialism.

The Maoist attack on the orthodox—or, as they prefer to call it, the revisionist—Communist party is relatively recent. So far it has made little progress within the CGT or the party cells. It has been more successful among the younger generation. Among

---

8. The crisis developed in earnest in 1962–1963, when the so-called Italians gained control of the orthodox Union des Étudiants Communistes (Union of Communist Students), or UEC, allowing the freedom of open debate. Of the groups mentioned later, both the Trotskyist JCR and the Maoist UJCML are splinters from the orthodox UEC. The former broke away at the beginning, the latter at the end of 1966.

students the first Maoist breeding ground for the Union des Jeunesses Communistes Marxistes-Léninistes (Union of Marxist-Leninist Communist Youth), or UJCML, was the highly selective school for future French professors, the École Normale Supérieure on Rue d'Ulm.[9] There and elsewhere some of the young men at the threshold of a brilliant future in academic officialdom chose work in a factory as a career. There is something of the Russian *narodniki* in the young Maoists. The former preached among peasants; the latter are going to the workers in order *To Serve the People,* to quote the title of their journal. Quotations from the little red book and the cult of Mao were not the ideal means of attracting critical students, but they were attracted by China's cultural revolution, with its antibureaucratic message and its appeal to youth. Their ideological enthusiasm and personal abnegation enabled the young Maoists to make substantial gains among university and high-school students.

Trotskyism is for the party-liners an old enemy. Trotsky, who was Lenin's partner in the October Revolution and the founder of the Red Army, was for years the hated heretic. The party-liners thought they had gotten rid of his shadow. The revolutionary lull and Stalinist methods made it possible to isolate the Trotskyists. Isolation in turn led to divisions and splits that seemed to the outsider to be quarrels among different sects. In the past few years, however, the shadow once again acquired substance. The ideas of Trotsky—his criticism of Stalinist bureaucracy and his concept of permanent revolution—found a new public, mainly among the young.[10] The divisions, nevertheless, remained and were reflected even among students, who had the choice of two groups of Trotskyist inspiration.

The first group, which had just taken the name Fédération des Étudiants Révolutionnaires (Federation of Revolutionary Stu-

9. The influence there of Professor Louis Althusser, keeper of Marxist purity, may have prepared the ground for a reaction against revisionism.

10. Here as elsewhere this revival was greatly assisted by the monumental trilogy in which Isaac Deutscher, an admirer but never hagiographer, raised the question of Trotsky's posthumous victory.

dents), or FER, was rigid in its organization and tended to apply old Bolshevik slogans rather mechanically. At the beginning of the crisis, the FER impressed some students by the discipline of its members; later, it failed to adapt itself to a dynamic situation and gained little ground. By contrast, the second group, the Jeunesse Communiste Révolutionnaire (Revolutionary Communist Youth), or JCR, proved more open in its theoretical approach, more flexible in its tactics, more aware of the specific problems of the student movement, and as such was to exercise a greater influence during the crisis.

Anarchism was the eldest of the heresies. Though French trade unions had been anarchosyndicalist until World War I—mistrusting political parties and waiting for the Great Upheaval through a general strike—anarchism was never so great a political force in France as it was, for instance, in Spain. Small groups used to meet in Paris, though few people knew about their existence. Naturally, when the barricades went up in May, the anarchists, for whom nothing is more precious than the very communion, the fraternity, of combat, were not going to let the side down. The forgotten black flags were one of the revelations of May. Yet more significant for the movement as a whole was the neoanarchism of the *enragés* from Nanterre. "We are more or less Marxists," claimed their best-known spokesman, Daniel Cohn-Bendit. Their political attitude was not determined by a study of Proudhon or Bakunin, Élisée Reclus or Kropotkin. Their anarchism reflected something different and was one of the symptomatic features of the May crisis. It combined hatred for Gaullist capitalism, disappointment with the Soviet experiment, and contempt for Communist bureaucracy, leading to a mistrust of any structured organization.

The fourth heresy is more of a mixed bag. One may put into it the student section of a small socialist party, the Étudiants Socialistes Unifiés (Unified Socialist Students), or ESU. Jacques Sauvageot was the best known of their members. One may also include the ex-Communist students, who had started on the heretical road under the "Italian" or liberal banner and moved leftward on the way, as well as the former advocates of the syndicalist line in the student union, some of whom just before the May upheaval founded at the Sorbonne the short-lived Mouvement d'Action Universitaire (University Action Movement) or MAU. All these veterans of previous battles, now in their mid-twenties and often postgraduate students or researchers, were to take the initiative in rank-and-file committees and play an active part in the propaganda of the movement. Last but not least, one must mention the high-school student organization, the Comités d'Action Lycéens (School Action Committees), or CAL, created shortly before the May crisis.

The numerical strength of all these groups should not be exaggerated. They naturally expanded during the revolutionary crisis, though on the eve each had only a few hundred members. What is more difficult is to assess their importance during the course of the crisis, the place that should be attributed to them in the narrative and explanations. To treat, say, Jacques Sauvageot and Alain Geismar or Alain Krivine of the JCR and Daniel Cohn-Bendit as the Lenin and Trotsky of an abortive October is plainly absurd. To dismiss them from the story altogether would equally be a distortion.

Within the student context the so-called active minorities did play a key role. They did not invent the movement nor order it about. But they spurred students into action, showed the way, channeled the disparate discontents into a whole, and gave it a sense of direction. Largely because of their efforts the rebellion against a repressive university was turned into a struggle against an oppressive society and the students looked from the start to the workers as the only allies who could crown their battle with victory. But once the struggle moved to the wider arena, students as such could not exercise a hegemonic function.

Yet even within the confines of the university, Gaullists and Communists alike had underestimated the influence of the "handful of *enragés*." Their initial membership was small, their divisions striking, their quarrels passionate. To grasp how their following grew, how the divisions, without vanishing, were overcome in action, how the movement gathered momentum, driven forward by incidents within the university and by echoes from the outside world, there is no better way than to consider what happened just outside Paris, in the faculty of Nanterre, where it all began.

You travel up the Champs-Élysées, past the Arc de Triomphe, and much later past the high buildings huddled near the Rond-point de la Défense, where the city planners, in an effort to diversify the French capital, sponsored a new business center. You have to go much farther westward, where new blocks of apartment buildings contrast with the old suburban villas. Suddenly on your left you discover a shantytown, still housing thousands of foreign, mainly North African, workers, and on your right, Rue de la Folie—Folly Street. This will take you to a vast conglomeration of haphazard modern structures, which even now gives the impression of an unfinished building site. You have reached your destination, the now celebrated faculty of arts of Nanterre la Folie.

With hindsight, everybody proclaims that it was folly to park thirteen thousand students in a semislum suburb with no life of its own and no attractions. The Latin Quarter, with its cafés, its entertainment, its atmosphere, was far away and not easily accessible. Everybody now also proclaims that it was double folly to build such a ghetto and fill it with students without providing the social and cultural amenities that would make up for the isolation. The library was still unfinished; there was no scope for any social life; as to political debates, they were forbidden, here as elsewhere, on the hypocritical excuse that the university was allegedly neutral.

All this, however is wisdom after the event. When the faculty was started, in 1964, it was hailed as an innovation, as a kind of French campus à l'américaine. Many professors and lecturers opted for this small faculty in order to escape from the impersonal and bureaucratic machinery of the enormous Sorbonne. The new dean, Professor Pierre Grappin, a former inmate of German concentration camps, was reputed to be a reformer, and the teaching staff at Nanterre was on the whole less conservative than the average French teaching staff. The government, if it thought about it, was not afraid of any great political unrest. In Paris, as in other capitals, the west end is the smart part of the town, and it could be assumed that the day students from well-to-do families, who outnumbered the boarders from more modest backgrounds, would set the tone.

It took some time for unrest to develop. The students' union and the existing political groups had serious difficulties in striking roots in this virgin territory. Only by 1967, when the campus got overcrowded and the disorderly reforms in syllabuses and teaching schedules created a climate of anxiety, did the spirit of revolt spread. In November of that year a wild strike shook the campus. As a result student-teacher commissions were set up, and students were granted a limited say in the running of the faculty. This did not lead very far. The authorities were not ready for radical reforms, nor prepared for serious concessions. The students were rapidly learning the limitations of gradualism.

The main field of political activity was still outside the campus. The Maoists preferred to make propaganda among the foreign workers in the neighboring slums rather than among students, and devoted most of their time to their own organization against the war in Vietnam, the Comités Vietnam de Base (Basic Committees on Vietnam), or CVB. Other militant students were active within a larger body called the Comité Vietnam National (National Committee on Vietnam), the CVN. At Nanterre itself, demonstrations for the free admission of male residents into the hostel reserved for women students provided splendid copy for the press and a reassurance for officials that it was all really just fun and games. In fact, it was part of a process of mobilization against repression in general, combined with a growing challenge to authority.

Events in distant Vietnam were to step up the pace. This is how an activist from Nanterre describes the psychological impact of the 1968 Tet offensive:

The "American way of life" and even American sociology were smashed in the process. Here they get bashed by the little Vietnamese who get out of their holes with little Chinese machine-guns and who muck it all up. This perishable aspect of American society, even of the ideology it was spreading, for many students it was a sort of breach through which quite a lot of stuff could be poured. . . .[11]

There was also a more direct consequence. The young members of the various committees wanted to express their sympathy and admiration for the Vietnamese in some striking way. In one of their sorties they demolished the Parisian office of the American Express. The police arrested several members of the CVN, including a young member of the JCR from Nanterre. On March 22 a few hundred students gathered together, determined to protest in a spectacular fashion. In addition to Trotskyists from the JCR and anarchists, there were all sorts of students who were involved in the campaign against the American intervention in Vietnam. The question was what to do? After much discussion the students opted for a symbolic act, the seizure of the administrative building; that is, the occupation of forbidden territory legally reserved for the authority. Once inside, drawing on the experience of the Sozialistischer Deutscher Studentenbund (Socialist German Student Federation), the SDS, they set up commissions—on student and workers' struggle, the class structure of the university, imperialism—produced a manifesto, and had time to depart before the police were called in. This was all. But the date is worth remembering. It marks the official birth of a political force—the March 22 Movement—that was to leave its imprint not only on Nanterre.

Its origins had a bearing on the style of the March 22 Movement. Militants from various groups with ideological differences, if one may paraphrase Lenin, had to think separately and strike together. They were not handicapped by the classical drawbacks of united action, the reduction of objectives to the lowest common

11. "Un Militant de 22 Mars Raconte," in Ph. Labro and others, *Édition Spéciale* (Paris, Publications Premières, 1968).

denominator. On the contrary, since it was not a case of elaborating and then imposing a joint program, but of offering the militant rank and file a worthwhile target, unity could only be achieved through increasingly radical moves.

Each action, whether big or small, had to be spectacular, so as to attract attention, and preferably be symbolic, so as to undermine authority either by revealing its repressive nature or by demonstrating its impotence. Above all, the action had to be instructive, pedagogical. Students, who had rebelled against the consumer society or, in their special case, against a university in which the master, the professor supposedly possessing all facts and theories, dispensed prescribed pills of knowledge to passive pupils, were not going to opt for politics from above. Minorities, however active, had no chance of success unless they could stir up the indifferent, awaken the apathetic, spur on the resigned. The main purpose of action was to mobilize, to turn passive onlookers into actors.

Within this context the effervescence of Nanterre makes better sense, and the "happenings" acquire a meaning. Take, for instance, the frequent interruptions during lectures. A sociologist explaining the American model of organization would suddenly be asked how this system functioned in Vietnam. Professors of Spanish would be interrupted by a petition for the victims of the Franco regime. These unexpected gags served many a purpose. The average French student, brought up in awe of his master, was at once taken aback and forced to think. It was not only the sacrosanct authority of the professor that was thrown into doubt, but also the contents of his teaching and the university as an institution.

Or to take the more complicated story, which started with allegations that students were being victimized, and culminated with the open intervention of the police on the campus. Whether or not blacklists of political troublemakers really had been drawn up rapidly became irrelevant. To cope with the unrest created by this affair, the authorities decided to seek the help of plainclothesmen. These gentlemen were in for a surprise. Pictures of them as wanted men now appeared on the campus bulletin boards. The proctors tried to tear them down. There were scuffles with students, and in the resulting panic the dean agreed to call in undisguised policemen. They stormed in with helmets, shields, and truncheons. The *enragés* had proved their point. That very day a handful grew into hundreds. The new tactics brought other dividends. Revolutionaries had made fools of empty-handed reformers. The lesson that soon spread throughout France was that only direct action paid off.

Direct action, guerrilla tactics, fully armed commandos—much was to be written and said about the military preparedness of the students. The truth is less exciting. Each group was in the habit of putting its tougher members in the front line. They had gotten their training from Communist stewards, who used to throw out heretics in May Day parades or beat them up outside factory gates. They polished their methods in skirmishes over Vietnam with the police and right-wing thugs. Their typical armor was a motorcyclist's crash helmet, tennis shoes for mobility, any stick or iron they could lay their hands on, and in some cases slingshots —David's weapon against the might of the fully armed Goliath. Yet it was not absurd to talk of guerrilla tactics so long as one was talking in political and psychological terms. Like guerrilla fighters they relied on surprise and mobility, on the unexpected blow that saps the authority of any established power. Their main weapon was daring—the classical weapon of the revolutionary always faced with a better-armed opponent.

A frontal crash was inevitable at Nanterre between the *enragés* now carried forward by a mounting wave and the academic authorities bewildered by the new forms of protest. How can one choose between the carrot and the stick, when one's young challengers want to take their rights rather than be granted concessions? They were finally given a hall for political meetings— which they promptly rechristened for Che Guevara—but this did not prevent them from interfering with lectures elsewhere. The climax came at the end of April with the proposal for two anti-imperialist days on May 2 and 3. There were all sorts of rumors that Occident, the extreme right-wing organization, had brought reinforcements from all over France to attack Nanterre. The faculty was mobilized for self-defense. In this excited atmosphere the dean finally decided to close the faculty altogether. Transplanted from suburban Nanterre to the Sorbonne in the heart of Paris, the crisis now shook the whole country.

Nanterre was not so much a microcosm of French academic life as a hothouse in which the revolutionary plant grew somewhat faster than elsewhere. The spectacular side of this growth, which was played up by the press, should not conceal its serious purpose. From the beginning, the politically conscious students were aware of their predicament. They knew that for them there was no radical solution within the framework of the university. This conviction is very well illustrated in a leaflet published by the March 22 Movement in the heat of the May battle:

> There are ten per cent of workers' sons in higher education. Are we fighting so that there should be more of them, for a democratic reform of the University? This would be better, but this is not the most important thing. These sons of workers will become students like all the others. That a worker's son should be able to become a director, that is not our program. We want to abolish the separation between labor and management.
>
> There are students who, on leaving the university, do not find a job. Do we fight so that they may get one, for a good employment policy for graduates? This would be better, but it is not the essential. . . . When a worker's son becomes a student, he leaves his class. When the son of the bourgeoisie goes to the university he may learn the true nature of his class, ponder about the social function for which he is destined, about the organization of society, about your place in it. . . . We want to build a classless society; the meaning of your struggle is the same. . . .
>
> Your struggle is more radical than our legitimate demands because it not only seeks an improvement of the worker's lot within the capitalist system, but it implies the destruction of that system. Your struggle is political in the real sense of the term; you are not fighting to replace one prime minister by another, but to deprive the owner, the boss, of his power in the

factory and in society. The form of your struggle offers us students the model of really socialist activity: the appropriation of the means of production and of the power of decision by the working people. . . .

The date of the student explosion could not be foretold, though it was obvious that when it came, the politically conscious elements would channel it in the direction of the working class. There is something in the political climate of a country, in its traditions, that seems to affect its collective unconscious. France had no beat generation, no hippies or flower children on any large scale. Those who found society unbearable did not, on the whole, try to opt out or to escape to some artificial paradise; they somehow assumed that it could be changed on broadly socialist lines.

After the event there is no shortage of well-wishers, of learned advisers to explain to the students that theirs was the first post-Marxist revolution, that they were their own vanguard or the vanguard of an intellectual movement. But the students clearly did not think that their struggle was a separate one. They wanted to break out of their ghetto and turn to the workers. Indeed, the desperate message of Marcuse, aimed at America, did not reach French youth till after the crisis. The revulsion against the repressive consumer society was not prompted by a special message. It was in the air. The authors whom the young revolutionaries read were Marx and to a much lesser extent Bakunin, Lenin, Trotsky, Rosa Luxemburg, Louis Althusser, Sartre, and, because of their involvement in the anti-imperialist struggle, Mao, Frantz Fanon, Régis Debray, Castro, and Che Guevara—hardly the stuff to prepare anyone for a managerial revolution.

Two partners are needed for an alliance. The fact that the students were likely to turn toward the workers did not mean that they would get on well together. The obstacles to an understanding were legion. It was not just a question of finding a common language between the rebel children of affluence and the newcomers to the so-called consumer society, of establishing confidence between the relatively privileged and the victims of the existing social order. The real trouble was not that the students were fighting to defend their privileges. Quite the contrary. If the students' union had only cared about its corporate interests, it would have been welcomed with open arms by labor unions, whose leaders were actually looking for such a "responsible organization" (the words are those of Séguy of the CGT) to do business with it at the top. The real trouble was that the students wanted to join in the common struggle; that they wanted to change society, not just the university; that the whole nature of their movement drove them to seek contact with the rank and file after their abortive attempts to push the union establishment into bolder action. No wonder that the Communist leaders, already shaken by the unexpected upheaval, did everything in their power to keep such carriers of revolutionary germs outside the factory gates. In May and June 1968 it was a strange and brief encounter. Its consequences are still to be measured.

We have put the accent, intentionally, on the particularly French aspects of the student revolt. We have seen how the growth in numbers produced qualitative changes, how a climate of uncertainty, anxiety, and unrest enabled a good proportion of the students to rise above their narrow interests and how active minorities helped this movement of discontent in the direction of socialist revolution. Here a reader familiar with student revolts all over the world will rightly object that although events are everywhere precipitated by specific, local causes, they are part of a bigger whole. Student unrest cannot be understood properly by just looking at the university or at one country in isolation. The French, like everybody else, are peculiar; they are not exceptional. Even in the United States, the dreamland of the European technocrat, such distant and different universities as Berkeley and Columbia have not escaped a similar fate.

True, American students in their revolt are still looking for allies among marginal social groups, among outcasts and outsiders. But the German students, with a greater theoretical bent and a strong Marxist tradition, like the French have their eyes fixed on the working class, though like the Americans they have no prospect of a *rapprochement* in the near future. The revealing feature of the French crisis was not that the students got an ambiguous response from the workers. It was that they got a response at all. Hence, we must now look at the economic and social conditions of Gaullist France to find out whether anything specific justified this historical exception to the rule hitherto prevailing in the western world.

DON'T CHANGE EMPLOYERS, *change the employment of life.*

—On the walls of the Sorbonne

Society in Flux

The image of France as a semirural country dies hard. The small Parisian restaurant, the *bistro,* the small local grocer or, better still, the open street market, confirm the nostalgic tourist in his impression that here at least things are what they used to be. But this is an illusion. Changes in the way of life tend to lag behind shifts in the pattern of production or the distribution of man-power. In fact, the economic and social shape of France has probably been altered as drastically in the last twenty years as

69

that of any other west European country except for Italy. Nor is this surprising. Partly protected by the tariff wall, prewar France had not gone as far in capitalist concentration as, say, Britain or Germany. It has been trying to catch up in the last two decades.

Migration from the land has been the most striking feature of this transformation. After World War I, in 1921, over 9 million French people were still working on the land. After World War II, in 1946, the number was still nearly 7.5 million. By 1968 their number had dwindled to 3 million men and women. Or to put it differently, farming accounted for over 41 per cent of total employment after World War I, for some 36 per cent after World War II, but for only 15 per cent in 1968. In France, as everywhere, the rural population is larger than the agricultural labor force. The figures are, nevertheless, sufficiently striking to destroy forever the myth that France is the land of the peasant.

Much less spectacular has been the modernization of trade. New forms of distribution, like self-service stores, have spread, and the number of shop assistants has grown while that of independent owners has been declining. But the small shopkeeper is still the rule rather than the exception, even if his share of the turnover is gradually dwindling. In industry, on the other hand, at least at the top, France has reached the highest stage of capitalist concentration, with the big firms not only swallowing the small ones but also devouring each other. Though takeover bids are still a novelty in France, each month brings news of more mergers, very often sponsored with the government's blessing. In steel and in electronics, in the car and aircraft industries, a few firms account for the bulk of national production, and they are encouraged to amalgamate so as to meet the competition of foreign, particularly American, giants. On top of this industrial structure both the joint-stock and the merchant banks have been concentrated into a smaller number of more powerful units. And the process is far from finished, since France still has far to go in order to catch up in most fields. Thus, in the United States, without even mentioning Britain, farming accounts for just over 5 per cent of the labor force; and, switching to industry, French firms still lag behind their German or British counterparts in productive and financial power.[1]

This reshaping has been taking place since the war regardless of the number worn by the French Republic. The squeezing of marginal farmers and tradesmen was already a feature of the Fourth Republic. Since nobody likes to be eliminated in the name of economic progress, the resulting discontent gave rise in the mid-fifties to a movement known as Poujadism, from the name of its leader, Pierre Poujade, a rabble rouser who explained to his followers that the root of all evil lay with tax collectors, egg-heads, and clever Jewish merchants. The Poujadists rallied massively to the Gaullist cause in 1958, hoping that the new regime would be more favorable to their interests. Their hopes, however, were bound to be disappointed.[2] Gaullism, if anything, quickened the tempo of concentration.

The Gaullist Republic had to speed up the process because it integrated the French economy more fully into the world market. The Treaty of Rome, setting up the European Economic Community, had been signed by General de Gaulle's predecessors, but it was he who brought France into the Common Market. In the ten years of Gaullist rule, the gross national product rose by 63 per cent. During the same period French exports more than doubled, increasing their share in the national product from 10 to 14.5 per cent. The increase was really more significant than it looked, since French trade had to shift during the same period from the sheltered colonial preserve to the more competitive European market.[3]

1. In the latest list published by *Fortune* (August 1969) of the top two hundred non-American firms only twenty-one French firms are included, compared with forty-seven British and twenty-eight German. In the top fifty there are six French and twelve German firms.

2. One of the explanations for the Gaullist seizure of power in 1958 is that the parliamentary Republic was not strong enough to preside over the process of economic modernization while extricating France from its colonial empire. A legendary hero was produced, a ruler capable of reconciling, at least temporarily, the inner contradictions of the system.

3. In 1958 the countries of the franc area still accounted for well over one third of total French exports, and members of the budding Common

The transfer was coupled with the liberalization of trade, the lowering of tariff barriers, and the lifting of exchange controls. Such an evolution was natural. It was in keeping with the letter and the spirit of the Rome treaty. Indeed, the French May explosion occurred just when the six members of the European Economic Community were going to abolish the remaining customs duties within the Common Market and surround it with a common external tariff. For France, which used to be a protectionist country, this outer tariff, based on the average among the six, meant a still further opening of its market.

France thus became much more sensitive to the fluctuations of the world economy, and whatever General de Gaulle's nationalist predilections, this could not but affect its economic policy. The transition is best seen in the changed emphasis in French planning. Since World War II all western states have been trying to instill some order into the anarchy of capitalist production. The French version of this attempt, which at one stage was being held up as a model, is known under the name "indicative planning." To put it crudely, officials sit together with representatives of employers' associations, trade unions, and other organizations in order to produce a detailed blueprint for medium-term economic development (four to five years). Employers cannot be given orders concerning what or how much they should produce —and in that sense indicative planning is just an exercise in coherent forecasting—but the state, with its power as producer, big customer, and lender, can influence their decisions.[4] For years, the accent in French indicative planning was on growth. In the most recent period, it has been gradually switched to price stability.

It is now customary to put the blame for the switch on General

Market for 22 per cent. By 1968 the share of the former overseas possessions had dropped to 13 per cent, while that of the Common Market had risen to 43 per cent (with Germany accounting for a fifth of French exports and a quarter of French imports outside the franc area).

4. But who is playing the decisive role? In Marxist terms, the state is defending the over-all interests of the dominating class. For that purpose, it may be forced not only to mediate inner conflicts within that class, but to impose concessions indispensable to preserve the system.

de Gaulle and on his financial battle with the United States. To attack the dollar, the Gaullists had to accumulate gold in the coffers of the Bank of France and therefore could not afford to incur trade deficits. This undoubtedly decreased their room for maneuver in domestic policy. But the General merely accelerated an inevitable trend. The reduced importance of national planning, the subordination of growth to stability, were really inherent in the liberal framework of the Rome treaty.

With their eyes fixed on the balance of payments, the French rulers got their country's economy infected with the so-called English disease, otherwise known as stop-and-go. As its name indicates, successive Tory or Labour governments had to halt Britain's industrial expansion as soon as it really got going in order to avoid trade deficits and a run on the pound. Though Britain presented the worst symptoms, it was not an exclusively English sickness. In the autumn of 1963, as the French economy was becoming overheated, Giscard d'Estaing, then Minister of Finance, applied the harsh treatment of a stabilization plan. The squeeze was not felt immediately, but from mid-1964 to mid-1965 industrial output was stagnant. Then for roughly a year production picked up rapidly, only to reach a new level and stand still once again. In the heat of the battle over the dollar price of gold—that is, over American domination of the western economy—the Gaullist ministers were unwilling to take inflationary risks to stimulate French production. They were waiting for Germany, France's chief customer, to recover from its own recession so as to stimulate production through exports. Thus, the upheaval of May 1968 occurred just as France was emerging from its second bout of stagnation.

A slower rate of growth, tighter financial conditions, increasing foreign competition, and the prospect of more to come—all this had an impact on French management. Mergers multiplied. Employers stopped holding on to labor during slack periods. Productivity rose faster than production. The French people suddenly rediscovered a forgotten fear, the fear of unemployment. While statistics in this field are extremely unreliable, particularly in France, it is officially estimated that in the spring of 1968 France had about 450,000 unemployed, accounting for 2.3 per cent of the labor force (or 2.6 per cent of total employment outside agriculture). Undoubtedly this was an exceptionally low proportion by American standards and was simply reaching the then British level. But for French people who since the war had lived in an era of what only economists can call overemployment, the psychological shock was serious. Unemployment once again began to look like a persistent phenomenon that particularly affected the young. Simultaneously, as a result of mergers middle-aged men in management or research also discovered that their jobs were not all that safe.

Discontent among the young, apprehension among graduates in industry—these two factors were to leave their mark on the May crisis. Yet these causes can provide only a marginal explanation of what happened. If each downturn in the cycle, each rise in unemployment, were to lead to an explosion, all western Europe, and Britain in the first place, would have had revolutionary governments for donkey's years. Having thus sketched the state of the economy on the eve of the crisis, we must look below the surface to see whether any deeper, more permanent changes in the social body determined France's social upheaval.

Throughout most of the postwar period France's civilian labor force averaged just under nineteen million people, over one third of them women. The inflow of foreign workers was roughly balanced by losses from an unusually old working population. Only in the past few years have total numbers grown, as the larger postwar generations started to enter the labor market. The previous overall stability in numbers, however, should not be confused with stagnation, with the absence of inner shifts and transfers. In France the major population movement from country to town, already mentioned, has prevented such social stagnation.

Historians may well stress one day that the years since World War II marked for France—and for continental western Europe—a new phase in the agricultural revolution. The spread of capitalist methods of production, the mass supply of tractors and fertilizers, brought about a faster increase in productivity in farming than in industry. While the agricultural population was more than halved, output per man during the same period more than tripled, thus raising the question of outlets. This, incidentally, was one of the reasons why the French government was interested in the Common Market.

France, which has roughly about half of the arable land of the European Economic Community, fought hard for an agricultural agreement penalizing food purchases from outside the EEC. Thanks to a complex system of levies on food imports, France's partners are encouraged to buy French surpluses or, alternatively, are bound to contribute to an agricultural fund, of which France so far has been the main beneficiary. Though this aid should not be exaggerated, the Common Market has in some respects helped France to cushion the shocks of its agrarian transformation.

Left to the free play of the market forces, migration from the countryside would have been much faster still. A system of price supports slowed down the exodus. Seen in perspective, this operation proved financially costly, socially unjust, but a politically paying proposition, at least in the short run. It was costly because average European agricultural prices were set fairly high, since in most countries farm lobbies still have political influence. As a result, production rose irrespective of demand, stocks accumulated, and surpluses had to be heavily subsidized to be dumped on the international market. Indeed, the whole European system was already bursting asunder when the French crisis occurred.[5] The system was unjust, because any system relying mainly on the maintenance of a fixed price in the final analysis merely confirms our society's Biblical dictum, "unto everyone that hath shall be given." Budgetary grants to keep up the prices of wheat, milk, and sugar beets have a different effect on

5. In December 1968, Sicco Leendert Mansholt, vice-president of the EEC, proposed a radical revision of the common agricultural policy. The main reason was financial. Agricultural subsidies by the six governments were estimated at $4 billion in 1968–1969, and, without a change in policy, were expected to reach about $10 billion in ten years' time. For the implications of this plan see pp. 223–231.

the marginal Breton farmer than on the big landowner of the
region north of Paris. They enable the former to survive at subsistence level and the latter, say, to purchase the most expensive
flats in the smart districts of the capital. Politically, however, the
system did work, since in the hour of reckoning the countryside
did not throw its weight onto the revolutionary side of the scale.

The policy had not always been so successful. The young
farmers who, encouraged to modernize, had bought equipment
on borrowed money only to find they could scarcely make ends
meet, would occasionally get mad, drive their tractors into neighboring towns, pour artichokes or new potatoes onto the streets,
and fight savagely with the police. Their exploits would then
make headlines in the international press. But when it came to
the real trial of strength, with very few exceptions they stayed
at home and thus propped up the regime. They behaved in this
conservative fashion for several reasons.

First, the emphasis on prices created the illusion of a joint
interest, of a farming community, blurring the real distinction between rich and poor. Secondly, the existence of a "European"
policy, worked out in Brussels, distorted the image of the conflict, allowing the government to parade as the defender of French
farming against unfair foreigners. Finally, the most dynamic elements in the countryside, regrouped in the Centre National des
Jeunes Agriculteurs (National Center of Young Farmers), or
CNJA, had been so busy collaborating with the government over
various schemes of reform that they could not contemplate throwing their troops into a decisive battle. Under the circumstances it
was not difficult for the government to frighten the rural population with stories about the car-burning Reds who, if they were
not going to nationalize wives, would certainly abolish private
property and grab the land from the farmer. For practical purposes the countryside remained quiet in May and contributed to
the Gaullist electoral victory in June.

The government cannot be certain that its agricultural policy
will always bring such dividends. Indeed, the European system
of price supports is too costly to be continued and, as we saw,

is already collapsing. The CNJA may well opt for a more militant leadership. Above all, a less improvised revolutionary movement is bound to learn from this spontaneous experience and seek allies in the countryside. Whatever the future holds, on this occasion it did work, bringing about a historical paradox. Though the motorized farmers of today are socially very different from their ancestors of a century ago, whom Marx in a famous passage [6] likened to potatoes in a bag unable collectively to defend their own interests, they actually performed a similar function. They helped to prop up the Gaullist regime as their forebears had propped up the empire of Louis Napoleon.

The radical difference is that the peasantry's ability to prop anyone up is very far from what it used to be. Taking simply the postwar figures, more people have left the land than are still working on it. The relevant question is, Where did all these uprooted peasants go? The men went mostly into industry, building, or transport. But the farmers were not the only ones to move. Detailed statistics reveal that the social makeup of the labor force is the result of a multitude of moves in various directions, of numerous shifts between branches, professions, and regions.[7] For our purpose it should be enough to consider the net transfers and the over-all trends summed up in Table 2 on the next page.

In the present ideological context, with so much talk about the twilight of the working class, the startling first conclusion to be drawn from these figures is that employment in industry has actually been rising. Naturally it has varied from branch to branch, going down in mining and textiles and moving up in chemicals and electrical equipment. Taken together, however, industrial workers now account for about thirty-eight per cent of the labor force and for substantially more if one includes those employed in transport and telecommunications. This is a bigger share than in the past, and leaving aside the vagaries of the cycle, it is expected to grow, admittedly very slowly, for some time to

6. In *The Eighteenth Brumaire of Louis Napoleon.*
7. See *Études et Conjoncture,* No. 10, October 1966. The entire issue is devoted to professional mobility in France between 1959 and 1964.

TABLE 2. TRENDS IN FRENCH EMPLOYMENT (in thousands of workers)

	1954	1962	1968 ‡	1973 (projection †)	1973 (per cent change, 1954 = 100%)
Farmers	5,175	3,878	3,087	2,183	42.2
Shopkeepers and assistants*	1,664	1,627	1,689	1,771	106.6
Transport and communications staff	1,299	1,386	1,495	1,609	123.9
Workers (including craftsmen)	6,685	7,050	7,364	8,319	124.4
Clerical staff *	1,507	1,850	2,254	2,731	181.2
Executives	304	378	463	646	212.5
Health services	250	346	500	618	247.2
Education	361	506	695	923	255.7
Technicians and scientists *	457	622	877	1,180	258.2
Total (including others)	18,949	18,956	20,002	21,500	113.5

* Excluding executives.

† Linear projection drawn up by manpower commission in 1966.

‡ Census figures for 1968 affected by squeeze.

come. Numerically, at least, the weight of the working class is not declining in France.[8] Prevailing theories about this supposed decline do not arise out of ignorance of statistics. They have an ideological base in a fashionable division of economic activity into three categories, crudely defined as primary (agriculture and mining), secondary (industry), and tertiary (including all the rest). While employment in farming has been going down, employment has been rising much faster in tertiary occupations than in industry.

The substitution of white- for blue-collar workers is a colorful

8. Employment figures in the population census of 1968 were affected by the economic squeeze. As industry did not provide enough jobs, the services were swollen artificially as a refuge from unemployment. France, it is now generally admitted, is insufficiently industrialized. International figures published by the OECD show that industry accounted for less than 41 per cent of French employment in the late sixties. The share was slightly lower than in Italy and much lower than in Britain or Germany (close to 50 per cent). True, industry accounts for only a third of U.S. employment, but this corresponds to a different stage. In France the growth of the tertiary sector is at one and the same time a sign of development and of underdevelopment.

though not entirely accurate description of this trend. The tertiary sector so loosely defined covers a strange range of occupations from charwoman to shopkeeper to chairman of umpteen companies. A social category that lumps together Baron de Rothschild and his footman or Mr. Rockefeller and his elevator boy must be analyzed in greater detail to have any meaning at all; and such a scrutiny reveals very significant divergences in the pattern of growth of various groups included under the same global heading. A clear distinction can be made between traditional services, which are stagnant or rising no faster than the economy as a whole, and the dynamic sections expanding at a much more rapid rate and accounting for the growing share of tertiary employment.

Thus, the classical services are losing ground. Domestic service, for example, is actually declining. Though in Paris Spanish and Portuguese women have taken the place of Breton maids, there are fewer domestic servants and charwomen in France than in the past. This reduction is barely compensated for by the spread of other personal services, such as hairdressing, cleaning, and so forth. Employment in trade, the other traditional outlet, is virtually standing still, though this stability, as we saw, conceals a gradual transformation; in the early 1970's France should, for the first time, have more shop assistants than independent tradesmen. Finally, the customary functions of the state, such as tax collecting, do not provide many more jobs. The numerical increase in the French civil service is accounted for partly by the post office and largely by the social services, with education showing by far the biggest increment (the bulk of French teachers are state employees).

If the traditional services expand very slowly, the growth of clerical and managerial work is much faster. The number of stenographers, typists, accountants, and other office workers will have nearly doubled in France over a period of twenty years. During the same period, the number of executives will have more than doubled. Under this heading are included the top managers in the private sector, who increase most rapidly; the highest civil servants, who do not increase so quickly; and the so-called industrialists, whose numbers are dwindling. This last contraction is the result of a double trend. Some disappear as a result of concentration. Many more change status for tax purposes, turning their private firms into companies and re-emerging as managers. Taking the executive group as a whole, these "top people," to use the deferential expression of a famous advertisement for *The* (London) *Times,* still represent less than three per cent of total employment.

But the pace of tertiary employment is set by two even faster-growing and most interesting categories. The first reflects the development of the two main social services, health and education. Employment in these two branches in France should soon top 1.5 million, or about seven per cent of the total labor force. The second category, also expanding at an annual rate of over five per cent, includes scientists and technicians. Included under this heading are scientific researchers, graduate engineers, highly skilled technicians, and draftsmen. Altogether they should soon reach the one million mark.

It is the social function of this fast-growing scientific and technical category that raised many discussions during the May revolt. Are they introducing technological change and improvements in organization that bring about higher productivity, or are they helping to increase the intensity of work and, therefore, doubly aggravating the exploitation of the workman? How much do their jobs benefit society as a whole, and how much do they simply swell the profits of their firms? Students, destined for such and similar jobs, suddenly revived in a new form the old dispute over productive and parasitical work. Their violent accusations against the existing order found an echo, and it rapidly became apparent that a similar test could be applied to the liberal professions, including teaching itself. A professor of, say, sociology can help his students to grasp the working of the social system and to question its very foundations. Alternatively, he can manipulate them in such a way as to rule out an alternative and turn them into efficient cogs in the established organization.

What is true of education is truer still of other professions.

Understandably enough, the revolutionary students did not question the need for spreading knowledge, nor did they oppose the trend that purported to reduce the part played by manual labor. They did question the use to which the huge surplus, resulting from the scientific revolution, is put in a market economy. A big proportion of white-collar work, they argued, is not designed to increase productive forces for human ends, to improve the labor conditions of manual and other workers, and ultimately to eliminate man's dependence on physical work. It is designed to exploit that labor, to impose a pattern of consumption, and thus to perpetuate a modernized capitalist system.

Putting on the agenda the issue of the ends of human activity, drawing attention once again to the difference between productive and parasitical work, to the clash between productive forces and social relations, the May Movement forced scientists, technicians, and teachers to think about their own function and to choose their side of the fence. It thus raised the problem of the future relationship between industrial workers, still by far the biggest and most coherent social class in the nation, and the fast-growing professional and technical intelligentsia invigorated by new blood coming from the universities. Much will depend on the nature of this relationship.[9]

Yet whatever the outcome, the structural changes that have taken place so far or are likely to occur in the foreseeable future do not preclude, on their own, revolutionary developments in France; on the other hand, neither are they specifically French. The mass substitution of white-collar workers for peasant farmers, or the slower transition from small tradesmen to shop assistants, far from ruling out revolutionary changes, improve the working class's chances of finding allies in its struggle. The phenomenon, however, is not typically French. This can best be demonstrated by reverting to the more usual division: employers, self-employed, and wage and salary earners.

At the opening of this century wage and salary earners ac-

9. We shall return to various aspects of this subject later in the book. See "The 'New Proletarians'?" p. 243.

counted for 58 per cent of the working population; at the end of
the last war, they still represented only 62 per cent of the total;
by the spring of 1968 their share had risen to over 76 per cent
and is still growing. But France is not venturing into uncharted
territory. On the contrary, it is following the trail set by Britain,
the pioneer of the industrial revolution, and elaborated by the
United States, Britain's western successor. Were it not for the
higher proportion of people still working on the land, the present
distribution of Frenchmen between occupations would not be
very different from the American pattern of about 1950.

Changes in the social structure of advanced capitalist societies
used to be given as one reason why revolutions could no longer
take place there. Since the French explosion this argument can no
longer stand on its own. In fact, it never could. It was always
coupled with the thesis about the social integration of the revolutionary class, about the *embourgeoisement* of the industrial
workers. This French term is now international currency, though
it has been converted in many ways. The loose concept has several meanings. One is that the proletariat, now that it is better
off, that it has more than its chains to lose, has also lost its revolutionary fervor. Another is that only the privileged sections of
the workers, a labor aristocracy, have a stake in preserving the
established order. A more sophisticated version suggests that
either the working class as a whole or just the labor aristocracy,
while acquiring higher standards of living, have also absorbed the
standards, the mentality, and the conservative outlook of the
lower middle classes. One must, therefore, look at wage differentiation in France, at gaps in income and consumption, to see
whether anything there explains the French exception to the alleged rule of a western world immune from revolutionary ferment.

Bare statistics, too, can be a method of distortion. To compare wages and salaries in a given country without a preliminary remark about property is to insinuate that the rich are only
richer because they get a bigger salary and to forget that they are
also wealthy because they own capital, because they own stocks
and other appreciating assets. In other words, it is to succumb to

the prevailing mythology according to which profits do not matter in modern monopolistic competition and property does not count in the age of big corporations, a managerial mythology of which John Kenneth Galbraith is only the latest prophet. However convenient, the myth, though based on elements of truth, does not correspond to reality in the United States, let alone in Europe.[10] Income is not the only yardstick of wealth, and salaries not the only source of income.

The second difficulty lies with the statistics themselves. The concept of wages and salaries, if socially more significant, is as loose and as all-embracing as that of a tertiary category of labor. It lumps together the unskilled laborer and the wealthy chairman of the board of directors. Tax laws being what they are, most French magnates are disguised as salaried managers (which, incidentally, accounts for the higher average income of top managers as compared with owners in industry and trade, whose average is brought down by the vast number of small tradesmen; and the latter, in addition, compete with some liberal professions for the title of champions in fiscal fraud).

Averages, in any case, provide a highly oversimplified picture. We know, for instance, that in 1966, the last year for which tax returns are available, 935 people had an average declared income of $240,000 (an average of $130,000 after taxes), whereas old-age pensioners were getting about $360 per annum. This huge range between top and bottom brackets is squashed in a tighter classification. Averages also conceal wage differences between men and women, as well as the more complex discrepancies between the young and the not so young. (As a rule, white-collar workers expect their salaries to rise with age, while blue-collar workers tend to find themselves in blind-alley jobs.) Provided that all its limitations are kept in mind, the following table gives an idea of the scale of wages and salaries in France.

10. For examples of controlling interest exercised with limited holding of stocks and for a general analytical criticism of John Kenneth Galbraith's *The New Industrial State,* see Ralph Miliband in *Socialist Register* (London, The Merlin Press, 1968).

TABLE 3. PERCENTAGE OF FRENCH EMPLOYEES IN INCOME BRACKETS, 1967 (in private and semipublic sector)

Net Annual Income (in dollars)	Higher Management	Lower Management	Other White Collar	Workers	Total (including others)
Less than 1,200	*	3.1	15.6	20.0	17.7
1,200–1,600	*	2.8	17.1	20.0	17.4
1,600–2,000	*	4.6	18.8	21.0	18.2
2,000–3,000	4.2	20.8	33.4	28.8	27.6
3,000–4,000	6.5	25.2	9.8	7.4	9.2
4,000–10,000	60.6	41.2	4.3	2.8	8.6
10,000 and over	26.7	2.3	*	*	1.3
Total	100.0	100.0	100.0	100.0	100.0
Number of Employees in Each Category (in thousands)	395	889	2,128	6,490	10,221
Average Wage or Salary (in dollars)	8,630	4,145	2,105	1,905	2,390

* Negligible.
Source: Institut National de la Statistique et des Études Économiques.

When in a country more than 40 per cent of the wage and salary earners get less than $1,800 per year—and such are the official estimates for France at the beginning of 1968—it is indecent to speak of an affluent society; the inaccuracies resulting from conversion at the official rate of exchange and the correction that should be made for the contribution of the social services do not alter the fact that for millions of Frenchmen the world of opulence is no more than a mirage. This impression is confirmed, though in less striking fashion, when looking at levels of consumption, even if, following the fashion, one looks at the ownership of those alleged symbols of affluence, the consumer durables.

At the end of 1967 a car, a washing machine, or a vacuum cleaner were to be found in roughly one out of two of France's 15.7 million households. Two thirds of the families owned a refrigerator, 60 per cent had a television set, and over a third had a record player. But only one household in four owned at one and the same time a refrigerator, a washing machine, and a television, while only one in five had all these and a car. Naturally the bulk of such families was to be found in the upper brackets, with an income of over $15,000 a year. That same year 43 per cent of all Frenchmen had a vacation, defined here narrowly as at least four full days away from home—which can also be read as meaning that at least one out of two did not go away for the briefest of vacations.

The difference between the haves and the have-nots did not disappear, though measuring the ownership of consumer durables is not the best way of drawing a line between them. So much attention has been focused on these symbols of affluence that they are often just symbols, absorbing a disproportionate share of a poor family's income. Television aerials in slums are a good illustration of this distortion. Housing, indeed, is often a much better guide to a country's prosperity, or rather to its people's comforts, and housing remains one of the worst black marks on the French economy.

A survey carried out at the beginning of 1967 showed that more than half of French dwellings had neither bathroom nor shower and no inside toilet. In rural areas, almost a quarter of the houses had no running water. About a fifth of all dwellings were considered rather crowded, and another 7 per cent badly overcrowded. At the other extreme, one-fifth had plenty of room to spare.

Was it then just a revolt of the have-nots, part of France's growing pains, an accident in the transition, which will be forgotten once the fast-growing production of durables throws some more goods onto the market? Nothing could be farther from the truth. The May Movement was not merely a struggle of marginal groups. If, in keeping with the Marcusian forecast, students acted as a spur, the other groups he mentions—"the substratum of the outcasts and the outsiders, the exploited and persecuted of other races and other colors, the unemployed and unemployable"—were not the driving force in the movement. And Europe, even if it is often ignored, does have such a substratum, consisting of men who perform the most unpleasant or the worst-paid jobs and who can be easily dispensed with when unemployment is rising. The European counterpart, though not the equivalent, of the Negro or the Puerto Rican is the foreign worker.

Greater dependence on foreign labor is the seamy, neglected side of western Europe's postwar expansion. The phenomenon is general, even if dependence varies from country to country. In Switzerland at one stage foreign workers provided a third of the labor force, foreshadowing a new Athenian democracy for citizens alone. Only in Britain, with its Indians, Pakistanis, and West Indians is the issue seriously linked with a color problem. On the Continent this aspect is secondary. In France, where foreign workers account for about eight per cent of the labor force, old layers of workers of Polish and Italian origin have been covered by successive waves of North Africans, Spaniards, and Portuguese, with now even a sprinkling of Yugoslavs and Turks and even more black Africans.

In Paris Spanish is now the main language among domestic help. Few Frenchmen are to be found employed on road construction teams. Foreign laborers are numerous in building, but they are also filling the predominantly unskilled jobs in various branches of industry, particularly where work is seasonal. Often living in slums, saving to send money back home, frightened of expulsion, trembling for their labor permit, the foreign workers are too vulnerable and too isolated by the language barrier to be the vanguard of a revolt. It is a measure of the sweep and scope of the May Movement that so many of them finally got involved. Yet, when in response to the student rising the general strike began to spread, the prime movers were French workers in relatively well-paid sectors such as the aircraft and the automobile industries.

Something deeper is therefore wrong with the affluent society, something that cannot be cured by the TV or the refrigerator. In May a notion of what prompted the workers to action could be obtained from leaflets and pamphlets, from numerous conversations, from ideas that were floating in the spring air unpolluted by any chimney smoke. The main resentment was directed against the factory itself, with its barrack-room discipline. A workman can feel in his bones that it is not his place but a strange surrounding in which he is a thing, an object, a commodity. The atomized, repetitive task is the more oppressive since the performer has the conviction that he can exercise no influence either on his own job or on the management of the factory as a whole. And this seemingly absurd activity must be carried on against the clock, at a nerve-racking pace. "Those infernal *cadences*" was the complaint recurring in every conversation. It is not only the rhythm and the condition but also the hours of work. A French workman may now be better off than before the war,[11] but he also works longer. This may sound surprising. The French government, after all, can claim to be a pioneer in vacations. Four weeks' vacation with pay is now the legal rule for all. Nevertheless, Frenchmen work more hours annually than they used to before the war. The forty-hour week, that great conquest by the popular front in 1936, is simply a limit above which overtime begins. In practice, French workers have averaged in recent years around forty-six hours a week. Add to it, daily, often a couple of hours in overcrowded public transport and it is no wonder that at the end of such a harassed day and journey most workers are fit only for the TV rather than for study or militant activity. No wonder, too, that suddenly something snaps.

Against this background it is easier to understand the am-

11. The real value of the hourly wage rate in France recovered its prewar level only in 1961. But social benefits (particularly family allowances) now account for a much bigger part of a workingman's income than before the war. Thus, to find out how much better off a worker is than before the war, one must know the size of his family. See *Études et Conjoncture*, No. 8, August 1965.

bivalence of the dialogue between students and workers, a dialogue bound to be awkward even without desperate jamming by the Communists. "Down with the degrading consumer society" was too sophisticated—or too crude?—a slogan to attract millions of workers who had only recently acquired a car or were aspiring to buy one secondhand. It was not too difficult to distort such a slogan as the raving of privileged intellectuals suffering from a surfeit.

And yet the wider message of the students also struck a chord. Many a workman felt that it touched the heart of the matter, that possession of more consumer goods, on its own, would not solve his problem, would not extricate him from the vicious circle in which the artificial paradise of leisure—*le weekend* or even the summer holiday—is supposed to compensate him for the frustrations of alienated labor and obviously cannot do so. Politically conscious workers were moved because the message reminded them of something they had once learned in their party cells. Workers at large were stirred because it was so clearly aimed in their direction. Beneath the romantic cover of moral indignation it echoed the Marxist appeal to the proletariat to accomplish its historical mission, to seize power in order to abolish class society. We have not heard the last of this ambivalent dialogue between students and workers even if in May the response was so muted that it all too often sounded like a shrill monologue by revolutionary students.

The unwritten premise is that May marked the beginning of a revolutionary era. Neither the example of the students nor the magic of their words alone could have driven the workers to strike on such a scale. The huge general strike was the outcome of accumulated discontent, itself the product of the conditions under which people work and live. What may come as a shock is that such conditions are the west European rule, not a French exception. Parallels with the United States are more complicated, since the United States has reached a different level of development. Comparisons with France's northern or eastern neighbors, allowing for the pitfalls of such an exercise, reveal nothing radically different, nothing that could justify contrasting behavior.

In the forms of property and organization of work, in conditions of life and labor, the patterns are basically similar. The hours of work per annum are roughly the same. The incomes—putting together the pay envelope and social benefits—are very close. The standards of living, taking into account national characteristics, are not very dissimilar. The French workman is not so well housed, but he eats better than the British or the German. Television is not yet as widespread in France as in Britain, but refrigerators are more prevalent, and France has marginally more cars per thousand inhabitants than either Britain or Germany. One could go on with such a balancing act without getting closer to an answer to the crucial question: Why was such a major strike possible in France whereas it still seems unlikely in Britain or Germany?

Part of the answer must now be sought in the political climate, in the general acceptance or rejection of choice. Nobody, not even the panegyrists of a "property-owning democracy," seriously believes that class struggle has vanished in the western world. The point is that in some countries, such as Britain or Germany, it has been institutionalized. Within the flexible limits set by the prevailing rate of profit, trade unions may bargain for a slightly bigger part of the cake. The latest attempt, prompted by the cost of long-term investment, is to institutionalize even the bargaining through an "incomes policy." The European trade-union bosses are not too enthusiastic about such a prospect, but they cannot even contemplate any solution outside the existing capitalist framework. The rank and file can fight, and even fight hard, within that framework. But the question of smashing it does not arise for the time being. In France or in Italy, on the other hand, the horizon is not so limited. There at the back of many workers' minds lies a belief in some kind of socialist alternative.

To seek the roots of this mood it is indispensable to glance, however rapidly, at the recent history of the French labor movement. Since the trade unions, through what they did or failed to do, were among the main actors in the May drama, it is necessary, if only for the understanding of the subsequent story, to provide the briefest of guides through the maze of French unionism.

THE GENERAL CONFEDERATION OF LABOUR . . .
brings together, irrespective of any political school, all the
workers conscious of the struggle to be carried on for the
disappearance of wage earning and ownership.
                              —First statutes of the CGT, 1902

"A Class for Itself"?

This article, proclaiming as its aim the end of exploitation of
man by man, still figures prominently on the statute book of
France's biggest labor confederation, the CGT.[1] The indifference
to "political schools" should not be taken to mean that the French
unions were originally nonpolitical. The texts of the documents—
such as the crucial Amiens Charter of 1905—show, on the contrary, that the labor unions considered themselves to be the main
political force. It was their job to carry out the "total emancipa-

1. But it was elaborated and reworded at the Thirty-Seventh Congress of
the CGT in November 1969.

tion" that could only be achieved through the "expropriation of capitalists." Once this was done, the unions were to be the chief organizers of production and distribution. And they were to accomplish their revolutionary task primarily through the weapon of a general strike.

Even if unconsciously, any movement is in some degree influenced by its origins. In May 1968 one could detect signs of the old belief in the *grand soir,* the day of reckoning, the belief in a sudden social upheaval, *le grand chambardement.* From their past French unions have also preserved the principle of separation between trade union and political party. No French confederation can have such open formal links with a political organization as the British Trade Union Congress has with the Labour party.

Yet the French labor movement cannot be explained in terms of its anarchosyndicalist origins. What matters are its current problems and its present position. The distinctive features of French unionism are its small membership, its split between various confederations, and its comparative weakness within the factory. Against this must be set the militant spirit of the workers, their sporadic outbursts and occasional big successes on a national scale. The relative backwardness of French capitalism, coupled with greater interference by the state, should also be taken into account. These are the problems that must be looked at to grasp the strategy and tactics of the French labor movement.

Out of France's fifteen million wage and salary earners less than a quarter belong to a trade union. The proportion would be closer to one third if one took the claims of the unions at their face value, and nearer to one fifth, if one accepted the estimates of skeptical analysts. In any case, the proportion is much smaller than in Britain, Germany, or the Scandinavian countries. The influence of the unions, however, extends beyond their membership (it could be measured in elections to social security bodies or factory committees). But this influence in turn is weakened by the divisions. French unions do not suffer from disputes between crafts. All confederations are run vertically by industry and horizontally by region. The division is between the confederations themselves, and it is political. The three biggest confederations are usually described, none too precisely, as pro-Communist, very moderately socialist, and ex-Catholic.

The first two spring from the same family. The CGT, united until World War I, has been split for most of the time ever since. That conflict dealt a double blow to the CGT. First, betraying its old principles of revolutionary pacifism, the confederation took an active part in the war effort, collaborating closely with the government. Second, the October Revolution gave birth to a new international movement with rules clashing with those of the CGT. For the Bolsheviks the trade union was only one of the instruments of class struggle, and a Communist within its ranks must not forget that he is a party member. Still, the split, when it became formal in 1922, was not so much between Communists and non-Communists as between revolutionaries and reformers, since many former anarchists joined the Communist minority in the breakaway union.[1a]

Fourteen years elapsed before the two rival groups were again merged, when the socialist and Communist parties got together in a popular front. 1936, with its great general strike, was the year of glory for the reunited CGT as its membership rose to a record level of over four million. Neither the new strength nor the recovered unity were to last long. The occasion for the new split was the Nazi-Soviet pact and the outbreak of World War II. Common resistance against the Germans prepared the ground for a second reunion, and the liberation of France inaugurated another spell of unity, of relative influence, and of reforms carried out with the help of a government that included socialists and Communists. (It may be argued that it was also another period of missed opportunities.) The third and still existing break came in December 1947. The CGT was a victim of the cold war and its division of the world. The majority of members chose Moscow rather than Washington.

In contrast to the two previous occasions, the Communists and

1a. Some left subsequently, others turned Communist like Benoit Frachon, who became secretary-general and is still the president of the CGT.

their friends gained the upper hand this time. They kept the name of the confederation and the bulk of its membership. Most workers chose to stay, not for reasons of foreign policy, but because the CGT was bound to be more militant than its splinter group. Party card-holders are outnumbered by seven or eight to one, and in a strict sense it is inaccurate to describe the CGT as Communist. On the other hand, the Communists are the only ones to have a line, an organization to carry it through, and trusted men in all key positions. When it really matters, their authority cannot be challenged. Hence, for the purpose of our story it is fair to refer to the CGT as a Communist-dominated confederation.

Communist authority is not seriously challenged because, whatever the theory, in practice decisions come down from the apex of the pyramid, in the union as in the party. The leaders must naturally take into account the mood of the rank and file, though the hierarchical structure provides distorted channels for its expression. Advancement on the union ladder is more dependent on approval from above than on support from below—hardly a system designed to encourage critical minds. The absence of genuine and open debate has made it easier to impose a line from the top. In the end the cumbersome CGT machine added its own dead weight to that of the party's bureaucratic establishment.

But this is only half the picture. The CGT would not be the power it is if its reputation as the most militant confederation did not attract the cream of the French working class. In addition to timeservers the CGT has in its ranks thousands and thousands of workers willing to sacrifice their leisure, their professional careers, and even their jobs for the sake of the class struggle. (Whether it will preserve this power of attraction is another matter.) On the eve of the May crisis the CGT had an estimated membership of over 1.5 million. In the last social security elections, in which all wage and salary earners were involved, it gathered about forty-four per cent of the votes cast. In polls taken at the factory level its share was substantially greater. Particularly influential in the automobile and aircraft industries, in engineering as a whole, but also dominant among railwaymen, miners, and dock workers the CGT is by far the most powerful of all the confederations.

Force Ouvrière (Workers' Force), which still uses the initials CGT-FO as its claim to the "old firm," is now much weaker. There is more often talk of Russian than of American gold as a sinister source of labor finance, but in the case of Force Ouvrière dollars were undoubtedly used to launch it on its way; the only doubt is whether CIA funds were actually transmitted through American labor-union channels.[2] FO, as we saw, was a product of the cold war, and as such has an uncertain future in a climate of coexistence. Its leaders are mild socialists who were quite close to Mollet's social-democratic party, though they could not follow it in its popular-front tactics because they have a professional stake in anti-Communism. For them, unity of action with the CGT would rapidly spell the end of their separate existence.

True to the syndicalist tradition, FO has no official links with any party and is mistrustful of planning, incomes policy, or any modern means for institutionalizing labor relations. At the same time, of the three big confederations it is certainly the one that is most eager to negotiate—whether with the state or the employers—and to reach a compromise.[3] This moderation has not paid off. In the spring of 1968, FO still had over half a million members, and in the last social security elections it obtained nearly one seventh of the votes cast. But it is gradually becoming a confederation of white-collar workers. Its strongholds are in the civil service and the post office. It has a small and narrowing industrial base.

In influence Force Ouvrière has already yielded second place

2. In 1967, after the sensational revelations made by Thomas Braden, Force Ouvrière denied having had any contacts with the CIA. This does not answer the question about the source of some of the money it received from the AFL-CIO.

3. It is dangerous to generalize. Some radical unionists refused to stay within a CGT dominated by the Stalinists. Force Ouvrière offered them more freedom of action. This is why one finds an entire federation of FO (in the chemical industry) or a regional union (Nantes) leading rather than lagging during the May crisis.

to the Confédération Française Démocratique du Travail (French Democratic Workers Confederation), or CFDT, a relative new-comer. Though founded in 1919, it had no real importance in the interwar period, when it was still called the Confédération Française des Travailleurs Chrétiens (French Confederation of Christian Workers), or CFTC, and was an organ of class collaboration run by the clergy. The change came with the advent of a new generation brought up in the Catholic working youth movement and hardened during the Resistance. The postwar growth coincides with the rise to power of this more radical generation, headed by the present secretary-general, Eugène Descamps, who was born in 1922.

By 1957 Descamps and three of his colleagues joined the directing body of the confederation, where they were still outnumbered by more conservative elements. By 1962 came the changing of the guard: The radical minority took over the leadership. Two years later the name was changed. The Christian label was dropped to show that the new leadership had a different conception and greater ambitions. By January 1966 the CFDT, which shares neither the prejudices nor the complexes of Force Ouvrière, signed an agreement for joint action with the CGT. The ex-Catholic confederation has roughly the same membership as the FO, though it already has a bigger following (more than one fifth of all the votes cast). Its strongholds are in engineering and in such modern branches as electronics. It is relatively influential among salaried staff and technicians.

In addition to these big three of the French labor movement, one must still mention a fourth power, the four-hundred-thousand-strong Fédération de l'Éducation Nationale (Federation of National Education), or FEN. Teaching does not fit into the established French pattern. The proportion of union members is very high within the profession, and the FEN was not torn asunder by the cold war. Instead it allowed the formation of organized factions, and their rigid, disciplined voting paralyzes to some extent the inner life of the movement. In the Syndicat National des Instituteurs (National Union of Elementary School

Teachers), or SNI, naturally by far the biggest member of the FEN, moderate socialists have a substantial majority and the pro-Communists (ex-CGT) come second, well behind. In the Syndicat National de l'Enseignement Secondaire (National Union of Secondary Education), or SNES, the two were still roughly balanced on the eve of the May crisis. In both there is a smaller faction called the Emancipated School, including anarchosyndicalists and Trotskyists.

The FEN is less strong among university teachers. Its union of higher education, SNESup, includes around a quarter of the academic staff. It is weaker among full-fledged professors than among associates and assistants, and this is why we shall refer to it later as the lecturer's union; the SNESup figures prominently in the events of May. Within this union the balance of forces was different, and in 1967 a radical coalition won a narrow majority. This is why Alain Geismar, its secretary-general, was able to throw the full weight of the union behind the revolutionary students despite the angry opposition of a substantial Communist minority.[4]

The conflict between a new radical left and the French Communist party is a feature of May, a problem for today and tomorrow. Rather than run ahead, we must now return to the labor movement proper and to the cumulative effect of its distinctive traits. The political division is certainly partly responsible for the small union membership. To give but one example, the closed shop (the exclusion of nonunion labor) is unthinkable in a French factory. But there are deeper reasons for the meager membership. In many small and medium-sized French firms the unions are being kept out by hook or crook. Even in big automobile plants like Citroën or Simca every effort is being made to limit workers' representation to "yellow" unions run by the management.

It is not so much through bargaining as through strike action, or the threat of it, that the French workers got their biggest gains. Their greatest conquests—whether in wages, welfare, or even

4. For subsequent change see p. 250.

union rights—were the result of battles on a national scale combined with political struggles. Admittedly, once the threat to the established order had been averted and the balance of forces restored, the alleged conquests always proved less impressive than they had been painted. Nevertheless, the pattern of struggle encouraged the workers to militancy and to questioning the whole capitalist establishment, which in turn discouraged managements from practicing collaboration inside the factory. The two trends fed each other, and in order to avoid explosive situations in France the state had to interfere more than elsewhere. It will be argued later in this book that Gaullism was partly the product of a stalemate between a potentially revolutionary working class and a relatively backward capitalism.

The French labor movement itself has not followed the same line throughout the postwar period. In the first couple of years after the war, while society was shattered and the business community, having largely collaborated with the Germans, was on the defensive, Communists as well as socialists were inside the coalition government, and the still united CGT was spurring on the workers to higher production in exchange for some social reforms. In 1947, the year of the Marshall Plan, of the final break between the wartime Allies, and of the expulsion of the French Communists from the government, the CGT launched its much delayed attack and, incidentally, lost its moderate wing in the process. French society had sufficiently recovered to withstand this assault, though the trial of strength in 1947–1948 was terribly tense. Even when the result was clear, the Communists did not let up on their political offensive. The CGT called on its members to strike and demonstrate in support of the peace movement, against American intervention in Korea, against "Ridgway the plague," and so on. Repetitive, unprepared, and unrelated to the direct, immediate interests of the workers, these actions wore out the rank and file and led to a big drop in CGT membership.[5]

5. The memory of this period renders all the more ridiculous the emphasis that Georges Séguy, its secretary-general, put during the May crisis on the nonpolitical nature of his movement.

Then came Stalin's death in 1953, which prepared the ground for peaceful coexistence, and General de Gaulle's seizure of power in 1958, which after a period of total isolation opened for the Communists the prospect of a left-wing coalition, of a new popular front. Since western capitalism appeared to have gotten its second wind and the French regime looked fairly stable, the labor movement had to adapt itself to this new situation. It was then discovered that behind the tactical moves of the labor movement there was really no strategic thinking. With a big Communist party still believing in Stalinist fashion that debate is a dangerous source of heresy and that a slogan is a perfect substitute for analysis, it was not strange that the French left should have been barren of ideas. Nor was it surprising that the ideas that did filter through came from Italy, where a more flexible Communist party forced the left to tackle problems. It was in Italy that the so-called strategy of structural reforms originated; in translation into French, it got the even more ambiguous name revolutionary reformism.[6]

The ambiguity lies not only in the title. In one sense, the new strategy was simply an adaptation to new circumstances, a refusal to fight yesterday's battles. To elaborate a program, to determine its alliances, to develop its propaganda, any movement must grasp the meaning of the changes in its environment. When throughout the postwar period western capitalism knows only recessions but no major economic crisis, when defense spending and state intervention reach new heights and industrial concentrations—a new pace when the Common Market provides a new supranational

6. For a radical interpretation of the strategy, those reading Italian can consult in *Critica Marxista* and *Problemi del Socialismo* articles by L. Basso, V. Foa, L. Magri, B. Trentin, and others. The great merit of André Gorz (author of *Strategy for Labor* [Boston, Beacon Press, 1967] and of *Le Socialisme Difficile* [Paris, Éditions du Seuil, 1967]) has been to introduce this subject matter to a wider European public. P. Naville, S. Mallet, and P. Belleville wrote about changes in the French working-class. For a reformist interpretation of the strategy see the writings of G. Martinet, and for a revolutionary approach toward similar problems see those of the Belgian Trotskyist, E. Mandel, author of the *Traité de l'Économie Marxiste*.

framework while the technological revolution reshapes the makeup of the labor force—when all this and more happens, if a socialist movement does not use the critical tools at its disposal to analyze the shifting situation, it abdicates its hegemonic revolutionary role. In the long run it means resigning itself to a purely defensive position, to a superior form of Poujadist protest.

But the strategy of structural reforms involved more than analysis. Its aim was to exploit the new contradictions, to offer counterproposals as part of a socialist alternative. The method was not without its risks. Were the changes to be carried out from within the system? Neocapitalism had shown its ability to withstand piecemeal attacks, such as partial nationalizations. In more general terms, workers cannot conquer economic power under capitalism as the bourgeoisie did under feudalism. Indeed, the more radical exponents of the strategy never contemplated a gradual transition within the system, which would ultimately result in the establishment of a socialist society. For them, each conquered position, whether in the factory or on the national scale, was a base for new advances; each action was also a recruiting drive for further offensives. A coherent socialist alternative was designed to show the workers and the mass of the population that the logic of their basic aspirations clashed with the inner logic of capitalism. Such mobilization was indispensable for a seizure of power that would open the way for a transition to socialism.

As its French title suggests, the strategy was also open to a more reformist interpretation. It could provide an ideological cloak for the tactics of social integration. This possibility was particularly real in France, where the party and the confederation that were reputedly revolutionary, namely the Communist party and the CGT, would have nothing to do with such innovations. When the Communists had defined Gaullism as "the rule of monopoly capitalism" or, to put it differently, as the government of big business, and added that the solution lay in the extension of "democratic nationalisation," they had done their theoretical homework. On the other hand, the labor confederation that was tempted by the new ideas, the CFDT, was suspected of reformism, and rightly so. The suspicion did not just rest on its Catholic origins of class collaboration. It rested on more recent experience. Until about 1965 the CFDT did try to elaborate a program of "democratic planning," including an incomes policy, within the existing system. The presence among the official technocrats of men with a kindred "progressive Christian spirit" helped to encourage its illusions. It was only the patent failure of this attempt that drove the CFDT to take a more radical line, to put more emphasis on the class struggle and on the incompatibility between its democratic socialism and the existing regime. Yet even then only a minority among its militants interpreted the strategy of structural reforms in a fairly revolutionary way.

The May explosion looked, at first sight, like a vindication of Communist skepticism. The workers, after all, were stirred to unprecedented action without any preliminary mobilization over structural reforms. A second look revealed the emptiness of the CGT arsenal. The biggest confederation had nothing to offer beyond wage demands and completely irrelevant proposals for a parliamentary coalition. The slogans of the CFDT were more in tune with the mood of the moment, but this, the second biggest, confederation had neither the following nor the confidence nor a sufficiently coherent line to take the lead on this occasion. The French workers were aware, however dimly, that they would have to seize power in order to consolidate their position, but for years nobody had told them how to set about it. The second part of this sentence indicates the limits of the May Movement, whereas the first part points to the fundamental difference between the French and Italian labor movements and their British, American, and German counterparts. In the Hegelian terminology of young Marx, French workers are closer to a "class for itself," groping, however haphazardly, toward political power; whereas the British workers are a "class in itself," which does not look beyond its immediate bread-and-butter interests.

Britain is the best choice for a comparison, since it does not share American illusions about classlessness. In the everyday social meaning of the word, no country is more class conscious than Britain, with its U and non-U patterns of behavior and its subtle shades of lower-lower or upper-upper middle class. Probably in no other country would a poll on social status get so many answers stating "working class," the subjective appreciation coming quite close to the assessment by the sociologist.[7] In a more political sense, too, British workingmen are quite class conscious. They know that their interests and strength lie in solidarity. Shop stewards have no great difficulty in bringing them out in sympathy strikes. Even a Labour government has not quite managed to break their militant spirit. Yet at this stage the bulk of British workers is not at all convinced that to alter radically their position they must seize power and do something about the system as a whole. (After the Wilson experiment nobody in his senses is likely to confuse the election of a Labour government with a threat to the capitalist order.)

This fundamental difference has a bearing not only on the workers themselves but also on the mental climate of the country. In Britain or the United States, the Marxist view of the class struggle has hitherto affected only a fringe. The dominant ideology reigns supreme. In France, its supremacy has always been questioned. Admittedly, the equation of socialism with the Soviet Union and the absence of creative thinking on the left have weakened the antidote in recent years. Nevertheless, throughout the postwar period the prevailing ideology has had to reckon with opposition. It is not a paradox to suggest that the student revolt, which rejected the established rules of the game and the conventional judgments of value, was more of a shock in the United States and Britain, where so far it has been contained within bearable limits. It was less of a shock in France, but there it cut across the heart of political life.

It is in this context that one can grasp the dual influence of official Communism. More by their image than by their acts, more by what they stood for than by what they did, the CGT and the Communist party have hindered the process of integration and

7. Which does not prevent a good proportion of such workmen from voting Tory, in keeping with the saying that "they know their station."

helped to preserve the revolutionary potential of French workers and their allies. The May crisis showed that they cannot use this potential. If the crisis should prove to be the beginning of a new revolutionary period, they will not be able to perform a dynamic role in the future. Later in the book we shall try to show why the French Communist party, unless it changes its nature and structure, is utterly unsuited for playing such a part.

At the close of this brief survey of France on the eve of the May crisis, the main peculiarity of France seems to lie in the unique political horizon of its labor movement. Two other points can be recapitulated briefly. France is in a process of transition. The exodus from the farms is not proceeding as fast as it did in the United States in the 1950's, but since the share of employment in agriculture was initially much higher in France, the proportion of peasants turned workers in its labor force is also much bigger. Less integrated, these newcomers not so surprisingly turned out to be more militant than other workers in the hour of crisis, though the importance of this factor should not be exaggerated.

Secondly, French big business is on the whole less powerful and less flexible than its western competitors. France still has a great number of medium-sized and small firms in industry as well as in distribution, and it has an explosive working class. Gaullism emerged as the product of this balance and of the vagaries of colonial withdrawal. Rather rashly, many saw in Gaullism a postparliamentary model, a form of technocratic rule for the age of big corporations. It did not quite come up to their expectations.

Gaullism, itself the result of a specific situation, in turn affected the course of events. A system of personal rule, in which all key decisions come from the top, tends to turn conflicts into crises. This may explain why a student revolt that elsewhere might have been handled at a lower level became an affair of state. It does not explain why France had a general strike. If the slow rate of growth of wages, for instance, had been the mainspring of workers' action, Britain rather than France should have been the site of the explosion—which brings us back to the political horizons of the labor movement.

French and Italian workers tend to be treated as an exception. It is more difficult to determine what the rule is.[8] Actually, each case should be treated in its context. Since an upheaval is also the result of specific circumstances against a given historical background, it would be rash to forecast for tomorrow a repetition of the French experience in, say, Germany or Britain; that now seems most unlikely. Conversely, it would be foolish to rule out a similar experience at a later date. If the equilibrium in the allegedly immune countries rests on nothing more solid than the capacity for social integration or the degree of political consciousness, its stability cannot be guaranteed. In France, too, after all, the crisis came suddenly and General de Gaulle was not the only one to miss the writing on the wall.

Wisdom comes after the event. Some experts now trace the warning signs back to February 1963, when the miners struck for thirty-five days, successfully defying the official requisition orders. But this was a rear-guard action in one industry, and a contracting industry at that. More significant, and more recent, was the stoppage in February–March 1967 at the Besançon and other works in the Lyon region of Rhodiaceta, a manmade-fiber firm belonging to the big Rhône-Poulenc group. Here, the strikers bothered less about wages than about security of tenure, the guarantee of employment. For this reason they questioned the policies of the management and asked for the books to be opened. There was already some friction between the more militant rank and file and the union leaders, while the interviews recorded on that occasion were a foretaste of the mood of May, with some young workers rebelling against the absurdity of their condition rather than simply complaining about the level of income.

8. It can be argued that the United States, like Britain in the nineteenth century, can absorb its working class for a time, thanks to privileges derived from its technological lead; that Britain goes on living, if not on the fat of the land, at least on conditioned reflexes; that the case of Germany is peculiar because of the aftereffects of Nazism and of the Soviet occupation, and so on.

More was still to come. In October 1967 Le Mans hit the head-lines not because of its twenty-four-hour car race, but because of a battle between workers from Renault, from Schneider and other factories in the area, and the police, a battle that raged for hours in the neighborhood of the *préfecture*. In January 1968 it was the turn of Caen in Normandy. During an unlimited strike at the Saviem truck factory a demonstration through the town ended in a violent clash between young workers and the riot police. Students for the first time were to be seen on the side of the fighting workers. They were to be seen again in March during a similar conflict at Redon. In all these struggles there was one common factor—the entry onto the stage of a new generation.

I WAS TWENTY. *I will not allow anyone to say it is the most beautiful age in life.*

—Paul Nizan, *Aden-Arabie*

The Dynamics of Youth, or Angry Young Men

They're coming. . . . Who? The invaders. Eight hundred and fifty thousands of them are coming of working age every year. Originally they were welcome, even eagerly awaited. The Gaullists, seeing greatness in numbers, were dreaming aloud of a France with a hundred million inhabitants. (Debré, when prime minister, was accused by the satirical magazine *Le Canard Enchaîné* of a rabbit philosophy, *le lapinisme*.) But the dream turned sour. The newcomers refused to take their appointed places. They

106

THE POPULATION OF FRANCE, MARCH 1968 (in thousands)

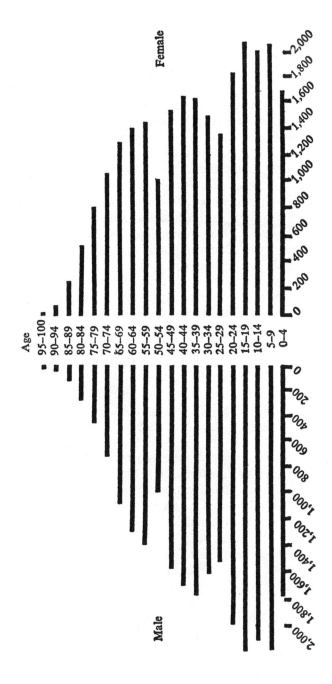

failed to conform to the nice image drawn up in a White Paper on Youth. They were not the nice boys and girls of the official fable, the socially obedient morons. Instead of just smashing chairs at a pop show, the new barbarians thought of smashing the regime. As shown in the accompanying graph, the population pyramid with its mighty base must now give sleepless nights to France's Gaullist rulers.

All over the world the powers that be are watching anxiously the growing generation. In France, where decades of stagnating population have bred a Malthusian mentality, the shock is particularly great. Once upon a time, when Bonaparte was crowned Napoleon the Emperor, there were 28 million Frenchmen, a multitude by the European standards of 1800. Though he bled his country white, by the middle of the nineteenth century France's population reached 35 million. Then, even without the pill, the size of the family started shrinking. At the turn of the century the total population climbed to just over 40 million. With only a fractional difference, this was the level of the French population at the end of World War II. Admittedly, in the meantime France had been decimated by World War I. Its ravages, however, were the more lasting since they affected a country with a stationary population. Without foreign immigration France's population would have actually declined in the first half of this century.

The trend changed abruptly after the last war. The postwar baby boom was reinforced in France by the introduction of substantial family allowances, and it took place in a country unprepared for the invasion, even though France had years to get ready. The slowly mounting wave reached the level of the labor market only in the early 1960's. By an international convention it is agreed that men between the ages of fifteen and sixty-four and women between fifteen and fifty-nine form a country's population of working age. By 1968 in France young people under twenty-five already accounted for more than a quarter of this potential labor force, and the balance was shifting every year in favor of this postwar generation. By 1978 those under thirty-five should account for about half the population of working age. Advancing inexorably, this young army might echo in a mocking fashion the last stanza of the "Marseillaise," the only postrevolutionary passage of the National anthem:

Nous entrerons dans la carrière
Quand nos ainés n'y seront plus
Nous y trouverons leur poussière
Et la trace de leurs vertus . . .

(We shall begin our careers,
When our elders are gone
We shall find their dust
And the trace of their virtue . . .)

Certainly richer than Job, but not so patient, the swarming millions have no time to wait for the dust to settle. As to the virtue of their predecessors, they only have to look around. . . . Under the weight of numbers, the foundations of French society are creaking.

Youth is not a class.[1] As soon as the young emerge from their apprenticeship, their school or faculty, they are driven to their places in society and to their potential side of the barricade. A revolutionary force cannot rest entirely on such a transient base. This is not to deny the special features of youth, even if these are unequally divided. Some are born old; in each grade there are schoolboys with the soul of the pensioner and the mentality of the stockholder. Conversely, and fortunately, there are plenty of people who preserve their unyielding spirit despite the passing of the years. Still, that spirit, and not only the impatience or the quest for the absolute, is usually associated with youth. Refusal is probably the key word: refusal to yield, to capitulate, to compromise.

1. For the opposite thesis, see John and Margaret Rowntree, "Youth as a Class," *International Socialist Journal,* Vol. XXV, 1968. In this very interesting essay the authors show the growing importance in the U.S. economy of the "defense and education industries," which help to absorb surplus manpower. It is in this context that they argue that the young are increasingly the main victims of exploitation.

Twenty, in Nizan's words, is not the most beautiful age, because the young man then discovers not only the tyranny of nature but that of established society, disguising its own dictatorship under the veil of technological constraint. He tends to rebel, to refuse concessions, and that is why the young are likely to be the dynamic element within their class.

We saw the revolutionary students rejecting wholesale the existing society. Behind them, ready to take over, stand the younger activists from high schools, serving their apprenticeship in the already mentioned School Action Committees, or CAL. Disgusted with the electioneering politics of the "respectful left," European students had to look to the oppressed of distant lands for a cause worth fighting for. Then they realized that they could also wage a different and yet identical struggle nearer home. Le Mans, Caen, Redon, pointed the way. In the militant young workers they saw their first potential partners.

Workers feel their alienation in their bones. It is part of their condition, their heritage. In France the young workingmen had their own additional reasons for discontent. The number of unemployed on the eve of the political crisis was put at around 450,000; it was also estimated that about forty per cent of those vainly seeking for a job were young people under twenty-five.

Lack of skill was not the chief obstacle. Indeed, it is among the skilled that unemployment was rising fastest. Many a young man unable to find employment had in his pocket his Certificate of Professional Aptitude, CAP. Many, in fact, kept their CAP's in their pockets and accepted jobs below their qualifications. Even those who got employment corresponding theoretically to their skill felt frustrated. More educated than their elders, they were also more aware of their productive potential, more conscious both of what they might have learned and of the limited use to which their knowledge was put. Between the young workingman emerging from technical school and the young student the gap was still relatively narrow.

At the political level, too, one could sense a cleavage between generations. The official adult left looked weary, battle-scarred, disillusioned. Its veterans could well remember the popular front of 1936, but also the Moscow trials and the Nazi-Soviet pact. For its middle-aged leaders the Resistance had been the great heroic period. Then, too, a generation was thinking of changing the world only to be frustrated and deprived of its victory. In the name of what had it accepted the lies, the half-truths, the rotten compromises? In 1956 like Alyosha in *The Brothers Karamazov* it discovered the stench of its saintly man's corpse. Three years after Stalin's death came Khrushchev's secret speech and then the Hungarian insurrection. Back home, this was followed by the failure to prevent the Gaullist takeover and by a half-hearted struggle against the Algerian war. The new generation is not burdened with such bitter experiences. Its veterans gained their spurs trying to intensify the fight against the war in Algeria. Admittedly, at the time of the May crisis the Russian invasion of Czechoslovakia was still to come. But then revolutionary youth is not burdened either with the Stalinist heritage or with any fidelity to the Kremlin.

In the factories, too, there were contrasts in mood. It is too simple to argue that the young are more daring because they have no wives, no children, no responsibility. This is not all. Youth takes a different view of its environment. For their fathers, the car and the television are the symbols of great achievement. For youth, they are part of the landscape. Young people cannot so easily be tempted to sell their political birthright for a gadget. True, the commercial society, neglecting no group that has money to spend, directed its advertising limelight on the young, and undoubtedly they were dazzled. But in a sense the young workers know even better than the students what social price has to be paid for the blessings of the so-called consumer society. Less integrated than their elders, unaffected by the Gaullist myth, questioning the virtues of their predecessors, including the authority of trade-union bureaucracy, the young workers formed a natural link between the revolutionary students and their own class.

History has a strange sense of humor. While this alliance was being forged, preparing the ground for the biggest strike in French history, the talk in Paris that spring was about the hopelessness of strike action. Trade-union leaders themselves seemed at a loss, not knowing how to cope with the intransigence of employers backed and guided by the state. From time to time, duly giving the newly required five-days' warning, they would call their troops out for a token twenty-four-hour strike. Occasionally they would combine it with a demonstration, in Paris a traditional march from the Bastille to the Place de la République. The militants would come, chant *"Pompidou—des sous,"* "Pompidou, give us dough," and go back home comforted by the fact that they had been so many.

But the day after, nothing would be changed. The learned were, therefore, writing about the end of the class struggle. The experts were pondering about the shape an incomes policy would assume in France. The Gaullists, untroubled by social unrest, were preparing for a splendid anniversary. It proved to be a hell of a birthday. The students provided the dynamite; the young workers, the fuse; their elders, the mass that had to be moved. Everything was ready for the explosion.

PART THREE
The Explosion

RUN, COMRADE, RUN, *the old world is behind you.* . . .
                                        —*Slogan revived in May*

The Student Uprising
(May 3–May 13)

THE STRANGE SIEGE *of the Sorbonne lasted only ten days.*
This first act was a curious mixture of the unexpected and the
inexorable. The rulers, bewildered, stumbled from blunder to
blunder. Political parties were completely taken aback. In this
spontaneous movement the leaders were those who sensed the
direction of the shifting tide. After merely a week, but what
a week, the night of the barricades marked the triumph of the
apparently vanquished students. The government then tried to

limit the damage by confining the victors to their academic ghetto—in vain. The mass demonstration on May 13 was the end of the first act, but also the beginning of the second.

May 3 started like any other Friday, with no visible sign of a gathering storm. The average Parisian found no warning in his newspaper of an impending crisis. The well-to-do, opening their *Figaro,* were reassured. True, the faculty at Nanterre had to be closed temporarily, but the paper's expert concluded with superb timing that the "revolutionaries" by their acts had managed "to strengthen the unanimity against the instigators of the movement." The Communist who was dutiful enough to read his party's paper had more food for thought. *L'Humanité* splashed across its pages a long article by Georges Marchais, vituperating against "False Revolutionaries to Be Unmasked." In this piece, which was to gain notoriety, one of the party's secretaries described Daniel Cohn-Bendit as a "German anarchist" and defined his friends of the March 22 Movement as "mostly sons of *grands bourgeois,* contemptuous toward students of working-class origin." It was a most revealing article,[1] but since the revolutionary students, according to the analysis of Marchais, were really serving the interests of big business and Gaullism, the regime had clearly nothing to fear from that quarter.

Newspaper readers were not the only ones to be kept in the dark. Most of the actors had no idea of what was coming. Alain Peyrefitte, the smooth Minister of Education, still in his early forties, could hardly imagine what was in store. As product of the École Normale and a diplomat by profession, he was one of those Gaullists of Bray, apparently destined for the highest honors under the Fifth, Sixth, or Seventh Republic. Despite his relative

1. The author foreshadows the Communist strategy in the coming crisis. He already accuses the students of "pretending to give lessons to the labor movement" and of attacks against the Communist party. He also gives away the reason for his piece and its timing: "more and more, they are to be found outside factory gates or in centers of immigrant workers distributing leaflets and other means of propaganda."

youth he had been the General's Minister of Information, then of Science, and was expected by many to hold the very top jobs. Could he guess that a "handful of troublemakers," to quote his own expression, would precipitate the beginning of the end of his career or at least the first break in an uninterrupted climb? On the other hand, Jean Roche, the rector of the Paris Academy, the Minister's chief representative in this crucial area, at the age of sixty-eight was clearly approaching the end of his academic career, begun as a professor of medicine. His prospects were retirement and a pension rather than a sudden and uncomfortable entry into the history books.

When the Latin Quarter itself woke up that morning, it presented no ominous sign of effervescence. Within this district on the Left Bank of the Seine are concentrated the bulk of the university buildings. To understand the importance of this concentration one must imagine, say, that a quarter of all the colleges in the United States were lumped together in New York around Columbia, or that Oxford, Cambridge, and London University were thrown together around Bloomsbury. Naturally, the 150,-000 Parisian students do not live in their *quartier* nor even all attend lectures there. The permanent inhabitants of the district are no builders of barricades. (After the crisis, as before, they sent a Gaullist deputy to the National Assembly.) But the students do consider the Latin Quarter, with its cafés, snack bars, and restaurants, its small cinemas, hotels, and bookshops, their own.

Its main artery is the Boulevard St.-Michel, familiarly known as the Boul' Mich'. The quarter is bordered on the north by the Seine, while to the south it stretches beyond the Luxembourg Gardens toward the Paris Observatory and Montparnasse, once the hunting ground of painters, poets, east European revolutionaries, and American expatriates. The frontiers are fluid. With a new faculty of medicine and the School of Political Sciences the student quarter now extends westward just beyond St.-Germain-des-Prés, known to postwar tourists for its "existentialist" cafés. Eastward it spreads to the new faculty of sciences erected on the site of the former wine market (*Halles aux vins*). But its heart remains the Boul' Mich' with its neighboring narrow streets. The foreign visitor is attracted by the bustle of youth rather than by such tourist landmarks as the Sorbonne or the Panthéon, where the French bury their famous dead.

Today, the Sorbonne is essentially the faculty of arts of the University of Paris. There are other faculties—law and economics, medicine, pharmacy, science—in this district full of academic institutions. The overcrowded Sorbonne, with its individual institutes and sections, had to spread, create annexes, invade other bodies. Still, the old Sorbonne building stands symbolically for Parisian student life. Old is not an accurate description. Though the Sorbonne can trace its origins to a theological school in the thirteenth century, its present building dates back to 1900. You can reach it from the boulevard by crossing a small square bearing its name, with a statue of Auguste Comte in the middle. Within ten days, this father of French positivism would be bearing a red flag.

Inside, in the main courtyard, there was some exceptional animation by noon that Friday. A few activists of the March 22 Movement from Nanterre, locked out of their own faculty, were meeting their Parisian comrades. Political groups with stronger roots at the Sorbonne, the two brands of Trotskyists, the Maoists, the left-wing socialists, and even at one stage the orthodox Communists, were represented. It was not a mass meeting, however, only a gathering of militants; there were about four hundred to start with, and some more turned up in the afternoon. Under the auspices of the students' union they had two urgent points to debate. The first was how to counter the offensive of the authorities at Nanterre. Not only had the faculty been closed, but eight students, including Daniel Cohn-Bendit, had been picked out as alleged ringleaders. The following Monday they were to face the disciplinary council of the University of Paris and the threat of expulsion.

The second, no less urgent, item on the agenda was how to reply to the planned attack of the extreme right-wing movement called, with unflattering symbolism, Occident. The fact that among its members former paratroopers were allegedly more numerous than students was, for fighting purposes, small consolation. A weekly paper, *Minute,* sympathetic to that movement, had just proclaimed: ". . . this Cohn-Bendit must be taken by the scruff of his neck and carried to the frontier without any formality. And if our authorities do not have the courage to do so, we know a certain number of young Frenchmen itching to perform this task of public health. . . ."

Occident itself was distributing leaflets claiming that "in agreement with all the Nationalists we have decided to bring to an end bolshevik agitation in the faculties *by all means*. We shall show on Friday the third that we are able to oppose Red terror and to re-establish order with the means required." The next few days were going to show who had a popular following in the Latin Quarter. Yet the threats of Occident were not entirely empty. Only the previous morning the offices of a student association had been burned and the arsonists had left their mark—the Celtic cross, sign of the Occident movement—on the wall. This accounts for the fact that the tougher attendants at the Sorbonne meeting had on their combat uniforms with crash helmets and sticks.

Did Rector Roche panic? According to most accounts there was no special trouble in the courtyard. The strongest allegations against the students were that they broke an old table in order to arm themselves with its legs. Even if true, this hardly explains the decision—if not entirely unprecedented, highly exceptional—to call the police force into the Sorbonne, where legally they have no right to enter without express permission. The rector could not have taken such a serious decision entirely on his own; he must have at least consulted his superiors at the Ministry of Education. One cannot, therefore, help a sneaking suspicion that the momentous move was the result of miscalculation rather than panic.

Here was the golden opportunity for teaching the *enragés* a lesson, for isolating the troublemakers and crushing them once and for all. The advisers in the Ministry of Education were reporting that with only three weeks to go before examinations, students were busy cramming and had no time for agitation or agitators. Most newspapers were giving the same impression— and not concealing their hostility. This looked like the moment to show force and make an example, to expel a few students and to intimidate the ringleaders through arrests, to prove that no nonsense would be tolerated and to do so amid applause ranging through the political spectrum from *Minute* to *Le Figaro* to *L'Humanité*. Magnificently Machiavellian? This splendid piece of formal logic rested on the false premise that the rebels were isolated. When this logical structure collapsed, it almost brought the regime down in the process.

Inspired or improvised, the move was made. Early in the afternoon policemen were out in the streets of the Latin Quarter in growing numbers. By 4 P.M. the Sorbonne was surrounded by a massive police force, helmeted, truncheons in hand, tear-gas grenades at the ready, prepared for battle. Inside, the students were arguing about what they should do. They decided not to fight. Stories differ as to whether they were given a formal pledge by the academic authorities that, provided they were peaceful, they would be allowed to leave freely. The truth is that as the police forced their way through one entry, at about 4:30, students driven toward another doorway were being picked up there by the gendarmes and thrown into Black Marias, or, as the French call them, salad bowls.

The news spread fast. From libraries, from cafés, from all over the place, students started moving toward the Sorbonne. For once the "troublemakers" were under arrest. No blame could be put this time on the "ringleaders." And here the unexpected happened. The students did not write an indignant letter to *Le Monde*. They did not circulate a petition. Nor did they call a protest meeting for the morrow at the Mutualité, where distinguished Nobel Prize winners could recall the Rights of Man and the Citizen while others could warn the government to beware. They did nothing of the sort. They simply thronged toward the police chanting "Free our comrades—*Libérez nos camarades*," the slogan that was to be the refrain of one memorable week. If this reaction was unexpected, the ensuing clash with the police was more predictable.

The cliché about each country having the police it deserves is really meaningless. It is more accurate to claim that the behavior of a country's police is rooted in tradition, that it reflects not only current tensions, but also the strains and conflicts of yesteryear. Having seen American cops, with their dogs, handling a civil-rights demonstration in the South or simply the 1968 Democratic convention in Chicago, European viewers know that the Americans need no lessons in toughness. In Europe, however, there are different patterns. The London bobby is still gentle by French standards (and since violence escalates, so is the London demonstrator). This is not due to any metaphysical cause, to French toughness or British gentleness, even if continentals are still puzzled by the story of the English policemen playing soccer with the workers during the general strike of 1926. The explanation is historical.

Bourgeois democracy has never struck such strong roots in France as in Britain. It was not only governments that trembled. Successive regimes felt ephemeral, their legitimacy often openly questioned by large segments of the population. They could not always afford the luxury of subtle domination. The police were not just for show or for traffic duty. More than potentially, they have always also been a weapon of civil war. Thus, of the forces that the Gaullist government had at its disposal during the May crisis, the best known, because of their sinisterly reminiscent initials, were the CRS. These Compagnies Républicaines de Sécurité (National Security Guards), founded after the war, had their baptism of fire in December 1947 in bloody battles with striking miners in the north of France. True, there was to be no such conflict with the workers for years to come, but in the meantime—until 1962—the French police fought on the internal front of a colonial war. For years their main task was to crush the Algerian National Liberation Front and its French sympathizers.

Admittedly, students are neither workmen nor Algerians.

Though traditionally there is no love lost between the students and the police, the myth of the students' privileged social origin still carries weight. You never know whether the young man you're clubbing will prove to be the son of some V.I.P. Usually it is preferable not to go to extremes. But this was no ordinary demonstration. The police were surprised by the angry response. Were the student gluttons for punishment? The truncheons and grenades only seemed to multiply the zeal and the number of demonstrators; from a few hundred they grew into a couple of thousand. The police had difficulty in clearing the boulevard. The students immediately revealed what were going to be their main assets: speed, fantastic daring, a flair for improvisation, and knowledge of the terrain.

Better armed and protected but less mobile, the policemen discovered that the struggle was not entirely one-sided, that it might be give and take. The gloves were off. An isolated student cornered by a few policemen had a fair chance of being a case fit for medical treatment. Many students proved elusive, and some policemen vented their rage on passers-by or even on the unlucky customers in neighboring cafés. The skirmishes lasted until dark. Shields, truncheons, and grenades on one side, the first cobblestones and even a token barricade on the other—all the ingredients of the coming confrontation were there. Blundering, through a complete miscalculation of the student mood, the government had precipitated the crisis. Spontaneously, the student rising had really begun.

Not everybody was aware of this dramatic change. The educational expert of *Le Figaro* thundered the morning after: "Students, these youngsters? Young guttersnipes, fit for the remand home, if not for a court of summary jurisdiction, rather than for the university." It was the turn of his Communist colleague on *L'Humanité,* while blaming police repression, to revive the theme of rebel isolation: "How to qualify those who, by their irresponsible acts, their violence, their insults, have provoked this situation? Already now, the great mass of students, including, we are sure, many of those who were led astray, can measure the serious consequences to which political adventurism inevitably leads, even if it is concealed behind pseudorevolutionary phrases."

The government, too, had not yet grasped the gravity of the situation. It still hoped to intimidate by a show of force. True, most of the arrested students were released during the night. But not all of them. While reinforcements were being sent to occupy the Latin Quarter in force, the arm of the law came to the rescue of the truncheon. The magistrates worked overtime, forgetting the weekend. On Saturday, though the prosecutor argued that "it must be known that here justice strikes," the accused were still given suspended sentences. On Sunday four demonstrators were sent to prison. The government was soon to discover it had awkward hostages on its hands. Within less than a week magistrates genuinely believing in the independence of their profession were to regret bitterly the Sunday zeal of their colleagues. But for the moment most outsiders—the government and the opposition, the politicians and the unionists—were still on the old wavelength and could not understand the new message from the Latin Quarter.

The academic world reacted more rapidly to the shock. Scarcely had the police ended their mopping-up operation on Friday night than the students' union called for a nationwide university strike to begin on Monday. Alain Geismar, in the name of the lecturers' union, issued a similar call, without bothering about the compulsory five days' notice. This was not the moment for legal niceties. In the Latin Quarter it was obvious that the times had ceased to be normal. Packed in the Black Marias, the student activists, the "leaders," could not believe their ears. When they learned that a major riot had burst out spontaneously, they felt their hour had struck. They were not going to miss the opportunity provided by the government's mistake and the explosive mood of the students. Hardly had they been released by the police than they held a late meeting on Saturday night to decide what to do next.

It is striking that from the very start the students did not bother about minor reforms, about corporate interests, syllabuses, or grants. Their three-point ultimatum was simple: The Sorbonne had to be reopened, the police force withdrawn, and the arrested demonstrators released. This last point was soon extended to demand the release of all demonstrators, whether students or not, whether French or foreign. For a radical transformation of the university system the students looked beyond the campus toward the factories. From the very beginning, in speeches, in debates, in the numerous leaflets soon to invade the French capital, the accent was on collaboration with the workers. "Long live the solidarity between workers and the fighting students," proclaimed one of the early leaflets. "The bourgeoisie fears above all," argued another, "that the student revolt will get linked with that of the workers."

Although they agreed on the strategy, on the need for joint action with the working class, the "grouplets" differed on tactics, on the best means for bringing such a junction about. The Maoists from the UJCML were in favor of leaving the Latin Quarter and concentrating their work on propaganda against repression through action committees in working class districts. The rigid Trotskyists of the FER wanted to exercise pressure through existing organizations: the students' union should somehow force or shame the labor unions into a joint strike and common demonstrations. The other groups—particularly the March 22 Movement, the Revolutionary Communist Youth (JCR), and the short-lived University Movement Action (MAU)—put more emphasis on the students as an autonomous force. Sensing that they could act as a detonator, they felt that the student movement had to play its own part to the full in order to have a chance of performing this explosive function. The students' union, influenced by the FER, first sent an appeal to all the labor unions. But it also called for a demonstration the following Monday. The mass of students was then to enter the arena and dictate, in a way, the course of the combat.

Monday the sixth was indeed one of the bloodiest days of May. As a rule, throughout this period fighting started in the evening. That day, it began almost in the morning. Paris was the "capital of peace," the meeting ground for North Vietnamese and American negotiators. But the Sorbonne woke up that morning looking like a fortress in occupied territory. Thousands of policemen were surrounding the university. The layman could hardly distinguish between the Paris police and its "special sections," the *gendarmes mobiles,* who are part of the army, and the CRS, the riot troops rushed in from the provinces. The first clashes occurred early in the morning as the "culprits" from Nanterre passed through the police cordon, singing the "Internationale," to face their judges.[2] For the time being the troops had orders to protect only the Sorbonne and its approaches. Dispersed, the students could regroup elsewhere and march through other parts of the Latin Quarter.

By noon there were several thousand on the embankment in front of the big modern building of the faculty of science. Were they to storm the Sorbonne or move into working class quarters to put across their case? Opinions differed. When the crowd began to move, they were still undecided. Their minds were made up as they faced a massive police barrier. The students were not yet ready for battle. They crossed the river and marched for a couple of hours through the center of Paris, chanting "Sorbonne for the students! CRS—SS! Down with police repression!" and so on. The general public was rather sympathetic. There was occasional applause and there were no boos. But the real test was still to come as the marchers got back to their own side of the Seine. An ominous silence fell as they approached the Rue St.-Jacques leading to the rear of the Sorbonne. What now?

All of a sudden the police charged with unexpected savagery. Several wounded students lay on the ground. The mass retreated. The zealous gendarmes had little time to savor their triumph. It was their turn to run under a rain of stones. Mad with anger, the students broke up the street for missiles. Learning from the enemy, they put the cars unlucky enough to be parked nearby in a staggered arrangement, a kind of quincunx. Tear gas could not dislodge them, and the police had to send other troops to threaten

2. The verdict, scheduled for the following Friday, will never be given.

them from the rear. Even then the students retreated in fighting order along Boulevard St.-Germain and dug their heels in at the Place Maubert. There it was a real battle, with charges and countercharges, cobblestones versus grenades. The air was thick with tear gas, yellowish with a sweet and acrid taste. Even the passengers in the subway below were crying. The police were bewildered by such stubborn resistance. They had to call for massive reinforcements, and after a couple of hours they finally managed to conquer the square.

They had not quite conquered. The students had vanished. Throughout the Latin Quarter the trek was now southward. From all over the place young men and women rushed toward the Place Denfert-Rochereau. It was there that the students' union had called them for a mass meeting at 6:30 P.M. The spot was well chosen. Near enough the Latin Quarter to show that the students were determined to recover their district, the square was vast enough to contain a big crowd. Its numerous outlets provided potential escape routes and were a puzzle for the police, who could not guess where the marchers would move. In the middle the statue of the Lion of Belfort—a smaller copy of Bartholdi's original—supplied a platform for men with a loudspeaker. Known once as the square of hell—Place d'Enfer—it was to be for a very brief season the meeting place of youthful hope.

Fresh from home or straight from one of the many skirmishes, the demonstrators were delighted to find themselves so numerous. They were already several thousand strong, and their ranks were still swelling. University students were in a majority. But there were also some young workers, high-school students, scientists, teachers, as well as a group of professors and lecturers answering their union's call, which had been issued in the heat of the afternoon fighting. ("We are asking university teachers to take their direct responsibilities, that is, to go out into the streets on the side of their students.") Ironically, the demonstrators raised their hands with ten fingers outstretched, chanting: "We are a grouplet, a handful of *enragés*." [3] Yet they knew they had not come for fun. Sporadic bangs from grenades exploding in the neighborhood were a reminder that this was no gentle stroll. And as the first rows of the marchers reached St.-Germain, they found themselves right in the front line.

That evening St.-Germain-des-Prés was no place for tourists. The Flore, the Deux Magots, the Mabillon—these well-known coffeehouses were in the range of fire. That night St.-Germain was not Greenwich Village nor Chelsea; it was a battlefield. The police could neither cope nor understand. Their forces were impressive and armed to the teeth. There was a time when, faced with such a black armada, the students would have turned and run. Now fear was turned into passionate determination, and they tended to run forward. In daring hands the cobblestone was a match for the hand grenade. *Le pavé*—the new hero of May, the Parisian paving stone, small enough to fit the hand, heavy enough to hurt, provided munition for the fighter and a brick for his barricade. It was also the symbolic stone thrown against the edifice of the established disorder.

A riot? No sir, it's an insurrection. Here, with the help of cars, billboards, railings, torn-off branches, trees, as well as cobblestones, the first serious barricade went up. Here a couple of buses serve as a barrier. There, two fire engines escorted by gendarmes are forced to fall back as students with only stones in their hands launch a successful counterattack. Faced by young men whose inventive fury could compensate for their inferiority in weapons, the police were driven to change their tactics. From then on they tried to avoid direct frontal clashes. The new method was to bomb first and mop up afterwards. The bombing was carried out preferably from a distance with grenade-throwers. Simple tear gas was soon backed up by more toxic varieties and supplemented by concussion grenades.

The second phase, the attack on broken up, isolated groups, was all the more violent since the strength of the resistance had

3. In France, under the decimal system instead of a dozen, you have a *dizaine,* hence the ten outstretched fingers.

been a shock to the police, who are neither used to nor designed
for an equal struggle. "Stop it, stop it . . ."—from time to time a
shrill voice would come from a window as the onlooker found it
unbearable to see a woman or a youngster clubbed into uncon-
sciousness. The main battle was over by about 10 P.M., though
sporadic fights and the chase after isolated groups lasted well
into the night. The official score for Bloody Monday was: 422
arrests; 345 policemen wounded, 24 of them taken to the hospital. The casualties among the demonstrators, higher still, could
not be calculated. Knowing by then what could happen to them
if they fell into the hands of the police, many students chose to
lick their wounds in private rather than to take that risk. But repression, once again, produced the opposite effect from what the
authorities had expected. The students were far from cowed, and
Bloody Monday was followed by Tuesday's Long March.

They were probably twice as many, some twenty to thirty thousand around the Belfort Lion on Tuesday evening. The revolt now
had its own paper, *Action,* and it sold like hotcakes. Leaflets
were also distributed, explaining how best to cope with tear gas.
More professors, workers, intellectuals, had come to express their
solidarity, but the students were still the most numerous and they
set the tone. The young march in a different way. Theirs is not a
stroll, a procession. They set off as if in a hurry to conquer something. From time to time they rushed, almost sprinting, their steps
responding to the *"hop, hop, hop"* of the cheerleaders, and the
successive waves then resembled the Japanese *zengakuren.* The
older marchers were not the only ones to be surprised by the
rhythm. So were the police, unaccustomed to demonstrators who
moved at such a pace.

The march was immediately brought to a first halt. The Latin
Quarter was forbidden territory, and near the Luxembourg Gardens its frontier was heavily guarded by massive trucks and bus-
loads of policemen. The students did not want a battle there and
then. The improvised stewards, holding hands, kept the crowd in
check and guided it backwards. At the corner of Boulevard
Montparnasse there was a moment of hesitation: eastward toward

the working-class districts, or westward toward the Champs-Élysées? The idea of parading red and black flags in the shop window of bourgeois Paris prevailed. The next moment of tension came when the demonstration reached the river. The bridge was blocked by the police. The long esplanade of the Invalides, with Napoleon's tomb at its back, was filled by the young crowd. A clash? No, both sides at that stage were trying to avoid one. The students turned right, and *hop, hop, hop,* they sprinted across another bridge toward the Concorde. The way toward the Arc de Triomphe was open.

In their rush the demonstrators had passed without any fuss in front of the National Assembly. Their contempt was symptomatic. There had been a time, under the previous Republics, when the Palais Bourbon—the seat of the lower parliamentary chamber—was a focus for demonstrators. Parliament had been the target for the protesters and the main headache for the police. The students, however, knew better. They did not attack the Élysée Palace, General de Gaulle's seat of presidential power, because they were not strong enough to face the bullets. They by-passed the Palais Bourbon because it was not worth storming. Ten years as a Gaullist rubber stamp had broken the remaining illusions about the importance of an already discredited institution.

"Power is in the street," chanted the demonstrators moving up the Champs-Élysées. The vast and elegant avenue had not witnessed such a parade for decades. Its lights were lit when, toward 10 P.M., the crowd filled the circular ending to the avenue, the famous Étoile, the undisputed star of wealthy Paris. Red and black flags floated in the wind, and the massed demonstrators roared the "Internationale" around the Tomb of the Unknown Soldier lying beneath the Arc de Triomphe. This was the supreme sacrilege, which in days to come would provoke indignant protests, because it is well known that the poor fellow got, along with a bullet in his head, a pledge not to be subjected to anything but patriotic prose and the national anthem.

After this iconoclastic climax the students marched back to their quarter, now turned into a police stronghold. The inevitable clashes started around midnight, though they did not reach the scale of the previous day. Many demonstrators had gone home, others were tired by the lengthy trek. The few dispersed fights, however, were violent, and some policemen were in a very ugly mood. Toward 2 A.M. a wooden framework was burning at one end of the Boulevard Montparnasse. Hooting ambulances overtook the black police-wagons. The ambulances were in a hurry. They stopped outside a coffeehouse, and the rescuers with the help of firemen broke its windows. Some of the customers staggering out had to be given oxygen. It was a near thing. The police had thrown gas grenades inside the café. Miraculously, the long march did not have a tragic ending.

Next day the political climate was visibly different. The stock of the students had risen considerably. They had shown courage and discipline. They had not yielded to blows; then they had proved they could stage a mass demonstration in an orderly fashion. Public opinion was shifting to their side. The middle classes were shocked by reports of police brutality, which could not be concealed. The workers were impressed by the fighting spirit of the students. The young men who had braved the truncheons and the grenades and came back asking for more were clearly no weaklings. The revolutionary spokesmen of the student movement and the professors associated with them felt carried forward by a tide that was not only Parisian. The news from the provinces was encouraging. From Toulouse and Marseilles in the south to Lille in the north, from Strasbourg in the east to Rennes in the west, came reports of solidarity meetings and demonstrations. Carried away by the enthusiasm—combined with the weariness of sleepless nights—the dynamic Alain Geismar proclaimed on Wednesday morning: "Whether the police frees it or doesn't, tonight the Sorbonne will be ours, it will belong to students and teachers."

Mixed with the feeling of strength there was a growing apprehension that the movement would be "reclaimed," its revolutionary force channeled toward reformist ends. "It's never for fun that one fights against a stronger opponent," *Action* had argued in its first issue. The revolutionary leaders now feared that their exceptional struggle could be diverted, channeled back into the established framework. They feared the government, which might seek a compromise through minor concessions, and also the opposition, which was eager to exploit the movement for merely parliamentary ends. For the time being, the government was still hesitating over the best method of getting out of its dilemma. It was still preoccupied with face-saving as much as with the task of placating the students.

The Communists proved quicker, or rather less slow, in sensing the change of mood. The day before, Séguy, the CGT leader, had vituperated against leftists who "have the unbelievable cheek to give lessons of revolutionary theory [to the working class] and pretend to lead its struggle." Next day in Parliament and in *L'Humanité* the attacks were aimed at the Gaullist government, while Communist students and teachers were for the first time urged to attend the mass meeting that the students' union had called, for a change, at the faculty of science on the embankment. If you can't beat them, join them and hope to swamp them in numbers.

It was raining in the evening as thousands gathered in the courtyard of the faculty, not knowing whether they would be led into yet another battle. The prospects were far from clear. Earlier, the communiqué published at the end of the Cabinet meeting had offered little hope. The Minister of Education had declared: "The government cannot accept that the tolerance and serenity indispensable for teaching and research should be replaced by fanaticism and violence." He had nothing to say about student demands. Professors of science, convinced that a new collision could lead to a bloodbath, sent a delegation headed by the Nobel Prize winner Jacques Monod, to persuade the Minister to change his stand. Peyrefitte then published a new declaration, which he was to repeat in the chamber, giving an assurance that "if these conditions are fulfilled [that is, if peace is restored] lectures could be resumed at the Sorbonne and at Nanterre as soon as the deans of the faculties think it possible, that is to say, I hope, by tomorrow afternoon."

However vague, this looked like an opening. The young men listening in the rain wondered about the next move, while spokesmen for various teaching unions expressed their solidarity. When the CGT delegate mentioned the name of Georges Séguy, his leader, he was greeted by some boos. But there were more important problems. Jacques Sauvageot and Alain Geismar confirmed that the three demands were inseparable and that even if the faculties were reopened, there would be no lectures so long as all the demonstrators had not been released. They also revealed that a representative of the Ministry of Education (as a matter of fact, the deputy rector) was in touch with them. Thus, the march began in an atmosphere of uncertainty.

Even before it started, a small incident had occurred that was a typical sign of the inner tensions. The orthodox Communists had brought along their deputies and municipal councilors of the Paris region. They tried to head the procession. This old maneuver was too obvious and did not work. Amid protests, the Communist dignitaries had to fall back into line. Crash-helmeted students moved ahead. Other stewards, holding hands, kept the marchers in on both sides. Though contacts had been made with the police and an agreement reached about the itinerary through the "forbidden" Latin Quarter, precautions were not superfluous, because with passions rising the smallest incident could get blown up into a bloody conflict.

The slogans were the same as on previous occasions, yet there was an uneasy feeling in the marching crowd, and when the demonstration reached the Luxembourg Gardens and the militants spread the order of the students' union to disperse, this feeling turned to disappointment. Many students lingered, and amid the groups that went on arguing despite the continuous drizzle, the prevailing idea was that they had been let down. Nobody was seriously suggesting that the Sorbonne, with its mighty police garrison, could have been stormed. Still, the students felt cheated, convinced in a curious way that the revolt was over, that it had been seized surreptitiously by parties, unions, organizations, and was now to be bartered away in some shady deal.

If the government ever had a chance of stemming the student tide, this was it. This was the moment to open the gates, release the prisoners, offer reforms. But the opportunity was not seized for all sorts of reasons. The Gaullists could hardly imagine what was still to come. The General talked of order and thought of prestige. The ministers, as usual in this regime, were mainly concerned with the General's opinion. And admittedly they were not given much time to act. While they quibbled over legal difficulties and bothered about what the students might do if allowed back into the Sorbonne, the revolutionary leaders recovered their bearings. Indeed, some students spent that Wednesday night debating how to repair the damage. When next day the police forces in the Latin Quarter, far from being removed, were reinforced, the student leaders sighed with relief. The General had come to their rescue.

On Thursday afternoon the Sorbonne was still in the hands of the police, with a number of students gathered just outside. Daniel Cohn-Bendit, with the voice of a tribune and the flair of a popular leader, proclaimed the street a lecture hall since the university was closed. With thousands just sitting down, the Boul' Mich' provided a stage for a lively teach-in. Alain Geismar publicly admitted he had made a mistake the previous day. Jacques Sauvageot explained the position of the students' union and took into account the criticism of it, since this was no passive assembly. Louis Aragon, the grand old man of French and Communist letters, seeking here the memory of his own surrealist and revolutionary youth, provided an interlude. He had some difficulty in getting a hearing, so strong was the resentment against Communist attacks. A party dignitary, he could not dissociate himself publicly from the official line, yet he promised to devote a whole issue of the literary journal he edited, *Les Lettres Françaises,* to the students.

More significant, however, was the decision of the JCR to accept Cohn-Bendit's proposal and open the meeting it was to hold that evening at the Mutualité to all the revolutionary groups. As the moment of decision approached and the movement gathered momentum, the "grouplets" could not preserve their sectarian predilection for cultivating differences. They either entered the mainstream or were thrown out, at least temporarily, onto the banks.

Differences, naturally, did not vanish. In the packed hall of the Mutualité that evening they became, on the contrary, quite striking as soon as the French militants took over after preliminary speeches by foreign friends. The Maoist spokesman for the UJCML summed up his outlook in a seemingly paradoxical formula—"Let's leave the Sorbonne to the gendarmes in exchange for their barracks at St.-Ouen" (a working-class suburb)—and dismissed other policies as petty-bourgeois attempts to isolate students from workers. The spokesman for the FER wanted to build a pyramid of strike committees in the faculties, headed by a national committee. Even Daniel Cohn-Bendit and Daniel Bensaid, though both members of the March 22 Movement, disagreed on one crucial point—the need for a revolutionary party (the former denied such a need, the latter considered a party indispensable). But both agreed that the immediate task was to unite, to carry on the struggle. They also agreed with Jean-Louis Peninou, of the ephemeral MAU, that the need now was for small action committees, regrouping the rank and file and thus encouraging initiative from below. Once again small groups went on discusing passionately well into the night. But whereas the previous evening the prevailing mood had been one of disappointment, that night there was a conviction that the showdown could not be put off for long.

Friday, May 10: Only a week earlier Rector Roche, by calling the police into the Sorbonne, had produced the unexpected, and now a major crisis was moving inexorably to its climax.[4] To understand why a showdown looked inevitable as well as to grasp the otherwise incomprehensible waverings of the coming night, one must ponder for a moment the positions of the contending

4. *Roche* means "rock" in French, and student wits protested that the rector was a mere pebble, though pebbles can occasionally distort the course of events.

parties. The student leaders were being carried along by a swelling tide, bigger each day and not just Parisian. But they could not afford to back down. The fiasco of Wednesday night was for them a lesson; a repetition, and either the tide would ebb or they would be swept aside. On the other hand, watching each day the tremendous police concentration, with reinforcements sent from the provinces, they could not ignore the risks of a massacre. The most lucid among them maintained that the risks, while serious, were limited, because they were students, not workers: The government could not open fire against "the future elite of the nation." In any case, the problem was not to storm the Sorbonne, but to march on and refuse to yield.

The government, from its initial blunder, was in a dilemma. It could not treat the students like workers for a combination of reasons. It was not just that most of the ministers had academic connections. (To take just one example, the white-haired Louis Joxe, acting as Prime Minister in Pompidou's absence, was himself a former professor and allied by marriage to the very academic Halévy dynasty.) Nor, as has been suggested, was it just that the rebellion was by their own children, by their own class. More important was the fact that until then student revolts had been treated as incidents and not as a major threat to society. Finally, the Gaullist system of government must be taken into account, a system in which the ministers are guided by what the General might think of them. On this occasion, General de Gaulle, preparing for his Rumanian journey, showed no sense of history. He simply told his ministers with soldierly wisdom that order must be maintained.

And so the government groped in all directions in search of a policy. Thus, on Thursday, after the improvised teach-in in the street, Peyrefitte announced that the Sorbonne would be closed "until calm is restored." That same day, Joxe was reported to be working on a compromise. To overcome the obstacle of the demonstrators in jail, the government advised the students' lawyers to lodge an appeal. The public prosecutor claimed their case could not be heard until the following Tuesday. The real snag was that the students could not be shot nor could they be clubbed into submission. The government was by then reluctant to wield the truncheon and loath to surrender. Within twenty-four hours it was to do both in quick succession.

"Free our comrades"—it was still the same slogan after a week's interval. Only this time the high-school students were the first to chant it sitting around the Lion of Belfort. During the past three days the strike had spread throughout the Parisian *lycées,* and their revolutionary organization, the CAL, brought its followers to Denfert-Rochereau at about 5:30 P.M. An hour later they were joined by the usual contingent of university students along with their intellectual and working-class allies. There was talk of an even wider coalition. The UNEF had reached agreement with the educational and labor unions for a joint mass demonstration the following Tuesday.

A peaceful parade, however, was not necessarily a panacea, and Tuesday was a long time away. A more urgent question was what was to be done that night. In keeping with the main demand, they should go and deliver their friends. But the central prison, La Santé, was too near and impregnable. The Sorbonne was out of bounds. As they began to move, most marchers were not certain whether they were going to the Ministry of Justice to demand the liberation of their friends, or to Broadcasting House to protest against the fantastic bias in the official television and radio coverage of the events. The positioning of the police, too, was bound to have a bearing on their destination. In fact, they set off on a journey to night's end.

It was a new route. Their itinerary took them this time through more popular quarters. There were more people on the pavement, more open windows. "Come with us into the streets. Your children go to school. You are all concerned." The marchers were visibly encouraged by the applause. Yet tension rose as through Boulevard St.-Germain they approached the Latin Quarter. Each side-street leading to the Sorbonne was filled with policemen armed for combat. Derisively, the students greeted them with the Nazi salute, roaring "CRS—SS." Between the demonstrators and the police there was only the thinnest line formed by young men and women holding hands and acting as stewards. There was hatred in the darkening air. The column stopped. Had the fighting started? No, it was simply that the gendarmes, backed by trucks, were blocking the way. The demonstration could not move forward nor could it turn right toward the Seine. It was only allowed to turn left and march up the Boulevard St.-Michel back to its point of departure.

The trap was obvious and so was the counter. Having reached the Luxembourg Gardens, the demonstration stopped. The leaders could not repeat Wednesday's mistake. They told the thousands massed in the boulevard to divide into groups and occupy the *quartier*. Did they also tell them to break up the streets to get ammunition? There was probably no need for such instructions. Faced with the police, not just outside the Sorbonne but throughout the district, and with the experience of previous days fresh in their minds, the demonstrators were not going to stand there empty-handed. Not everybody agreed. The orthodox Communists protested and walked out.[5] What is certain is that the next logical step—the feverish building of barricades—was entirely spontaneous, a sheer invention of the crowd.

The official spokesmen who were soon to talk of "experts in urban guerrilla tactics" had a strange sense of humor. No expert would have chosen as the central axis of his defense system a vast avenue (Rue Gay-Lussac opposite the Luxembourg Gardens), thus allowing the enemy scope for bombing and room for maneuver in attacking; the barricades that resisted longest were in narrow, climbing streets. Built with passion and ingenuity—but then young students and workers lack neither—the fifty or so barricades were located haphazardly. They were the product of circumstances, as was the police (or rather governmental) deci-

5. *L'Humanité* of May 11, having along with the other papers been put to bed too early to report the whole of the night's events, put the blame on "Trotskyist and anarchist groups." But the incident was quickly forgotten. That same day, the Communist party published a communiqué putting the blame squarely on the government.

sion to allow them to go up. But they were also a political act and a symbolic reminder. They were a sign that the students, while not attacking, would not yield until their demands were met. They proved, though only later, to have a special appeal to the collective memory of French workers, whose grandfathers had fought in the Commune. The impact was the greater since, if not the whole nation, still a great many Frenchmen stayed up to listen. The night of the barricades was also the night of the transistor radio.

A digression is here necessary. Everybody knows that France's state television and radio (Office de Radiodiffusion-Télévision Française, or ORTF) are fully under government control. They are their master's voice. France, however, has also its commercial radio stations. Two in particular have a big following, namely Europe One and Radio Luxemburg. To claim that they are independent would be an overstatement.[6] Let us say that they are influenced in less direct fashion and have, therefore, more scope for maneuver. Add the element of competition, and the skill and courage of reporters with a love for their jobs, and you get a night of dramatic reporting that kept millions of Frenchmen awake. That night was certainly no exception to the rule that "truth is revolutionary."

Radio Luxemburg even acted at one stage as an open go-between. The recording of this abortive negotiation on the air is quite a valuable document.[7] It makes the official case, which alleges that the students had "refused the dialogue," sound rather

6. The state, for example, holds nearly half the stock in Europe One. The other main stock holder, Sylvain Floirat, is a millionaire who is also the owner of Matra, the aircraft and missile company heavily dependent on government contracts. Besides, though the transmitters of both stations are outside French frontiers—which is why they are called "peripheral"—the government can cut them off at will.

7. Most of it can be read in the brief but excellent *Insurrection Étudiante*, a critical collection of documents edited by Marc Kravetz (Union Générale d'Éditions. 10/18. Paris, 1968). This was published immediately after the events. Now the researcher has at his disposal the impressive and scholarly volume *Journal de la Commune Étudiante*, documents selected by Alain Schnapp and Pierre Vidal-Nacquet (Paris, Éditions du Seuil, 1969).

hollow. The experiment started exactly at 10 P.M., when demonstrators and the police were facing each other in the dark. The news editor had just read a statement by Rector Roche, offering to meet the student leaders within the Sorbonne in order to discuss conditions for the resumption of lectures. One of his reporters in the crowd got hold of Alain Geismar, who was asked to comment.

Rising to the occasion, Geismar put over the student case with perfect clarity. The gist of his argument can be summed up as follows: The student leaders are with the demonstrators, while the rector is with the police; the student spokesmen do not intend to change sides. The real problem is simple. The government has offered to grant two of the student demands; it has refused to accept the third. When this proposal was offered to students at Denfert, they answered unanimously: *"Libérez nos camarades."* The only question is whether the rector has anything to add on this point.

Deputy Rector Claude Chalin replied that he could not answer without consulting the Minister of Education. Urged to hurry, he promised to bring an answer within ten minutes. Fifty long minutes later he came back on the air to repeat literally Rector Roche's previous statement. Only that and nothing more. After all the tense expectation, this was a terrible letdown. For the listening millions it had not been a waste of time.

The demonstrators had not wasted theirs either. The barricades were going up and up, some of them reaching a height of about three yards. Anything could serve the purpose. Automobiles were often a foundation. A neighboring building-site was a real treasure. The most precious find there was an air hammer, which once mastered made it possible to open up the streets wholesale. The paving stones then went from hand to hand. Young men and women were seized with a building fury. Not everybody shared their enthusiasm. Just before midnight a few hundred militants of the FER arrived with red flags from their separate meeting. Appalled by the size of the police concentration, they argued that to stay there was to invite a massacre. Their alternative was to

go to working-class districts with the slogan "Half a million workers into the Latin Quarter." And so they went. But their example
was not followed. The atmosphere behind the barricades was one
of determination, exhilaration, and also optimism. In this not-so-
red quarter people were coming down with sandwiches, drinks,
chocolate. As the hour advanced, it was increasingly difficult to
believe that the troops would attack. Would they have waited for
so long?

The time factor was also the argument used by Maurice Grimaud, the prefect of police. With every hour his task was becoming more difficult. The government, however, hesitated. Later the
story was spread that it could not reach a decision because General de Gaulle had gone to bed at ten. Students are too clever to
swallow such *muzhik* tales about the good czar and his bad ministers. In fact, the General was represented in all the negotiations
by the Secretary of the Presidency, Bernard Tricot, and by his
trusted lieutenant, officially charged with the affairs of the French
Commonwealth, Jacques Foccart. Just after midnight acting Prime
Minister Joxe moved into the Ministry of the Interior where, with
the latest information from the "front," the Gaullist caucus held a
permanent council of war.

Joxe, who was personally inclined toward diplomacy, had little
scope for initiative. The General had said that order must be restored. Desperate phone calls were pouring in to all the ministers
from all the glorious names of French science. A delegation of
six professors and students, including Cohn-Bendit, made a last
attempt to persuade Rector Roche to demand the withdrawal of
the troops—in vain.[8] By 2 A.M. Christian Fouchet, the Minister
of the Interior, had carried the day with Prefect Grimaud's argument that if any more time was wasted, he could not guarantee
that the streets would be cleared by the morning.

A quarter of an hour later the troops had their marching or-

8. The only result was an appeal, issued after the police had moved
into action, asking the students "to stop spontaneously the conflict." For
a report by one of the professors in the delegation see *Le Nouvel Observateur*, May 15, 1968.

ders. Several hundred CRS were the first to move. The small barricades in the square facing the Luxembourg Gardens were cleared rapidly. But to attack the main obstacles in the Rue Gay-Lussac the police resorted to its new tactic of preliminary bombing, first with grenade-throwers, then with hand grenades. It has been suggested that five thousand grenades were used on that night alone, and the authorities after initial denials had to admit that in addition to the traditional tear gas, the CS grenades, which American troops had experimented with in Vietnam, were that night used for the first time in France.[9]

Thump, thump . . . "Arise ye damned of the earth" . . . bang, bang . . . "De Gaulle murderer" . . . whamm, whamm . . . *"C'est la lutte finale"* . . . the noise was deafening, breathing difficult. A blinding cloud of gas and smoke rose above the first barricade, whose defenders wore handkerchiefs and had their faces covered with baking soda. A change of wind and the first wave of police was driven to retreat, suffocated by its own gas. (Policemen, too, were later treated for eye-burns.) Soon they were on the attack again, trying to storm the main barricade in the Rue Gay-Lussac, but also to cut it off through a side street, which was defended with equal passion. To help the besieged, buckets of water were poured from neighboring windows in the hope of clearing the atmosphere. This did not last because the police started throwing grenades into open windows. The wounded, the blinded, those who could not stand it any more, were taken to the rear and replaced by eager young men rushing up from barricades lying farther back. The first line of defense was not easy to break.

The police now attacked from all sides. Only live broadcasts on Europe One and Radio Luxemburg gave sporadic news from all fronts. And in between the reports came a series of desperate appeals. The academic world was shaken. Many professors had

9. Since in our civilization burning a car is apparently a much graver political and moral sin than breaking a skull or raping a girl, one is bound to report that the first cars to blaze were set on fire by the police when gas tanks burst after being hit by exploding grenades. It was only later that the defenders set cars on fire to slow down the police while they were retreating.

come out into the streets to be with their students. The glorious names of French science were trying to make use of their prestige. Two famous mathematicians threatened publicly to resign if the assault did not stop. Professor Monod begged for a truce so that the injured could be evacuated. Hospital orderlies had to brave the truncheons in their efforts to drag the wounded out of the clutches of the police. Another professor of mathematics was wounded trying to prevent the gendarmes from entering an academic building. For the battle was now drawing to an end.

Superior force had prevailed. By 5 A.M., most barricades in and around Rue Gay-Lussac had fallen. By 6, though there were still pockets of resistance, particularly near the hilly area around the Mouffetard Market, Cohn-Bendit broadcast an appeal to his friends to break off so as to avoid a slaughter. The battle was over, but not the mopping up. The cruel manhunt went on. The police were enjoying their revenge. There were no sanctuaries. Policemen, rifle or gun in hand, barged into private homes and dragged out refugees whom they clubbed into Black Marias. The image that sticks in the mind is of a young woman, dragged naked into the street and then into a distant van by representatives of law and order who were yelling "We'll teach you, you whore." For many of the prisoners arrest was only the beginning of a ghastly ordeal.[10]

It's morning. Paris wakes up. Though streets are still disem-

10. The police are doing their "job." Their official superiors, from the prefect upward, are doing theirs in praising the police for their worthy restraint. How do they square such statements with thousands of eye-witness reports? Beatings-up in the street are dismissed on the ground that they took place "in the heat of battle." But what about the sadistic treatment—there is no other description for it—of arrested men and women, boys and girls, inside the police stations or in the regrouping center at Beaujon? The horrifying descriptions by victims and witnesses are recorded in *Le Livre Noir des Journées de Mai* (Paris, Éditions du Seuil, 1968). The government threatened to sue the authors for slander. It never even contemplated a public inquiry into the behavior of the police. *The Black Book* and its sequel, *Ils Accusent* (also published by Seuil, 1968), are indispensable reading for anyone who wants to have a complete image of the May crisis. They should be compulsory reading, too, for all those who lecture about "intellectual terrorism" and "student violence."

boweled and carcasses of cars give a junky air to fallen barricades, order reigns in the Latin Quarter. Outside the Luxembourg Gardens one sees the picture typical of the end of all battles—a host of defeated prisoners, haggard, their eyes still red, being pushed with rifle butts into departing vans by the victors. Only the picture this time was deceptive. The vanquished were the winners, and the "victorious" troops had inflicted on their masters a terrible defeat. The government, the opposition, the nation at large, were all aware of it on Saturday morning.

Nothing revealed the government's disarray more clearly than this unofficial communiqué published by the French News Agency, Agence France-Presse (AFP) early that day: "It is being stated this morning in French governmental circles that one can detect in last night's demonstrations in the Latin Quarter, while talks on Vietnam are taking place in Paris between the Americans and the North Vietnamese, the intervention of forces hostile to the re-establishment of peace."

To stoop to such patently ridiculous explanations [11] a government must feel it has no case and that public opinion is swinging wildly against it. The opposition grasped this, too. Forgetting their reservations and objections of yesterday, all opposition parties now stood behind the students and violently condemned the government for its "brutal repression." Within hours the labor and teaching unions agreed with the UNEF to stage their joint demonstration a day earlier, on Monday, May 13, and to couple it with a general strike. Teachers, who are civil servants, and workers in the nationalized industries decided not to bother about the compulsory five days' warning.

For the Gaullist government it was now urgent to redress the situation. With its policy lying in ruins, the need was for an immediate substitute. "I have an idea," claimed Georges Pompidou, getting off his plane at Orly on Saturday evening after a nine-day

11. *Le Monde* coupled this gem with the following comment: "Is it necessary to observe that this *ex post facto* explanation does not stand up to a moment's reflection, since the bulk of students and their organizations are favorable to peace in Vietnam?"

official visit to Iran and Afghanistan. The Prime Minister had been lucky. He had been able to proclaim *"Zalmota salam,"* which means "Hello, young ones," in Afghan, while Parisian students were shouting in plain French, "Down with the police state." Naturally, the Prime Minister had been in constant touch with his colleagues and, therefore, entirely responsible with them for the conduct of policy. Yet the absentee landlord—the *"miraculé de Kaboul,"* the man miraculously healed in the Afghan capital, as Mitterrand later called him—was in a more comfortable position than other Gaullists to preside over the inevitable change of line. For the next six weeks, the Prime Minister was to be the key figure in the Gaullist camp, if not more important at least more active than the General himself; and it is, therefore, worthwhile to glance at the man before we look at his "idea."

When back in April 1962 Georges Pompidou was appointed Prime Minister and his dark face with its bushy eyebrows and a sly peasant smile was first splashed across the newspapers, the opposition thundered "What is good for the Rothschilds is no good for France." It could have added: Caligula had appointed his horse; General de Gaulle, his private secretary. Pompidou, who at the time had not been elected to any political office, could have been described as a self-made man were he not so much the product of the General's patronage.

The main exception to the French rule of social immobility is the rise through three generations: from peasant through teacher to anything. Georges Pompidou is a striking illustration. Born in 1911 in the Cantal village of Montboudif into a teacher's family, this young champion at passing examinations passed brilliantly through the classical gateway to an academic career, the École Normale Supérieure. Yet, nothing seemed to destine the leisurely young *professeur,* with no Resistance record whatsoever, to a political career through Gaullism. The old school tie did the trick. One of his fellow *normaliens* was on the General's staff in liberated Paris and brought Pompidou along. The newcomer had little time to run through his paces, but he was sufficiently appreciated to be rewarded with a nice job in the civil service (the

Council of State, dealing with conflicts involving the state) when the General retired in January 1946. Pompidou showed there his adaptability and capacity for quick work, since he combined his new job with permanent duties for the master-in-exile.

Since the Fourth Republic refused to surrender, it had to be taken by storm. During the storming by the troops of the Gaullist Rassemblement du Peuple Français (Rally of the French People), or RPF, Pompidou was kept in the background, at the General's headquarters. The tottering Republic showed an unexpected capacity for passive resistance. By 1954 the General had to admit failure and bide his time. Once again the master's retreat led to a change of profession for his faithful secretary. In the financial committees of the Rally, Pompidou had worked with a director of Rothschild Frères, who thought his skills would be an asset to the bank; and there, too, our champion climber got to the top without forgetting his Gaullist duties. In 1958 the years in the wilderness were over. The Algerian *putsch* brought the General back to power, with Georges Pompidou as his Directeur de Cabinet. Another spell at Rothschilds' and in 1962, after the end of the Algerian war, the private secretary was turned into Prime Minister.

General de Gaulle had not chosen a lame horse for Premier. After a brief apprenticeship Pompidou found politics no more formidable than banking or constitutional law. For the General he was a perfect lieutenant. But appetite, say the French, grows with eating. Our professional climber gradually started dreaming of the summit. Behind the easygoing manner there is an iron will, behind the leisurely detachment a great deal of ambition. The man was intelligent enough to know he could not inherit the Gaullist legend, the Bonapartist appeal. He could only succeed on the slogans of law and order and the stable franc, as leader of a conservative coalition. Georges Pompidou began to have his own political interests and ambitions. Rushing back to defend the regime in danger, he was rushing to preserve his own heritage.

The returning man's gamble was the logical sequel to the utter failure of the previous martingale. He said in effect, since the policy of repression has ended in disaster, let us now see what can be salvaged through concessions. Instead of keeping the Sorbonne out of bounds, let it be turned into a student sanctuary. Let students and professors stew for a while in their own juice. Throw one vital ingredient—the examinations—into the melting pot and the odds are that the dish will ultimately have a reformist taste. If the university is overhauled in the process, so much the better, though the immediate task is to prevent the revolutionary unrest from spreading.

The Prime Minister was in a hurry. That very Saturday, after a brief Cabinet meeting and having obtained the green light from General de Gaulle, he appeared on television just before midnight, full of heartbroken sweetness, the reasonable peacemaker revealing his plans. The Sorbonne would be opened on Monday. That very same day "the court of appeal will be able to give a ruling, in keeping with the law, on the requests for release lodged by the condemned students." And thus the allegedly insurmountable obstacle, which was the result of the independence of the judiciary, vanished at once. Nobody had any doubts about what this ruling would be, and the common surmise was rapidly confirmed.[12]

Pompidou in his broadcast gave some clues to his tactics. He reassured the candidates for examinations that special circumstances would be taken into account and concluded with a plea to students and their representative associations "to reject the provocations of a few professional agitators." With hindsight, it is easy to show why the gamble failed. The Gaullist government, too, was aware of the handicaps it now had to overcome. The loss of face by the judiciary was the least of its troubles. The discontent aroused within the police by the sudden *volte-face* was already more worrying. The ordinary policeman took it as a slap in the

12. The four demonstrators sentenced to jail obtained their release on parole on Monday; all the others held in custody had been released on Sunday. The land of Montesquieu is not a country with illusions about the separation of powers.

face, as a public indictment of his actions.[13] Still, that damage could be repaired. What Pompidou did not bargain for was the contagious effect of the student example. For his scheme to work, the university had to be isolated. For the second time in this crisis, the Gaullist calculation rested on a false premise. In fairness, it must be admitted that at the time not many people expected unrest to spread so rapidly from campus to factory.

The mass demonstrations throughout France on the following Monday acted as a link between the two movements, a transition between the two phases of the crisis. Their preparation was no easy matter, and the bargaining between students and labor organizations took a great deal of time on the preceding Sunday. The Communist-dominated CGT, with its mighty machine, was hitherto accustomed to running the show. The students, however, on this occasion were in a strong position to impose at least some of their conditions. It was finally agreed that the march, starting in the working-class districts, would cross the Latin Quarter and culminate in Denfert; that union leaders would lead the demonstration, while politicians would walk farther back in the crowd; that students, to show the autonomy of their movement, would have their own meeting place and their own stewards. For the Communists, who for most of the previous week had complained about the ultrarevolutionary style of student demonstrations, this was a lot to swallow. But the moment, however transient, was one of awkward reconciliation, and nobody at this stage could deny that the students had earned their place.

The weather was on the side of the victors. On Monday afternoon the sun shone on the biggest demonstration Paris had ever known. How many were they? Half a million, a million?—nobody

13. On May 13 the union including most uniformed policemen published an angry communiqué. To start with, it recalled that the occupation of the Sorbonne had been carried out on the government's orders. It went on to say that it viewed "the declaration of the Prime Minister as an admission that the students were in the right and as an absolute disavowal of the action of police forces ordered by the government," and it then expressed its astonishment that "an efficient dialogue with the students had not been sought before the regrettable clashes."

can really say.[14] It was a human sea or, to be more accurate, two huge rivers joining each other rather than merging together. The students, teachers, lecturers, scientific workers, who started flocking toward the Gare de l'Est soon after midday, were too numerous to hold a serious open-air meeting. The "grouplets" had grown into a mass. An even bigger crowd was beginning to gather nearby, around the Place de la République, the rallying point for the labor unions. The meeting between the two was not entirely smooth. The CGT stewards tried for a while to take full control of the operations but, seeing that rough tactics would lead to unwanted trouble, gave up the attempt. It was getting near 4 P.M. when, slightly behind schedule, the actual march began. At about 5:30, when the first rows reached Denfert, the bulk of the tail was still standing around the Gare de l'Est. It was well after 8 when these tail-enders reached their destination.

Opening the march were crash-helmeted students carrying red and a few black flags. Just behind, beneath a banner proclaiming "Students, Teachers, and Workers Together," walked the student and labor leaders. In the crowd packing the pavements all along the route people showed each other the three young men whose figures had become familiar: You see that smiling redhead? It's Cohn-Bendit. And the small but stocky chap with a babyish face? It's the prof, Alain Geismar. And the handsome one, a bit of a matinee idol? It's Sauvageot. The names of the three young people remained in the news. Soon, however, they were joined in the limelight and even eclipsed by a couple of middle-aged men, more neatly dressed, marching in the same row. One was Eugène Descamps, forty-six, a lively northerner and leader of the CFDT. The second, walking awkwardly with the students, was a sober southerner, Georges Séguy, only forty-one years old but with a

14. The competent police forces proved beyond doubt on this occasion that their function was not one of assessment, but of psychological warfare. With scientific precision they estimated the number of marchers at 171,000. The figure was then quoted on television as emanating from United Press International. The wire service issued an indignant protest. The figure did actually occur in its dispatch, but along with the source—the police forces —and a comment expressing astonishment that they were putting it so low.

long career behind him. Only the previous June this man of the apparatus had taken over as secretary-general of the CGT from the veteran Benoit Frachon. The political leaders, such as Rochet, Mitterrand, and Mendès-France, were lost behind in the crowd.

This was not only the biggest demonstration ever. It was also the most dynamic in years. There were more red flags than in the past, more fists were clenched above heads in the revolutionary salute, and the "Internationale" was sung time and again. The mood of the students was to some extent infectious. The jolly slogan obvious because of the date—"Happy birthday, mon General"— was coupled with the more political "Ten years, that's enough." The students, nevertheless, set quite a different tone, chanting "All power to the workers," "Socialist revolution," "Power lies in the streets," and for the first time in a mass demonstration the slogan that in the days and months to come would be sung, whistled, or clapped by all those who wanted to emphasize their revolutionary determination, the jerky *"Ce n'est . . . qu'un début. . . . Continuons le . . . combat."*

Standing on the sidelines as the march went on and on, one was struck by two features, both pointing to the future. The first was the gap between generations. The mood was so exhilarating that many demonstrators, having walked their five miles or so, went back part of the route to watch the rest of the parade. It was noticeable that the young workers were clearly drawn toward the most militant students. They would walk along for a while singing the "Internationale," shouting slogans, clenching their fists. The younger elements in the working class, at least, were attracted by the idea of carrying on the struggle. This impression was the more significant since the ceremony was not simply a Parisian one. Similar marches were being held throughout France. Reports were soon pouring in about record attendances. The improvised general strike was only a semisuccess, but demonstrations were everywhere exceptionally big. Sixty thousand here, seventy thousand there . . . From Toulouse, from Marseilles, from other towns, came stories suggesting that nothing so important had happened since the liberation of France.

The second striking impression was of the divorce between the revolutionary students and the Communist party-liners. Even on this occasion the provisional coexistence between them was visibly strained. One could see the anger of CGT stewards when, say, passing in front of the Palais de Justice the students pulled down the official flags and replaced them with red banners. There were no police in sight along the route. The government wished to avoid any clashes this time, and the CGT was not looking for trouble either. An incident can easily happen and then escalate. One did, in fact, happen toward the end of the demonstration as a police ambulance drove into the crowd packed at Denfert. The driver panicked and wounded some demonstrators. Frightened, the other policemen started shooting. Only the intervention of the stewards prevented the policemen from being lynched. When hundreds of thousands are involved, an incident can suddenly change the course of events, and that is what the Communists wanted to avoid. The demonstration had to be peaceful and orderly, a show of strength that could somehow be put into the kitty for future use in political calculations or bargains with the employers. The students, on the other hand, meant what they were chanting: They wanted to carry on.

They literally wanted to march on from Denfert. But here the CGT machine was in action. Stewards channeled the crowd. Loudspeakers repeated orders to disperse, along with instruction on which streets to take. The students were no match. They found that only a few thousand among them were prepared to go on toward the Champs de Mars. This was not enough to march on "to the Élysée," as some in their enthusiasm were urging. And so, rather bitter, they sat where they were for yet another improvised teach-in. The day, however, did not end on such a sour note of division and disappointment. From the Champs de Mars most of the demonstrators moved on to the Sorbonne. They did not have to storm it this time. Already, on Saturday, the students had occupied the faculty of science and the Censier annex of the faculty of arts. That Monday morning a group had marched from Censier to take over the Sorbonne, where an improvised meeting heard

Jean-Pierre Vigier, the militant physicist and secretary of the Russell Tribunal, explain that the movement was not ending with this first victory. Yet it was only that night, after the mass demonstration, that the Sorbonne really opened.

Did the regime hope to enclose the students in their ghetto? They answered by opening the university to the world at large and to the workers above all. When you made your way through the dense crowd that night, you were greeted by the libertarian motto "It is forbidden to forbid." If imagination had not yet seized power, it had already taken possession of the walls. In the courtyard Pasteur and Victor Hugo, dressed up in red for the occasion, could not believe their eyes. The atmosphere, those in the know were suggesting, was reminiscent of Havana after the fall of Batista. Somebody had even brought a band. Inside in the vast lecture halls students served their apprenticeship in direct democracy, with some young workers, rather bewildered, trying to join in.

In smaller rooms the more conscientious militants discussed the organization of their "Red base" and the forthcoming tasks. Some of them actually had little patience for the folklore, for the *kermesse héroique* outside. But after the tension of ten unbelievable and unexpected days the students had the right to celebrate and even to dream for a moment. Tomorrow would come with its harsh facts and struggles. Now, exhilarated by their victory, they wished to believe for an instant that the words written on the wall were true, that everything indeed was possible. As this triumphant night was coming to an end, many a student or worker sitting in the courtyard of the Sorbonne could echo the words of Wordsworth:

> Bliss was it in that dawn to be alive.
> But to be young was very heaven.

THE WORKERS *will take from the fragile hands of the students the flag of the struggle against the antipopular regime.*

—On a banner carried by students

The Workers Take Over
(May 14–May 27)

THE CRISIS NOW SPREAD *from campus to factory, from Paris to the whole of France. After the unexpected student rising came the unprecedented general strike. All the elements in the drama were there from the very start. Those who would, couldn't; those who could, wouldn't. The Communist leadership tried desperately to keep the torrent of class conflict within established, institutionalized bounds. It almost succeeded. But this was a curious crisis, with its own logic and its sudden twists.*

*When everything seemed to have been settled around the
conference table, the workers refused to play their appointed
part, thus upsetting the plot and forcing the politicians to perform
in a third, dramatic act.*

The words on the banner, if touchingly naïve, accurately marked
yet another turning point in the crisis. It was Thursday, May 16,
and the dusk had just fallen when the banner, surrounded by red
flags, emerged from the Sorbonne. Its bearers and a small crowd
behind them were going to leave the "free" Latin Quarter and
cross Paris westward in the direction of Boulogne-Billancourt.
Once again, everything seemed possible. The marchers, many of
them inspired by the history of the Russian revolution [1] may well
have thought they were living through their own October. They
were not Blok's symbolic Twelve, guided by Christ, crossing revolutionary Petrograd. It was Paris that the students had set on
fire, and they were going to hand over the revolutionary torch to
the only class capable of completing the job. Their destination in
Boulogne-Billancourt was a stronghold of the working class, the
Renault car factory, with its thirty-five thousand employees, who
that very afternoon had stopped work. The wave of strikes, which
had started in the west near Nantes, had reached Paris and would
soon engulf the whole of France.

History is not a succession of *images d'Épinal*. The transfer of
the banner, the revolutionary torch, was no grandiose ceremony
to be recorded in the textbooks. It was a semiflop, and its mixed
reception reflected the inner contradictions of the May Movement. When the students finally arrived—some on foot, some by
various means of transport—it was dark, and they found the shutters drawn. True, a number of young workers standing on the
roof greeted them enthusiastically. Slogans were chanted, and
they all sang the "Internationale" together. Quite a few workers
came outside the factory gates, and in the square opposite, the

1. The improvised expedition was sponsored by the Trotskyist FER.

Place Jules Guesde, small groups timidly tried to start a dialogue. Students also walked along the walls of the factory, and at the rear gate near the river other discussions began between workers standing inside and students just outside. This awkward dialogue in the night across iron bars probably provides the most accurate image of this historic encounter.

The awkwardness was not accidental, and the relative failure of the first improvised meeting was not due to lack of preparation. The unions later explained away the closed gates on the apparently reasonable grounds that visitors inside factories might cause disturbances. But the CGT quite clearly wanted to reduce contact at the base, among the rank and file, to a minimum, and Boulogne-Billancourt was its fief. (Before the crisis the CGT used to collect about four fifths of the votes cast in factory elections.) This was made plain the day after when the students' union tried to repeat the performance, only on a grander, more significant scale. The CGT imposed its veto; it distributed in the Latin Quarter a leaflet "advising the initiators strongly against the maintenance of their initiative" on the grounds that "it could facilitate a provocation leading to an intervention by the government." [2]

Taken aback, the students hesitated. There were orders, counterorders, soul-searching. The CGT had in a sense succeeded in preventing a mass demonstration. Nevertheless, in the end a few thousand students led by Jacques Sauvageot and Alain Krivine of the JCR marched to Billancourt. Now the roles were reversed, and the CGT was embarrassed. In the prevailing mood of sympathy for the students, it was difficult to admit that the Communists had tried to prevent them from coming. Some party-liners even pretended for a while that the leaflet was a fraud. A meeting was ultimately held, with somewhat greater success than on the previous evening, but it was obvious from the start that relations between the two potential partners were very strained indeed.

The Communists could put down the shutters. They could not

2. The leaflet claimed that the student decision had been made without consulting the three unions of the Renault works. The two smaller unions countered this by issuing a leaflet welcoming the march.

prevent contact altogether. For the next few weeks the Place Jules Guesde was a small forum, a minor Hyde Park. It was also the image of what was happening throughout France wherever students were within easy reach of a factory. But Boulogne-Billancourt gave a slightly distorted picture, because it was a showpiece and the CGT could mobilize many militants to put its case over there. The students, as a rule, did not have the upper hand in the argument. Their best dialecticians were busy elsewhere. Those who came were full of revolutionary fervor, but this was not a substitute for strategy. They were also often overawed, treating each workman as if he were the embodiment of the historical role of his class.

The CGT spokesmen in each debating group soon discovered an argument that carried weight. They played on the deeply ingrained feeling among workers that they need a strong organization to defend their interests. Any criticism of the conduct of the CGT was thus presented as a whim of the petty bourgeois, who could indulge in individualism.[3] It often worked. What CGT militants had more difficulty in explaining away was their union's reluctance for contact and discussion at the base. Why, argued the students, if your union is democratic and the leaders truly represent the rank and file, why do they want to limit exchanges to the top, to the summit, to the respective hierarchies?

Part of the difficult answer naturally lies in the bureaucratic structure of the CGT—but only part. The passion of the Communist attacks against the revolutionary students at this time, the violence of the CGT's reactions to "leftist" interference, can only be understood against the background of an exceptional situation. Georges Séguy and his CGT colleagues were faced with an unexpected, overwhelming crisis that did not fit at all into their strat-

3. Every day Communist speakers and papers argued that the students were splendid, only their organization (the UNEF) was not. Whenever students dared to suggest that while the workers were magnificent, their party or union did not pursue, at this stage, a policy suited to their vital interests, the insolent outsiders were accused of teaching the working class what it ought to do. It was a good example of the Stalinist double standard.

egy. Their almost openly avowed task was to channel the torrent of class conflict into parliamentary waters, to keep it within capitalist bounds. Whatever their motives—"betrayal of revolution" to some, cautious wisdom to others—it was a very difficult job, and interference by "leftist adventurers" did not make it any easier. To grasp the meaning of the moves by all the parties in this tense struggle, one must look first at the strike itself.

In one way, a general strike on a national scale defies any comprehensive description. In each factory, even in each shop, in each plant or office, it has its own roots, its own background, its own peculiarities. A complete account can only be a collective work, filling volumes. At the same time, the characteristic of a general strike is that it all happens together, each stoppage being nourished by its predecessor and influencing the next one. The essentials can thus be summed up by studying its birth and the special features of its development. The rest, up to a point, is the story of a country's creeping paralysis. (The analyst has few precedents to draw upon. The May–June strike was the first to occur in Europe on such a scale since the war and the biggest France and probably any country has ever known.)

It all started the day after the mass demonstration of May 13. It began in the nationalized aircraft factory of Sud-Aviation at Bouguenais, near Nantes. At first sight it was possible to treat the stoppage simply as an incident. The Nantes–St.-Nazaire region is known to be particularly tough (an exception to the general rule: The local branch of Force Ouvrière, influenced by anarcho-syndicalists and Trotskyists is more, not less, militant than the CGT). Besides, the conflict had been brewing for some time. Hours of work had been reduced, and the workers were claiming a rise in hourly rates sufficient to compensate for the loss. After a closer look, the novelty of the strike and its direct link with the previous day's demonstrations was more apparent. The strike was not launched by the unions, but precipitated by young workers who occupied the factory and locked in the manager. Probably unconsciously, the new generation was reviving the sit-down methods of the previous great upheaval, the general strike of 1936.

The students, by occupying their universities, may well have served as a reminder.

Next day, Wednesday, May 15, the new trend was confirmed. The second blow was struck in Normandy, near Rouen, in the Renault factory at Cléon. By setting up their modern subsidiary in a predominantly rural area, and by bringing the managers and overseers from Paris, the directors may have hoped to avoid social unrest. Such hopes were now destroyed. The factory employed a high proportion of young people, many of them doing jobs inferior to their qualifications, and here again the angry young men were the prime movers in an action that led to the siege of the management office and the occupation of the factory.

The government was still unaware of the crucial new twist to the crisis. General de Gaulle took off for his Rumanian trip on the very morning of the first strike, leaving Georges Pompidou to cope, as they both thought, with the students. The trade unions were more sensitive. On Wednesday evening, after Georges Séguy had consulted Eugène Descamps, both unions issued instructions to their militants to swim with the tide. The following evening the CGT published an open appeal calling its members into action.

It was high time. The tide now began to come in very fast. On Thursday, May 16, not only Renault-Billancourt went on strike, but all the other branches of the nationalized car firm, notably at Flins and Le Mans. On May 17, sit-in strikes spread throughout the engineering industry and on to the chemical industry. Trains all over the country came to a halt, and post offices ceased to function. The area affected by stoppages also increased rapidly. After the industrial parts of Normandy, and Paris with its "Red belt," Lyons and its region, the heart of the French chemical industry, were hit. On Saturday, May 18, when General de Gaulle returned from Rumania one day ahead of schedule, it was the turn of the mines, and of public transport in Paris and several big towns. Utilities, such as gas and electricity, were also taken over, though with an eye on public opinion the strikers decided at least for the time being not to cut off supplies for domestic consumers.

Within a week the tide had swept over the whole of France

and paralyzed the bulk of basic production. Reporters, trying to keep up with the ever-growing number of stoppages, had now to speak of "several million strikers." The psychological effects began to be felt. There was a run on food shops as housewives stocked up on fats, sugar, and pasta in preparation for a long siege. The prospect of a stoppage at the Bank of France and in the Central Savings Office precipitated a run on the banks, which often had to limit withdrawals to five hundred francs (a hundred dollars) even before they were themselves directly affected by the strike. Drivers rushed to gas stations, which dried up even quicker than they should have. Although for the time being ordinary daily life was not very greatly disturbed except for difficulties of transport and the collection of garbage, France was getting mentally prepared for a major upheaval.

Having within the first week paralyzed the bulk of the country's industry and transport, the wave of unrest did not recede or even stop. It went on massively to complete its job, overflowing into outlying areas and the remaining sectors of economic activity. Small factories followed in the wake of the big ones, and new branches of industry were drawn into the wake each day. On Tuesday, May 21, the textile mills, which had hitherto been largely spared, were brought to a halt. That same day all the big Parisian stores—from the Galeries Lafayette to the Samaritaine—closed their doors. The following day the teachers went on strike, though in obedience to the instructions of their unions some of them went to school and remained in touch with the pupils. Since many high-school students had been active in the movement from the start, they now had plenty of opportunity to influence general assemblies and other meetings in strike-bound *lycées*. The conservatives, incidentally, were right, from their point of view, in raising hell. Open politics—as opposed to the subtle weight of the establishment—and the questioning of hierarchical orders made a spectacular entry into French schools, and the authoritarian *lycée* will never recover from the shock.

The professional intelligentsia, profoundly stirred by the student revolt, was given new courage and new impetus by the crippling power of the workers' movement. Thus action broke out almost simultaneously in the most unexpected quarters (around Tuesday, May 21). A group of doctors, inspired by students who were debating a reform of their profession, occupied the premises of the Medical Order. Architects, following the lead of the rebel students who were occupying the School of Fine Arts, proclaimed the dissolution of their own corporate association. Painters sought the best way of proclaiming solidarity with the movement. Actors went on strike and closed all the theaters in the capital. Even writers found something to take over: They occupied the house belonging to the Society of Men of Letters. At the same time the young executives bearing the mysterious name of C4 [4] decided to introduce some practice into their theoretical discussions at the Sorbonne, and staged two token occupations: They seized for a while the building of the Conseil National du Patronat Français (National Council of French Employers), or CNPF, and then took over the premises of the corporate Confédération Générale des Cadres (CGC), who were dismissed by the rebels as too conservative and too narrow-minded.

All this was effervescence, the symptom of a mood, the froth on the wave. But for the Gaullist government, still trying to gain time, the flood was getting dangerously close to its own home. It was natural that most scientific workers employed by the state-financed Centre National de la Recherche Scientifique (National Scientific Research Center), or CNRS, should have felt from the start a strong sympathy for the students and the radical professors. Now their main union, in order to keep up with its more militant members, called on all laboratories to imitate the pacesetters by electing management committees as a first step toward a democratic overhaul of the country's scientific policy. On May 21 all the unions within the Commissariat à l'Énergie Atomique (Atomic Energy Commissariat), the CEA, called on their members to strike; all military institutions were thus to follow the example of such civilian bodies as the nuclear research center at

4. From the initials of Centre de Coordination des Cadres Contestataires.

Saclay. In the turmoil not even General de Gaulle's cherished project was spared.

Soviets at Saclay? [5] What next? The government did not have to wait long for an answer, since on the same Tuesday stoppages began in the ministries of Equipment and Social Affairs, while several hundred of the strikers in the Ministry of Finance paraded, chanting slogans, outside their office. Pompidou, and the employers, could no longer hope to wear out the strikers. Things were moving so fast that the General's policy of wait-and-see was threatening the foundations of the regime. When, on Friday, May 24, the government finally invited all the unions and the employers' federation to join it in round-table negotiations that very weekend, the economic life of the country was virtually at a standstill, and the number of wage and salary earners involved in the stoppage was loosely estimated at between nine and ten million.

"Those who can remember tell us that the 1936 popular front strikes were nothing by comparison," the young workers were claiming with pride. And indeed, in scope and sweep the movement was unprecedented. Yet what part did the trade unions play this time in launching and consolidating this exceptional movement? Trade unionists in general, and the CGT spokesmen in particular, angrily reject the familiar charge that they had climbed on the bandwagon only to put on the brakes. In a way, quite a strong case can be made for their thesis. True, the first strikes broke out spontaneously, having been precipitated by the young workers, and the unions were faced with an accomplished fact. But then a mass strike is not a military operation that can be called at will or forecast with precision.

It would be absurd to suggest that the strikes were merely an echo, a response to the student rebellion. A general strike is a frontal battle in class war, and all the previous class skirmishes—even at the shop level—can be treated as training for the mass confrontation. The unions can rightly claim that without their

5. To quote the title of a book describing what actually happened, *Des Soviets à Saclay?* (Paris, Maspero, 1968).

years of routine work the army of labor would not have been ready for such a struggle. Finally, it can be argued that the vague instructions issued by the CGT, its bread-and-butter program, and its emphasis on wage demands helped in the initial stage to speed up the movement. A general strike, at least to start with, feeds on past grievances and gathers momentum through the accumulation of a host of ordinary discontents. The CGT and the Communist party can thus pretend that far from acting as a "brake," they contributed to the rapid spread of the strike.

Yet to stick to such a mechanical assessment is to miss the difference between a skirmish and the main battle, between the daily struggle and the historical occasion; it is to confuse the general strike, political by its very nature, with an industrial conflict in, say, the American steel industry, where both sides are well aware in advance that the nature of the economic system is not in any way at stake. For a revolutionary party, the general strike provides a unique opportunity for mass propaganda and mobilization. With the dominant ideology shaken and temporarily on the defensive, the workers gathered in their strangely idle factories can learn in weeks more than they had grasped in years gone by. The general strike can be a school of class consciousness, a school attended by eager millions who in normal times are not within reach.

Nine to ten million strikers is inevitably an abstract figure. In every stoppage there are the militants, the sympathizers, and a passive fringe following sometimes against its will. The peculiarity of the general strike—and the French example, in this respect, was no exception [6]—is that usually passive masses are drawn into

6. See Rosa Luxemburg, *The Mass Strike, The Political Party and The Trade Unions*, for a descriptive analysis of the Russian wave of strikes in 1902–1906. In an interesting footnote she attacks the attitude toward the mass strike of the opportunist elements in German social democracy and gives a few examples of this open opportunism. All the passages she quotes with indignation—such as "the political mass strike can only be victoriously carried through when kept within strictly legal means"—have a familiar ring. They all could be underwritten by Rochet, Marchais, and Séguy. Opportunism does not even change its vocabulary.

action and that the newcomers tend to be more militant than veteran trade unionists. To harness their energy, however, it is necessary to give them room for initiative so that they can run the strike through daily meetings of a general assembly and through a broadly elected strike committee permanently responsible to that assembly. The task of the revolutionary party or union is simply to advise, co-ordinate, suggest, to venture beyond the confines of the factory, and on a national scale to provide a political lead and see how far the movement can be carried. To hide behind the classical excuse that the masses are not "ripe," when one has done everything to stunt their growth, is to crown past failure with supreme hypocrisy.

An allegedly revolutionary party that allows the initiative to flow from below inevitably runs the risk of being driven beyond its original intentions. The alternative, chosen by the CGT and the Communist party, was to run a general strike in a more military fashion, from above. Trusted trade unionists were picked for strike committees and tried to get their policy endorsed. Mobilization of the workers was limited to the necessary minimum, to the numbers needed for such indispensable duties as picketing. Workers were allowed to drift home, while those who stayed in the factory were encouraged to play games rather than to indulge in dangerous debates. At moments one began to wonder whether the sit-down strike was designed to prepare the workers for the offensive or to isolate them from the outside world with its leftist germs. Exceptions to this rule occurred in plants where all kinds of heretics—leftist sections of the CFDT or Force Ouvrière, Trotskyists, Maoists known as "proletarian syndicalists"—attempted to drive the strike forward so as to create a base of dual power in the country. These exceptions will be studied in the next chapter and will show that the general strike could have had a different social and political content as well as a different outcome. Technically it is arguable that the CGT helped to spread the strike. In historical perspective, to tax it simply with "braking" is a gentle understatement.

Why should the CGT be singled out as mainly responsible for

the nature of the strike? For the obvious reason that it is not only the biggest and strongest of the French labor unions, but also the only one to pretend to be "truly revolutionary." In the past it had opposed structural reforms in the factory or the system as a whole because its avowed aim is the abolition of capitalism, the elimination of wage labor and of private ownership of the means of production (*salariat* and *patronat*). It denies to anybody the possibility of overtaking it on its left. When the "revolutionary" CGT revealed itself in this crisis, for whatever reasons, as a pillar of the established order, the "reformist" CFDT appeared radical by comparison.

The motives of the ex-Catholic federation may certainly have been mixed. Some of its leaders, linked with the Parti Socialiste Unifié, or PSU, the small but active left-wing socialist party, really saw in the crisis an opportunity to start a transition toward socialism. Many of the militants were stirred by the students and by their rejection of existing social relations. Undoubtedly, Descamps and his colleagues perceived also an opportunity to attract young workers who were repelled by the bureaucratic caution of the CGT. But the main reason was contained in the situation itself, because it was so obviously exceptional. A breach had been wrought in the existing system. Here was a unique occasion not just for bringing Gaullism down, but also for widening the breach in the capitalist structure, for breaking the omnipotence of the employer in the factory and attacking the power of the state, the ultimate protector of existing property relations. In such circumstances, to stick to quantitative demands, to limit the struggle virtually to wage claims, was to choose the battlefield most suitable for the opponent, to allow the tottering enemy a chance to recover after a temporary defeat.

Admittedly, the CFDT did not have a consistent strategy either. It was never quite clear whether it was advocating *cogestion* (workers' share in management) or *autogestion* (which sometimes sounded like workers' control over management and on other occasions could be interpreted as the management of the factory by the workers themselves). Nor was it crystal clear

whether such factories run by workers were to be the exception
to the rule of private ownership, or if they were to be the rule,
how they would coexist with a capitalist state. All the ambiguities
of "revolutionary reformism" came to the surface, and making it
more convient for the Communists to dismiss the strategy as
empty talk. But the Communists made no effort to put some content into it, to provide an alternative program, to give the French
proletariat a political lead. The only message was: danger ahead.
It can be illustrated by the remarks of Georges Séguy: The
CGT "has no vocation to lead the movement to its political conclusion"; the working class could be "dragged into an adventure";
"one should not take one's desires for realities." [7] Driven forward
by events, the Communist leaders had their eyes fixed from the
start on all the possible avenues of retreat.

It used to be an old Stalinist trick to describe dissenters as
agents of the government or the police, and French Communists,
as we shall see, fell back easily into this habit. If one were to follow their example, the obvious explanation of their self-defeating
policy would be that Séguy was an agent of Pompidou or that the
party leader, Rochet, had strict orders from Moscow to preserve
the Gaullist regime. It would be an utterly absurd conclusion.
Bewilderment rather than betrayal provides the key to Communist action. Amid the classical accusations, turned into clichés
through repetition, "parliamentary cretinism" fits better the conduct of the French Communist leadership than "revolution betrayed."

At a time when the crisis revealed the real balance of social
forces, showing the basic weakness in the country of their social-
democratic partners, the Communists continued to cling desperately to their electoral strategy, to the vision of a popular-front
coalition with Mitterrand's social-democratic federation, the
FGDS. In a situation when it seemed possible to forge a much
more radical alliance from below, they went on pressing for a

---

7. The last was a reply to a question about action designed ultimately
to lead to the abolition of capitalism. All are taken from public pronouncements on May 17 and 18. The examples could be multiplied.

joint electoral platform reached at the top. The snag was that for their parliamentary ends they had a revolutionary weapon at their disposal, because a general strike, however much you try to conceal its nature, is not an electioneering weapon. The red flags flying over occupied factories were a reminder that what was at stake was not just a majority in Parliament.

Georges Séguy and his colleagues were thus in a dilemma. They had to keep the strike going so as to force the employers and the government to negotiate, while simultaneously preventing it from reaching its full political dimension. For the CGT a rapid conclusion was the best possible way out. Georges Pompidou and the employers' federation (the CNPF), however, were aware of the Communist dilemma and therefore began by playing for time. For the CGT this involved the risk of being overwhelmed by revolutionary elements regrouping themselves around the students— hence the violence of the Communist attacks against the students and other "adventurers." The Communists' refusal to carry the strike to its political conclusion was only fully apparent in the second week, when it became plain to all that the stoppages were neither regional nor ephemeral; but the party's cautious strategy could be discerned from the very beginning through its conflict with the students. The controversy acquires a meaning as a symptom and must be viewed as such. First, however, we must turn back to the students and see what they had been doing during the ten days when the center of gravity was shifting from the campus to the factory.

We left the students on the night of Monday, May 13. They were masters of the Sorbonne but still had to face a more awkward situation inaugurated by Pompidou's policy of concessions. Next day it was not just a question of the Sorbonne or the other Paris faculties; virtually all French universities were Red, or Pink, bases occupied by the students. Their revolutionary leaders now had to solve three complex and closely connected problems: First, they had to combat the Gaullist attempt to keep them in splendid isolation; second, they had to elaborate a university program attractive enough to draw the reformers and radical enough to clash with the inner logic of capitalism; last but not least, they were determined to link their struggle with that of the workers. As the strike spread, it was this last point that gradually dominated all the others.

Parisian students, flushed with their victory, were naturally driven to extend their base. Two days after the seizure of the Sorbonne, on Wednesday, May 15, to be precise, a cultural commando unit began to put into practice the assertion that "since the National Assembly has become a bourgeois theater, all bourgeois theaters should be turned into national assemblies." It struck next door and took over the Odéon, or Théâtre de France, a national theatre run by Jean-Louis Barrault and Madeleine Renaud, the celebrated actor-and-actress couple. From then on, for nearly a month, the show was not on the stage but in the audience. Almost all day and night anyone could stand up from his seat and declare what he pleased. As a nonstop happening, the show was unique. As a sign of people's urge for self-expression, it was interesting. As a political outpost, the Odéon brought the students little benefit. Politically inoffensive, it attracted among its spectators not a few snobs from smart districts; it thus provided an excuse for the charge that the students were organizing a circus for the middle classes.

Snobs were undoubtedly also to be found among the crowds who invaded the Sorbonne every evening, walking in the courtyard, with its portraits of Marx and Mao, Lenin, Trotsky, and Che Guevara, and its knots of political groups debating or just reading poster newspapers and wall inscriptions. May, incidentally, was a month of self-expression, with countless unknown authors scribbling their thoughts, feelings, passions, on all available walls, and not merely within the university. The graffiti ranged from the epigrammatically topical remark ("Amnesty— an act through which sovereigns most often forgive the injustices they have committed") to the eloquently revolutionary adaptation ("Mankind will not live free until the last capitalist has been hung with the entrails of the last bureaucrat").[8] Yet it was the spoken word that dominated. Each evening the visitor to the Sorbonne had a choice of subjects, as several debates were carried on at the same time in the big lecture halls. Very occasionally there was an important guest such as Jean-Paul Sartre. Most of the time there were passionate political or social discussions, with everyone entitled to have his say. It may be objected that considering the circumstances, there was more passion and illusion than practical work. Still, it was a great experiment in freedom.

The presence in the vast crowd at the Sorbonne of members of the "smart set" (to whom could be added police informers and plain gapers) has been played up by ill-wishers to discredit the student venture. To point out that the number of snob spectators declined as the class struggle heightened is only a partial reply. This was the price students had to pay for their ambitious design of opening up the university, for their dream of closing the gap separating them from the workers. The dream did not really come true, and the Communist party shares some responsibility for the failure. The symbolically closed factory gates blocked the passage both ways. Most of the young workers who nevertheless came to the Sorbonne were either the politically conscious, defying the party line, or the young rebels, the unemployed, the social outsiders. A tiny minority was to cause trouble, cleverly magnified, when the tide was receding, to "justify" the reoccupation of the Sorbonne by the police. The interesting thing was how many of the alleged misfits found a purpose in action and a sense of discipline. In any case, the students could not proclaim their social and libertarian objectives and shut themselves out from the outside world.

To those who focus attention on the spectacular, it is easy to retort that morning and afternoon in the same large lecture halls, throughout the day in all the small halls of the Sorbonne, in other faculties, in all the universities of France, much work was being done by improvised committees and commissions. Indeed, more

8. The most complete collection is in *Les Murs Ont la Parole, Mai, 1968* (Paris, Éditions Tchou, 1968).

ideas were produced, more reform projects drafted, within a few weeks than within the ten years of the Gaullist regime. It is therefore easy to answer the critics. But the answer does not go to the heart of the matter. The students were, in fact, faced with a dilemma. In drafting their programs, they were working in a void. They could not know for certain into what social framework their projects were to be fitted.

In the abstract, this is no problem. It was enough for the drafters to produce the outline of a progressive university that would harmonize with a socialist society. If Gaullism won and the established order survived, the inevitable conflict between the logic of the blueprint and that of the system would drive the reformers to join the revolutionaries. But there is a world of difference, if not between theory and practice, between such an abstract proposition and the concrete circumstances of May. If Gaullism triumphed, the main problem for the students would be to preserve the university as the source of revolutionary ferment, as a shelter in which some theoretical work could be developed and taught. If the regime were to collapse, opening up an era of transition, the revolutionary students would wish to turn the universities into Red bases, from which they could take an active part in the reshaping of society. As the general strike did open up such a prospect, the most dynamic and most sophisticated students turned their attention to the struggle outside the university.

In the absence of a revolutionary party the students had thrust upon them a hegemonic role for which they were socially unsuited and for which most of them were theoretically unprepared. All the divergences between anarchists, Trotskyists, Maoists, and whatnot, which had been somewhat submerged while the student wave was mounting, now returned to the surface. They were enlarged by doctrinal and practical differences on what was to be done. Roughly speaking, there was a split between those who sought the absolute, wishing to change man and society here and now, or, alternatively, were ready to lose rather than to indulge in organizational compromises; and those with an eye on the polit-

ical main chance, sensing in May an unexpected and almost un-
hoped-for opportunity for raising the issue of state power.

One point, however, united all the divided groups. They were
all convinced that the revolutionary upsurge could only be the
result of action from below, and this conviction was strengthened
by the conduct of the Communist party when it tried to control
the movement and keep it in check. The students, for their part,
opted for grassroots work, for the mobilization of the rank and
file. The small, flexible action committees were born at the same
time as the student insurrection, though it was only after May 13
that they really grew in importance. These would-be soviets of a
potential revolution will be studied in the next chapter as one of
the original contributions to the May Movement. One of the
features of their development must be mentioned at this stage.
They grew like mushrooms in university districts, flourished in
several popular quarters, but penetrated with great difficulty into
factories where they had to meet organized party and union resistance.

All the drama of May was here in a nutshell. The Communists,
who could carry the movement as far as it would go, were determined to check it. The students and their political allies, eager to
push it to a revolutionary conclusion, had neither the equipment
nor the following to perform the task. Their only chance was to
lead into action the masses usually guided by the Communist
party. The clash between the two partners was thus inevitable,
even though the student leaders tried for a time to preserve at
least an appearance of unity. The Communists and the CGT had
no such scruples, and they attacked viciously from the very beginning. Some of the attacks must be mentioned here, and not
just for the record.[9] Their very viciousness was a sign of the pres-

9. Though they should be recorded so that future socialist generations
should know to what depths a "truly revolutionary" party can descend
after years of Stalinist demoralization. Conditioned reflexes die hard. In
fairness, it must be added that some of the student leaders did not mince
their words either. The most famous example is Cohn-Bendit's reference,
on May 13, to the "Stalinist scoundrels," hardly a diplomatic epithet. But

sures under which the Communist leadership was working at this point.

The first clash occurred almost at the same time the general strike began. The occupation of the Odéon was only a beginning for the students; the theater, right in the Latin Quarter, was still in their ghetto. Their next target came straight from the textbooks. On the following day, May 17, they proclaimed that next day they would take over Broadcasting House. They were advised against this step by technicians and radio journalists, who were already on a partial strike, and television journalists, who were soon to join the stoppage. The Communists condemned the initiative with the utmost severity. The students were forced to give up their project, and their *volte-face* was facilitated by an official move that the government thought a clever gambit.

That same Thursday, late in the evening, Pompidou suddenly addressed the nation, assuring it that the government would do its duty. He called on Frenchmen to listen to the "voice of reason" and not to follow the *enragés* whose "avowed aim is to destroy the nation and the very bases of our free society." To strengthen this argument and frighten the audience, the three best-known leaders of the student insurrection (Cohn-Bendit, Geismar, and Sauvageot) were put on a program preceding the Prime Minister's broadcast. So that the point should not be missed, Pompidou, referring to the *enragés,* duly insisted that "we have shown you some of them." The thickly laid plot, however, did not work. The young men not only brought some fresh air into television. Casting aside the usual rules of the game, they ridiculed the journalists who were supposed to show them up.

Only the Communists behaved as if they had misunderstood the clumsy trick. That same night the CGT published a vehement protest asking why the government, which was not allowing the labor unions to express their views, was "putting television at the

---

the basic difference is that on no occasion did the students appeal to the established (bourgeois) authorities with the charge that the Communists were either lawbreakers or foreign agents.

disposal of those who openly propose to take over the ORTF."
Thus, the Communists were not appealing to the labor movement,
branding the students as hotheads. They were appealing to the
government and branding them as lawbreakers. Nor was it an
isolated incident. A few days later the Communist daily [10] questioned publicly the Minister of Youth on his contacts with Daniel
Cohn-Bendit and the amount of subsidy he had granted to the
March 22 Movement. The day after at a press conference Georges
Séguy went one better when speaking of Cohn-Bendit: "It seems
that the warnings we had issued even before the Prime Minister
hinted that the individual in question belonged to an international
organization are now being confirmed."

Thus, the secretary-general of an organization belonging to the
World Federation of Trade Unions was accusing Cohn-Bendit of
foreign links. A Communist described internationalism as a sin.
The Communist party was competing with the government in
making insinuating allegations and accusing it of tolerance toward the breakers of bourgeois law and order. The Communists
were soon to show that they could stoop lower still, yet all this
within one week was a pretty sample of what they could do when
under pressure from their left—and that pressure was now mounting.

There was a striking contrast between the cautious, moderate
tone of the CGT and the much more radical appeals coming
from other quarters. The PSU, for instance, was proclaiming:
"Those who would try to deflect the movement toward purely
quantitative demands, without questioning the present power-
structures, would bear a very heavy responsibility." Alain Geismar, still secretary of the lecturers' union, added: "Together with
the reform of the university, we consider that radical anticapitalist transformations are indispensable to get the confidence and
support of the popular masses for any new regime, which implies
a socialist domestic policy and a resolutely anti-imperialist foreign
policy." Even the CFDT stated plainly that the action of students

10. *L'Humanité*, May 22, 1968. The author of this masterpiece in in-
sinuation did not have the courage to sign his name.

and workers must take as its target "the economic, social, and political structures of capitalism."

All this was the sort of language likely to find an echo among the Communist rank and file, and precautions were therefore taken well in advance. The CGT had sponsored a major festival of young trade-unionists on May 17. Since the date coincided with the beginning of the general strike, it was quite natural to put the jamboree off because the young militants had more important work in the field. The delegates, however, were already in Paris, so they were able to get together quickly to discuss the tactics and strategy for the coming crucial period. But the CGT chose to disperse them at once, because it was unwilling to run the risk of leftist contamination. The infection was, however, slowly making its way. On May 23, André Barjonet, for years secretary of the Center of Economic and Social Studies of the CGT, resigned from the union and then from the Communist party. Three days later an important group of Communist intellectuals sent a letter to the party leadership, accusing it of cutting the party off from "a great force of socialist renewal." By then, however, both Georges Séguy and Waldeck Rochet thought they were firmly back in the saddle. The unions, the employers, and the government were then sitting around a conference table.

We have intentionally kept the limelight so far on one side of the barricade, because little of real interest was happening on the other. Whenever an old ruling class is faced with a new and overwhelming social phenomenon, it is at first bewildered, passive, reacting to events rather than guiding them. Gaullism followed in this respect the illustrious precedents of Louis XVI and Nicholas II. Indeed, the early period can be described as the period of absent rulers. In the first week of the crisis it was Georges Pompidou receiving the applause of Afghan students, while their more numerous French counterparts were threatening the regime. Then it was the turn of General de Gaulle to win laurels from Rumanian workers, while French factories were being decorated with red flags. The General is a stickler for protocol, preoccupied with rank and fascinated by foreign affairs. This helps to explain why he did not want to give up his Rumanian trip. Yet incomprehension also played its part, and this was shown on his return.

Back in Paris a day ahead of schedule, on Saturday, May 18, the General presided next day at a special Cabinet meeting. He then summed up the situation with soldierly vulgarity in a formula—it can be rendered roughly as "Reforms, yes; dirty mess, no"—which provided scope for etymologists [11] and a proof that at this juncture he had not yet understood the nature of the upheaval. His decision to wait a few more days before addressing the nation was a sign that he still hoped the unwelcome strike would somehow fade away.

Pompidou, who was coping directly with the crisis, and the employers' federation, which was getting the pulse of the country from its members, were both by then losing this illusion. In an upheaval that threatens the foundations of the system, big business and a bourgeois government have both common and divergent interests. For the business leaders, the vital aim is to preserve the main features of the capitalist order. A government or even a regime can be sacrificed on this altar. A Prime Minister, inevitably, has a different stake. Pompidou was fighting for his political life. In defending Gaullism, as we saw, he was defending his own heritage. These diverging interests appeared later in the crisis and even led to divisions within the ruling majority. For the moment both partners, surprised at first by the scale of the strike and rather incredulous, had to resign themselves to the fact that a price would have to be paid for survival. On May 21 the employers' federation put out its first feelers, trying to find out whether the CGT meant what it said about sticking to purely economic

11. In French "Les reformes, oui, la chienlit, non." *Chienlit* means literally "he who shits in bed." It originally referred to the gay dog returning from the party so drunk as to foul his bed. Its meaning then was "masquerade." Now it is used as a loose and vulgar equivalent for disorder. Those who believe in the social significance of a man's vocabulary may be interested to know that the same rare term had been used at the beginning of the crisis to describe the student disorder by the extreme right-wing paper *Minute*.

demands, because in that case the two sides could do business.[12]
That same day, Georges Séguy had let it be known in public that

> If the government and the employers are ready to have a dis-
> cussion with the CGT, recognizing at last its authority and com-
> petence, we are ready for such a debate and will pursue it
> without interruption until an agreement is reached or a dis-
> agreement recorded. We shall then go back to the workers on
> strike and shall consult them about what decisions to take. . . .
> This is not a time for empty talk about profound transforma-
> tions of society into which everyone packs whatever he likes. . . .

The official answer to this invitation was bound to be positive.
True, some ministers, notably Michel Debré, in charge of finance,
were still making normal calculations about what could be
granted to the workers without upsetting existing plans. Pompidou
knew better. He knew that his government was half crippled, ruling in a void in a paralyzed country. He knew that an inflationary
package was not too high a price to pay for survival. His only
consolation was that his most powerful opponents, the Communists, were for their own reasons playing according to his rules.
Before the negotiation proper started, it was therefore useful to
show them who was the master in parliamentary terms. The day
Séguy extended his public invitation, the National Assembly began discussing a motion of censure that was put down by the opposition.

The two-day parliamentary debate was the farcical interlude
in this drama. The Palais Bourbon used to be called a "window-
less house," and it now fully deserved its nickname. The visitor
coming in from outside had the strange impression of having gone
to the wrong show. The trouble was that it was the right one, the
ritual censure debate with actors failing to rise to the occasion.
The result—a Gaullist victory—was a foregone conclusion, since
the followers of Giscard d'Estaing and the deputies of the center

12. See André Barjonet, *La CGT* (Paris, Éditions du Seuil, 1968), pp.
154–155. For alleged contacts between Secretary of State for Employment
Jacques Chirac and the CGT see P. Alexandre, *L'Élysée en Péril* (Paris,
Fayard, 1969).

had no intention of submitting themselves to the voters. More damaging was the contrast between the parliamentary antics and the situation outside. On the second day two fellow-travelers improved matters to a certain extent. An oldtimer, Pierre Cot, a former Radical Minister now elected with Communist support, made a speech bearing some relation to the crisis, while Edgar Pisani, a former Gaullist Minister, attracted attention when he explained why this was his Finland Station. On the whole, however, after years of unimportance the deputies had probably gotten used to the idea that they did not matter. They were so strikingly out of tune with events that the television officials, who had more or less insisted on the telecasting in full of the debate, unwittingly contributed to discredit still further France's parliamentary institution.

Only two points emerged on the second day of the debate. One was expected and was made in the Chamber: Pompidou expressed his readiness to talk with the unions. The second was so surprising that when it reached the lobbies it was greeted with disbelief. Daniel Cohn-Bendit, temporarily out of the country, had been declared an "undesirable alien" and would therefore be expelled should he try to come back to France. The move was bound to launch the students into action, and coming from a government unable to assert its control, it gave rise to all sorts of rumors. Some argued that the measure had been taken by a minor official and the government was forced to endorse it. Others whispered knowingly that the decision had been made by the General himself out of spite. Such rumors could not be checked, but if one assumes that the government was not yet too bewildered to be Machiavellian, the move fitted nicely into Pompidou's plans. The Prime Minister assumed that things would be fairly safe as long as the Communists stuck to their part of the tacit agreement. The job was to keep the nominal Reds separate from those who were really determined to embark on a revolutionary road. Nothing could be better designed to keep the Communist leadership and the students apart than to throw the Cohn-Bendit affair between them.

Reputations die hard, and the student leaders had to take into account the fact that in popular esteem the CGT was "revolutionary" while the CFDT was "reformist." On the eve of the parliamentary debate the students had a meeting with the latter. In the press conference that followed, both sides insisted that their views were identical. Sauvageot, speaking for the students, stressed that their "struggle would have no future unless it opened on to the struggle of the workers." He nevertheless had to add that no special agreement had been reached with the CFDT, since in any case collaboration with the workers would not be the outcome of some deal reached at the top. He was to make the same point a couple of days later, when the idea of a similar meeting with the CGT had to be dropped. Indeed, in a most violent communiqué the CGT attacked Jacques Sauvageot, who ". . . had the unbelievable cheek to pretend to discuss the conduct of the working-class struggle and its objectives and affirmed his intention of appealing to the workers above the heads of their unions." Simultaneously, the indictment went on, the leaders of the students' and lecturers' unions "were organizing lightheartedly a demonstration of a provocative nature, to which they were calling students and workers." The conclusion was inescapable: "A serious and responsible organization, the CGT can only deal with serious and responsible partners." (This, as every good Stalinist can testify, was a perfect example of noninterference in another organization's affairs.)

With the haven of negotiation in sight, the last thing the Communists wanted was another Bloody Friday that could give new impetus to the revolutionary movement. The demonstration to which the CGT had referred was sponsored as a protest against Cohn-Bendit's expulsion. The students, in any case, wished to stage some action that could link them with the mass of the workers. The government, through its expulsion of Cohn-Bendit, left them no choice. In fact, a few thousand people protested almost spontaneously on the Wednesday (May 22) when the act of expulsion was made public. It was this young crowd, incidentally, that on its way to the Palais Bourbon switched gradually from

"We are all undesirable" to "We are all foreigners" to "We are all German Jews."

Though the student leaders, who were conserving their energy for Friday's mass demonstration, had no wish for trouble, that night and the next were to witness scenes of violence in the Latin Quarter, which were splashed next day across the world press. To understand why and how the fights started, one had to be literally on the spot. The Latin Quarter, it must be remembered, had become a sort of free republic, with the students themselves running traffic while law and order were maintaining themselves. There was no trouble so long as the police stayed discreetly at a distance. All changed when massive police forces ostentatiously crossed the "frontier" and parked at the bottom of the Boulevard St.-Michel. A crowd gathered and jeered. There was probably no need for a provocateur. The very sight of the hated policemen in full armor drove somebody to throw a stone. The police replied with tear gas. The escalation was on. After a time the police charged. Young people then flocked from all over the place, rallied by the cry "They're taking over the *quartier.*" This is the script that was rehearsed on Wednesday and acted to the full on Thursday. Tension was naturally high when it came to Friday's demonstration.

The government tried to keep people away by means of scare stories. The Communists tried to entice them away by sponsoring two demonstrations of their own in Paris. That this was their purpose was made plain when one of the Communist marches was suddenly diverted from its original destination, the Gare d'Austerlitz, because only a bridge had to be crossed from there to rally the students at the neighboring Gare de Lyon. All this proved insufficient. There were many young workers and quite a few Communist intellectuals in the crowd—estimated at some fifty thousand—that thronged toward the Gare de Lyon that evening from all over Paris.

Once again, people were visibly delighted to find themselves so numerous. It was a militant, determined mass that set off toward the Bastille chanting slogans, thunderingly proclaiming itself German Jewish.[18] At 8 P.M., as the demonstration was marking time, its front ranks blocked by the police, some people listened to their transistor radios. General de Gaulle's long-awaited broadcast came almost as an anticlimax.

What the General was going to say was predictable. He claimed that the state had to preserve public order, but also to think of reforms "involving a more extended participation" of Frenchmen in running their affairs. His solution was a referendum, through which the French people would give the head of state "a mandate for renovation." If they failed to do so, he would naturally resign. The most caustic summary was soon to be written on a wall: "He has taken three weeks to announce in five minutes that he is going to undertake within a month what he has failed to do in ten years." The speech fell flat, and many blamed a failure of the General's magic for what happened later. This is naïve nonsense. The speech was neither better nor worse than others he had made in the past, but the situation was different. The General was not faced with narrow-minded military commanders or weak-kneed politicians. He was faced with a social movement that was still on the rise.

"*Adieu, De Gaulle, adieu . . .*" a waving sea of white handkerchiefs rose above the marchers. There was little time, however, for funeral orations or fun. In the front line the skirmishes had started, and police charges began to break up the demonstration into segments. It was the beginning of a bloody night known as the Night of the Bourse because of the token fire started in the symbolic temple of French capitalism. The breakup of the march was not entirely an advantage for the police. The fast-moving marchers regrouped in several demonstrations. A small party took over the Bourse by surprise and set some telephone boxes on fire. Most of the demonstrators paraded along the big boulevards and marched toward the Opéra. The police were outflanked and overtaken by the speed of events. Had they chosen to, the demon-

13. A nice twist was added to the now celebrated slogan by Aimé Césaire, the Negro poet and progressive deputy from Martinique, who whispered: "I am quite willing to shout it, only nobody will believe me."

strators might well have penetrated into the neighboring Ministry of Justice or, possibly, into the Ministry of Finance. Just before midnight, having heard reports of fighting in their own area, most demonstrators marched back to the Latin Quarter, crossing the Seine by a curiously unguarded bridge. From then till the early hours of the morning it was an almost classic battle in the student quarter, with concussion grenades and small barricades set on fire to slow down the advance of the troops. The mopping up was particularly savage, and all that has been said earlier about the sadistic beatings inside police stations could be repeated here in stronger terms.

Looking back on the last Bloody Friday, one can distinguish two conflicting interpretations. Many of the participants argue retrospectively that it was a mistake to go back to the Latin Quarter, that ministries might have been seized and that an opportunity to start an insurrection was missed. Other commentators claim that the government manipulated the situation cleverly and allowed the demonstrators to rampage all over Paris so as to frighten the middle classes with an invasion of the "scum," "the underworld," to use the vocabulary of Fouchet, the Minister of the Interior. Both versions seem to miss the main point. But first, Fouchet's accusation must be dealt with.

Throughout this crisis the press, including liberal papers, based their comments on a strange assumption. Only the students had the right to rebel. Whenever men not in their early twenties or youngsters visibly not with an academic background were discovered in the fighting crowd, the immediate reaction was to speak of the mob and of subversion. The implicit logic was that students had the right to lose heroically in splended isolation as long as they did not upset the wider social order. Naturally the students did not share this view. On the contrary, their spokesmen insisted that their battle only had a meaning if linked with the struggle of the workers. They openly appealed to the latter and got some response from the younger generation. Amid the young rebels from the working-class suburbs, often in conflict with the authorities, love for the cop was certainly not the dominant feeling. But these were not gangsters, and looting was not a feature of the French riots. The men from the underworld know on which side their bread is buttered. The gunslinging professionals appeared on the stage only in June amid Gaullist election squads and the strikebreaking fighters for "freedom of labor."

Such reasoning is not to be expected from a Minister of the Interior. The Gaullists tried to make the best of a bad job. Official propaganda used whatever it could—burned cars, the rising scum, the underworld—to sway public opinion. Yet it would be absurd to suggest that the authorities stage-managed, or even welcomed, a night like that. The police were exhausted, overextended, and had not yet recovered their faith in their masters. Nor was Paris alone. That very night there was bloody fighting in Lyon and Nantes. Indeed, the first two fatal casualties were added to the long list of wounded that night. A policeman was killed in Lyon by a truck, and a demonstrator in Paris by a fragment from a grenade.[14] The government was not sufficiently in control to be able to get away with many such nights.

The converse is not true either. The students could not start an insurrection. They were not prepared for it, and the conditions were not propitious. Even if they had seized public buildings, they would have been driven out. Pompidou could still feel fairly safe because the mass of the workers was not involved. On Saturday afternoon, with the Boulevard St.-Michel barely cleared of barricades, attention again shifted to a neighboring district of Paris, to Rue de Grenelle in the ministerial quarter. There, at 3 P.M., in a small Louis XV-style palace, the Hôtel du Châtelet, delegates of all the labor unions and the employers' federation joined Pompidou and his colleagues for some twenty-five hours of bargaining, and Frenchmen were taken back thirty-two years to another upheaval in their history.

Major crises prey on the collective mind of a nation, and in 1968 many Frenchmen tended to view current events through

14. It was reported at the time that he was killed with a knife, not a police weapon, thus suggesting a settlement of accounts amid members of the "underworld."

the prism of 1936. Once before, France had been paralyzed by a general strike, even if not quite on the same scale. Once before, the official leaders of the labor movement—at that time socialists and Communists—saved the existing system around a conference table in neighboring Rue de Varenne, only in a different palace, the Prime Minister's Hôtel Matignon (hence the name Matignon Agreements). But there was one basic difference. The socialist Léon Blum was then presiding over the government. The popular front of Communists, socialists, and Radicals had won the election before the strike. In fact the workers occupied factories because they felt they had won and thought they had seized power. They hadn't. Even so, the capitalists then had to pay quite a price for survival. Collective bargaining, a forty-hour week, two weeks holiday with pay, to mention but a few of these gains—these were considerable conquests for that period. This time the workers did not trust the Gaullist government in power. What were they to be offered for giving up the strike and the occupation?

In preparation for the negotiation, two of the unions—the CGT and the CFDT—produced from the drawer their two-year-old agreement and brushed it up. Five items were put on the agenda. The first concerned social security. Under the French system of medicare, all wage and salary earners are insured. They pay their doctor or chemist and are then reimbursed a percentage of the fixed, or "conventional," price. The insured used to get eighty per cent back, but in 1967 the government reduced it to seventy per cent by a decree that also deprived the labor unions of their control over social security. It was this decree that the unions wanted to get repealed. Most of the other items do not need any special explanation. The program included demands for higher wages, for shorter hours without any reduction in pay, for a policy of full employment, and last but not least for a "free exercise of union activity within the firm." On this last item the two confederations diverged seriously, the CGT merely insisting on the extension of the undoubtedly limited freedom of action allowed French unions within the factory, the CFDT groping toward some kind of "union power."

On the eve of the talks the CGT, at least verbally, hardened its position.[15] The details of the twenty-five-hour negotiation, with its breaks, impromptu statements, and changes of mood, need not be chronicled. It seems agreed that it was essentially a match between Georges Pompidou and Georges Séguy. At one stage, on Sunday afternoon, there were signs of deadlock when the leader of the CGT declared that his delegation had an "imperative mandate" to obtain a sliding scale for wages to guarantee their purchasing power, payment for the period of the strike, and abolition of the decree on social security. By the early hours of Monday morning, to judge by the contents of the package, the imperative was no longer so categorical.

In the draft agreement reached, the biggest gain for the workers was in wages, particularly for the lowest paid. The minimum guaranteed hourly rate was to be raised by over a third, from 2.22 to 3 francs (roughly from 44 to 60 cents). This applied fully to some 200,000 people in industry and commerce earning the previous minimum, and to about 600,000 earning less than the new one. In addition, the minimum was also to be increased for agricultural laborers. The rest of the labor force was promised a 10 per cent wage increase for the year as a whole, in two installments. This was about 4 per cent more than the usual average in nominal terms, and somewhat less in real terms, since prices were likely to rise faster than usual. The package also included the outline of an agreement on trade-union rights within the firm,[16] the promise of a gradual reduction of working hours, and a pledge to increase medical reimbursements from 70 to 75 per cent. The decree on social security was not abolished, and the sliding scale was forgotten. As to the hours lost because of the

15. In a press conference on May 23, Jean-Louis Moynot, a secretary, declared: "The general strike is the decisive lever to force the employers and the government to yield." Georges Séguy added: "Only a *national negotiation* can solve the crisis. . . . When we shall have obtained *satisfactory* answers to *all* the questions put, we shall go back to the workers to consult them." (Italics mine.) The statement is interesting in view of the subsequent course of events.

16. The law was to be voted in December.

strike, the workers were to be given half their pay on account, to be compensated for, at least in principle, by overtime.

Judged by normal standards, the unions could welcome the agreement as very successful. But the times were not normal. The unions could not claim to have obtained anything spectacular, nothing comparable to the forty-hour week or the holiday with pay of 1936. The main gains were in wages, and they were sub-stantial—substantial enough to be swallowed up partly by infla-tion without a radical change in policy designed to consolidate the shift in incomes. If, for revolutionary socialists, the Matignon Agreements had been a farce, the Grenelle Agreements were the parody of a farce. Yet the negotiators, having hurried through the night, sounded rather satisfied on Monday morning. Pompi-dou explained that "only the extraordinarily serious nature of the current crisis has made it possible to reach such important con-clusions." The employers' federation added that it had entered the negotiation "acutely conscious of the gravity of the situation." The union leaders were slightly more balanced in their judgment. Georges Séguy said: "Demands that had been rebuffed by the government and employers have found a partial, if not total, so-lution. Much is still to be done, but the demands have been granted for a great part, and what has been decided should not be minimized. However, we cannot give an answer without consult-ing the workers." Eugène Descamps of the CFDT made the same point, claiming that the delegates must now find out "whether we have defended [the workers'] interests correctly." Radio com-mentators were not so meticulous. They were already announcing the end of the crisis and speculating about the time needed for work to resume. At 8 A.M. all was over bar the formality of con-sulting the workers. A couple of hours later nothing was over.

The workers' veto was first expressed at Boulogne-Billancourt. The union leaders who went there straight from the talks could not expect any enthusiasm for the package. They had visibly rushed things through and in their strange hurry had dropped al-legedly "imperative" demands. There were already rumors that Renault workers from the provinces had called up to say "Go to hell." The young CGT secretary at Billancourt who opened the mass meeting had to repeat the local demands, and it was clear that the gap with the Grenelle protocol was too wide. What the top CGT leaders apparently expected was a *Non, mais;* that is, an agreement to take the Grenelle propositions as the basis for further discussion. The bargaining could thus be switched from the national to branch or even factory level, and once this happened, the situation would have ceased to be explosive. In their scheme the CGT leaders made only one miscalculation: They misjudged the mood of the workers.

That something had gone wrong could be sensed throughout the mass meeting, for instance when the veteran Benoit Frachon waited in vain for applause at the end of his peroration against those daring to give lessons to the working class, or when André Jeanson, chairman of the CFDT, was loudly applauded for speaking about the convergence of the fight of the students and that of the workers. But the real turning point came in the middle of Georges Séguy's speech. It was a balanced speech, explaining that more could have been achieved if there had been but one union facing a left-wing government. In his description of the agreements he came to the point of pay for days lost: "We have fought to obtain payment for the days of the strike. This is an expression bosses do not like; they prefer to call it something different. After a long discussion the employers' federation has agreed to pay fifty per cent of wages for the duration of the strike, with arrangements for making this up that vary according to cases . . ."—interrupted by whistles and boos, he tried to go on—". . . according to cases, listen. . . ." The booing gets louder and louder. Seguy has sensed the mood of the crowd: ". . . a method of recovery depending on cases, and after what has just happened, it will not be the case for Renault." [17] Amid shouts of "Don't sign" the CGT leaders were obliged to learn their lesson. It was not a diplo-

17. A recording of the speech is published in Bauchard and Bruzek, *Le Syndicalisme à l'Épreuve* (Paris, Éditions Robert Laffont, 1968), pp. 108–109.

matic, polite *Yes, but* or *No, but*. It was a violent refusal that altered the political equation.

The *Non* from Renault was only a prelude. Radio reporters now brought an echo from all the strongholds of the working class, from Berliet near Lyon, from Sud-Aviation near Nantes, from Rhodiaceta. And smaller factories soon followed the same line. It was No. The attempt to solve the crisis within the system had failed. Frenchmen, and the world at large, were beginning to wonder whether power was not really in the streets, and who, in that case, was going to pick it up?

WORLD STRUGGLE *would indeed be very easy to make if the struggle were taken up only on condition of infallibly favorable chances.*

— KARL MARX *to* L. KUGELMAN, *April 1871*

How Not to Seize Power
(May 27–May 31)

THE MYTH IS NOW SPREADING *that the key to the French crisis lies in the magic of the word. General de Gaulle lost his verbal spell on Friday, May 24, and the regime was shattered. He recovered it on Thursday, May 30, and Gaullism was triumphant again. The myth is really a fairy tale for romantic historians. The snag is that the General did not win, or rather that he won by default: The other side lost. We saw this defeat of the left developing throughout our narrative.*

*Yet the left had a second chance thrust upon it. How this
chance was squandered is a dramatic, though rather complex,
story. It begins the very day when the veto of the French
workers tore to pieces the compromise between the unions
and the government.*

Charléty Stadium is a student sports ground in the south of Paris.
The crowd that packed its stepped rows of seats on Monday evening, May 27, had not come to watch athletics. The marchers
who were soon to fill the arena carrying red banners and a few
black flags were no ordinary sportsmen, either. This was a political meeting of the dynamic wing of the May Movement, and despite official scare stories about the risk of shooting and stern
Communist warnings against provocation, it attracted tens of
thousands. The speakers represented most sections of this eager
public that listened attentively to Jacques Sauvageot of the students' union and a spokesman of the March 22 Movement; to
Alain Geismar, who had just left his post in the lecturers' union
to concentrate on political action; to André Barjonet, who had
resigned from the CGT in protest; to Maurice Labi, from the
chemical and glass industries union, a leftist branch of Force
Ouvrière; and to others. The recurring refrain linking most of
these speeches was the Cuban motto: "The duty of a revolutionary is to make revolution." But how and with whom? The meeting did not really answer these questions.

A man standing near the speakers' corner illustrated part of
the dilemma facing the movement. He had marched with the
marchers, but was not going to speak, though he was the only
internationally known figure in the crowd. It was Pierre Mendès-
France, who during his brief spell as Prime Minister back in
1954 had made peace in Indochina and captured his country's
imagination. He was now sixty-one years old, and during the
Gaullist decade he had not only been in opposition but often
quite intentionally out of the limelight. Nevertheless, he was one
of the very few political figures not included in the popular con-

tempt for politicians, and probably the only one respected by
many young Frenchmen. His prestige was based on a reputation
for intelligence, courage, and personal honesty. Yet this man of
integrity was now the man of the hour in an ambiguous position.
For some he was, metaphorically, a Kerensky who would simply
pave the way for real revolutionaries. For others, he was French
capitalism's last chance to survive through reforms.

Confusion was confounded because this former Radical now
belonged to a leftist socialist party, the small but influential PSU.
The PSU itself was the result of many mergers. Some of its founding members had come from the orthodox socialist party, the
Section Française de l'Internationale Ouvrière (French Section
of the International Workers' Association), or SFIO. They had
been against Mollet's colonialist policy and had found it too much
when in 1958 he rallied to the victorious General de Gaulle. The
other founding family was itself an amalgamation of various small
groups of France's new left. Add to it leftish Radicals personally
faithful to Mendès, a few Communist dissidents, a sprinkling of
Trotskyists, and you get quite a mixture.

Among French parties the PSU was closest to a position of
"revolutionary reformism." It tried to adapt its strategy to structural changes in society. It offered counterplans to governmental
programs and attempted to elaborate a socialist alternative. Still,
with stronger roots among the professional intelligentsia than
among industrial workers, it was often suspected of technocratic
temptations, and the presence of Mendès-France strengthened
such suspicions. "Modern," after all, is not always synonymous
with "socialist." Whatever the grounds for such mistrust, during
the May crisis the PSU under the leadership of its young secretary, Michel Rocard, backed the students from the start, and
most of its members took an active part in the movement. Could
Mendès-France, a famous but marginal figure, neither leader nor
an ordinary militant of this small party, could he, too, be linked
with the May Movement? [1]

1. On the strained relations between Mendès and his party see Gilles
Martinet, *La Conquète des Pouvoirs* (Paris, Éditions du Seuil, 1968), pp.
28–31.

The man was obviously a problem. Whereas a number of his former followers had jumped onto the Gaullist bandwagon and quite a few were drifting gradually towards the center, Pierre Mendès-France was driven by the logic of his honest opposition farther and farther to the left. Whether he could be called a socialist depended on the meaning one gave to the term. If it meant simply state intervention against the abuses of private capital, reforms to modernize the economy and eliminate the most glaring social inequalities, Mendès could certainly be called a socialist.

Yet could one imagine this Radical bred in the parliamentary tradition, this French New Dealer with a neo-Keynesian outlook, attacking the foundations of France's bourgeois order? Men are often what circumstances make of them, and some Frenchmen genuinely saw in him the gravedigger and others the savior of capitalism. Mendès, the symbol of clear choice—known for his formula "To govern is to choose"—was now being carried forward under a cloud of ambiguity. (For all the difference between the two men, his situation bore some resemblance to General de Gaulle's ten years earlier, when the General was climbing to power in shapeless disguise.)

Mendès-France was at Charléty but he did not speak. Had he done so, he would have made an open bid for the leadership of the dynamic wing of the movement. Since this gathering was unmistakably hostile toward the Communist hierarchy, he would have reinforced the already strong Communist opposition to himself as head of a popular-front coalition. He had his own reasons for not speaking. Nor is it certain that he would have been welcome to this predominantly revolutionary crowd. It had nothing to do with personal esteem, but a great deal with the nature of the Charléty gathering.

An organized, disciplined party can set itself limited, immediate objectives. It can calculate that at this stage the important thing is, say, to bring Gaullism down and introduce a number of reforms. In that case it can rely on the social weight of its organization to influence the new balance of forces and, if possible, to upset it once again. Such tactics are outside the scope of an en-

tirely spontaneous movement. Many in the crowd gathered at
Charléty thought that either the Communist party or its traditional followers could still be dragged into revolutionary action.
If that hope was unfulfilled, quite a few were convinced that for
the long-term victory of socialism it was more important to show
up the Communist leadership in its true colors than to patch together a compromise solution. Altogether, most of the Charléty
crowd was not particularly interested in a parliamentary way out.

With Gaullism apparently crumbling, not everybody shared
this indifference. Politicians now tried to move to the center of
the stage. The morning after Charléty, it was the turn of François
Mitterrand, chairman of the social-democratic FGDS, to hold a
press conference and make his own bid for the succession. Taking
the General's words at their face value, he started from the premise that De Gaulle, defeated in the referendum, would depart. He
added the legally doubtful argument (but who were the Gaullists
to give lessons in legal respectability in exceptional circumstances?) that the Prime Minister would then resign and the
President of the Senate, acting as temporary head of state, would
call on the left to govern during the interim period. Mitterrand
put himself forward once again as a candidate for the presidency
of the Republic. In the meantime, however, before the presidential election, somebody would have to govern and settle the crisis.
For this purpose he suggested a "provisional government," headed
by a man like Pierre Mendès-France and with ten ministers
chosen "without any bar." This, in the code language of French
politics, meant that Communists could join such a government.

Mitterrand was no mean politician. It is this astuteness that
had enabled the fifty-one-year-old leader of a small splinter group
to re-emerge, first as the only candidate of the left in the presidential election of 1965, and then, having performed better than
expected, as the head of a federation that regrouped Mollet's socialists, the Radicals, and his own followers from "political clubs."
In the process he had sponsored the idea of a new popular front
and favored the Communist comeback into parliamentary politics. Mitterrand's calculation was simple. France, he realized, was

moving, if not toward a two-party system, at least toward a system of two coalitions; and in electoral terms the left could challenge the Gaullists only if it had Communist support.

His strategy, elaborated with Guy Mollet, rested on two additional unwritten assumptions. The first was that the Communists would accept the rules of the bourgeois game; the second, that in this parliamentary game they would be junior partners in the coalition. The May crisis confirmed the first assumption, with the Communist party behaving in a perfectly reformist fashion. But it shattered the second. The limelight shifting from parliament to country revealed the real balance of forces. The FGDS, Mollet's socialists, the Radicals, were shown up for what they really were, essentially electioneering cartels. The Communist party, by contrast, showed its power, even if it did so in a negative way. The powerful suitors were still pressing for the parliamentary match. The FGDS, conscious of its weakness, was growing increasingly reluctant, playing hard to get. Many socialists and radicals were looking wistfully to their right, seeking additional support to redress the balance.

The Communist leaders were in an awkward spot. If they had studied their Marxist classics, they would have known that their conduct in this crisis fitted perfectly into the definition of "social-democratic opportunism." They had fought throughout on the ground of their class enemy. The trade unionists were guilty of "economism," sticking to wage demands within the capitalist system. The political wing limited its horizon to problematical electoral gains within a bourgeois Parliament. And the party did not transcend such deviations; it had no strategy that would bind the two fronts into a coherent plan. At first the CGT was pushed into the foreground in the hope that the general strike could be limited to quick material gains. The party, during this period, was merely echoing its normal slogans about the need for unity on the left, for a more elaborate joint electoral platform.

As time went by and other groups, advocating a more radical policy, began to gain ground, the Communist party tried to counter by setting up its own committees "for a popular government of democratic action." Since the Grenelle negotiations, far from ending the crisis, had given it a new political impetus, the Communists put pressure on the FGDS to hurry up with strengthening the alliance. But as the Communists were still bargaining in parliamentary terms, their would-be partners kept the upper hand. The paradox of the situation was that the Communists could have swept Mitterrand and Mollet into an alliance or into oblivion with ease. For that they had to take the leadership of the movement, to attract the radical forces linked with the students, to run the strike in a different fashion, to show themselves as the main anticapitalist force; in short, they had to be what they were not, namely a revolutionary party.

There remains the puzzling question, Why did the Communists decide not to play the Mendès-France card? Their hostility was unconcealed. The day after Mitterrand's suggestion of a "provisional government," *L'Humanité* mocked Mendès in an editorial: "Thus the providential man has not yet left the Élysée when another savior is being called for." Communist propaganda tried to convey that like the Charléty crowd, the party was worried by the capitalist support for Mendès-France, by his lack of socialist zeal. This was sheer hypocrisy. Mitterrand and Mollet, its chosen partners, were even less suited for the role of gravediggers of capitalism.

One is left with two possible explanations. The more charitable one is that the Communists preferred a weak rather than a strong ally and feared the personality of Pierre Mendès-France, particularly if the government brought to power by the strike was also dependent on the dynamic forces revealed in the struggle. Which brings us to the less charitable explanation: The Communists may well have feared that a Mendès-France government brought to power in such a fashion would not be the end of the matter, that there were risks of the crisis continuing. Was it not more comfortable and safer to remain the "truly revolutionary" opposition within the Gaullist regime? Only Gaullism at this point gave the impression of vanishing, and the other risk was of finding oneself the cuckold in the affair of the succession to Gaullism.

To avoid this danger and remind everybody who was the chief force—or the main weakness?—of the French labor movement, the CGT forgot for a moment its alleged political allergy and called on its followers to demonstrate on Wednesday, May 29, not only for "workers' demands" but also "to contribute toward a political settlement."

All these antics, these strange hesitations about filling a vacuum, can only make sense against the background of crumbling authority, against the décor for the twilight of a reign. One lesson to be drawn from the events was the unsuspected fragility of the seemingly mighty modern industrial state. Ten days of student rebellion followed by ten days of a general strike, and Gaullism was falling apart. The feeling of anarchy was all the stronger since no parallel power was taking the place of the stumbling governmental machine. For some days now, if you went to see a minister, the old usher could not conceal his surprise that somebody still wished to see the man allegedly in office. Pompidou, mustering the government's forces, had the uncomfortable feeling that he could rely only on a small handful of his colleagues. The levers were failing to respond in the most unexpected quarters. Television was on strike, and the government could only put on a token news program. The transmission services of the Ministry of the Interior were on strike, too. To illustrate symbolically the helplessness of a once arrogant power, the banned Daniel Cohn-Bendit reappeared at the Sorbonne at midnight on Tuesday, May 28, and held a press conference.

As long as the strike looked provisional, employers could put up with it. But after the *Non* from Renault they began to take the red flags flying over their factories seriously and to wonder whether the Communist party would not be dragged or driven to a new line of action. Money was flowing out, and the bank strike, paradoxically, was hindering a bigger outflow; it was probably more effective than the loose exchange-control introduced as an afterthought on June 1. The leaders of French business were divided about the best course to follow. The interregnum was too short to measure the exact strength of the different groups, though three broad schools of thought could be distinguished.

One school was ready to ditch the wavering General in favor of Georges Pompidou or anybody else who looked capable of redressing the situation. A bigger group was convinced that the legendary hero was still useful at the top, while what was needed quickly was a change of government and of Prime Minister; a less committed man like, say, the clever Edgar Faure might still be able to resolve the crisis by widening the coalition as far to the left as possible. A growing number of businessmen, however, were giving up such hopes and coming to the conclusion that the Gaullist regime would have to be thrown overboard in order to salvage what could still be salvaged of the system. The Mendès-Mitterrand tandem, the possible winners of tomorrow, was looked upon as a lesser evil, under the circumstances, by these people who were beginning to find out what guarantees the new regime could offer.

Similar cleavages had appeared among politicians and could be detected in private, in anxious telephone conversations and in the parliamentary lobbies. Men close to the very top were lamenting in whispers that General de Gaulle had lost his nerve, that he was complaining of sleeplessness and talking of himself as a man of the past. The meaning of such hints was obvious. At the same time, pressure within the majority for Pompidou's departure was getting stronger and louder. On Thursday morning, Giscard d'Estaing, former Minister of Finance and the still youthful leader of a group whose votes the Gaullists required to keep their parliamentary majority, proclaimed that "at this moment, when everything is breaking down, including elementary fidelity," the President should stay, while a new government with a wider base should prepare a general election. On the previous afternoon one of Giscard's followers had told Pompidou plainly during a meeting between the Prime Minister and representatives of his majority that he should go and leave room for Edgar Faure.

The Gaullists had not altogether given up hope of clinging to power. On Monday, when the expectation of a negotiated agreement with the unions proved vain, the men in charge speeded up the mobilization of Gaullist networks old and new. Enough gasoline was found to bring truckloads of the faithful to Paris in preparation for an eventual counterdemonstration. By Wednesday, however, hope had turned to despair, and many members of the majority were also turning to Mendès-France.[2] Wednesday, May 29, was a day of panic, hope, and illusion. It was also the real day of decision.

Just before 10 A.M. ministers arriving at the Élysée learned with surprise that the ministerial council scheduled for that morning was cancelled. The President's sudden decision had only been passed on to the government a few minutes earlier, so that not all those concerned could be warned. Surprise turned to real anxiety among Gaullists when news flashes announced by about 11:30 that General de Gaulle and his wife had just left the Élysée for Colombey-les-deux-Églises, their private home in the country. That at least is what the harried palace press service said was their destination, adding that the President would be back next day for a Cabinet meeting. Rumor immediately had it that the General had retired to the country to prepare his message of resignation. Yet the real shock was still to come, when reporters phoned from Colombey to say that there was no presidential helicopter in sight. The General had vanished into thin air, and for over six hours France did not know the whereabouts of its official head of state.

It was not just the general public. The government knew nothing either, and General de Gaulle's closest collaborators could not help, claiming that they were not in on the secret. At Matignon, the Prime Minister's office, delegations came and went. Ministers and deputies pressed, implored, gave advice. Amid the coming and going, Pompidou also had to decide how to advance in the dark, ignoring the General's intentions. Just in case, he booked a tentative television appearance for 8 P.M. He already had a problem on his mind—the mass CGT demonstration scheduled for the

2. Who could provide a very interesting list if he decided to publish his memoirs.

afternoon. The day before, for the first time since the beginning of the crisis, the suspicion had been raised in the highest Gaullist quarters that the Communists might be tempted to try to seize power. Since the CGT march was going to pass not very far from the Élysée, it was decided to mass police forces in the area and give them orders to shoot if it proved necessary. But the Minister of the Interior was now bringing persistent and alarming reports that it was the Hôtel de Ville, the city hall, that the Communists intended to seize. Should one shoot there too? The government need not have bothered, yet it was a sign of the prevailing disarray that no decision was made about whether or not to defend the Hôtel de Ville, in the heart of the town, the traditional seat of revolutionary power.

Fouchet's informers were wrong. The Communists had no intention of seizing anything. The CGT and the party wanted to show their strength in the greater Paris region, and they did. They brought several hundred thousand people into the streets for a demonstration that they alone had sponsored. The talks with the students' union over the vexing problem of the correct "attitude toward repression"—in plain terms, over Cohn-Bendit—had failed, and the other labor unions seized on this pretext not to march with the Communists. Quite a lot of students were there, nevertheless, but this was no great fusion of the two wings of the movement.[3]

The CGT was undoubtedly the mightiest wing. Its march was powerful and for the first time plainly political. The workers were not clamoring just for higher wages. They were clamoring for a different government capable of applying a different policy. The march was powerful, orderly—the demonstrators obeyed with discipline the loudspeaker instructions for a quiet dispersal—and as equivocal as its main slogan, "Popular government." Many marchers had no doubt that this meant their own government, imposed by their own action in the factories and, possibly, in the

3. The UNEF and Sauvageot were later blamed for the decision. However wrong, it did not matter tremendously, because Communist strategy would not have been altered in any case.

streets. But for the organizers, this "popular government of democratic union" was a parliamentary solution worked out with Mitterrand's FGDS, in which, however, the Communists should have a place corresponding to their impressive numbers. By what parliamentary magic this new government would come into being, or how the Gaullist incumbent would be removed, was never made clear, though that afternoon everybody seemed ready to believe in miracles.

Everybody was also busy jockeying for position. Barely had the CGT begun its first political demonstration, at 4:30, than Eugène Descamps, leader of the CFDT, in an impromptu press conference committed his union politically much farther than ever before in its history. His starting point was that what one was faced with was no longer a political crisis but a crisis of the regime. The events of the last few weeks had revealed new political forces demanding radical reforms in the structure of society. The Communist party and the FGDS, for all their worthy efforts to produce a common program, were not able to integrate these new forces and to satisfy their objectives. For the bulk of the CFDT leaders and militants, Descamps concluded, Pierre Mendès-France was the only man capable of doing so and therefore of "assuming the responsibility of power" with the help of the left, old and new. Breaking with its tradition of political neutrality, the CFDT threw its full weight behind Mendès-France.

The would-be Prime Minister of the left was, meanwhile, consulting his allies. He was locked in a Parisian flat with the leaders of the FGDS: François Mitterrand, the socialists Mollet and Gaston Defferre, as well as René Billères, the Radical. The talks were not easy, and it was past 9 P.M. when Mendès-France, accompanied this time by three leaders of his own PSU (Rocard, Heurgon, and Malterre), went to the National Assembly to make a statement to the press. In the present dramatic and fast-changing circumstances, he argued, the left had to offer immediate measures and a progressive long-term policy. The accent had to be put on what united its forces. Trying to practice what he preached, Mendès-France stressed that he was ready to head a transitional government provided it represented "the whole left," which meant Communists included but also the "live forces of the nation," which was a sign that Charléty had not been forgotten. He was not, however, preaching to the convinced. Neither the Communists nor the PSU showed a great deal of enthusiasm for his proposals.[4]

While left-wing politicians were looking this gift horse in the mouth, the fickle animal was already on his way. While they were pondering how to divide the spoils, victory was eluding their grasp. By the time Mendès-France had read his statement, General de Gaulle, back at Colombey since just after six, was getting ready for a good night's sleep for the first time in days. Since the "vanished" General had spent his afternoon with military commanders, was it their investiture that had given him his renewed confidence? Not quite. The military were only part of a broader reappraisal of the situation, which must have convinced him that he only had to counterattack and his chief opponents would run for cover.

We now know that instead of going by helicopter to Colombey, General de Gaulle had traveled first to St. Dizier, where he apparently met his fellow generals, including the military commander for eastern France, and then to Baden-Baden, the French headquarters beyond the Rhine. There he talked with General Jacques Massu, commander of French troops in Germany.[5] History has its revealing ironies. Ten years earlier, paratroop Brigadier Massu, known for his guts rather than this brain, had been

4. That same evening the PSU, in a communiqué, expressed its disapproval of any solution "which would not alter fundamentally class relationships and would not attack the capitalist social order." The morning after, *L'Humanité* was still attacking the idea of a "providential man."

5. But we still know very little about this episode. French specialists in instant history such as J.-R. Tournoux (*La Tragédie du Général*, Paris, Librairie Plon, 1969), Claude Paillat (*Archives Secrètes*, Paris, Denoël, 1969), and P. Alexandre (*L'Élysée en Péril*, Paris, Fayard, 1969), give conflicting versions of the trip and the conversations. The participants have not spoken yet, and in any case they will have an axe to grind. But this factual gap is not very relevant to our argument.

a key figure in the Algerian *putsch* that brought General de Gaulle back to power. When, a couple of years later, the colonels on his staff wanted to repeat the performance, this time against General de Gaulle and his Algerian policy, the faithful Massu—iron in the soul, if such a metaphor can be applied to a paratroop commander—would not join them. His fidelity had been rewarded, since he was now a five-star general. Yet General Massu was a living illustration of the split in the French army caused by the Algerian war, and of the wounds still unhealed.

A suggestion from General de Gaulle that he would let bygones be bygones, grant amnesty to the remaining prisoners from the Secret Army Organization (the Organisation de l'Armée Secrète, or OAS), and let exiles such as Bidault and Soustelle return, was certainly welcome to the military. In fact, such promises cost General de Gaulle nothing. If he did manage to have an election after all, he would require the support of all the French right, from its liberal wing to its fascist fringe. All the wartime collaborators as well as the former advocates of *Algérie française* would have to be wooed in any case. Nor was the promise indispensable. Against the "Red peril," against an attack from the left, the General could rely on the military commanders. But could he rely on the army?—that was the question.

Ten years earlier France had a colonial army perfectly suited for civil war. Since then the General had not neglected the armed forces—far from it. But in their modernization the accent was put entirely on the nuclear striking force, and the conventional troops were the budgetary Cinderella. General de Gaulle was the author of a celebrated prewar book on the professional army, *Vers l'Armée de Métier.* He had not forged for himself such a weapon for civil strife.

At the time of the crisis, operational French troops on the Continent—that is, both at home and in Germany—were estimated at about 260,000. The army accounted for 168,000 men, but some 120,000 of those were draftees. There was as yet very little unrest in the armed forces and almost no revolutionary propaganda. Still, to use a predominantly conscript army as an instrument for civil war would have involved a tremendous risk. The military commanders could offer some shock troops—such as paratroopers or navy commandos—to protect public buildings or means of communication; this was already being done. They could bring some units on maneuvers back to the gates of Paris as part of their psychological warfare. They were in a position to counter a *putsch*. But they had no troops to break a determined general strike.

Why, then, was General de Gaulle full of confidence at the close of that Wednesday? According to cross-checked accounts, he had left the capital that morning in a state of high excitement.[6] Was he really fearing a Communist coup and refusing to end his career in bloodshed? The vanishing act, in any case, had other advantages. It heightened the drama. The meeting with the military commanders, which was not kept secret for long, played on the fear of civil war. Above all, by the end of that eventful day the General had sized up his opponents and realized the error of his tactics. Hitherto he had tried to stop a social movement with words, while his Prime Minister was trying to settle matters with the Communist leaders. As social forces failed to respond to his incantation, the movement was gathering momentum and pushing the reluctant Communist leaders forward. Now the General was going to attack the Communist leaders directly and leave it to them to break the strike. His new gamble depended on the Communist reaction. General de Gaulle had a quiet night's sleep.

Indeed, the day after, back in Paris, he was in no mood for concessions. It required the pressure of the Prime Minister to make him agree to throw the opposition a bone to pick, to substitute for the referendum a general election.[7] Pompidou saw the

6. When he rang up Pomidou just after 11 A.M. without telling him about his German trip, he apparently mentioned three sleepless nights and is reported to have ended the conversation in a most unusual way: "I am the past, you are the future, *je vous embrasse*." When he called again around 6 P.M. from Colombey, he had regained his self-control.

7. Usually there is a difference between an election and a referendum, which is really a plebiscite. At that point, the difference was unimportant. The question was, Who would be in power at the time of the vote? What mattered was the strike.

General at 2:30 P.M. and duly handed in his resignation; after all, a Prime Minister is expected to know his master's intentions and whereabouts. The resignation was duly turned down; the lieutenant could still serve for a few weeks before being discarded as too big for his boots. General de Gaulle signed the letters dissolving the Assembly, presided over a brief Cabinet meeting, and then recorded his short message to the nation, announcing that he was soldiering on. The message was broadcast at 4:30 sharp; it was as tough as it was brief:

In the past twenty-four hours the General had contemplated "all possibilities," but he had decided not to resign. He had proposed a referendum. It visibly could not be held on schedule. He now offered a general election, which would be held rapidly unless an attempt was made to "gag the French people," to prevent them from expressing their views as they were being prevented from learning, teaching, or working "through intimidation, intoxication and tyranny" exercised by groups directed from afar and by a "totalitarian party." Should such an attempt be made, he would resort to "other ways than an immediate vote." He also called on the French people at once to organize "civic action" to help the government and its servants in the struggle against subversion, which would rapidly lead to the victory of "totalitarian Communism." But, he concluded, "the Republic will not abdicate."

Scarcely had the General finished than his supporters flocked to their own demonstration. The reinforcements brought from the provinces proved superfluous. The frightened, the frustrated, the men who had been seething with indignation during the past few weeks, were filling the Place de la Concorde, ready to march up the Champs-Élysées toward the Arc de Triomphe. How many were they? Probably not so many as the marchers on May 13, even if the police, looking through magnifying glasses, for a change, spoke in millions. The exact amount did not really matter. It was a huge crowd, politically and socially very mixed, the sacred union of all shades of the right. Former collaborators from Vichy marched with veterans of the Free French; men carrying the United States flag walked behind Gaullist ministers and deputies, self-proclaimed fighters against the "American hegemony"; advocates of colonial liberation marched side by side with *Algérie française* fanatics, and mealy-mouthed liberals with fascist thugs.

Socially it was a mixture, too. The smart districts had come out to parade. Elegant hostesses, more often seen at cocktail parties than in political ones, company directors, high officials, well-off tradesmen, and retired army colonels made their debut in the streets. Alone they could not have amounted to much. But in the crowd they were likely to meet their concierge, their waiter, their butcher. The typists, the shop assistants, the junior office clerks, who dream of social climbing but know their place, were there, too, together with angry shopkeepers and patriotic saloonkeepers. The demonstration was a rendezvous for all that part of the lower middle classes that fits so well into Heine's formula, "a skein of fear filled with prejudices." There was also more than a sprinkling of well-dressed youth to remind one of the obvious, namely that one can be young and counter-revolutionary.

Their slogans ranged from the traditionally jingoist—"France for Frenchmen" and "The flag is blue, white, and red"—to the memorably odious—"Cohn-Bendit to Dachau." [8] In between there was also the ridiculous: The passionate fashionable ladies, the new *merveilleuses,* and company chairmen shouting "Freedom of work" and "Set the factories free." "Our factories" would have been more accurate, though the poor darlings would have been in a fix if they had been free to run them on their own. Herein lay the class difference between the two demonstrations and their respective significance. In electoral terms, the discrepancies were only marginal: One crowd roughly equalled the other. In productive terms, in terms of social conflict, the "human dust" parading on the Champs-Élysées weighed but little on the scales.

8. The slogan was not only shouted. It was immediately recorded in *Le Monde.* Undoubtedly most of the Elysean marchers could swear that they were not in favor of gas chambers. To the best of my knowledge, not one of the leaders or organizers published a word of protest or proclaimed publicly that there was no room for fascist thugs in their movement. It was not the moment to be choosy.

This is why only superficial observers can take the Gaullist demonstration as the new turning point in the crisis.

Let us forget for a moment all that we now know about the strategy of the Communist leadership and its determination to avoid a showdown. On Thursday evening, after General de Gaulle's speech, the situation did indeed look dramatic. Some even wondered whether the Communists had not been trapped into action. They had put a political foot forward into the apparent void and received the "totalitarian" brick. Could they retreat without reply? From other quarters the first reactions to the message were pretty strong. "It's the voice of dictatorship," claimed Mitterrand. It is "the declaration of war on the people," echoed the leader of the Federation of National Education. Was it the eve of a clash, of a conflict between the soldiers and the strikers, between the armed forces and the army of labor?

It never was quite so dramatic as that. We have seen that the military commanders were unable to supply the General with troops that could break the strike, and even if the exhausted police forces [9] were added, this still was not enough for the job. The main questions remained essentially the same: When would the elections be held, and who would run them? Would the general strike continue on a national scale, paralyzing the country and, by the same token, squeezing the government out? In other words, would General de Gaulle, ten years after his seizure of power, be paid back in his own coin?

Now dressed in the democratic mantle of the defender of the Republic, General de Gaulle knew well what it was all about through his own successful experience. In the mid-fifties Gaullism was a spent force. In the parliamentary elections of 1956 its score was insignificant. Then came the Algerian *putsch* of May 1958 and the chance the General was not going to squander. He used the threat of a military invasion to force the cowardly government of Pierre Pflimlin to step down and hand the reins over to him, pre-

9. 13,500 CRS; 14,700 plainclothes and 54,900 uniformed policemen; and 61,000 gendarmes. But the latter belong to the army. Figures quoted in *Le Monde* on May 25, 1968.

serving legal forms. Once in power, the General staged a referendum and pocketed eighty per cent of the votes cast. He well
knew, therefore, that it mattered whether you faced the electorate
as the vanquished or the winner. Paid back in his own coin? Not
quite. There was one basic difference between the two May crises
ten years apart, the difference between mercenary soldiers and
the working people, between a host of paratroopers and millions
of strikers.

Under such circumstances you do not need to reject an election,
appearing to fear the verdict of the people. You simply choose
your own time and your own terms. A shrewd observer [10] mentioned three conditions the opposition might have made for taking part in an election: a change in the prerogatives of Parliament
(why, after such a crisis, should one vote for a powerless assembly?); a reform of the electoral law and boundaries, favoring the
majority; an extension of the voting age to, say, eighteen so that
the young, so active in the crisis, should also have their say. It
was possible to invent many other conditions. The opposition, for
instance, could claim that a regime that for ten years had manipulated public opinion, notably through its control and use of radio
and television, could not be trusted with running a fair election,
that the Ministry of the Interior, the Ministry of Information,
and the regional prefectures should first be put under popular
control. The key was not in the preconditions themselves; it lay
in the continuation and strengthening of the strike.

Admittedly, the strike had to harden to counter the Gaullist
offensive. If the police tried to break through picket lines and to
occupy, say, post offices, the strikers would have to use the weapons they still had in reserve by, for instance, cutting off gas or
electricity. Altogether, to keep a general strike, now in its third
week, going it was necessary to alter the tactics, to mobilize the
men fully, to tell them frankly what it was all about, to develop
wherever possible the provisional organs of dual power. All this
involved more risks. Were the Communist leaders and the CGT

10. Lucio Magri in his penetrating *Considerazioni Sui Fatti di Maggio*
(Bari, De Donato Editore, 1968).

ready to assume them now, or was General de Gaulle right when he took his gamble? Anyone who still had doubts about the answer on Thursday night could have none left on Friday, when Georges Séguy issued the orders of retreat for the army of labor and dotted the i's on the order:

> As it has never ceased to declare, the CGT is ready to pursue this negotiation at the level of the government and the employers' federation as well as at all other levels so as to reach an agreement acceptable to the workers. At present, it is the intransigence of the authorities and the ill-will of the employers that paralyze in many cases the normal conduct of negotiation. . . . In order to remove any misunderstanding about its objectives, the CGT declares that it has no intention of impeding in any way the conduct of the election.

May 31: This was the real end. The day before, the army of labor, several million strong, had been fighting on a national front. The day after, the dispersed regiments, battalions, companies, would try to get the best possible terms in their retreat. The global trial of strength would be over. The Communist leadership opted for the safety of "parliamentary battles between frogs and mice." It chose the road of electoral defeat.

IL FAUT SAVOIR *terminer une grève. (You must know how to end a strike.)*

—MAURICE THOREZ, *1936*

From General Strike to General Election

THE OUTCOME *was now inevitable. The left did not stand a chance. A general strike is not an electoral gadget. You either win and then get your victory endorsed, or you lose. A left that had proved in the crisis that it neither would rule nor deserved to could not seriously expect a mandate from the electorate. The June episode can thus be described briefly, though it should be very roughly divided into two parts. The first is still one of tension, connected with the gradual breakdown of the strike.*

When two workers were killed on June 11 and the CGT got away with a token strike, it became obvious that the Communists would not be overwhelmed in this crisis. The second phase was mainly electoral. The campaign had its farcical side. There were the Gaullists, tongue in cheek, painting the Communists ultra-Red, while the alleged disciples of Lenin paraded as champions of bourgeois law and order—not a common sight. It would have been funny had it not been sad. The crisis that began with a bang ended with an electioneering whimper.

Symbolically, the so-called consumer society scored its triumph on Tuesday, June 4, at the close of the Pentecost weekend, with a monstrous traffic jam. The trade unions had made the psychological mistake—but was it really unintentional?—of allowing gas stations to refuel. Millions of Frenchmen rushed out for the long weekend. When they came back, with public transport still paralyzed and policemen too busy for traffic duty, cars lined up for hours. Paris experienced possibly the worst traffic jam in its history. Was France back to normal? Not yet. The strike was still general, and efforts to bring it to an end were still meeting considerable resistance.

All the actors stayed true to form. The revolutionary students and their allies tried to keep the strike going and the workers mobilized; they offered their services wherever they were needed for resistance. The Communist hierarchy was equally determined to end the strike. Once bitten, twice shy, it was not going to repeat its mistake; a second disavowal could be disastrous. The Communists, however, were now in a more comfortable position. Once the general strike was divided and bargaining shifted from national to branch level, the risks of a general conflagration were much smaller. The CGT tactic was to get something better than the Grenelle Agreements so as to allow *L'Humanité* to announce day after day the news of a triumphant return to work.

The government, to begin with, was also in a hurry to remove the serious political danger. In order to end the complete general strike, it made quick concessions in the public sector, granting two or three per cent more in wages and agreeing in some cases to pay full wages for the days of the stoppage. By June 5 the strike was drawing to an end on the railways, in the post office, in gas, electricity, and the coal mines. Then, sensing the change in the balance of forces, both government and employers hardened their positions, particularly in those branches involved in international competition. This was notably true of engineering, and the automobile industry once again became the test case. On June 6 the government felt strong enough to attempt to break the strike by force. The gendarmes were sent to take over the Renault works at Flins. The factory was craftily chosen. Renault symbolized a stronghold of the working class, but Flins, though only some twenty-five miles from Paris, was isolated in a predominantly rural area.

Police forces managed to occupy the factory, but they could not get it to work. They had reckoned without the resistance organized by young workers and CFDT unionists, who called on the students to come and help. Despite police blockades all the way from Paris, despite numerous arrests, the students did come to offer their services and their experience. For the next two days the Latin Quarter was transplanted to rural surroundings, with truncheons, grenades, and the lot, as young workers and students fought with the gendarmes, first outside the factory, then across cornfields. The strikebreaking operation failed, though a high price was paid to frustrate it. The troops mobilized for the operation were many. For days, within an area stretching well around Flins, no mercy was shown to the young, particularly if they resembled a cop's image of a student. On June 10 in neighboring Meulan a high-school student and Maoist militant, Gilles Tautin, was drowned during a manhunt in circumstances that have not yet been cleared up.

The government was already trying its luck in another provincial car factory. That same night, gendarmes and CRS attacked the Peugeot works at Sochaux. Students could not be blamed for the resistance there. The workers, thrown out of the factory, came back with bolts and anything else they could lay their hands on. The "forces of order" replied with bullets. Two workers were killed, and several were wounded. The government realized that its second venture was getting too dangerous and withdrew the troops. It was after this shooting that the CGT would not go beyond a symbolic token strike, thus proving that nothing would drive it off the electoral road. It was on the same Tuesday, June 12, that the UNEF staged its last street demonstration, which included a protest against the drowning near Flins and the killing of workers at Sochaux.

"Abortive" demonstration would be a more accurate description. The Gare de l'Est was surrounded by massive police forces to prevent the would-be demonstrators from reaching their meeting place. Thousands of them instinctively moved toward the Latin Quarter, but there, too, the police were numerous and ready for the fray. And so it was on the periphery that sporadic battles raged until the morning, as small groups of demonstrators, prevented from joining forces, fought the police with desperate fury. Paris was kept awake all night by concussion grenades, and the vestiges of the struggle were left there in the morning for the onlookers to see. The Gaullists, regaining control of the situation, wanted to make political capital out of the troubles. Gaullists and Communists alike were by now mainly concerned with the coming election.

During this first half of June inevitably there were open hostilities between the Communists, persuading their followers to resume work so as "to confirm and strengthen their victory" at the polls,[1] and the revolutionary students, loudly proclaiming that to abandon the strike for the election was both defeatism and treason. Pretenses were no longer being kept up by either side. On June 1, at the close of the march from Montparnasse to the

1. Were the Communists blind, or were they deceiving their readers on purpose? The question is not unfair since the editor of the paper making such optimistic forecasts, René Andrieu, claimed later that the Communist party had expected an electoral defeat. See his interview in *Le Nouvel Observateur,* September 1968.

Gare d'Austerlitz described at the opening of this book, the Communists were openly branded as strikebreakers. The students rejected the charge of anti-Communism. "True anti-Communism,"
retorted Alain Krivine, "is the work of those men at the head of
labor organizations who refuse to see that a socialist revolution is
possible." [2] The Communist papers were full of success stories and
descriptions of the joyful return to work. The workers, in fact,
were dragging their feet; this was made clear by the mounting
attacks against revolutionary elements in the same papers. Thus,
on June 6 in a box under the heading "Vigilance," *L'Humanité*
took to task "leftist groups . . . [that] intervene violently to oppose
the will of the workers to resume work." The comment was funny
in two ways. First, if "Communist" were substituted for "leftist,"
it could have been published in any Gaullist paper. Secondly, for
anyone even vaguely acquainted with the relative strength of the
CGT apparatus and that of the "grouplets," the image of the poor
cégétistes being bullied to strike by ultra-leftists was hilariously
hypocritical, a pure flight of fancy.

L'Humanité got even shriller during the Flins episode, because
there students played their part against the wishes of the CGT.
The paper's readers could hardly decide who was responsible for
the fighting, the police or the "militarily organized commandos"
led by Alain Geismar. For the orthodox Communist the answer
was simple: Both were guilty, because they were accomplices.
The police only "claimed" to have blocked the road. "In fact,
their activity fits into the plan of the government." After Cohn-
Bendit, it was now the turn of Alain Geismar to be branded as a
Gaullist agent. Once again, however, it was Georges Séguy who
went one better and, after de Gaulle's appearance on television
on June 6, put the blame squarely on the General: "But he did
not point out those really responsible for the troubles and provocations, whose activity, including their agitation against a return

2. A public meeting was held later that evening to found a *mouvement
révolutionnaire*. Strategic differences were one of the reasons why this
attempt never got very far.

to work, is covered by a strange complacency on the part of the authorities."

Séguy, the Communist leader of the CGT, did not hesitate to point with an accusing finger, and when within a week the government took the hint and on June 13 outlawed all revolutionary groups and arrested many militants, the Communists did not utter a word of protest. How could they, when they had aided and abetted?

If the second half of the month was mainly concerned with electioneering, the strike was dying only slowly. The Renault workers went back on June 17. Other big engineering firms followed suit. Many small factories in all branches of the industry went on resisting for a time. The return to work was neither "triumphant" nor too depressed. The strikers felt frustrated but not defeated. The only ones to feel humiliated were to be the radio and television people, who stayed out longest and lost. Theirs was a most unusual stoppage, for some thirteen thousand technicians, producers, and journalists struck not really to get more money, but because they could bear no longer to be an obedient tool, to put on ministerial speeches instead of pictures of Paris in revolt. In this industry, too, the unions exercised a restraining influence. An attempt was made for a while to run an objective radio news program that refused orders from above. It worked for a time, though not for very long, and the striking radio journalists finally had to get off the air. Their television colleagues, the stars of the profession, later joined the strike and disappeared from the small screen, leaving the government to put out the news with the help of scabs.

The radio and television strikers were popular. Their campaign was inventive, with slogans such as "The police on the screen means the police in your home." At the beginning of June they launched Operation Jericho. Each day different social groups—writers, scientists, students, and so on—circled silently around Broadcasting House to express their sympathy. On the seventh day . . . coachloads of policemen were there instead of trumpets.

It was the day after the last student demonstration; all meetings had been forbidden, and the organizers called the march off.

As June was drawing nearer to its end, the technicians gave up the strike. The radio journalists lasted a few days longer; those from television stuck it out until July 12. Mass firings were the government's reply to this struggle for independence. The journalists paid a heavy price. Yet their studied insistence on the non-political nature of their strike seemed strangely naïve under the circumstances. It was more serious to attack walls with trumpets than to expect triumphant Gaullism to abandon its favorite weapon of propaganda.

All month the regime gradually recovered and regained lost ground. On June 14 the police took over the Odéon, on June 16 the Sorbonne, on June 27 the School of Fine Arts, where students and artists working collectively under popular control and responding to the demand of the moment had revived an art form, the political poster. It was the seizure of the Sorbonne, its manner and preparation, that showed that things were coming back to normal.

Give a dog a bad name, and then hang him. It was preferable to discredit the students before kicking them out, and this is where the episode of the *katangais* fitted in nicely. They were neither black nor foreign. Among the outcasts finding shelter at the Sorbonne was a group headed by Jacky, who claimed to have served in Katanga, hence the nickname of the gang. They had helped the students to fight with the police and keep order inside the university. Then they began to act as if they were the masters of at least part of the place. There were stories of beatings and of drugs. The problem was real. But there was a surprisingly coordinated look to the press campaign that revealed it to the world.

Revolution, orgies, mercenaries—what splendid copy. Many foreign journalists lapped it up. Their French colleagues, who should have known better and guessed the object of the operation, did the same. In fact the students kicked out the *katangais* themselves and started washing and cleaning the Sorbonne. This did not prevent the police from walking in, first alleging that they had a reason, then dropping even this pretext. The last students and professors were ejected after offering only passive resistance. Outside a crowd gathered and was dispersed with the usual mixture of truncheon and grenades. That Sunday night the Latin Quarter once again looked like occupied territory. But this time it was an end, not a beginning. The government would not tolerate any "Red bases" or summer universities that included workers. As to the bourgeois press, having been shaken for a moment in May, it was also again running true to form. It could not raise a protest; it had spent its passion in Katanga.

We have almost forgotten the election, so unreal it seemed in this climate and so certain its result. The electoral campaign opened officially on June 10, though General de Gaulle had inaugurated it four days earlier with a long appearance on television, one of those studied "improvisations" with a stooge providing the cues. The General had recovered his poise and set the tone of the campaign. He did it by describing a painting that shows a crowd being led to hell by demons and brandishing its fists against a solitary angel. A friend of the General, he told us, had imagined a happy ending, with the crowd stopping on the edge of the abyss, leaving the demons and running toward the angel. "Totalitarian communism" represented the demons in this allegory, and there was no need to spell out the name of the solitary angel. It was not all so corny. Indeed, the General showed that he had understood better than many of his lieutenants how deeply French society had been shaken and that once power was regained, Manicheism would not be enough. It would have to be replaced or completed by the magic formula of participation.[3]

Meanwhile, the main job was to win the election. The masterminding of the campaign was left to Georges Pompidou at the head of a reshuffled Cabinet; ministers too obviously connected with the crisis—those responsible for the interior, education, social affairs, information—were cast aside. The Prime Minister

3. The students wittily conjugated its capitalist meaning: I participate, you participate, he participates, we participate . . . they profit.

duly did what was needed to reclaim the extreme right. While the revolutionary groups were being banned, room was made available in jail by the release of General Salan, Colonel Argoud, and other champions of French Algeria and military subversion. Georges Bidault returning to Paris without any trouble opened the exiles' trek back.

This was not sufficient to mobilize fully the huge party that General de Gaulle himself had allegedly described as the "party of funk." After such a strike and such a crisis, to frighten the middle classes out of their wits was not too difficult a task. Instead of talking about their own record, the Gaullists brandished the flags, red and black, and showed behind them the barricades with burning cars, the anarchy, and at the back of it all the totalitarian menace of a Communist dictatorship. Later, in private, they were quite willing to admit that their electoral version of the events bore little relation to reality. What did you expect us to do? To wage the election campaign against the "grouplets"? The Communist party was a sitting duck. Fiction sometimes sounds more real than fact.

And yet fear alone would not have been enough. A regime usually does not rest just on a truncheon. Only in major crises, as in May, does it reveal its true foundations. In normal times a system cannot function without an inner coherence, a set of values, at least an appearance of logic, rationality, and purpose. The Gaullist system was clearly not very well integrated, since it could explode in such a fashion. Its spokesmen were now busy putting the pieces together. In their difficult job they were helped tremendously by the nothingness of the other side. The Gaullist system, however bad or disliked, had the merit of existing. There seemed to be no alternative on the electoral horizon. Fear was reinforced by the fear of the void.

This time the emptiness of the left could not be concealed by a makeshift electoral platform between the Communist party and the FGDS. Experts wondered why the left was so visibly out of step, why the Communists had refused to let the united left have a single candidate in each constituency, why the FGDS was glancing anxiously to all sides, why Michel Rocard of the PSU had stated openly on television that "the Communist party . . . has deliberately chosen to contribute to the survival of the Gaullist regime." The surprise of the experts was surprising. If the left had an alternative, a purpose, a strategy, it would have been in power by then. Fortune, claimed the Romans, favors the bold. History has no obligation to provide electoral compensation for those who fail to seize their chance in the field.

The Communists made frantic efforts to reassure, to appear champions of stability and paragons of patriotism. They drowned the "Internationale" in the "Marseillaise" and wrapped up the red flag in the national tricolor.[4] So strangely attired, Waldeck Rochet, the secretary-general, recited in his slow Burgundian accent that his party was "the party of order." The words that recurred in his speeches were discipline, calm, responsibility. All to no avail. The Communists splashed their posters with the information that they had been the first of all to condemn revolutionary "adventures" and all the disorders—but in vain. For whatever their part in the conduct of the general strike, they could not obliterate it. Above all, they were paying a price for their origin, their reputation, their power, a penalty for what they might have been. It was the farce of the sheep in wolf's clothing.

It was not even a successful farce. For those who opted for bourgeois order the Gaullists with a truncheon remained a safer bet. Many sympathizers, on the other hand, must have stayed at home, disgusted by such unprincipled antics. Thus the Communist party lost both ways. Its partners fared no better. The efforts of the FGDS to appear as the potential leader of the left now looked ridiculous. It was too obviously inconsistent and undecided. As to the PSU, its roots in the nation were too thin and too recent for rapid electoral growth. Besides, many people who might have backed it were either too young to vote or politically in favor of boycotting the election.

4. ". . . the Paris proletariat sought to secure the advancement of its own interests *side by side* with the interests of the bourgeoisie, instead of enforcing them as the revolutionary interests of society itself, and it let the *red* flag be lowered to the *tricolor*." Marx, *Class Struggles in France*.

Altogether, considering its disarray, the setback suffered by the left at the polls on June 23 was not sensational. Compared with the previous election, held in March 1967, the Communist share of the vote dropped from 22.5 per cent to just over 20 per cent; that of the FGDS from nearly 19 to 16.5 per cent; while the PSU, despite a higher number of candidates, did not quite double its share, from just over 2 to nearly 4 per cent. This would have meant roughly a 3 per cent swing away from the left, but the Gaullists, squeezing the center, gained more. They reached 43.6 per cent of the vote on their own, and close to 48 per cent together with those followers of Giscard d'Estaing, who did not have the official Gaullist label.[5]

Under the present French electoral law there are two ballots for deputies. On the first, when there are many candidates and an absolute majority is required, the voter is supposed to *choose*. In the second, when only two or three candidates remain in most constituencies and a simple majority is enough, the voter is supposed to *eliminate* the man he does not want. The second round can thus weaken or reinforce the trend of the first. On this occasion, it was bound to strengthen it.

A year previously, the popular-front alliances—that is, agreements between left-wing parties to keep only the best-placed candidate in the field in each constituency—were on the whole endorsed by the electorate. This time the wastage was greater. Many socialists and Radicals chose not to vote for the Communist, while even the Communist electorate did not show its traditional discipline. In addition, the voters of the center altered their pattern. In 1967 a fair proportion of such floaters had abstained or even voted for the left rather than back the Gaullist candidate. This time, they were frightened, and so they rallied massively to the Gaullist camp. The combination of such shifts and of the electoral law helped to turn a victory in votes into a triumph in terms of

5. In absolute figures the Communist party dropped from 5 to 4.4 million votes; the FGDS from 4.2 to 3.7 million. The PSU got 874,000 votes compared with 378,000. The Gaullists with the official label climbed from 8.4 to 9.7 million.

seats. With 294 deputies in an assembly of 485 members, the orthodox Gaullists had a comfortable majority on their own.

As one left the ministry where the results were being announced and where Gaullists were toasting their victory in champagne, several cars passed, hooting *ti-ti-ti-ta-ta*, the signal for French Algeria with which the followers of General de Gaulle had already triumphed ten years earlier. On this Sunday night of June 30, 1968, all Paris seemed to resound with the words of Rimbaud:

> *Société, tout est rétabli; les orgies*
> *Pleurent leur ancien râle aux anciens lupanars,*
> *Et les gas en délire, aux murailles rougies,*
> *Flambent sinistrement vers les azurs blafards. . . .*

It was but the mood of the moment: so superficially true, so fundamentally wrong.

A full stop can be put here even if the climax of the story was reached much earlier and its sequel is still to come. At this point the reader should be able to make up his own mind about what was or was not possible and about the very nature of this strange upheaval. Although masses of books have been written on the subject and all sorts of theories elaborated, it might nevertheless help a little to dispose of the more absurd explanations and to put in perspective one controversy that became counterproductive. The explanations that can be simply dismissed are all those that tend to reduce the whole complex phenomenon to a conspiracy, whether domestic or foreign. This is not to deny the interdependence of world events. It is to deny that history is purely the handiwork of 007 or 008.

A conspiratorial mind will reduce anything to a plot. Even so, it requires a great deal of fancy to imagine that Mao Tse-tung precipitated the Paris riots in order to block the peace talks on

---

* Society, all is restored: orgies, brawls;
   Screams, groans choke the lupanars once more,
   And maddened gaslight on blood-stained walls
   Lights the blue dark with a sinister glare. . . .

Vietnam, or that the CIA did it to bring General de Gaulle down a peg. There remains the Cuban alternative, which assumes that such a little island has not enough on its hands already with Latin America and that it mass-produces guerrilla fighters for the whole of Europe; it also assumes that the French crisis was the work of guerrillas. All such nonsense, emanating from some Gaullist quarters, is not simply the product of conspiratorial minds. It is a useful substitute for an analysis of the roots of the crisis. Since everything was for the best . . . only a wicked plot could have shaken the Gaullist paradise.

Even more ridiculous is the early Communist suggestion that the French government did it on its own. The editor of *L'Humanité*, in a book [6] published quickly in order to give the Communist version of the events, devotes the bulk of a chapter to an extract from the memoirs of a former chief of security police, according to which in 1827 barricades were erected in Paris, people were killed, and the whole thing was an electoral plot perpetrated by the police. This passage was not included to state the obvious, namely that if the police were doing their work, there were undoubtedly many informers and not a few provocateurs in the crowds of the Latin Quarter. But it fills almost the entire chapter on the night of the barricades and more than hints that this, too, was the work of the police. Presumably, to precipitate the largest mass demonstration and the biggest general strike so as to annoy the CGT.[7]

If the method is contemptible, the suggestion is plain stupid. Admittedly, the proletariat does not have the unenviable privilege of occasionally acting as if it were unaware of its class interests, nor does the party claiming to be its guide have the exclusive

6. René Andrieu, *Les Communistes et la Révolution* (Paris, Julliard, 1968).

7. Since our learned Communist historian is so interested in *agents provocateurs,* he certainly knows the story of Roman Malinowski, member of the then tiny Central Committee and head of the Bolshevik faction in the Duma (parliament), who was a paid agent of the Okhrana, the czarist police. What epithets would he use, and rightly so, about a writer who would pick on this as a basis for insinuating generalizations about the nature of the Bolshevik movement?

right to blunder. The bourgeoisie, too, is often shortsighted. Indeed, the main function of its state is to defend such long-term interests. Naturally, anybody can make serious mistakes. It is, nevertheless, silly to suspect your opponent of sheer idiocy. What could Gaullism gain from the crisis? A bigger parliamentary majority? In a country where no general election was scheduled for another four years and where, in any case, Parliament matters but little, was it worthwhile paying such a price for such a miserable reward? And what a price. . . .

By price is not meant here simply the rise in the wage bill or the loss of some five billion dollars worth of gold and dollar reserves. The flight of capital was an aftereffect, the combined consequence of temporarily reduced profit margins and of fear about the future. The biggest price was what the crisis revealed. Everybody was able to observe the unsuspected fragility of the state and draw from it his own conclusions. The ruling classes emerged from the ordeal shaken, not knowing how best to recover their position and confidence. The industrial workers were bewildered, too, but for the opposite reason. They were stunned by the rediscovery of their strength—and they still are. Not only students, but thousands of technicians, scientists, teachers, remain tempted by what might have been. The elaborate electoral calculations worked out before the crisis no longer have much significance. Society, contrary to Rimbaud's lines, has not been re-established.

This should not be taken to mean that France has undergone a revolution. Those who saw none, not even on the horizon, can put up a very strong case. There was nobody in May with a strategy capable of uniting the various forces in the movement and of leading them toward a successful conclusion. It can even be argued that for years no serious preparatory work had been carried out that would have allowed the workers at least to grope toward a strategy. That is why in the middle of this story they appeared at a loss: They wanted the moon and were told to count their pennies.

The whole controversy over a revolutionary situation is a quarrel over words. It all depends whether you mean by it that all the favorable elements—the pent-up forces, a movement to guide them, a staggering opponent; in short, almost certainty of success —that all such factors are combined, or simply that the situation itself is explosive enough so that it could be harnessed for revolutionary purposes. One can leave such worries to experts in semantics, and conclude by paraphrasing Trotsky: In May the piston may have been missing in France, but there was a surprising amount of steam. This unexpected volume of revolutionary steam suggests that Europe has re-entered the age of conflict and possibly the era of revolution. We shall try to elaborate this point in the last part of the book. But before dealing with its significance for the world at large, we must still look more closely at the contents of this revolutionary steam.

PART FOUR
The Fallout

"IT LOOKS DIFFERENT FROM LYON," *a colleague, sent to the provinces to report on the last stages of France's general strike, cabled triumphantly. And it certainly looked more routine, more dreary, less dramatic from any other part of French territory than from the vantage point in the capital, where the whole scene could be surveyed. It is a feature of a general strike that the addition of seemingly ordinary stoppages creates an extraordinary situation. By keeping the eyes fixed on an isolated instance, one ran the risk of repeating the experience of Fabritius in Stendhal's* Charterhouse—*he just missed the Battle of Waterloo.*

A bird's-eye view is preferable to myopic concentration on one spot. It is not sufficient on its own. A wood is also made of trees. Once the broad picture is drawn, the canvas can be usefully completed by paying greater attention to some selected aspects. In this part of the book, it is proposed to tackle some issues raised by the May crisis that have a bearing on the future and a significance extending beyond French or even European frontiers.

THE PEASANT'S TITLE TO PROPERTY *is the talisman by which capital held him hitherto under its spell, the pretext under which it set him against the industrial proletariat.*
—KARL MARX, *Class Struggles in France*

No Peasants on Their Backs

It did look different seen from Paris. It will always appear more dramatic in the capital; as long as there is a centralized state, it is in the capital that the struggle for power must culminate. True, this time once again Paris was undoubtedly more radical than most of the country. Yet it would be wrong on this occasion to speak of Red Paris and the white—or true blue—provinces. The contrast was not so striking. In its first, student, phase the crisis was essentially Parisian. The dramatic clash began in the capital,

223

where more than a quarter of French students are concentrated.
But their uprising was not isolated. It set alight most universities
throughout France. The second phase, namely the general strike,
actually originated in the west of the country and reached the
Red belt of Paris by way of northwestern France.

In this second stage Paris was still the focus of the political
struggle, though the intensity of the conflict varied from region
to region, depending on the background, the temper of the workers, the control exercised by the unions. There was more effervescence in university towns, where revolutionary students could
exercise an influence on the course of events, but on the industrial
front, where it really mattered, the strikes were toughest in those
factories in which militant groups managed to force the hand of
the cautious union establishment.

Geographically two broad regions lagged behind the rest of
France. As might be expected, one was the east, orderly, reli-
gious, traditionally conservative, and solidly Gaullist. The unexpected laggard was the south, leftish in its reputation and, until
then, quite resistant to Gaullist infiltration. But on second thought,
it is not so surprising that the May Movement did not carry along
with it the areas of old-fashioned rural radicalism. The south of
France is still largely rural, and the May upheaval was essentially an urban phenomenon. Only once, on May 24, did the
farmers demonstrate at the same time as the workers and students, though even then their official spokesmen took pains to
emphasize that this was pure coincidence, that the farmers were
minding their own business and were not adding their support to
the struggle against the regime. Only in Nantes on that occasion
did the farmers driving to town on their tractors look like potential allies in a revolutionary battle. The menace of a second front
in the countryside was not a serious threat for the government,
at least not in May 1968.

We saw earlier some of the reasons why the farmers did not
get involved and some of the policies that had enabled the government to neutralize the countryside. But we also saw that the
framework within which the regime could develop such policies

was cracking, and mentioned the Mansholt Report as a warning of the framework's impending collapse. How the recommendations in this explosive report will be applied depends on all sorts of political unknowns, yet whatever the decisions, the Mansholt diagnosis itself foreshadows a new phase in the transformation of agriculture within the Common Market. The reduction of employment in farming is expected to proceed at a faster pace. What is more important, to modernize European farming it will no longer be sufficient to supply more equipment and fertilizers. It will now be necessary to amalgamate the small farms into much larger units. This inevitable concentration may well revive social conflicts in the countryside.

According to the Brussels experts, the number of people working on the land in the European Economic Community is expected to decrease from about ten million in 1970 to around five million in 1980. The reduction should particularly affect the big three of the EEC, where the bulk of the peasant population is still concentrated; that is, in descending order, Italy, France, and Germany.[1] The drop should be the result a combination of two trends. While marginal farmers will go on being squeezed out and forced to seek alternative employment, roughly as many elderly people are expected to leave the land. Figures of declining employment in agriculture usually conceal one important feature, namely that farming has to a large extent become the occupation of the aged, who hang on at the subsistence level, awaiting an old-age pension or supplementing it. More than half the farms within the EEC are run by men who are over fifty-seven years old. The Mansholt Report suggests various pension schemes that could help them to retire and induce them to do so.

The overhaul of the existing farm policy of the EEC is dictated by financial considerations. On an average, the six countries spend nearly five per cent of their budgets on agriculture, and as things stand, the prospect is of even higher subsidies solving no

1. The share of agriculture in total civilian employment was in 1968 still over 22 per cent in Italy; 15 per cent in France; and just over 10 per cent in Germany.

problems. The situation has become urgent because of the milk glut, the surplus of butter outstripping the stockpiling capacities of the EEC.[2] The Mansholt remedy is to spend slightly more now in order to reduce expenditures in the 1980s, and to spend the money differently, investing it mainly in structural changes. Up to now a great deal of money has been used to step up output by intensifying production within existing units. Since the farms were on the whole very small, both men and equipment now tend to be underemployed. To cut the losses, adapt production to the pulls of the market, and bring farm incomes into line with their counterparts in industry and trade (whatever such vague "parity" may mean), the Mansholt Report recommends a drastic redistribution of land. Should its recommendations be followed, the landscape of Europe's continental countryside will be entirely reshaped, the millions of small farms being replaced by incomparably larger "production units."

Such units are to be specialized, and their size should vary accordingly. The report specifies an optimum range for all specialties. Thus, if a farm is to specialize in meat, it should have between 150 and 200 bulls or between 450 and 600 pigs; for poultry and eggs, the recommended figure is 10,000 hens; for milk the target is 40 to 60 dairy cows; and for crops, between 80 and 120 hectares (roughly 200 to 300 acres). To reduce risks, several production units can be regrouped into a "modern agricultural enterprise." In any case, it is proposed to limit financial aid by 1975 to units with a development plan showing that they are aiming at the prescribed target.

How big the gap is between the economic optimum calculated by the experts and the present level of Common Market agriculture can be illustrated by one set of figures. Two thirds of the farms within the EEC still have fewer than 10 hectares (about 25 acres) of land and fewer than five cows. To move within a few years from small- to large-scale farming implies a massive redistribution of land, which in turn contains the seeds of social upheaval.

2. Which does not prevent butter from being a luxury in Europe.

Take France, for instance, and its postwar changes in the countryside. The tiny dispersed plots, which are the result of France's inheritance laws,[3] have to some extent been consolidated. Some small farms have vanished, some big ones have grown bigger, and some estates have acquired additional land. But there were legal restrictions on these transfers, and changes in property relations did not keep pace with the growth of output. The best proof is that the number of farm laborers has declined even faster than total agricultural employment. While old men stayed on the land, the younger ones, whether family help or hired laborers, were driven to try their luck elsewhere. The tractor provided a partial substitute for farm labor.

As if all of this were not enough, what is in store is politically much more explosive. The old boundaries must now give way. Even in France, which has more arable land than its neighbors, only five per cent of the farms own more than 50 hectares (about 125 acres), though admittedly they account for a quarter of the total output. The reform could thus be simply designed to strengthen the large estates and consolidate the well-to-do farmers. On the other hand, it could have a different effect.

The issue is not an abstract one. The amount of money involved is huge, and the redistribution contemplated is on a massive scale. If the scheme were to be carried out, something like 50 to 60 million acres of land would change hands within a few years. Will tremendous public funds be used to subsidize big landowners and to create a new class of super-*kulaks,* or will the land made available in this way help to lay the foundations of co-operative farming? The Mansholt Report skates around the issue, insisting only on the fact that farmers must have freedom of choice, that they will not be compelled either to leave the land or to join production units. It does not commit itself as to the social context in which this "freedom" will be exercised. From the English enclosure movement of the sixteenth century up to

3. The Napoleonic Code of 1804 abolished the law of primogeniture and led to the division of the succession between all children, hence the splitting of plots.

our day the towns have been filled by peasants uprooted in the name of freedom.

In west European farming concentration is inevitable, and it offers a revolutionary movement new scope for propaganda and action. It gives it a chance to revive class struggle and consciousness in the countryside. The notion of the poor or middle-level peasant is relative. It must now be adapted to entirely new standards. A hundred hectares (about 250 acres) of arable land could soon be the norm for crop growers. Production units of that size can be part of much larger estates, and there is no guarantee that by 1980 the targets set by the Brussels experts will not have been rendered obsolete by further technical progress. If things were left to themselves, in such a context only the top fifteen per cent of the farms within the Common Market—those of more than 50 acres—would have a serious chance of survival. For the rest, and particularly for the two thirds of the farms that have fewer than 25 acres of arable land, the only chance for some of them, at least, to stay on the land would lie in a deliberate policy, in the determination of a government to use the land released through public subsidies for setting up producer co-operatives for poor farmers. A socialist regime could even exploit such a situation to drive home to the peasant Marx's lesson that "the title to property is the talisman by which capital held him hitherto under its spell."

To assure the small farmer that he can cling to his plot and get a decent living thanks to a generous policy of price maintenance, as the French Communist party has done up to now, is a blind-alley policy. It would be both more honest and more rewarding to admit the need for a radical transformation and to put the accent squarely on the nature of the reform, to ask who will carry it through and in whose interests. Some of the objectives set in the Mansholt Report are perfectly laudable, at least on paper. To bridge the gap between town and country has been an old socialist dream. To insure for people staying on the land regular hours of work, including a weekend's rest, to provide them with social and cultural amenities—there is nothing wrong with that.

Equally praiseworthy is the idea that care should be taken of those who are obliged to leave the land, the old being given a decent pension and the young sufficient training to acquire skills for alternative employment. The snags lie not with the promise, but with those chosen to fulfill it.

Is a bourgeois government likely to forget its motto—that the rich should "enrich themselves"—and lay the foundations of co-operative farming, which could serve as a base for socialist agriculture? Relying traditionally on "freedom of movement" to get cheap labor from the countryside, can a capitalist regime be expected to mend its ways, to supply migrants with sufficiently broad general skills, to increase their bargaining power, doing incidentally for the children of peasants what it has not done for the sons of the workers? The damaging criticism can be carried further, into the field of distribution, which weighs so heavily on the little farmer that it is slowly strangling him, whatever his rise in productivity. Will a capitalist government attack the big middleman, hit the powerful commercial interests, and help the co-operatives to seek new social channels of distribution? In demanding answers to these questions, the revolutionary movement can find new allies in the countryside, because most of the peasants are destined to be the victims of the land reform if it is carried out by the present rulers.

West European governments are frightened by the prospect of higher social tensions in the countryside. This is why they have handled the Mansholt Report as if it were political dynamite. They can delay decisions, blunt the edges of the plan. They cannot ignore much longer the issues it raises. The problem is not the invention of a mad Dutchman. It is the logical consequence of economic change. The EEC cannot afford to dispense with the advantages of large-scale production in farming and stay in competitive business. Sooner rather than later, it will have to move to a new phase in the modernization of its agriculture, a more explosive stage, involving the amalgamation of farms and the redistribution of land. Provided the revolutionaries do their job in the countryside, the French regime, to take an example, will no longer be sure that next time too everything will be quiet on the rural front.

All the genuine revolutions of this century—from Russia to China, from Vietnam to Cuba—achieved victory with the support of land-hungry peasants. Once the revolutions had triumphed, this mass support proved a mixed blessing. They all had to start building socialism in primitive surroundings, burdened by a host of peasant farmers. No west European revolution can rely on comparable backing, for the simple reason that farming accounts for a much smaller, and a fast declining, proportion of the total employed population. The support need not be nil, as it was in France during the May crisis. It cannot be so massive as it was for its predecessors. For the same reason, however, a successful revolution in an advanced country would be in a much more comfortable position once victory had been achieved.

Lenin warned his comrades not to expect a rapid transition to socialism. It would be a slow process, he argued, not only in Russia, but even in the advanced countries of western Europe, because after seizing power the revolutionaries would still have to bear the dead weight of the peasantry. Britain, with relatively few small farmers, was in his view the exception, though a qualified one, since it had a great number of small property owners outside the countryside. At the time when Lenin was thus singling out British agriculture, it still accounted for about twelve per cent of the country's labor force. Such will soon be the average for the whole of the Common Market. By 1980 even Italy should be approaching a similar proportion, while the average for the EEC, at about six per cent, should then be close to the present American pattern.

Continental Europe is on the eve of a possibly dramatic change in property relations in the countryside. The rulers will do everything in their power to slow down the process and soften its political effects. How explosive the situation gets will depend on their moves, but also on the action of their opponents. The second round in France may see tractors rolling into town, and not only in Nantes. And should revolution triumph throughout western Europe, the winners for the first time this century would not have to drag millions of reluctant *muzhiks* on the road toward socialism. What looked like a major liability in May can still be turned into an asset and finally prove a blessing in disguise.

TWO POWERS *cannot exist in a state. . . . The dual power expresses but a transitional stage in the development of a revolution.*
—V. I. LENIN, *The Tasks of the Proletariat in Our Revolution*

Anarchy and Dual Power

"Anarchy" is one of the most fashionable words of our time. It was flogged in France during the May crisis, though clearly not to death, since it lives on in every newspaper and flourishes in conservative conversation. This abuse of the word should not be confused with any renewed interest in the doctrine of anarchism, in the controversies between Marx and Bakunin, between socialists and anarchists, over the way to get rid of the state. The Leviathan is stronger than ever, the problem of its "withering away" is still very much with us and will emerge later in the story. But the censorious defenders of the established order are not concerned with such theoretical issues. "Anarchy" is for them a synonym for "disorder" and is used with its traditional companions—"nihilism," "mob," "social envy"—as a verbal first line of defense against the challenge to authority. Its current fashion is an obvious symptom. Those in power do feel challenged.

No wonder that the French government in May vociferously proclaimed the threat of anarchy to conceal its impotence and rally support. The red flag looking innocuously pink in official Communist hands, the black flag of anarchy came in handy to revive the ancestral fears of the middle classes. The Gaullists, however, were not the only ones to raise the alarm. The Communists tried to outbid them as the chief enemies of anarchy and the staunch upholders of order. In their zeal they even forgot which order they were defending. They also forgot the elementary lessons of revolutionary theory and bolshevik practice.

Anarchy, according to *The Oxford English Dictionary,* is "Absence of government; a state of lawlessness due to the absence or inefficiency of the supreme power." A revolutionary looking at a political strike draws a similar conclusion from a different angle. "The power of the strike lies in the disorganizing of the power of the government. The greater the 'anarchy' created by a strike, the nearer its victory." These are the words of an expert, the conclusion drawn by Trotsky from the experience of the abortive Revolution of 1905. However brilliant Trotsky's record was in the two Soviet revolutions, orthodox Communists are not yet ready to accept him as an authority. But they cannot reject Lenin, from whom the lines quoted at the opening of this chapter are taken. Between February and October 1917 the dual power uneasily shared by the provisional government and the executive committee of the (Petrograd) Soviet was not for Lenin a subject of abstract speculation. He both studied and tried to influence the shifting balance between the two as well as changes in their respective power base, so as to carry the revolution to a successful conclusion.

Lenin's lesson, namely that two sovereign powers cannot co-exist forever in a state, is self-evident. But this more or less transient period of dual power is probably an inevitable stage of any real revolution. A *putsch*, a palace revolt, can be carried out overnight by plotters and paratroopers. A revolution, involving broad masses of people, requires time for mobilization, for getting millions ready for the final assault. Parallel power must first be built and then strengthened. Dual power is an advanced stage, when revolutionary and counter-revolutionary forces wrestle for supremacy. It may be ventured that the outcome, its manner, its more or less violent nature, depend to a large extent on the preceding buildup.

If dual power cannot last forever, a vacuum is bound to be even more ephemeral, and in France the May crisis seldom went beyond the stage of a void. When the government was not in a position to enforce its decisions, when power was slipping from the hands of the ruling class, the other side was partly unable, and largely unwilling, to take it over. For the rulers, disobedience to their laws is lawlessness. This should not be confused with disorder. Indeed, if parallel power were to fill the vacancy, there would be less risk of disorder. There could be no disorder at all, and it would still be anarchy from an official viewpoint. Anarchy, with its double meaning, was thus a useful cover. The Gaullists entertained the confusion for obvious reasons. The Communists played the same game in order to camouflage their categorical refusal to transgress the bounds of bourgeois legality, of Gaullist law and order.

A situation is sometimes stronger than the wishes of the protagonists, and there were moments when legality cracked under pressure. Thus, when the unions launched their one-day national strike on May 13, they did not bother about the five-day notice legally required of the public sector. The duly enacted deterrent failed to deter and remained a law simply on paper. For a time the Sorbonne, the Odéon, most university buildings, had ceased to be under Gaullist jurisdiction. The Latin Quarter for a spell was out of bounds for the police. The general strike, with its paralyzing effects, occasionally prompted an inevitable transfer of power. The unions, and not the official authorities, determined to whom electricity would be supplied. It was also their decision that banks should open to pay the strikers. When in Nantes the delegates of strikers acted as price inspectors in the market, when there or near Le Mans they imposed a graduated toll tax rising with the horsepower of the car, they were taking over prerogatives legally reserved for the state and its representatives. Yet these were sporadic cases of a transfer of authority, improvised on the spur of the moment. They were not part of a coherent, nationwide effort to open the way for parallel power. On the contrary, they had to be done in the teeth of conscious Communist opposition to any such excursions onto a potentially revolutionary road.

The general strike itself was in a sense a challenge to established law and order. Two basic principles are safeguarded in all our western constitutions, written or unwritten. One is the principle of private property, including ownership of the means of production. The second is the principle of freedom, particularly the freedom of people to sell their labor and of the employers to hire it. In the more democratic versions, these basic principles are tempered by the right of organized labor to strike. There is no real contradiction. The right may interfere with the principles, but it is assumed that it will do so only locally and temporarily. It is viewed as no more than a bargaining weapon. Should it be used to challenge the system, to paralyze the country, to threaten its institutions, there are plenty of weapons in all constitutional arsenals, ranging from emergency regulations to martial law. When this point is reached, however, the outcome no longer depends on constitutional niceties. It depends on the balance of power in class struggle. And this point is reached very, very seldom.

An unlimited general strike, with the occupation of factories by the workers, can easily be turned into this rare conjunction. Not only does it prevent the exercise of what the Gaullist demonstrators called "freedom of work," the employer's freedom to hire and fire. It also casts a shadow over property itself. Will the workers occupying a factory turn it back to its "rightful" owners and agree that things should go back to "normal"? Threatening, as it does, the two sacrosanct pillars of the capitalist system, the unlimited general strike is by its nature political. The Communists found it very difficult to pretend otherwise.

In 1968, as in 1936, the striking workers kept the equipment in the factories spick and span. Modern workers are no Luddites. *L'Humanité* waxed lyrical over the care with which they were polishing "their" tools. All the ambiguity of the Communist attitude is contained in this possessive pronoun. In order to have collective control over the factory and their environment, the workers would have had to carry out a successful revolution, and as the precedents show, even this would not have been the end of the struggle. And the "tools" have become such a complex matter. A medieval craftsman knew what "his" tool was. The workman in the early, manufacturing, stage of the industrial revolution still had a notion of his skill, though he was losing the meaning of his part in the process of production. In our age of computers and automation, the workman, and not only the workman, is completely at a loss, overwhelmed by the complexity of the process in which he is involved. The machines seem to be alive and he a hopeless appendix. And yet the workers, collectively, also know that the whole complex machinery cannot function without them. They never know it better than during a general strike.

When everything is at a standstill, when the machines are strangely idle, the masters gone, the chain of command temporarily broken, and the barrack-room discipline lifted, the factory is a perfect place in which to tackle this complex issue, starting from the practical end. The workers can begin by discussing their own management, the extent to which, say, job evaluation corresponds to technical needs or to the requirements of hierarchical discipline. Should accounting books be available, they are a great help in a factory teach-in of this kind. But gradually the workers have to extend beyond their factory gates in order to understand their own feeling of divorce from the product of their labor, the deeper reasons for their alienation. By now it requires quite an effort to perceive that the productive environment in which we live and work is not just dictated by technological progress, that it is historically determined, a manmade system for the exploitation of man by man. Factories during a general strike could be most useful schools of socialism. Great pains were taken in May to see that in most cases the education should not go much beyond picketing.

In most cases, though not in all. Take the example of the Vitry branch of Rhône-Poulenc, the big chemical and artificial textile trust.[1] The Vitry factory supplies essentially chemical raw materials and has, therefore, a high proportion of researchers. Out of a total staff of around 3,600, the workers account for only half, and the technicians for some 1,000 men. The rest is divided between overseers and various executive grades. Until the May strike it was a quiet place, with little political activity and a very small union membership (thirteen per cent of the labor force, taking all unions into account). The CGT, the least weak of the unions, thought it was safe in such a factory to mobilize the men. It was agreed to set up basic committees regrouping all the strikers in each of the thirty-nine factory buildings. Each committee elected four delegates. Half of them at a time sat on the strike committee, acting as a link in permanent and open session. As a precaution the CGT managed to put on top of this structure an executive committee exclusively made up of trade-union delegates and designed to negotiate with the management. What the CGT did not bargain for was the extent of the active participation in the strike. More than half the staff took part in the occupation and, therefore, in the work of the committees. For a couple of weeks the executive committee was bound to endorse the decisions of the strike committee.

The inspirers of this movement from below do not attempt to hide its weaknesses. Its main strength, and surprise, was the deep involvement of the rank and file. It proved that when matters con-

1. See *Cahiers de Mai*, No. 2, July 1968.

cerning them are not decided by distant proxy, the allegedly apathetic workers take a keen interest in their own affairs. Against this strength must be set the drawbacks. The division into committees along factory buildings maintained artificial separations and did not help to bring workers and technicians together. It also strengthened the tendency to concentrate on narrow, corporate subjects. Only a very active minority was ready to look beyond their factory. And yet, despite this apparent isolationism, the mood was inspired by the outside world. The enthusiasm of May was dampened in June. The turning point, significantly, was not General de Gaulle's speech on May 30. It was the following Pentecost weekend, with its exodus to the country and its rumors of a return to work. The morale went down as the prospect of real change disappeared over the electoral horizon. Nevertheless, the CGT, which tried to end the strike there and then for electoral reasons, had to wait till June 13 before it was able to break the resistance briefly born of hope.

Although not the rule, the relatively active strikes, like the one at Vitry, were not an exception either. The history of the general strike is still to be written. Detailed reports and analyses are still scanty and dispersed.[2] Nonetheless, it is quite easy to quote a score of examples of strikes run by basic committees or by general assemblies meeting every day. There were such strikes in the chemical industry, and also in the electronics industry, particularly in the many factories belonging to the two (now amalgamated) big firms in the sector, Thomson-Huston and the CSF (Compagnie Sans Fil). There were active strikes in offices as well as in factories. At the Ministry of Equipment and Housing, for instance, in addition to daily assemblies there were also commissions discussing such subjects as civil-service reform. Several institutes of economic research tried to combine their own meetings

2. Plenty of books have been published on the student and political sides of the May crisis but very few about the strike itself. This is why reports by participants published in *Cahiers de Mai* are so valuable. One should mention the books describing the strikes at Flins and Cléon published in the series *Cahiers Libres* (Paris, François Maspero, 1968).

with a more general gathering of workers in the social sciences. Many of the laboratories of the National Scientific Research Center elected their own management committees, while at the headquarters a central action committee tried to spur the originally reluctant unions into bolder moves.[3] And one could go on quoting examples.

How to change society? How to run our own affairs? These were the twin themes of May, with a natural emphasis on the second. In the strike-bound nation it was more a case of theory than of immediate practice. At very few factories was production actually restarted by the strikers. The only known example of this at a relatively big firm was at the CSF plant at Brest, which produced some walkie-talkies during the strike. This, as we saw earlier, did not prevent *autogestion* and *cogestion,* self-management and a share in the management, from being at the heart of debates as passionate as they were confused. And the confusion was all the greater, since the debates were part of the crisis and their conclusions were bound to be greatly affected by its outcome. The theoretical schemes would have to be applied in a real world, a world that would be different according to which side won.

Once the crisis was over and production restarted, the difficulties connected with securing a share in the management were rapidly discovered. One illustration should be enough. In an electronics plant in the Paris region, the strikers returning to work were determined to show the bosses that things would no longer be the same. They had set up basic committees and were determined to preserve these popular bodies and force the management to run the factory in a different way. The management, still on the defensive, gave the impression of yielding. The strikers soon found out they were on the verge of falling into the trap of participation. "We thought of replacing factory discipline by self-

3. For the problems still raised by scientific researchers at a later stage, when the tide had turned, see *Recherche et Contestation* (Paris, Anthropos, 1969). This is a report of the proceedings of a conference held in July 1968.

discipline," an activist put it bluntly, "only to discover that we were doing the overseer's job with a smile."

Similar risks were involved in schemes for improving the way the works were run. Technicians and *cadres* were often particularly eager to show that they were capable of managing the firm better. But better for whom? For the owners or for the workers? Without a decisive voice—not just a say—in the organization of work and the distribution of the proceeds, the elected representatives of the workers would be merely the free agents of the owners. The committees were thus rapidly reduced to a different choice: either to fall back on the more consistent line of workers' control, asking for the maximum information but fighting for the best terms from the point of view of the wage earners; or to be driven to ask, not for a share in management, but for full control.

Even then the troubles and ambiguities would not be over. The slogan of *autogestion* was really symptomatic of the May Movement. It reflected its hopes and illusions, its profound aspirations and its limitations. Self-management, on its own, is no panacea. Proudhon's associations of freely contracting workmen, Utopian a century ago, would be absurd in our age of intricate economic structures. To get factories to work does not solve the problem of the social organization of production, distribution, the allocation of resources, and so on. Take an individual factory run by the workers themselves: At best, they could eliminate all the arbitrary elements of the employer's exploitation. But the technical division of labor within the factory is also largely conditioned by the social division of labor outside. Without conquering at least the "commanding heights" of the economy, the workers would be rapidly prisoners of their own environment, unable to offer an alternative rationale to the whole process of production and distribution. If a share in management led logically to *autogestion,* the latter immediately would raise the question of the conquest of power.

Was *autogestion* then an empty slogan? Far from it. The experience acquired by the people in running their factories and offices would have been useful whatever the outcome. If the

Gaullists won and the factories went back to their owners, the workers would still have learned a great deal that would come in useful for the daily struggle ahead and for future counteroffensives. Besides, getting even some factories started again would have raised the strike to a higher level. It might even have led through parallel power to victory. Then *autogestion* would have come into its own as part of a bigger project. Victory could only have been a beginning. To consolidate it, the workers and their allies—the technicians and the scientists, the students and the teachers—would have had to embark on the gigantic task of re-shaping social control over production. They would have had to seek new methods of planning that genuinely matched technical possibilities with the aspirations of the producers, dropping the artificial divisions between production and consumption, between labor and leisure. In other words, they would have had to start building what up to now exists only on paper, a society run by the working people for the working people.

Why *autogestion* remained an empty slogan in May is easy to see. To start a factory going, to use raw materials and distribute the finished products, would have involved a really revolutionary blow against the pillars of property. The union leaders were not even ready to take the much more elementary measures needed to keep the strike going, or at least to show their determination to take them. As time went on, the strikers were threatened by lack of resources (the French trade unions are notoriously poor) and by the boomerang effects of the paralysis gripping the country. If they intended to stick it out and counter such prospects, they had to exercise an increasing control over transport, food supplies, prices, and so on. But to assume such functions and claim such authority, it was in turn necessary to strengthen their new sources of power, to mobilize support. It was indispensable to spread genuine strike committees throughout the factories, to co-ordinate their work, to set up action committees or popular councils throughout the land from local to national level, and to rely on this new network of authority. To put it bluntly, the need was to organize "anarchy" into parallel power. The political and union leaders who got hold of the movement in the second half of May chose to denounce anarchy rather than organize it. The Communists opted for the vacuum and defeat rather than dual power, for bourgeois law and order rather than the Leninist conception.

A great deal has changed over the last fifty years, and circumstances were naturally different in May 1968 from what they had been in Lenin's time. Yet the road to revolutionary victory probably still leads through organized anarchy and parallel power. How far the French May Movement could have traveled on this road it is impossible to tell, since the Communist leaders consciously blocked this way from the start. How far such a movement will go next time depends on the lessons it draws from its negative experience. Defeats, too, can be instructive if their lessons are properly digested.

WE DON'T WANT *to be the watchdogs or servants of capitalism.*
—May slogan

The "New Proletarians"?

Are we witnessing the birth of a new revolutionary class? Can the students and teachers, technicians and scientists, be described as the "new proletarians," destined to carry out the radical transformation of capitalist society that industrial workers have failed to achieve? Put so bluntly and crudely, such questions can only get negative answers, particularly in the French context. Yet worded in a more sophisticated fashion, roughly the same argument is to be found at the heart of some of the original thinking about the French crisis.[1] Nor are such unorthodox theories surprising. The crisis itself followed a far from orthodox pattern.

It started not among industrial workers but among students, and it is among them that it found its most radical expression. The politically conscious students rebelled against society as a whole, against its hierarchical structure, against the foundations of private property on which the edifice rests, against its vulgarly aggressive commercial façade. Only when the rebellion spread throughout the country, when it gathered political momentum, switching from university to factory bench, did it lose its revolutionary impetus. The labor unions, admittedly after some delay and frantic efforts, had managed to turn a struggle *against* the system into a battle *within* it.

The other departure from the pattern, providing scope for theoretical innovations, occurred during the second phase of the crisis. During the general strike, the traditional dividing line between wage and salary earners was blurred. Salaried employees, whether in technical, scientific, or managerial jobs, did not this time rally collectively to the employers' side. Many, as usual, did act as the upholders of capitalist law and order, but quite a few did not. Siding this time with the workers, they took an active part in the strike. The emergence of such an activist minority marks a break with the past and an interesting pointer to the future.

Interesting, because these *cadres,* as the French call them, are the fastest-growing section of the labor force and because the rapid expansion of this professional intelligentsia is a common feature of all advanced countries. Everywhere numerical growth is coupled with social differentiation. A fraction of the newcomers can be absorbed at the top of the establishment and get real executive functions. The majority must resign themselves to jobs increasingly distant from the real centers of decision-making, to

1. This point is made, though still cautiously, by J.-M. Coudray in Morin, Lefort, Coudray, *Mai 1968: La Brèche* (Paris, Fayard, 1968). It is carried to its logical conclusion in Alain Touraine, *Le Mouvement de Mai ou Le Communisme Utopique* (Paris, Éditions du Seuil, 1968).

being the recipients of orders handed down from above, to a narrowing scope for genuine initiative; in short, to a form of alienating work that was once thought to be the exclusive prerogative of the laborer. Gradually they lose the feeling, or rather the illusion, that they are an integral part of the ruling class. The malaise of the *cadres* resulting from these frustrations is international, though under normal circumstances it is difficult to gauge how widespread and deep this feeling is. The French upheaval provided a unique opportunity for seeing how these pent-up passions express themselves in a time of crisis and for drawing distinctions between behavior of various groups lumped together under the generic name professional intelligentsia.

The whole movement started among the would-be *cadres,* among students who rejected the future that society offered them. They found some allies in the university. For a time the support of the teachers looked massive. But sympathy for the victims of police brutality should not be confused with solidarity with their struggle. The liberals rapidly fell by the wayside. Only a section of the teaching staff, particularly the young lecturers, shared the critical vision and the radical objectives of the revolutionary students. To these could be added the scientific researchers working in close connection with the university. In this first phase the crisis was confined to the academic world.

The technical and managerial employees whose jobs were directly related to the country's economy became really involved only when this machine came to a stop. Naturally they were not indifferent to what was happening in the Latin Quarter, and individually they were quite stirred. They had to make up their own minds, however, only in the second half of May, when the general strike had paralyzed the country. The reaction of the salaried employees can be summed up roughly in three categories. The first includes the more or less active strikebreakers, ranging from men who were ready to lead scabs into action, to less zealous servants who simply assured employers of their eagerness to work. The second and biggest group can best be described as passive strikers. The conflict between the employers and the workers imposed on them a period of unwanted leisure and gave them time to ponder their own uncomfortable position on the fence. Finally, there were those who broke with precedent and took an active part in the strike.

The activists were still a minority. By itself, this fact in no way invalidates the thesis that a new revolutionary class has appeared on the horizon. A movement must start from somewhere, and political class-consciousness is not acquired overnight. But there is another reason why it is difficult to treat the *cadres* as a homogeneous, collective category. Their reaction to the strike did not only vary depending on the local political climate, the size of the firm, the kind and efficiency of its policy of "social relations." It was also determined, as a rule, by their function in the process of production and social organization.

Active strikers were to be found mainly in the modern branches of industry, such as electronics and aircraft, chemicals and parachemicals. These are science-based industries, in which technical and scientific workers account for a substantial, occasionally predominating, share of the labor force. They are closer to wage earners than to overseers. The limit is reached in laboratories or research sections of vast corporations. There, the scientists and technicians feel that they have little say on the framework within which they operate, that the bias is clearly in favor of the managers and salesmen. Frustrated and grouped together, they not surprisingly contributed numerous strikers. One example should be enough to show the contrast between the researchers and the overseers. At the Renault plant at Boulogne-Billancourt, only a handful of technicians and engineers joined the strike. In the neighboring technical division at Rueil, the majority voted, at least to start with, in favor of the strike.

On the basis of the French experience one is tempted to draw some tentative rules. Top managers and men in true executive jobs have few reasons to rebel against the system. Scientists and technicians are more likely to join in the protest if they are victims of the social division of labor (and conscious that the imperatives of technology are only a disguise), and less likely to do so if they are isolated supervisors in that division. Men working in research and development tend to be more critical of the capitalist establishment than those in management and distribution. But even this general rule must immediately be qualified. If sales managers and salesmen stayed aloof, or were hostile to the strike, economists, sociologists, and statisticians working in market research or other economic and social institutions were among the most radical participants in the movement. There is an obvious link here with their colleagues in the civil service, the strikers in the ministries of finance or housing. In both cases the men and women involved in the strike were questioning their own function in society. In both, they were echoing the student protest summed up in the slogan "We don't want to be the watchdogs or servants of capitalism."

Indeed, the division among the professional intelligentsia, as well as the emergence of a revolutionary minority, reflects a trend that is more easily discerned among the students. It will be objected that the mood of the students during the May uprising was too passionate to serve as an accurate guide. But to confirm this trend, we have at our disposal a poll taken not in the spring of 1968, but in the following winter; that is, when the revolt had been crushed. The victors, it will be recalled, were clever enough not to rely exclusively on repression. While police forces were being massed in the neighborhood and "muscled proctors" were making their entry into the university, that most flexible of politicians, the adroit Edgar Faure, was appointed Minister of Education. The newcomer was allowed to imitate the language of the protesters and even to steal some of their slogans. He was given scope to change the structure of the university and to introduce a degree of autonomy. His task was to isolate the revolutionaries and reassure the bourgeoisie that there would be no more explosions. The demonstration that most students were "reasonable" when their "legitimate grievances" were removed was to be provided through their mass participation in the elections to the newly created councils with a say in the management of university departments.

Everything was mobilized to insure a good score. The papers were singing the praise of reformism, with the Communist *L'Humanité* joining in the chorus, and the only criticism in the national press was that the scheme might be too bold. The pressure on public opinion and, through it, on the students was tremendous. One could barely hear the arguments of radical students refusing to take part in a farce. The councils, they pointed out, would only have the appearance of power. The students could never have a majority nor could they have any influence on what really mattered, such as the content of their education. To vote, in their view, meant merely to legitimize a fraud.

A boycott is never an easy line to advocate. It was particularly difficult then, with the tide receding, the horizon apparently blocked, and the various radical groups quarreling among themselves over strategy and tactics. In addition, Communist students were preaching participation in the name of the alleged principle of struggle from within. Yet, for all this, Faure could not get the majority of French students to the polls. To claim that fifty-two per cent of them had cast a vote, he had to rely on the ingenuity of his statisticians.[2]

For our purpose, the tricks of the statisticians are less important than the results, however twisted. These results, while confirming the survival of a strong revolutionary potential, also show that voting percentages do not vary haphazardly. On top of the nuances resulting from regional differences, the political complexion of the students seems largely influenced by the subject they are reading and, indirectly, by the job that awaits them. Throughout the country some of the faculties are predominantly Red, while others are rather blue; the former boycotted the poll, while the latter participated in large numbers.

Not surprisingly, Faure registered a success in the faculties of

2. If you can't get more people to vote, you can reduce the number of registered voters and thus "achieve" a higher percentage. The number of students in France suddenly dwindled, but who will bother about the big discrepancy between two sets of figures? After all, they were needed for different purposes.

medicine. Because of the high cost of extended study, medical students tend to be recruited from a particularly privileged background. More important still, once they have gone through their examinations, they are destined for a relatively well-paying job in a liberal profession. During the May crisis, many medical students took part in commissions attempting to reform syllabuses or the scope of their studies. A few months later, most of them responded favorably to Faure the reformer. They felt no overwhelming professional reasons for reshaping society.

Future lawyers participated with the same zeal. Here, however, one must draw a distinction. In keeping with an old custom, French faculties of law also house the departments of political science and economics. Whereas students of law voted as massively as their medical colleagues, the economists did not. Indeed, wherever they had been politically active in May, for instance in Paris, they abstained as massively as their colleagues in arts and science.

The faculties of arts and science remain the bastions of revolt. It is there that the growing battalions of protesters are still being recruited. But these faculties are very big, and a closer analysis, wherever it is possible, reveals further differentiation within the student body. For instance, in the faculty of arts, the most radical departments are those of philosophy, psychology, and sociology.[3] Students supposed to learn about the meaning of the world and the workings of our society in order to acquire a *weltanschauung* and transmit the ruling ideology or assist in social integration are the most numerous to rebel against the system. Science students, resenting their appointed place in the allegedly technical division of labor, and the prospective manipulators of this social division, form a growing revolutionary nucleus.

3. The liberal Faure even threatened to abolish sociology for undergraduates with a typically subtle argument. He was not going to suppress it because there were many protesters among sociology students. Heaven forbid. But the great number of protesters was a sign that there was something wrong with the studies. That is why . . .

Admittedly, students still being groomed for the mincing machine have a capacity for violent reaction much greater than graduates who have gone through it. Their mood cannot be taken as an accurate expression of the temper of the professional intelligentsia. An allowance must be made for society's power of absorption and man's capacity for resignation. Yet, even the mood of the students, as illustrated in the French university poll, does not foreshadow any global revolt of the nation's *cadres*. It rather suggests a deepening split, a cleavage within the professional middle class, and the formation of a revolutionary minority.

A similar conclusion is suggested by recent changes within unions of intellectual workers. We saw earlier that France's biggest union of university teachers—the SNESup—was controlled, even if with the barest of majorities, by the radical new left, which made it possible for its secretary to throw his union's weight on the side of the students during the May crisis. Immediately after the battle the leadership was confirmed, again by the narrowest of margins. In the following months, which were traumatic for some of the teachers faced for the first time with students openly questioning their authority, the Communists managed to mobilize the more conservative elements, particularly in the provinces, and seize the leadership with the help of a corporatist coalition. But it is a most unstable balance that can be tilted in the opposite direction by something less than a gale of discontent.

The process has not gone so far among teachers of lower grades. Until a few years ago their unions were dominated by mild reformers linked with the moderate socialist party. Since then the Communists and their fellow-travelers have gained control of the union for secondary education and have made progress among primary-school teachers. This development is quite logical, since the Communists now not only appear, but act, as the representatives of narrow, corporate trade-unionism. They are taking over the positions of social democracy and some of its following. But their progress is paralleled by the reappearance of a new radical left, which in France has been branded *gauchiste* [4] (ultra-left) and does not seem to mind this nickname.

Possibly still more significant is the political crystallization among scientists employed in laboratories and institutes run by the state through the National Center of Scientific Research, the CNRS.[5] Most of them belong to the Syndicat National des Chercheurs Scientifiques (National Union of Scientific Research-ers), or SNCS, which until the May crisis had no inner political alignments. It was vaguely leftish, with the Communists, thanks to their organization and discipline, occasionally pulling the strings. They pulled one too many in May 1968, when the student upris-ing began, by trying to push the union toward the Communist party line. They provoked a spontaneous revolt by the rank and file, which not only forced the leadership to stick with the stu-dents throughout the crisis, but also led to political divisions at the ensuing congress. For the first time the delegates had to choose between three different lines: the Communists, presenting an es-sentially corporate platform; undecided reformers temporarily regrouped around the Swedish model for socialism; and the ultra-leftists. The latter, to their own and everybody else's surprise, got a slight edge and were entrusted with the secretariat of the union.

Nothing so spectacular occurred in the big unions of profes-sional, scientific, and managerial employees. There, too, inevi-tably the crisis had left a ferment. The Communist-dominated CGT had trouble with its social scientists. The reformist CFDT had to proclaim that the "subversive" views of its branch in the

4. *Gauchiste* and *droitier*, ultra-left and ultra-right, are Communist terms for deviations. They imply that there is a just policy somewhere between the two.

5. The nearest American equivalent would be the National Science Foundation, but the CNRS includes researchers in all branches of science and the arts. At the last congress of the FEN, in November 1969, the moderate majority's share of the vote declined (from 62.46 per cent to 55.96 per cent); the pro-Communists barely increased their percentage (from 31.41 to 31.79), while the so-called ultra-left doubled its share (from 6.13 to 12.25). What the Communists gain on their right they lose on their left.

petroleum industry did not represent the opinions of the confederation. Even the moderate and respectable Confédération Générale des Cadres, or CGC, had some internal troubles. Yet all this did not culminate in the formation of a radical nucleus. Should one, therefore, conclude that the professional intelligentsia, far from being a revolutionary vanguard, was really a social laggard, precipitated temporarily into the movement by an unprecedented storm? After all, the sweep of the general strike was such that other groups who by tradition have remained aloof—shop assistants in big stores, taxi drivers, news vendors—were also drawn into it.

It would be a wrong conclusion. There are many reasons why revaluation of values is a slow process among the *cadres*. For many engineers, technicians, and managerial employees working in private industry the very fact of belonging to a union, other than the respectably inoffensive CGC, is in itself a professional risk. They are prisoners of their environment, but also of age-old illusions about their status and social position. That some of them nevertheless sided with the strikers, while others showed no hostility toward the movement, is in itself a turning point. The guarantee that there will be further repercussions lies in the very nature of modern economic development. The ranks of the professional intelligentsia are being swollen at a rate that will make it increasingly difficult for its members to preserve their traditional illusions.

Even if the phenomenon is real and historically significant, it does not herald the advent of a new revolutionary class. The thesis seems far-fetched not only because, as we saw, the professional middle class is likely to be split in the process. There are two other reasons for rejecting it in this extreme form. The first is practical and is revealed when one analyzes the sequence of French events. The second is more theoretical and emerges when the premises of the theory are reset in an international context.

It is at once natural and strange that such a thesis should have been inspired by the French crisis: natural if the analysis is focused only on the university; strange if it takes into account the country as a whole. Outside the academic world and its periphery intellectual workers were not the initiators of the movement. They were its fellow-travelers. Individually, many *cadres* were profoundly shaken by what was happening in the Latin Quarter, and quite a few were to play a dynamic role in the strike. As a social group they were only drawn into the strike when the industrial workers had paralyzed the country. The May crisis was actually a reminder of the social weight of the proletariat. Undoubtedly science is now incomparably more important in production than it used to be, and the university therefore has a much more vital function for the economy. Nevertheless, a month of academic strikes throughout the country would only cause a stir. A general industrial strike, crippling the economy, rapidly raises the question of political power in the country. May was also a reminder that the weight of a class is not only measured by numbers.

But maybe the theory is not destined for France. If teachers and technicians, scientific and social workers, are the revolutionary class of today or tomorrow, then North America should figure at the top of the revolutionary agenda. It is in the United States rather than in France that the premises of the theory are fulfilled. There, with no untapped reserves of farm labor to draw upon, the relative share of industrial employment is actually declining. The technological transformation has gone farther than anywhere else, and the number of white-collar workers is rising fast. The proportion of college-trained graduates in the economy is also much larger than, say, in France.

True, the American university is in a state of revolt. But for the time being the upheaval has not spread far enough to undermine the foundations of society. Equally true, the professional intelligentsia is uneasy. Its unrest is illustrated by writers and painters. It occasionally expresses itself through gestures of sympathy for the civil-rights movement, through protests against the Vietnamese war, through understanding of the student revolt. Yet this undeniable discontent shows no sign of finding an organized political outlet. The professional intelligentsia in the

United States lacks a prospect and a potential partner that could carry it into battle.[6]

Projecting current American trends into the future, it is not impossible to imagine a situation in which the apathy of the traditional American working class would cease to be a major obstacle to revolutionary developments. If continued economic concentration and the connected streamlining of organization reduce the growing mass of white-collar employees to conditions of work that, at least in terms of lack of initiative, were hitherto associated with the factory; if scientific progress and the spread of automation reduce drastically the number of unskilled, and even skilled, workers in industry and replace them with a college-trained labor force,[7] then these scientific and technical workers —the new producers, newly alienated—could become the driving force of historical change.

We are not there yet. It is even debatable whether we are inevitably heading in that direction. Nevertheless, a practical program based on such a vision might, in the American context, give a progressive lead. For radical students trying to break out of their isolated campuses it may suggest other allies in addition to "outcasts and outsiders," allies closer to production and, therefore, to the mainstream of American capitalism.

In Europe, on the other hand, and particularly in France and Italy, a similar theory is at best ambiguous. It is positively harmful when coupled with a distorted image of the American future. Property and profit have not ceased to be the mainsprings of American society. The United States is neither postindustrial nor postcapitalist. The hierarchical clash between the rulers and the ruled has its class roots. To assimilate in such a way the American and the Soviet equation means to accept the fashionable idea that

6. To object that the American workers are not revolutionary either is simply to shift the argument one remove. Because in some European countries the working class preserves the belief, however vague, in its revolutionary role, the rebellion of the intelligentsia acquires a different significance there.

7. In other words, if capitalism manages in its own degrading way to eliminate the differences between manual and intellectual labor.

today's conflicts are merely the result of a stage reached in technological development, and, by the same token, to perpetuate confusion.

Indeed, ambiguity and confusion were the striking features of the debate among the professional intelligentsia during the French crisis. We are not talking here about the *cadres* who stayed at home and trembled throughout the crisis, hoping it was only a nightmare. We are referring to the men who took sides, made personal sacrifices, attended assemblies in occupied factories or at the Sorbonne.[8] Even in their case, sympathy for the students and solidarity with the strikers were mixed in varying proportions with elitist dreams, technocratic ambitions, and corporate interests.

One of the recurring complaints of the contesting *cadres* was their lack of information, the extent to which they were kept in the dark about their company's affairs. They clamored for a share in decisions. Some were hankering after the lost paradise of the small enterprise, in which *monsieur l'ingénieur* mattered; and they were looking toward an idealized American corporation, in which all the *cadres* were miraculously of crucial importance. Management, one of those American words that acquire a magic meaning on crossing the Atlantic, often sounded like a panacea in the mouths of confused protesters. Accompanying it was the symptom of native ambiguity, as in the frequent references to François Bloch-Lainé, the French ideologist of "participation" in the capitalist framework.[9]

Some went a step farther, hinting that the *cadres* should be the real masters of the firm. The workers, the argument ran, cannot grasp the intricacies of production, and the owners are too preoccupied with immediate profit. The salaried employees would run it better, more efficiently. Such claims were seldom coupled

8. For extracts from tape-recordings of some of these meetings see A. Willener, C. Gajdos, and G. Benguigui, *Les Cadres en Mouvement* (Paris, Les Éditions de l'Épi, 1969).

9. High civil servant, now chairman of the Crédit Lyonnais, a nationalized bank, author of *Pour une Réforme de l'Entreprise* (Paris, Éditions du Seuil, 1963).

with serious explanations—better for whom? more efficiently by what criteria and at whose expense?—and this was logical, since their authors seldom looked beyond their factory or their immediate grievance to question the workings of the system as a whole.

Finally, there was the obvious corporate argument. The industrial workers, through their organization and struggle, have improved their position and increased their power in the factory. The *cadres,* through their gentlemanly dilly-dallying, have lost both in power and prestige. They also should organize and fight, not so much for money (the question was rarely raised) but for greater influence within the firm and within society. Should they also use the workers' struggle for their own ends? Such an objective was never spelled out at the time, though it may be guessed that part of the professional middle class listened with interest to subsequently elaborated theories purporting to prove that the working class had outplayed its historical role, that it was today's equivalent of the peasantry in the nineteenth century, at best capable of supplying the infantry for somebody else's victory. It is tempting to dream of climbing to power on somebody else's back.

Such a brief summary of the debate within the professional intelligentsia is one-sided and distorted. It misses the spirit of revolt that swept through France during the period. On the other hand, it is not surprising that the professional middle class should have carried into its revolt the prejudices and clichés prevailing in its environment. Revaluation of values is an intricate process. The capitalist system, built up over centuries and modernized in the past few decades, overwhelms and dwarfs the individual with its air of apparent inevitability. Normally nothing seems possible beyond superficial tinkering.

To step outside, to look critically at the system as a whole and at one's own function within it, requires courage and imagination. By its tradition and upbringing the professional middle class is hardly prepared to do this. If the ruling ideology is the ideology of the ruling class, the *cadres* of a nation are its main victims— or accomplices. They are designed to peddle the ideas, manage the organization, supervise its workings. (The supreme hypocrisy is that they are brought up to do so with a clear conscience, in the belief that they are doing a socially useful job.) The extraordinary thing about the French crisis is that so many of them rebelled and that a minority within the minority carried its task of criticism and self-criticism to its logical conclusions.

For sociologists and economists it was fairly easy to perceive that their jobs were, as a rule, connected with the functioning of the established society, the perpetuation of privilege. For scientists working in their laboratories, it was more difficult to grasp that their research was conditioned, limited by a social framework, and that it would be exploited within that framework. It was more difficult still for the engineers working in their plants to admit that they were not just neutrally applying the laws of technology but were also instruments of exploitation. Yet such indictments were heard during the French crisis, and they were delivered by the men involved. The process of debunking has begun.

When a society is shaken but not destroyed, it instinctively produces mechanisms for its own defense. Since the whole western establishment could be threatened by the massive revolt of its young graduates, it must find new means of absorbing them. Money will not be enough. They must be given a feeling, if not of freedom, at least of importance and prestige. The new ideological offensive should have some success. Some of the young graduates may hope that the big stockholders and their associates will co-opt them into what C. Wright Mills called the "power elite." They may aspire to be senior civil servants, top managers, academic mandarins, or they may be content with less exalted positions in the service of the ruling class. Many budding doctors and dentists, lawyers and accountants, will do no more than grumble about their lot. Advertising agencies and supersalesmen will even praise it. Some of the liberal professions have not yet been crushed by concentration, and even when squeezed by the economic machine, not all men will rebel. Thus, in industry, many engineers, particularly those who have risen from the ranks, are quite ready to trade submission for material gain. What is more difficult to preserve is the prestige, the feeling of belonging to an elite. You can hardly persuade the mass-produced graduate that he gets McNamara's passport to power along with his diploma, that he too is destined to be boss at Ford and then Secretary of Defense. A growing number see themselves for what they are: white-collar workers with a longer educational apprenticeship, superior cogs in the machine.

And the counterpoison is working, too. The ferment introduced by the students is spreading. Young people, while questioning their own position, are also questioning their environment. It is becoming increasingly plain that the struggle against the military chain of command in industry, against the hierarchical, impersonal discipline in economic life as a whole, is indivisible, that it must be global or in vain. One can imagine an army in which the general staff would reach collective decisions and superior officers would have considerable room for maneuver. One can hardly envisage an army where everything would be jolly and collective down to the level of noncommissioned officers, with Prussian discipline below. And every year the universities are throwing onto the market a host of NCO's. Herein lies the chief ally of "subversion." The McNamara myth carries less conviction with the college-bred sons than the Ford myth did with their fathers. It is not difficult for the politically conscious among them to prove to the rising generation that the choice is between submission to the hierarchical order or a radical overhaul of social organization, between command by the very few or a share in collective decisions for all.

For relatively privileged intellectual workers to opt against the existing system is only the beginning of a long road. The relatively easiest next step is to accept a leveling of wages, which some French *cadres* welcomed during the general strike on rather moral, or charitable, grounds. To be consistent, they should agree to a more painful application of the egalitarian principle. They must learn to view their chief asset, superior education, as a temporary advantage, a windfall that improves their advising capacity but nothing more. The struggle they join is for a society in which, in the long run, after the disappearance of private ownership of the means of production, differences between intellectual and manual labor will also disappear. The ultimate choice for the *cadres* is between a mythical managerial revolution and a genuinely socialist one, the search by collective producers for new ways of organizing their labor and leisure, the bold bid to reshape their life.

Such an alternative is bound to split the professional middle classes. It has already begun to do so. Some students and teachers, technicians, social and scientific workers, are already reacting as intellectual wage-earners. They are still few, though their numbers will grow. Because their alienation is not a heritage of generations, as in the case of the traditional proletariat, it is more acute; because the revolt against their own condition is linked with a fairly conscious indictment of the system, they are likely to be found in the front rank of the struggle for a radical transformation of society. Socially, they provide the bulk of the membership of what is now called throughout the western world the new left, at odds with the traditional parties and unions, reduced by the vagaries of history to marginal skirmishes. The new intellectuals do not have to rebel for marginal gain.

Is this then the embryo of the new revolutionary class foreshadowed by its prophets? Youth, students, new intellectuals—all have had this title bestowed on them, together or in succession. Yet if the main actors in the French May drama have learned and taught something, it is that they cannot do it alone, that their battle against the hierarchical order is inseparable from the workers' struggle for emancipation. The ideologists distorted the meaning of their action when in a flight of fancy they set it in the imaginary context of "postindustrial" society. On the other hand, by focusing attention on the students and their closest allies, the new intellectual workers, they have emphasized a development relevant not only for France—the changing nature of class conflict in a changing society. But their diagnosis needs to be corrected. Advanced capitalism has not eliminated its old contradictions. In trying to grow out of them, it has sown additional "seeds of its own destruction."

I DON'T WANT *to die an idiot.*
      —Title of a post-May play by cartoonist Wolinsky

Cultural Revolution

China's historic upheaval still had such an impact on the political vocabulary that metaphors borrowed from it naturally sprang to mind when people commented on the French crisis. The writings on the walls of the Sorbonne were likened to the *ta tse bau* of the students in Peking, and the French rebels were described as Red guards. Had they not risen against bureaucratic authority and established rule? Were they not determined to build on the ruins of bourgeois culture? The analogies, if sometimes instructive, were on the whole superficial. China had embarked on an unprecedented experiment. A ruling Communist leadership, in a determined bid against the inevitable growth of bureaucracy, had dared to initiate a purge that, though inspired and to some extent controlled from the top, had to be carried from below by the masses.[1] In France, the concept of cultural revolution could only be applied in a quite different sense. The name fitted a revolt against a way of life, a social organization, a civilization. A cobblestone thrown against the smooth surface revealed an unsuspected depth of discontent, and this is where the French lesson is relevant for the western world.

The poster, as we saw, was the only form of art the protesters reinvented at once, while the impact on literary expression of the sudden outburst of free speech remains to be seen. As to the providers of culture, the intelligentsia in the narrow sense of the term, they were split by the conflict in the traditional way. The upholders of established values were temporarily silenced. The cleverest among them were shouting with the chorus in the hope of so distorting the message of protest as to render it innocuous. If there was a novelty, it was the violence of the protest itself, which reflected the intellectual's predicament in what is allegedly a society of mass culture.

Until our times, the class nature of culture was unconcealed. Thus, France's great literary achievement of the nineteenth century was the bourgeois novel, and there was no pretense that culture was for the masses. The subsequent spread of education and literacy did not remove class barriers or bridge the cultural gap. It did not forge a common language. If anything, specialized progress has only provided additional obstacles to communication.[2]

1. For this crucial aspect missed in most western comments on China's revolution, see K. S. Karol, *China: The Other Communism* (New York, Hill and Wang, 1967).

2. When one talks now of "two cultures," the reference is usually to the divorce between scientific and literary culture or, in more sophisticated arguments, to the incommunicability between mathematical and verbal language. See an essay on this subject in George Steiner, *Language and Silence* (New York, Atheneum, 1967).

Classless mass culture is still so distant that we cannot even imagine what form it will take. What passes for it, in an intentional confusion, is the mass production of cultural goods and their commercialization on an unprecedented scale.

The creative artist or critic is faced with awkward choices. He can stick to his trade, express the anxiety of the epoch for the few, experiment with his tools, hoping for a breakthrough that will suddenly re-establish contact. He can withdraw into his tower, keep there some solid assets that are threatened with devaluation by commercial and political pressures, and somehow preserve them for the future. But if his commitment drives him to seek a wider public now, he must compete with the commercial record, permanently playing all the variations on the theme that capitalism washes whiter. The painter is tempted to shock so as to stir, the writer to shriek so as to be heard, the film-maker to smuggle his message in a cartoon strip. Whichever way he chooses, the dissenting intellectual feels thwarted, frustrated, unfulfilled. It is out of derision that our age has been called the century of mass communication.

"To live without selling," if one may borrow the title of an essay,[3] was certainly one of the aspirations of the May Movement. But intellectuals are no longer innocent. They have no wish to replace the rule of the salesman with the tyranny of the uncultured, or even the cultured, commissar. Revulsion is not the same as revolution. Surprised, like everybody else, by the crisis, the intellectuals had little time in which to improvise new structures. Where immediate action was required—addressing workers through posters, entertaining strikers, filming demonstrations—there was no serious difficulty. But in the turmoil of the fast-changing situation the assemblies of writers, critics, artists, and actors, ill equipped for the task, could only grope toward the solution of their professional problems. Essentially, the intellectuals merely echoed the main message of May, the violent protest against the existing social order.

3. Raymonde Moulin, in *Art et Contestation* (Brussels, La Connaissance, 1968).

The cry against the stupidity, hypocrisy, and meaninglessness of our social life was loudest at the Sorbonne, but it also reached the industrial suburbs. Indeed, it was probably the main link between the two. To the Republic reciting its slogan Liberty, Equality, Fraternity, the angry echo replied Injustice, Inequality, Idiocy—this last being the inseparable companion of the other two. For months afterward, the absurdity of existence was to be summed up in a simple formula scribbled all over the Paris underground: *métro, boulot, métro, dodo* (subway, work, subway, sleep). Why? What for? What is the meaning of it all? The violent French outburst against the crippling society, however incoherent, was a reminder that millions of people are not resigned to having no share in the shaping of their own lives. (They do not want to die, let alone to live, as idiots.)

Though it was foreshadowed by student unrest from Tokyo to Berkeley, from Berlin to Rome, the violence of the French revulsion still came as a surprise. The shock was the greater since it could be argued that in the "permissive sixties" the western ruling class had succeeded in evolving a system capable of integrating, or at least neutralizing, all forms of social protest. Back in the days of the cold war George Orwell, his eyes fixed on Stalin's Russia, had painted a nightmarish world of mental manipulation in which even inner dissent was impossible. At the close of his *1984,* the revolutionary leader himself was so broken that he not only whispered "I love Big Brother"; he genuinely believed it. But the most ruthless form of domination is not always the most efficient. Had Orwell concentrated on his own environment, he might have imagined a more subtle and more sophisticated model. Have you ever heard anyone proclaiming "I love Big Business"? Expressing his fondness for freedom or enterprise?— quite often; his passion for the big corporation?—never. A domination is not less effective because it is not clearly perceived. Quite the contrary.

The new western ideology rested, and still rests, on the twin pillars of pluralism and growth. The doctrine of pluralism starts from the undoubted fact that in advanced western societies dissent is tolerated, various classes and groups can express their opinions and compete. The emphasis on competition, however, makes it possible cleverly to conceal the extent to which powerful biases are built into the system so as to insure the survival of capitalism,[4] or, to put it in Orwellian language, the extent to which one class is much, much more equal than the other.

But is capitalism a relevant factor at all? The task of the twin doctrine of growth is to transcend such vulgar issues as property, the distribution of wealth and income, the mainsprings and purposes of growth itself. The rich and the poor, the employers and the employed, the haves and the have-nots, are somehow reconciled by their common interest in higher output. What matters is the size of the cake, not its taste nor the size of different slices. The "invisible hand" of Adam Smith will no longer do. In the pragmatic theory of growth the new rulers thought they had devised a seemingly classless ideology.

Whether expounded in academic treatises or distilled in popular newspapers, this ideological medicine could not have worked alone. To spread and to overcome serious resistance, it had to be mixed with a good dose of resignation, with a feeling of hopelessness produced by the absence of any alternative. Here in recent years the Soviet Union has been made to perform a dual function. On the one hand, examples of Russian repression, preferably taken out of historical context, have been amply used as a warning of what happens when a country gives up pluralism, and pluralism in this argument is subtly interchangeable with private property. On the other hand, clumsy Soviet attempts to extricate the economy from the Stalinist strait jacket—Libermanism, the emphasis on profits, the idea of wider powers for managers—have been hailed as a proof that the social system is irrelevant, that technology imposes a similar pattern whatever the regime. There is no Siberia in the advanced western countries. The dis-

4. For a penetrating and devastating analysis of the hidden as well as the open biases, see R. Miliband, *The State in Capitalist Society* (London, Weidenfeld and Nicolson, 1969).

senters are allowed free expression. It seemed, for a while, that they could only cry in the wilderness.

You do not have to declare that you love the big corporation. You may even proclaim that you hate it. You can contract out, pray to alien gods, make your choice between yoga and Billy Graham. You can complain about the rotten state of society and work toward the moral improvement of man as a means toward altering it. But if you choose to act, if you try to reshape your social environment, you come up against a political framework that allows for no more than marginal change. The system is fool-proof, or rather it looked as if it were until the French crisis revealed that it was loaded with gunpowder.

The system clearly has a great capacity for recovery, and the skill of its repairs-engineers should not be underestimated. In France, for instance, the glimpse of a different future that drove millions to action was cleverly replaced by the electoral map with its calculations. The Russians obliged with timely assistance. The Soviet tanks entering Prague made it easier for western propaganda to proclaim that socialism is incompatible with freedom. Nevertheless, the chief ally of all western establishments is the power of inertia, the overwhelming weight of the prevailing environment. When there is no prospect of radical change, man cannot be expected to brood permanently on the seamy side of his life. He is tempted to fit as best he can into the existing structure, and he is conditioned to do so by all sorts of devices. The Daily Drug on the way to work, the TV back home, almost everything he lays his hands or eyes on imperceptibly relays the newly recorded message: Capitalism washes whiter. . . . The last washing may not have been perfect, but with its new enzymes, capitalism washes whiter, whiter, whiter than anything else.

Outwardly, the machine is working as smoothly as before. The French precedent is a warning not to trust appearances. The apparently resigned can suddenly rebel, showing the depth of their hidden discontent. The system is vulnerable and now known to be so. The French uprising, though abortive, thus marks a break in Europe's postwar history, foreshadowing a new age of conflict. Not everybody is fooled by the lull.

André Malraux, former novelist, former Communist sympathizer, but still General de Gaulle's Minister of Culture at the time of the crisis, was not able to stoop to the level of some of his colleagues and dismiss this historical turning-point as the mischievous work of some foreign agents. Unwilling to condemn the regime he was serving, he raised the French conflict to its international dimension and described it in apocalyptic terms as part of the general crisis of civilization, of the inability of modern culture to keep pace with technological progress. So far, so good. Had the author of *Man's Fate* drawn on his smattering of socialist knowledge acquired in earlier days, he would have tried to go to the root of the trouble, to the clash between the mighty productive forces and the obsolete social relations. With nuclear power offering new sources of energy, the computer opening up new vistas of automation, with fantastic scientific possibilities within human reach, everything seems to be ready, and more than ready, for a complete reorganization of life by, and for, the collective producers. Capitalism is inherently incapable of meeting this challenge, and Russia's failure to respond to it in no way removes this incapacity.[5]

Student unrest, spreading from country to country, is a sign of cultural revolution, a symptom of disease in societies sick not only in their bodies but in their heads. Morons and misfits, unable to appreciate the sacrifices society has to make for their sake— thus thunder the loudspeakers of international propaganda. Its manipulators know better. They know that it is the most lucid

5. The story used to be told about an American team of specialists visiting Soviet railways. Asked about their impressions, they first told their beaming hosts that the track seemed excellent. They then expressed timidly their surprise that during the three days of inspection they had not seen a single train on the track. Back came the angry reply: "And what about the oppression of the Negro in the United States?" Now, one has often the impression that "What about freedom of expression in the Soviet Union?" is an equally relevant reply to questions about western failures.

who rebel against the social order and their place within it. This does not mean that the system will collapse through a brain strike, through the mass desertion of its elite. Enough newcomers will be wooed or bribed into running it. The *clercs* will not fail to fulfill their treasonable function in exchange for crumbs of power and prestige. The big stockholders will find enough recruits to fill the managerial jobs in the big corporations, in the civilian and military apparatus of the state, in the increasingly important ideological factories. But the mood is now changing. The cultural revolution led by the younger generation is depriving the ruling class of its supreme hypocrisy, the inner conviction that what is good for General Motors is good for society and the world at large.

How nice it was to parade as the party of progress, leading mankind to the moon and beyond. The ideological fortress of growth was impregnable as long as it was only being attacked by reactionary romantics fighting in the name of an idealized past. Indeed, the attackers were really allies. Abstract depreciation of the value of earthly goods made it easier to suggest that running other people's affairs, and those of the country, was no privilege but the rich man's burden. Now that young students and workers have made breaches in the walls, the defenders of the established order have to put up with a different kind of assault, coming from all sides. The so-called economy of growth comes under fire for its injustice, its inequality, its very purpose. Growth for whom and for what? Progress to produce what kind of social and individual life?

Horizon 1980, Year 2000, the postindustrial society, the scientific Utopia—all such futuristic flights cannot conceal the fact that what is being projected is the same class society, based on profit, privilege, and passive acquiescence. Its beneficiaries and their servants thought they had invented a magic machine—fed by technological innovations and oiled by advertising—that could run forever. The French students and workers rising against the absurdity of their life have not only upset the Gaullist imitation of this machine. They have pointed out the weakness of its model, the assumption that the producers of this world can be driven for ever as a herd of passive consumers.

The two pillars are interconnected. If the concept of growth can no longer keep up the ideological edifice, the scope for pluralism will also shrink. If people cannot be fooled into resigned co-operation, they will have to be forced into obedience. The truncheon of law and order is beginning to take precedence over the ideological weapons of pluralism and consensus. Such a shift is a sign of weakness. Illusions are preferable, and concealed domination is more efficient. The rulers are determined to cling to power, but they are shaken. Their arrogance is feigned, and their self-confidence an act. Look at them carefully. They're trembling. These are not the puritan captains of industry convinced that they are building a New Jerusalem. They are cousins of the French aristocrats of the second half of the eighteenth century and of the czarist camarilla in the years preceding the Russian revolution. They are witnessing the twilight of a reign.

But when a ruling class has outlived its time, it does not bow out gracefully of its own accord. It has to be removed more or less forcibly. Has the French May crisis also outlined the instruments indispensable for such a historic takeover?

THE ACTION COMMITTEES *are the expression on the political level of the fundamental democratic need of the masses. . . .*

—Draft of a platform, May 1968

The Would-Be Soviets

A movement finding no ready channels for its expression is driven to seek its own new ways. The instruments for action it forges in the process are improvised. They reflect the strength of the movement but also its weaknesses, difficulties, and ambiguities as well as its deep aspirations. The French May Movement, born outside the traditional parties and destined to grow in spite of their opposition, invented the *comités d'action* (action committees), to carry out its tasks.

269

The movement and the instrument were almost born at the same time. The first skirmishes outside the Sorbonne took place on May 3. The day after, we find the first trace of the committees in a significantly worded appeal: ". . . join the action committees that are being created in the faculties. Take the initiative. . . ." [1] On May 9, during the meeting held at the Mutualité, which was mentioned earlier, Jean-Louis Peninou [2] could already speak on their behalf and define their line: "What we need are basic committees to organize the unity of the base [of the rank and file] through action and particularly *for* action." But it was only after the following night, the night of the barricades, after the mass demonstration and the general strike that followed, that the action committees spread, rising rapidly from half a dozen to several hundred, concentrated mainly in the Paris region. At a general assembly held on May 19, some 148 Parisian committees were represented by delegates. Not all the committees were represented, since it should not be forgotten that all such meetings were being improvised in a general climate of excitement and confusion.

The confusion extended to the label itself. "Action committee" became so fashionable a term that it would have surprised nobody if the employers' federation had set up an action committee at the time. Before one analyzes the nature and function of the action committee, it is therefore necessary to enumerate a few bodies that belong to the same family and separate it from those that simply borrowed the fashionable title.

Thus, in addition to the action committees proper, which had their co-ordinating center at the Sorbonne, there were the student-worker action committees, which moved their headquarters to the Censier annex of the arts faculty. These were close cousins,

1. Leaflet published by the Mouvement d'Action Universitaire. For the documents see the excellent *La Sorbonne par Elle-Même* (Paris, Les Éditions Ouvières, 1968). See also Alain Schnapp and Pierre Vidal-Nacquet, eds., *Journal de la Commune Étudiante* (Paris, Éditions du Seuil, 1969).
2. Along with Marc Kravetz, best-known spokesman of the so-called syndicalist left in the student union at the end of the Algerian war. Both were to play a prominent role in the co-ordination of action committees.

with the more specific task of strengthening the link between university and factory. The action committees, by definition, were not connected with any political movement, as they were open to all militants without distinction. Yet some committees that were so connected should, nevertheless, be included in the same category. First, there were the action committees against the repression, turned later into Committees for the Support of the People, which, as their name rightly suggests, were run by the Maoists. The latter could claim to be the initiators of such grassroots implantation, since their own basic committees against war in Vietnam had been set up along similar local, neighborhood lines. But the real inspirers of the idea of transcending political nuances through action were the students of Nanterre, and the March 22 Movement sponsored its own Comités d'Action Révolutionnaires (Revolutionary Action Committees) very early in the May crisis.

The frontiers between these various organizations were not very rigid, and it was often by chance that a man seeking an outlet during the crisis joined one instead of another. An abortive attempt was actually made, on June 2, to merge all these committees together. They were all, in their way, part of the May Movement. The same could not be said, for instance, of the Action Committees for a Popular Government of Democratic Union, which, again as the title suggests, were a front organization for the Communist party. Alarmed by the progress of the spontaneous outburst, the Communists launched their committees on May 21, not to push the movement forward, but to channel it into parliamentary waters. The name was the same, the purpose diametrically opposite.

The action committees proper were designed as instruments of struggle. They were advised from the beginning to stick to small groups from ten to thirty people. The only other recommendation provided by the first general assembly was that they must also be political. The meaning of that word was made plain: "They must aim at the overthrow of the regime and the opening of a revolutionary way for the transformation of society." The committees were not concealing their determination to mobilize all those who were not satisfied with the conventional action of the traditional left-wing organizations. "The problem is not to demand a bit more of this or a bit more of that," one of their early leaflets proclaimed, "it is to demand *something else*." As the crisis deepened and the established parties of the French left showed no intention of taking advantage of it for any "transformation of society," the gap between them and the committees deepened, too. Since the Communist party was the only organized force on the left, the committees were bound to enter into conflict with it, whatever their original intentions.

From the very start, the action committees had a problem of their own. They were faced with a dilemma over organization, or, to be more accurate, they had the difficult job of organizing spontaneity. By their very nature they were opposed to bureaucracy; they were born out of a reaction against it. They tried to avoid this danger in their own ranks. There were three types of committees: local committees, based on a small district, a neighborhood; university committees divided by branch; and work committees in factories and offices. Yet all were small enough to meet at least once every couple of days, to make collective decisions and implement them together. Their function was to intervene rapidly whenever required in their own area, to counter official indoctrination, to stir people into thinking and thus spur them to action. If one may apply to them a Communist term, it was largely a job of agit-prop, of agitation and propaganda.

Snags began to occur, along with the growing need for linking the activities of the various committees. Each committee sent delegates to a general assembly, and three such Parisian meetings were held in May. Yet decisions could not be reached easily by such a big and disparate gathering. Besides, it was a most clumsy and slow way for taking initiatives in a situation that required rapid reactions. Plans were therefore drawn to set up intermediate organs, based on the district or branch and regrouping from twenty to fifty committees each. There was not enough time, however, to put such plans into effective practice.

At the middle level, not to say at the top, much scope was

therefore left to an organ plainly called co-ordinating—much scope but little power. The co-ordinating body could issue slogans or calls to action. It was not sure of getting a response. In the draft program it was specified that each action committee would decide on its own whether to follow leads given on a Parisian or national level. As one of the most active members of this co-ordinating organ put it with sober wit: "We were like a central committee but in the sense the word had at the time of the Paris Commune of 1871 . . . without power but with all the initiatives." [3] Things worked all right as long as the main requirements were for explanations, debunking, and counterpropaganda. The co-ordination of committees fulfilled these tasks with skill and imagination. So did the journal *Action,* which became the mouthpiece of the movement. But as events quickened pace, the need was felt for a political platform and lead.

The need was the more urgent since the action committees were torn between two temptations. They could become the nucleus of a new kind of organization, of a new political movement, since they, on the whole, rejected the idea of a party. They could also provide, or rather stimulate, the embryo of parallel power. This was the direction in which they moved first. In a country paralyzed by the general strike they thought that the best way for mobilizing people was to deal with immediate difficulties, starting with such simple tasks as the clearing of garbage or the setting up of kindergartens, and moving on to price control and then to the establishment of a parallel market. Such and similar initiatives did find an echo, but it was quickly found out that in the vacuum that was being created, potential followers were asking for more. They were asking for a political alternative.

When did the activists begin to feel this pressure? Probably after May 24, the Night of the Bourse, when they themselves became aware that the movement was lacking a sense of direction; certainly three days later, when the rejection of the Grenelle compromise by the workers raised the issue of state power in the popular mind. Yet when it came to supplying a political direction,

3. Speaking with the author well after the events.

a platform, a strategy, serious cracks appeared in the action committees. Many members were opposed to the very idea of greater power for a central body, however democratically chosen. Some "grouplets" also saw here the danger of political competition. The reader can be spared the details of squabbles over such apparently trivial issues as the signatures on a poster. The sects had been swallowed by the movement. They had not been digested. It may be added that the attempt to widen and streamline the action committees probably came too late. The general assembly that failed to do it took place on June 2. The tide had already turned.

The action committees did not vanish with the ebb. On the contrary, they were very prominent in the last phase of the crisis. The Communist party was now openly urging the workers to go back, and young men from various committees rushed to help all the remaining pockets of resistance. They were to be found not only in the battle at Flins but also in a host of smaller factories where workers struggled on without much publicity. Indeed, the action committees have not vanished yet. The local committees that had struck stronger roots have survived up to now, obviously in more modest size than in May. By June it was clear that the committees could not relaunch the movement there and then. They were no match for the combined forces of the Gaullist government and the Communist party.

In retrospect it is easy to minimize the importance of the action committees, to claim that organization is all and spontaneity leads nowhere. It is equally easy to stress the heterogeneity and incoherence of the committees, their lack of a strategy, their indecision as to their own role. The fact remains that along with the March 22 Movement they made an original contribution to the May crisis. Their function at that stage was to awaken rather than to lead. Admittedly, their ambitions proved greater than their possibilities. Yet their approach, even their very existence, was a sign of the utter inadequacy of traditional parties for the tasks of our day. Even the hesitation of the committees over the part they had to play—nucleus of a political movement or embryo of parallel power—are symptomatic. Like the slogan *autogestion,* they too have a prophetic air about them. Maybe entirely new forms of organization are required to allow a revolutionary movement to start from below and to begin building socialism at once. Like the soviets of 1905 the *comités d'action* may still prove to have been forerunners of something bigger.

One important reason must still be mentioned for their failure to expand further in May 1968. In a text published at the time by the Censier committee, a rather bold claim was staked: "What one must organize now is the power of the working *classes.*[4] The action committees are the appropriate instrument to achieve this in the present period."

They were not capable in May of organizing the power of the working *class* in the singular. They had more success with students and the radical intelligentsia than with industrial workers. They spread more easily locally, in the various districts of Paris, than in the factories. This does not mean that they made no progress there at all. Far from it. Action committees were formed at Renault, Citroën, in many plants both in Paris and the provinces. They contributed to give dynamism to the strike. But in the factories their activity met the stubborn and organized resistance of the CGT. The counterpower of the Communist party is a factor that cannot be discounted.

4. Italics mine.

WE KNEW *we could not make a revolution without the Communists. We now know we cannot make it with them.*
— *Les Temps Modernes, June 1968*

The Negative Hero

Between the promise of a new French revolution and its fulfillment stands the French Communist party. The PCF has appeared from the beginning of this story as the villain, as the main obstacle to a revolutionary conclusion, or, depending on your standpoint, as the hero, the unexpected pillar of the regime, the surprising darling of the traditional upholders of capitalist society.[1]

---

1. See frequent references to its seriousness, responsibility, sense of the state and of national interest, in such newspapers as *Le Figaro.*

This image is obviously oversimplified. Only in Victorian melodrama or the Zhdanovist versions of "socialist realism" can the protagonists be described thus in black and white. To do it justice, the PCF ought to emerge as the negative hero of this story.

The PCF ought to emerge as a hero because it is the main actor, or if you prefer, nonactor, in the drama, because its role, however passive, was more important for the course of events than the speeches of General de Gaulle, the antics of his ministers, or the marches of his supporters. With its 300,000 or so members, with its five million voters representing between a fifth and a quarter of the French electorate, with the support of the biggest labor confederation, the PCF was, on paper, the only force capable of carrying the May Movement as far as it would go. It was, however, a negative hero, because it failed abysmally in its historic task and actually prevented the movement from gathering momentum. The noun in the definition is a statement of fact, an objective assessment of the party's importance. The adjective is a judgment of value, based on certain standards, indeed on the standards of revolutionary socialism that the PCF claims to incarnate. To put the blame on the Communist party is in a sense a backhanded compliment; it shows that its claims can, or could, still be taken at their face value. The conduct of the PCF provoked surprised relief or indignation. The behavior of the social-democratic FGDS was greeted with unsurprised indifference.

In the Orwellian newspeak of our times some political words have lost all links with their original meaning. Social democracy no longer has any connection with socialism. It is one of the methods, applied usually in moments of stress, for managing the capitalist economy. The point has been made so obvious in Europe by the performance in office of Harold Wilson, Pietro Nenni, and Willy Brandt that it would now require a good dose of naïveté to whip up passion if any of these should miss the opportunity of a revolutionary transformation of society. Mitterrand and Mollet, their French counterparts, belong to the same family. They, too, have served in bourgeois governments and shown

what they were capable of doing.[2] The social-democratic leaders
are now so ostensibly an integral part of the capitalist system that
they are well past the stage of "revolutionary betrayal." The
Communists are not, or not quite.

The PCF is a negative hero because, as we saw earlier, it
partly helped to create a situation in which its revolutionary impotence was revealed. In this respect, the analogy is with German
social democracy, though not with that of today but that of the
years preceding World War I. The comparison is rather flatter-
ing to the French Communists. They have no Kautsky surrounded
by a galaxy of brilliant Marxist scholars. They cannot claim to
have spread socialist education among the masses on a scale even
comparable with the early German achievement. But their rudi-
mentary propaganda has helped to perpetuate a revolutionary
conscience among the workers and a belief in many other sections
of the nation in the hegemonic role of the proletariat. It helped,
therefore, however unwittingly, to prepare the ground for the
May crisis, which found our hero utterly wanting. Yet because
of the political climate of France, the Communist party cannot
admit its bankruptcy as a revolutionary force. In its dealings with
its social-democratic partner, the PCF can now be sweetly reasonable. In its controversies with the new left it has revived old
Stalinist methods, including lies, slander, and fisticuffs. This passionate reaction makes sense. For the first time since its creation
the PCF is faced with a threat from its left.

A party cannot proclaim a state of collective amnesia. It cannot easily forget its recent past. The ultra-leftist slogans that the
party in its new respectable posture condemns with such vehe-
mence are usually its own, often from yesteryear, sometimes from
yesterday. It has not been so long since the Communists were
violent demonstrators against *"Ridgway la peste"* and the main
target of the police. Farther back, Communist militants sat in
jail because of their struggle against colonial rule or against

2. Guy Mollet, for instance, was the Prime Minister during the Suez
expedition and French repression in Algeria before rallying in 1958 to the
victorious General de Gaulle and serving in his first government.

French militarism. Watching young students and workers marching behind their red banners as if they were setting off to conquer
the world, middle-aged Communists cannot help thinking, with
nostalgia or with rage, about their own youth. Their leaders cannot help wondering whether this new wave will not invade their
own territory as they themselves once invaded the territory of
their social-democratic predecessors.

The gray functionaries who now sit at the top of the party
machine were not born functionaries. The oldest of them, like
Benoit Frachon, can retell, admittedly in their own fashion, the
last fifty years of struggle of the French labor movement. Even
a younger man, like Georges Séguy, who cut the most reactionary
figure in the May story, started his political life as a heroic member of the Resistance against the Germans.[3] Lower down in the
hierarchy there are thousands of influential members who, after
some of the party's *volte-faces,* thought they had reached their
Finland Station and yet stayed on in the ranks because on balance this was the only place where they could soldier on, because
with only sects on their left and Mollet's repellent socialist party
on their right, there seemed to be no alternative. The rank and
file had no such qualms of conscience. For a long time they did
not know the seamy side of official Communism and shrugged
off the allegations about it as bourgeois lies. They had accepted
party discipline and in exchange had been offered comradeship,
the dignity of a man who is no plaything of fate, the pride of one
who helps to shape the world's destiny. And they were in safe
hands, since the party was the authorized practitioner of the
"science of revolution."

Critics from both left and right now tend to lump orthodox
Communists as timeservers or seekers after a parallel career.
For most of the membership this assessment is as insulting as it
is dangerously inaccurate. A social climber in France can find
plenty of less awkward and more rewarding ladders. A link with
the party used to be, as a rule, a handicap. For many a working-

3. But he also made his whole union career as a man of the apparatus.
He was climbing simultaneously the rungs of the party and union ladders.

man, membership in the party, or even in the CGT, used to mean the sack. It still means harassment and obstacles to promotion. For most nonmanual workers, the party card is a drawback rather than an asset to advancement. For workers and intellectuals alike, belonging to the party takes up time, requires devotion, involves sacrifices. Undoubtedly the Communist militant resembles less and less Lenin's conception of a professional revolutionary. But he is still different from the member of an ordinary bourgeois party, although the May crisis may speed up the change toward the social-democratic model. What the party machine does to this human material is another matter, but the impulse that drove most members to take the party card is the very opposite of careerism. Even in its Stalinist disguise revolutionary socialism attracted until recently the most dynamic and politically conscious elements among French workers.

In this context the gloomy conclusion drawn by *Les Temps Modernes* in the hour of collapse can be qualified. May did not show that a revolution cannot be carried out with the Communists. It proved that it could not be completed in spite of them, or rather against them. The negative hero was not a clumsy and inefficient participant in the May Movement. It was a conscious opponent, throwing from the start the might of its machine across the path that might have led in a revolutionary direction. We are thus left with the original knowledge that no revolution can hope to succeed in France without Communist support. This, too, must be elaborated. In a revolutionary movement Waldeck Rochet, Georges Séguy, or Georges Marchais can be easily dispensed with. The dynamic forces that still back them cannot— which inevitably raises the question, Why do some of the most politically conscious elements in France still back such a leadership?

Warned by the jingoist bankruptcy of the Second International in 1914, the founders of Communist parties took great pains to avoid a repetition of the mistakes of the past. Since middle-class intellectuals—lawyers, professors, journalists—had so often in the past betrayed or distorted the interests of the labor movement, care was taken to prevent their supremacy. Great emphasis was put on factory cells so as to assure the predominance of the proletarian element in the party.[4] To avoid the embourgeoisement of the dignitaries, the corruption of a new labor aristocracy, the salaries of the highest officials were kept down to the level of a skilled worker. (Communist deputies hand their salary to the party and get in exchange a much smaller allowance.) Yet all these precautions did not prevent a different kind of degeneration. Why?

This is not the place to retrace the detailed history of the PCF, with its chapters of glory and its pages of shame, to set its daily struggle in defense of the workers against the background of the evolution of French capitalism, the absorption of the Socialist party into that system—which all helps to explain why the attraction of the PCF prevailed over its repellent features.[5] The short answer must be that like other Communist parties, it is now paying the price for over a quarter of a century of Stalinism.[6]

After years of ventriloquism it is difficult to recover one's own voice, more difficult still to recapture one's capacity for original thinking after a long spell of imitation. Marxists, seekers after dialectical truth, were turned into peddlers of authorized truth, while Moscow enjoyed a monopoly on orthodox pronouncements. One of the features of monopoly is that when the headquarters

4. Yet in 1967 the works cells accounted for less than 27 per cent of all the cells. For figures and an analysis of the problem see Annie Kriegel, *Les Communistes Français* (Paris, Seuil, 1968).

5. For the insertion of the party into French politics see Jacques Fauvet, *Histoire du Parti Communiste Français,* 2 vols. (Paris, Fayard, 1964–1965). For a brief "ethnographic" study by someone knowing the party literally inside out, see Annie Kriegel, *op. cit.* Also *Le Communisme en France,* a collection of papers (Paris, Librairie Armand Colin, 1969).

6. It is fashionable to write that the PCF was turned bolshevik ("bolshevized") after 1925. Since at that time Stalin had already gained the upper hand in Moscow and since the French party acquired its real shape during Stalin's rule, it is more accurate to speak of its "Stalinization." There is more often than not a political purpose in the preference for "bolshevization" as a term.

fail, all the branches are driven to the wall. This bankruptcy could, and still can, be the source of a revival of creative thinking, without which there is no scope for an autonomous strategy adapted to the tasks of the day. But in the French case such a resurrection is made impossible by the survival of monolithic structures that stifle internal debate.

On paper, democratic centralism allows for a two-way traffic of ideas, for fruitful discussions at all levels within the party, just as the Stalin Constitution of 1936 provided for the exercise of democracy in the Soviet Union. In fact, the theory, like the orders, flows from the top downward. The debate, if any, takes place behind closed doors. From time to time a member of the political bureau is blamed or warned or expelled. A purge reveals a past conflict. A new twist is given with or without explanation. The new line is then handed down with a full blast of propaganda. It is a binding law, but it was not elaborated collectively by the party, and the dissensions within the leadership were given no publicity. In the slightly more relaxed atmosphere of the last few years the cells, or lowest organs of the party, are no longer quietly obedient, and reasons for unrest have not been missing. In 1956, after the double shock of Khrushchev's "secret" indictment of Stalin and of the Hungarian insurrection, and even more in 1968, after the twin shock of the May crisis and the invasion of Czechoslovakia, many cells were shaken by bitter debate. This soul-searching, however, can never transcend the level of the section, the local body just above the cell. The leadership can impose its ideas, isolate the dissenters in their cells, shroud its own divisions in mystery, and prevent any open collective debate that would determine the party line from below.

Stalin's system, if damaging in the long run, was at least more consistent. Moscow was the capital of the socialist fortress. It was also the headquarters of world revolution. The national parties were, in theory, regiments in the army of world revolution; in practice, their function was limited to the defense of the fortress. In any case, it was Moscow, or rather its "leader of genius," who determined strategy and issued orders, which were then transmitted downward. The system was logical and demoralizing. Each Communist party, which in Antonio Gramsci's conception was to be a "collective intellectual," was turned into a collective marcher, or rather into the strangest of puppets, full of its own energy, without which it could not survive, and yet with no mastery over its essential movements. Socialism was supposed to lift the masses, to develop the political consciousness of the workers and thus give them a sense of direction. Stalinism changed this awakening into a disciplined routine. Marching to orders is not sufficient training for finding one's way. When the monolithic system collapsed, Communist parties, guided by nothing more than conditioned reflexes, found themselves in the wilderness.

The price they had to pay was very heavy because when the obsolete and artificially bright façade was partly dismantled, it became plain that all the fundamental problems of socialism in Russia and in the world were still unsolved. Rather than meeting the challenge and tackling the real problems, the PCF chose not to look and not to listen. When Nikita Khrushchev delivered his indictment against Stalin, French Communists tried as long as they could to ignore the "secret" speech, and when this was no longer possible, they seized on the Russian version of the personality cult as a substitute for an analysis of the roots of the trouble. The man who was once the source of all wisdom was now the source of all evil. A balanced judgment would have been a more dangerous exercise.

French Communists backed the Russian intervention in Hungary. They did not combine this support with a thorough analysis of what had gone wrong with a "people's democracy" that after twenty years in power had to face a popular uprising. The PCF took Russia's side throughout the Sino-Soviet conflict, without ever starting a real debate on "peaceful coexistence," which lies at the heart of the quarrel. When the conflict threatened to degenerate into an armed clash, French Communists had a ready answer to the theoretically complicated question of how two socialist countries could have reached such a pass: China had ceased to be socialist, and it was all Mao's fault. (Dialectical materialism used to be accused of underestimating the role of the individual in history. Today its alleged interpreters tend more and more to explain events in purely personal terms.) The Russian invasion of Czechoslokavia, for all sorts of reasons, proved too much even for the faithful French. For the first time in its history the PCF dissociated itself from the Soviet Union on an important issue. It even publicly "deplored" the Russian action. Yet even then it reduced the whole matter to a "mistake." Anything rather than going to the heart of the matter.

On all these major issues the PCF has staged no genuine, open debate in which the two sides of the case could be argued from a socialist viewpoint. Take coexistence as an example. A case for the Russians can be made by underlining the destructive power of nuclear weapons, pointing out the need for caution, and emphasizing the importance of consolidating "socialism in a single block." Conversely, it can be argued that the fear of nuclear weapons should work both ways and that a nuclear stalemate could be used as an umbrella to protect the revolutionary movements in the third world. It is theoretically true that socialism will ultimately have to prove its superiority as a more advanced form of economic and social organization. It is equally true that there is at least a potential contradiction between coexistence with the United States and maximum aid for revolutionary movements in Asia or Latin America struggling against American imperialism. The argument could be continued, yet to raise it at all is to question a basic principle inherited from the Stalinist era, namely that the interests of world revolution and of the Soviet Union are identical. How could it be otherwise, since Russia is a socialist state? Once started, the debate leads logically to the rejection of an even bigger taboo.

If Russia is a full-fledged socialist state, the crimes of the Stalin era must be explained as the ravings of a madman, and the invasion of Czechoslovakia must become a "mistake"—two explanations highly unsatisfactory to a Marxist. If the Soviet Union is simply a "postcapitalist" state with some socialist features, the situation alters radically. The critical tools of Marxist analysis can be applied to its society. Its policies, whether domestic or foreign, are no longer progressive by definition; nothing can be taken for granted.[7] One can no longer get away with a story about the initial difficulties of backwardness, encirclement, and so on. What matters now is whether or not Russia's present institutions and policies are an obstacle to its socialist development. The role of the bureaucracy, the state that does not wither away, the absence of a workers' democracy—these are some of the questions that require analysis. They are also some of the crucial questions of our time. In refusing to raise them in the Russian context, a Communist party deprives itself of an opportunity to discuss its own postcapitalist prospects. It is unable to construct an up-to-date model for the transition to socialism and, by the same token, cannot really take on leadership at home.

French Communists took a long time to grasp the consequences of the post-Stalin era. At first, as we saw, they were more Stalinist than Khrushchev and tried to ignore the change. Then their attention was absorbed by domestic problems. The PCF can now proudly proclaim that in 1958 it was the only big party to oppose the Gaullist takeover. But all the same, at the time General de Gaulle's victory was a great defeat for the Communists. It cost them votes and seats and increased their isolation. The isolation, on the other hand, had the advantage of not raising problems. Things changed suddenly in 1962, when a general election showed that the Gaullists, by swallowing the other conservative groups, were emerging as a potential majority party. In purely electoral terms this meant that the divided left would always remain in opposition. Guy Mollet, the veteran socialist leader, had been until then one of the most virulent anti-Communists in Europe. But he could also count, and his arithmetic led him to make a spectacular *volte-face*. Between two ballots in the same election Communists and socialists improvised popular-front alliances, standing down in favor of each other. More was to come. For the presidential election of December 1965 the Communists agreed

7. This, incidentally, does not rule out the principle of the defense of postcapitalist Russia against a capitalist attack.

not to put up a candidate of their own and to back François Mitterrand as the candidate of a united left without any prior agreement on a common program. For the general election of March 1967 the Communists actually signed an electoral pact with the recently created FGDS.

This was not the first time that French Communists had entered bourgeois politics. They had backed the popular-front government of socialists and Radicals in 1936 and had put their own men in office under the three-party coalition after the last war. At the time, however, it could have been argued that their tactics were to a large extent determined by Moscow's over-all strategy. Now the PCF had to make up its own mind. The parallelism between its own soft line and the Soviet coexistence line was largely a coincidence. French Communists now had to decide on their own how far they were willing to get involved in the running of a capitalist society. The electoral pact they had signed with the FGDS was merely a catalogue of points of agreement. When they came to working out a program of government, the potential partners had even more difficulties with foreign than with domestic policy. True, they differed, for instance over the amount of nationalization, since the Communists naturally asked for more than the FGDS. Still, a bargain could be struck on this issue, as it was implicitly agreed that a popular-front government would manage a "mixed," that is, a predominantly capitalist, economy.

What was implicit on the home front could not be so easily concealed in foreign affairs. The Communists' social-democratic partners were both "Atlantic" and "European." In the political climate prevailing in France at the time, they were probably resigned to toning down their pro-Americanism. They were not ready to make any important concessions over Europe. For the Communists, on the other hand, to accept the liberal framework of the Common Market was publicly to admit that they were ready to act as the reformist managers of capitalism. They weren't quite.

Still, events were pushing them in that direction. The alliance of 1967 was a semisuccess. The prospect of a popular-front victory in the next election was a genuine one. Thus the Communist leaders were thinking in electoral terms when the May crisis faced them with an entirely new situation. We saw earlier how they sacrificed all revolutionary potentialities for the sake of the shadow of a popular-front government. Scarcely was the crisis over when the Russian invasion of Czechoslovakia threatened their opening to the right. If they had not blamed the Russian move, they would have found themselves without any perspective, either revolutionary or reformist. Their historic refusal to toe the Moscow line was not, therefore, so surprising. Whatever its motives, it might have marked the beginning of a healthy departure, the opening of a useful debate. There was a great need for explanations. Many faithful members, particularly of the older generation, who had been taught for years that the land of the workers, the socialist fatherland, could do no wrong, were deeply shocked. A collective discussion would have been the only sound treatment. The leadership chose the opposite course of hushing up the whole affair and blaming the "extremists." Roger Garaudy, who had backed the Dubček regime too loudly, was warned to keep quiet. Jeannette Veermersh, widow of the party's chief leader, Maurice Thorez, resigned from the political bureau to express her disagreement with the new line and her fidelity to Moscow. And that was it.

Not entirely. Alarmed by the unrest spreading in the cells, the leaders decided on a period of retrenchment. The popular front that they had sponsored with such zeal vanished temporarily from the horizon. The FGDS fell to pieces, and time was needed to put it together under some new label. In the meantime, the PCF was able to harden its line, at least on paper. In November 1968, at the end of a special session of its central committee held at Champigny, it proclaimed that the "peaceful road" to socialism should not be confused with an exclusively "parliamentary road." Forgetting its own performance in May, it now spoke of the decisive action of the masses. Under the new slogan of "advanced democracy" it produced an indigestible hodgepodge with liberal ingredients borrowed from its socialist allies and the classless concept of the "state of the whole people" clearly pinched from Stalin's epigones. What this new Communist program, bearing the proudly evocative title Manifesto, showed above all was a state of intellectual disarray that could no longer be concealed by Stalinist orthodoxy. A western Communist party stifling all original research to fill the vacuum,[8] not even trying to perform the function of a "collective intellectual," is now the victim of two dominant ideologies, not just one. Its mind is split between the all-pervading ideology of its capitalist environment and the ideas of Russia's ruling bureaucracy.

That the refusal to allow any creative research was a deliberate policy was confirmed almost immediately. At the end of 1968, shaken in their convictions by the presence of Soviet troops in Prague, a number of Communist intellectuals, predominantly "liberal" or "rightist," decided to take a new look at some of the fundamental questions of our day. Together with some faithful fellow-travelers and a few sympathetic social-democrats, they founded a monthly magazine, *Politique Aujourd'hui*. It was a cautious, almost an innocuous, affair, which threatened no more than some friendly criticism of the party line. But it could be the thin end of the wedge, and the leadership reacted vigorously by requiring all party members to sever their links with the journal. They were asked to do so on the apparently reasonable ground that the Communists should present a united front to the outside world and thrash out their differences within the party. The tragicomedy of it all is that Communist intellectuals were driven to seek an outside platform because of the absence of inner debate.[9]

8. An exception can be made for Louis Althusser and his followers, whose ambition is to restore the original thought of Marx. After years of accretions and falsification this could be a valuable performance. Yet, once cleaned, the tools are for use and Althusser cannot use them without clashing with the party line; hence his silence, or trite orthodox pronouncements, on all key contemporary issues from the Sino-Soviet conflict to the May crisis.

9. The way in which Roger Garaudy was removed from all his posts at the party's Nineteenth Congress at Nanterre in February 1970 does not alter the diagnosis. True, for once, the accused was allowed to speak in his defense. But the case was prejudged. The leadership had condemned

In the hour of mortal danger, in 1918, when the Germans were at the throat of the young Soviet republic, the Bolsheviks were not afraid to start an open and bitter controversy over the Peace of Brest-Litovsk. What is the PCF so secretive about? Is it afraid that its intellectuals will reveal the route of an illegal demonstration, the hiding place of some underground fighters, the date and plans of an insurrection? Let us be serious. All they can reveal are the shaky ideological foundations of the party. The aging bureaucratic leaders are consistent in excommunicating dissenters. They are fighting for their own conception of the party, in which truth is revealed from above, the leadership can do no wrong, and nothing creative can come from below—the conception of a party unable to lead a socialist resurrection.

When Stalin's statue was toppled from its pedestal, when the international Communist monolith was subsequently shaken by Chinese blows, there were great hopes of a socialist revival. There was also much talk of each country seeking its own way to socialism. Whether the search for socialist solutions can be confined to national frontiers is another matter. The great opportunity was not seized. Having failed to provide themselves with the structural means for seeking a new direction, the Communist parties of western Europe now stand bewildered at the crossroads between the neo-Stalinist blind alley and the old beaten track of social democracy.

The conduct of the PCF in May 1968 was no aberration, no slip by a revolutionary party that misjudged a situation. It was the natural behavior of an organization intrinsically incapable of evolving a revolutionary strategy. Crippled by the organizational structures and habits inherited from the Stalinist era, the PCF is in no position to assume a hegemonic role. It cannot, to repeat Marx's quotation, enforce the interests of the French proletariat

---

his heretical views (see Roger Garaudy, *Le Grand Tournant du Socialisme* [Paris, Gallimard, 1969]) and the debate was simply to confirm this verdict. Not one of the 960 delegates at Nanterre dared to speak in his favor or against the party line. The manner is slightly different, but the substance unchanged.

"as the revolutionary interests of society itself." It is unable to
foreshadow a different kind of society or outline means for achiev-
ing it, and by the same token it is unable to harness the discontent
expressed in the cultural revolution or to attract the growing radical elements within the professional intelligentsia. In short, the
PCF seems to have outlived its historically progressive function.
Here lies the second analogy with German social democracy.
Future historians may treat the May crisis as a revelation of the
real state of the PCF, as the outbreak of World War I was for
the outwardly healthy German social-democratic party.

An actor no longer fit for his role need not necessarily leave
the political stage. He can be recast. He can keep his part, preserving the illusion that he is carrying on, until a vigorous newcomer pushes him aside and takes over. Thanks to force of habit,
but also to its experience, its apparatus, the devotion of its militants, the importance of its daily work, the PCF can preserve the
illusion and continue to perform as the "false conscience" of the
French proletariat. How long it will manage to do so depends on
the pressure of outside events and the stature of the would-be
competitor. May revealed embryonic forces on the party's left
and stirrings within its own ranks sufficient to frighten, though
not to budge, the leadership. Indeed, May confirmed the lesson
that a social upheaval can only be successful if it draws the millions still influenced by the PCF, and therefore paralyzed, into
the mainstream of the revolutionary movement.

Can this transformation be achieved from within or from without? The question is one of practical politics, not of morals or
principle. The theoretical work, the proper assessment of the
balance of power and the movement of social forces, is vital. Yet
the best theoretical workshop will prove of little use if its products cannot be submitted to practical tests involving contact with
the masses. The best channels for such contact will vary from
country to country and differ depending on whether one tackles
the union or the party political front. Take France and its labor
unions. The revolutionary socialists had several opportunities to
continue their efforts after May. Most of them decided to brave

the Communist control of the CGT and to remain in touch with the most active workers in the biggest confederation. Some opted for the greater freedom of maneuver offered by Force Ouvrière. And yet others chose to exploit the opportunities provided by the leftist temptations of the CFDT. Whether these various trends will one day merge, along with comparable trends among teachers, technicians, and researchers, to form a single union is a matter of time and of the progress achieved in their respective fields. A new labor confederation cannot be built overnight. Nevertheless, considering the influence exercised on the May-June strike by small "grouplets," by a handful of activists, bigger pockets of militants within all the unions could change the shape of the next crisis. Trade-union bosses are not unaware of their new predicament.

At the party level, the question is tactically different. The problem for the revolutionary militant is whether he can exercise any influence within the organization and whether the organization is worth influencing. Thus, for instance, although the Labour party in Britain does not impose strict discipline on its members, it has been turned into an electoral machine with little hold on the real political life of the country and no bearing on the policies of its own government. Each case, in fact, must be treated on its merits. Even the two big Communist parties of western Europe—the French and the Italian—do not present revolutionary socialists with the same dilemma and, therefore, with the same choice. For all sorts of historical reasons connected with the development not only of the country, but also of the party itself—the intellectual influence of Gramsci, the long period of underground activity during the fascist era, with less direct control from Moscow, the adroit leadership of the subtle Palmiro Togliatti—the Italian Communist Party (Partito Comunista Italiano, or PCI) was never so rigidly Stalinist as its French counterpart, and for that very reason was better prepared for the transition.

More flexible, more tolerant, the PCI is usually also described as "softer," less "revolutionary" than the PCF. This oversimplified judgment rests on the unfounded assumption that a certain

freedom of discussion, a clash of ideas, favors the right within
the Communist movement. Neither the assessment nor the premise
stands the test of facts if one compares the development of the
French and Italian parties. When the leader of the right within
the Italian party, Giorgio Amendola, floated the idea of a reuni-
fication of the working-class movement, arguing that both socialists and Communists had made errors in the past, and his venture
was clearly leading in the direction of parliamentary reformism,
the protests throughout the party were so loud that he was forced
into a hasty retreat. In general terms, the more monolithic organization of the French party makes it possible for the leadership
to march its followers to the right with only a whisper of protest,
whereas the Italian hierarchy would run the risk of an outcry.
Luigi Longo, the middle-of-the-road party secretary, or Enrico
Berlinguer, his deputy and heir, know that they have to reckon
with their left—if not so much with Pietro Ingrao, the left's
spokesman within the leadership, then with his more radical supporters. If they dared to behave as preposterously as their French
colleagues behaved in May, they would run the risk of an open
split in the party, and such a threat might be enough to affect their
decision. In fact, the PCI has so far taken an incomparably more
flexible and conciliatory position toward the students and the
spontaneous strike movements.

Actually, it is the Communist new left that has the intellectual
initiative inside the PCI, that stirs up ferment and forces the party
to think. Its spokesmen, though not numerous, turned the party's
twelfth congress—in February 1969 in Bologna—from a traditional ritual into an event that will mark a date in the post-Stalinist development of international Communism. Luigi Pintor, in an
original analysis of his country's position, argued that class struggle in Italy had shifted from trench warfare into a war of movement, imposing new tasks for a party determined to be the chief
revolutionary force. Among its duties, he mentioned the weaving
of a pattern of workers' democracy, linked with the students and
trying to act as a "counterpower"; the search, not for accidental
allies, but for partners ready to endorse a similar strategy; the

elaboration of new forms and new content for socialism in advanced countries. The Soviet model was openly proclaimed inadequate in its conception as well as its application. Where he left off, another member of the central committee, Rossana Rossanda, picked up the thread in a speech that would have been even less imaginable in the French party on a similar occasion. She based her argument on two points: first, the significance of peaceful coexistence and its relationship to revolutionary developments; second, the lessons to be drawn from the Czech conflict. Refusing to treat the invasion as an "error," she was led to question the nature of the Soviet system and to reject the Khrushchevian treatment of its ailments as inadequate because it did not deal with the roots of the illness. Thus, all the fundamental questions of a socialist revival, which it is normally the aim of a Communist Congress to drown in a sea of words and messages of congratulation, were put plainly on the agenda.

It remains to be seen how far the new left within the PCI will be allowed to seek the answers, to brush aside all taboos in its search, to publish its findings, to advocate new methods; in short, to change the nature of the party through its theoretical and practical advance.[10] For a revoluntionary socialist in Italy the question of whether he can accomplish his task within the Communist party is still an open one. In France, May provided the final answer, shattering all previous illusions. Under the prevailing rules the leadership cannot be shaken from below. The voice of protest cannot echo beyond the level of the party cells. The dissenter, who does not dare to defy the rules for fear of excommunication, might as well stop deceiving himself that he is work-

10. Barely were these lines written when the leadership of the PCI proved that even the flexible Italian party could not tolerate such a revival. In a special session, in November 1969, its central committee decided to "cancel the party membership" of Rossana Rossanda, Aldo Natoli, and Luigi Pintor—all three members of the committee—and of Lucio Magri, coeditor with Rossanda of *Il Manifesto,* the monthly review launched the previous June to express the views of the new Communist left. It is still too early to say how deep is the current crisis within the PCI. For a summary of the events leading up to the exclusion, see *Il Manifesto,* Numero 7, December 1969.

ing toward a revolutionary transformation of society. The lesson
of May seems plain. The PCF will not change—its nature and
not just its line—without a major external shock combined with
an open revolt from below, breaking the rules and sweeping aside
the existing structures as well as the leadership. The heretic may
stay inside the party by force of habit, to carry on his daily tasks
or because he sees no alternative. If he is waiting for a smooth
internal transition, he might as well be waiting for the Redeemer.

Even if it is accepted that our negative hero has outlived his
historic function, allowance must be made for one important
exception. The PCF may still play a leading part in a defensive
action. Its capacity for rear-guard struggle is not really surprising. Self-imposed intellectual paralysis has prevented the Communists from coming to grips with their new capitalist environment. Unable to work out an up-to-date strategy, they have been
in no position to launch an effective offensive against neocapitalism. The party has, on the other hand, been able to resist the
daily encroachments of neocapitalism and to fight its biggest battles in defense of existing society: against fascism in the 1930's,
against Nazism in the Resistance, and, less successfully, against
the Algerian settlers and colonels in 1958. Considering the absence
of a revolutionary perspective among French Communists, it is
not entirely paradoxical that they should feel most at ease in patriotic dress, clad in the tricolor as the leading defenders of bourgeois democracy. They probably could take up this struggle
tomorrow if France were threatened with a regime of colonels.

Fascism is not yet looming on the French horizon. The economy does not look like collapsing. The middle classes, however
discontented, do not seem ready to run amok and cannot put the
blame for their trouble on "Marxist parties" in power. The classic
ingredients are still missing. Yet if France were to be threatened
with a fascist or semifascist regime, the Communist party would
be among its first targets. When big business resigns itself to such
a solution as a last resort, it must be determined to break any
form of labor organization, however cautious, orderly, and mod-

erate. The Communist party and the Communist-dominated union, for all their lack of revolutionary zeal, remain the main ramparts of French labor. Hitler did not spare German social democracy. French colonels would be bound to strike at the PCF.

Left-wing divisions have always helped to pave the way for fascism. German social democracy wrote some of its most shameful pages after World War I. Afterward the Stalinists committed the folly of equating Nazism with social democracy as "twin evils." If history teaches anything, the militants of May will not repeat the same folly. Nor will they repay the Communists in their own coin, keeping silent with a smile if the PCF should be banned, as the French Communists kept silent when the "grouplets" were outlawed. A ban on the mass Communist party would mean the proclamation of a totalitarian regime. The PCF could still turn out to be the leading force in the struggle against the colonels. The negative hero, or rather his devoted supporters, could once again prove his capacity for heroic action.

Le fascisme ne passera pas, Non passeran. . . . These defensive slogans have often been the tragic prelude to defeat. Even if in France they were to be, as in the thirties, the slogans of a successful resistance, the PCF is ill equipped to turn defensive into offensive, to switch from the defense of bourgeois democracy to the battle for socialism. Yet this is the task that the French spring has put on Europe's agenda. The crisis has suggested that a socialist movement can get hold of power in an advanced capitalist country if only it can show what it will do with it, if through its action and inner behavior it foreshadows the beginnings of a new society. The negative hero may still be able to fight the battles of yesteryear. May has revealed a fleeting glimpse of Europe's future.

THE THEFT *of somebody else's labor time, on which wealth now rests, appears a miserable base compared with the one big industry creates and develops itself. When labor in its immediate form ceases to be the main source of wealth, working time will cease and will have to cease to be the measure of work. . . . The surplus labor of the masses will no longer be the condition for the development of general wealth as the leisure of the few will cease to be the condition for the full development of the human brain. . . .*

Real wealth is the full development of the productive force of all individuals. Hence, its measure will be disposable time and not working time. To take working time as the standard of wealth, it is to base wealth on poverty and to treat free time only by opposition to surplus labor; it means reducing time as a whole to working time and degrading the individual to the simple role of working man, dominated by his labor. . . .

The real economy consists in saving labor time. . . . Saving working time means increasing free time, that is, time devoted to the full development of the individual who is the supreme productive power and who, in turn, acts upon productive forces. . . . Free time—which is at once leisure and superior activity—will naturally transform its beneficiary into a different individual and it is as such that he will re-enter the process of production. . . .

—KARL MARX,
Grundrisse der Kritik der Politischen Ökonomie

DO NOT *consume Marx.*

—*May slogan*

PART FIVE
In Search of the Future

NOBODY PRETENDS *that democracy is perfect or full wise. Indeed, it has been said that democracy is the worst form of government except all those other forms that have been tried from time to time.*

—WINSTON CHURCHILL

WE HAVE NEVER BEEN IDOL WORSHIPERS *of formal democracy. Nor have we ever been idol worshipers of socialism or Marxism either. . . . [We] have always revealed the hard kernel of social inequality and lack of freedom hidden under the sweet shell of formal equality and freedom—not in order to reject the latter but to spur the working class into not being satisfied with the shell, but rather, by conquering political power, to create a socialist democracy to replace bourgeois democracy —not to eliminate democracy altogether.*

—ROSA LUXEMBURG

The End of Marginalism

They propose nothing and respect nothing. They are vandals who can only destroy. At their age we were fighting for God and Country. With no such outlet for their aggressive instincts, the youngsters of today are just wrecking for the sake of wrecking, for the fun of it. The student rebels are ungrateful nihilists.

Translated into French or German, Italian or Japanese, the indictment required no more than idiomatic variations. Everywhere the tune was the same. But as the culprits were not im-

299

pressed, as they failed to respond to the appeals of liberal preachers, the tone got harsher. By now the young rebels are no longer
simply hooligans. They are Red fascists and left-wing Nazis.[1]

The main sin of the rebels is that they do not respect the established rules of the game. The increasing anger with which their
exploits are greeted is the anger of the managers of a well-run
gambling house faced with intruders who accuse them publicly
of cheating. But this is a legitimate business, they retort with indignation, blessed by the Church and the moralists, not only
squared with the authorities but devised in collaboration with
them. Everything looked so quiet and safe. Even the victims
seemed to consent. They could grumble. They never dared to
question the complicated rules and regulations. Although the
takings might vary from year to year, the profitable game was
destined to last for ever. Its organizers were entitled to believe
that they had found the magic formula to fool most of the people
all of the time. But suddenly the intruders barged in, threatening
to upset the painfully constructed system.

No wonder the violent attacks against the disrespectful outsiders sounded more or less the same all over the world, since
those horrible intruders had dared to take on the international
capitalist syndicate and expose its tricks in different countries.
They had loudly proclaimed that the French emperor was naked,
that British democracy was a sham and the American dream a
fraud. They did something more dangerous. They publicly de-
nounced the rules of the game as twisted, as designed to produce
one possible result. Heads—you win, tails—we lose; we're not
playing. As in France and Italy young workers echoed the slogan
of the subversive students, all those with a stake in the capitalist
racket began to take the threat seriously. If such ideas were allowed to spread, the game would be up.

1. The sincerity of such accusations can best be gathered in Germany,
where many righteous critics are former members of the Nazi party.

The Rules of the Game

Soviet Communism tolerates no internal opposition to its system. The western powers, whatever their colonial exports, reserve "democracy" for domestic consumption. Is it then fair to suggest that here, too, devices more subtle than the Russian guarantee the survival of the system, that is, the perpetuation of capitalism? After all, conflicting parties can put out propaganda, seek popular support, compete in elections. Indeed, in western Europe, socialist parties have actually been voted into office. But the answer does not lie in a name. The test lies in what a party does and what it is allowed to achieve if it sticks to the rules.

Take a nominally socialist party or a left-wing coalition assuming office in, say, Britain or France. The odds are that it was voted into power after the bankruptcy of a conservative government. Its official task is, therefore, to increase production, cut down consumption, and encourage exports. Pundits will give it friendly advice to introduce an incomes policy, which in plain language means to freeze wages or at least to keep them in check. If, fresh from its electoral victory, the government is still sufficiently confident, it may be "radical" enough to bring dividends under control as well as wages; dividends, but not profits, since higher profits are the main source of bigger investment. The fact that a government elected to defend the interests of labor is thus driven to protect capitalist privileges is perfectly logical. It is one of the rules of the game.

A left-wing government cannot follow a middle course for long. It is rapidly forced to decide whether it is going to work within the system. If it decides that it will, it is bound to move from surrender to surrender. The expert advice is right. A capitalist economy can only be run on capitalist lines. A "socialist" government sticking to the rules of the game can only be marginally different from its conservative predecessor. If it should depart from the pattern and attack the vital interests of the business community, it would have to take increasingly radical steps to resist the counteroffensive launched by domestic capitalism and its foreign allies. Before the war, many members of the Labour party, such as Professor Harold Laski, doubted that the ruling class in Britain would stick to parliamentary rules if its vital interests were threatened. It proved an abstract debate. In principle, the British House of Commons can decree that all the redheaded men in Great Britain should be sentenced to jail. In practice, a Labour majority in the House cannot hurt business interests sufficiently to put the issue to the test. The 1960's, with a Labour government in Britain and socialists in office in Germany and Italy, have dispelled the last remaining illusions about the threat these parties allegedly represent to the capitalist establishment. The differences between Europe and the United States in this respect are merely quantitative. American capitalism does not require the services of social democracy to integrate its working class.

These parties do not attack the system because they have no popular mandate to do so—thus runs the official argument. (It is, incidentally, amusing to note that when a left-wing government carries out a right-wing policy nobody bothers about its mandate.) As the self-perpetuating nature of the western system became more obvious on both sides of the Atlantic and led to more direct attacks against the foundations of capitalist society, its defenders donned the mantle of democracy and branded the iconoclasts as men with no respect for the rule of law and the rule of the majority. It is significant that this outburst of liberal wrath was not sufficient this time to frighten and silence the radical minority. On the contrary, it was greeted with derisive laughter and a polemical verve reminiscent of the old days of socialist self-confidence.

We are glad to learn—retorted the radical critics—that Messrs. Rockefeller and Rothschild have no more right than the poorest of their fellow citizens to sleep on the benches in the park, and we highly appreciate this equality before the law, but do you imply that because these gentlemen have no more than one ballot paper each, they have no more influence on lawmaking than any Tom, Dick, or Harry? Do you venture to suggest that any workingman or student can found a newspaper empire and sway public opinion like Hearst, Lord Thomson, or Springer? Do you dare to suggest that in this age of mass manipulation, when advertising can sell any product, money can buy everything except political power? [2]

A century ago the call for universal suffrage made rulers tremble. Now, at least in the western world, it appears to be the rallying cry for the upholders of the status quo. The paradox is important. The argument carries weight. It sways the judgment of millions of decent and honest people who have no privileges to defend. In their opinion, the radical students may have a strong case; the young revolutionary workers may be the standard-bearers of the future, but this does not entitle them to ignore the will of the majority, the will of the people. One man, one vote, is too precious a principle to be squandered. Since this is a most telling argument, let us stop for a moment to see how this precious principle really functions in our society.

To pick on Gaullist France—with its television openly used as an instrument of government propaganda, its semiofficial candidates backed by the administration, and so on—would be too easy a test and therefore unconvincing. The liberals would approve the indictment and conclude that nothing was proved except that Gaullism was not a model of democracy. So let us take Britain, the birthplace of parliamentary democracy, where the Labour party is supposedly free from procapitalist bias, and a lady, Barbara Castle, who rose to fame on the progressive or Bevanite wing of the labor movement. In 1969, as Minister of Production, she showed such passion for democracy that she de-

2. They occasionally dare. In June 1969, during the French electoral campaign, Jean-Jacques Servan-Schreiber appeared on television to praise the virtue of the Swedish formula. The gist of his argument was that the rich should keep their economic power and the poor should be compensated with political power. As the author of the *Défi Americain* preached this doctrine with real conviction, one wondered what to admire— his innocence or his hypocrisy. The same premise, incidentally, is to be found in the much advertised manifesto he produced in 1970 as the new program of the old Radical party.

cided to spread it to industrial relations.[3] To prevent wildcat strikes, a cooling-off period was to be introduced and a ballot taken among the men to decide by majority rule whether to strike or not. Let us forget that Tory enthusiasm for this introduction of compulsory balloting into a factory had rather undemocratic motivations.[4] The idea itself sounds reasonable. A strike is an important act for a worker, and therefore it seems fair that a decision to embark on one should be taken collectively by a majority vote.

But why stop there? Let us imagine that a government, in its zeal for democracy, tries to extend it to the boardrooms, to impose a compulsory vote on all major decisions concerning investment, profits, wages, job evaluation, assembly lines, and so on. The principle of the vote would no longer be one man, one vote, but one share, one vote. Let us proceed still farther. The strikes are only a reaction to the very decisions mentioned above. The workers are very much concerned about them, yet it would not cross the mind of our zealous democrats to register the workers on the electoral lists of the firm and then apply the rule of one man, one vote.[5] Where real power is at stake, we are still living in the era of suffrage qualified by wealth.

Periodically, every four or five years, the omnipotent citizens are given the right to choose between Humphon and Nixrey, between Ted Wilson and Harold Heath, between Pom-poher and Pom-pidou. In principle they are not compelled to elect a candidate of the "consensus," yet this is where double insurance guar-

3. The project, presented under the title *In Place of Strife*, visibly inspired by Nye Bevan's *In Place of Fear*, had finally to be dropped because the resistance of the labor movement proved stronger than its leaders had reckoned.

4. Two of the biggest labor unions had switched from right-wing to left-wing leadership. It was no longer possible to rely on their bosses to prevent strike action.

5. The idea of a vote by the workers would make sense in Russia, where private property was abolished. Unfortunately, there are no signs there of the advent of a workers' democracy. The snag with Britain's Labour government is that it defends the so-called national interest, but would like to be treated by the workers as their own, as the representative of the working class. The ambiguity works, but only for a time.

antees the survival of the capitalist system. In the first stage, the forces of capital are kept intact, and in the second, they in turn can use the power of wealth to influence public opinion so as to prevent a clear anticapitalist mandate from being given and, certainly, from being carried out.

What looked like safety to the rulers appeared a vicious circle to their radical opponents. The road toward a majority seemed blocked. Yet when a political system cannot be conquered from within, pressure builds up to attack it from without. This has begun to happen throughout the western world. At first, the non-parliamentary opposition tried to expose what was really going on. Resistance was designed to reveal the repressive nature of the regime, the seamy side of the liberal façade. It was rapidly driven to direct action at the grassroots. In general elections or presidental polls the exploited are easily taken in by the correct-sounding slogans produced by the smooth and mighty party machines. The center of power is distant, the issues at stake somewhat abstract and easily distorted. Men cannot be deceived so easily in their own environment, in matters concerning their daily work and life. The struggle was gradually switched to the lecture hall, the office, the shop floor. Democracy had to be reconquered starting at the base. The new radical opposition, seeking a way out of its dilemma, stumbled on the basic difference between the revolutionary and the reformer: "Not through a majority to revolutionary tactics, but through revolutionary tactics to a majority —that is the way the road runs." [6]

It also ran straight into the liberal framework of capitalist society. As long as the opposition was keeping to the rules, it was not only tolerated. It was welcome and almost indispensable for the working of the system. It gave warning of tensions, allowed concessions to be made on time, and provided a temporary alternative when inner pressures reached too dangerous a level. The loyal opposition was all that, and it was harmless too. It helped the system to change, to adapt itself to new circumstances, without ever threatening its foundations. The new radical opposition

6. The formula is Rosa Luxemburg's.

offered a different challenge and got a different response. The advocates of global, as opposed to marginal, change, hailed from the start as the enemies of freedom, have since then been branded as the evil apostles of violence.

Our rulers and their spokesmen have not been converted to Gandhiism overnight. There is violence and violence. The millions of bombs poured over Vietnam can be described as Indian *ahimsā,* nonviolent resistance; so can the hundreds of thousands of alleged Communists murdered in Indonesia as an incident in the re-establishment of democracy; the American paratroopers sent to the Dominican Republic as messengers of freedom. Men who through their perfectly legal investments prop up apartheid in South Africa are "honorable gentlemen," while the students who in ungentlemanly fashion try to prevent them from doing it are "fascist thugs." Nor is this a classic example confirming that you can be a scoundrel abroad as long as you behave decently in your home town. "Thou hast committed fornication, but that was in another country and anyhow the wench is dead." Similar double standards are being applied to the domestic situation.

That in most countries five per cent of the population owns three quarters of a nation's wealth,[7] that everything is designed to preserve the interests of this minority, that the owners of capital, their associates, and their servants determine the rhythm of our work, shape our lives, condition the pattern of our behavior —this hardly concealed dictatorship is taken for granted and treated as a realm of freedom. Any outburst against this repressive society is branded as violence. A gate broken at the London School of Economics, a lecture interrupted at the Sorbonne, a building occupied at Columbia, let alone a factory occupied by the workers—these are subjects for hysterical headlines and bouts of indignation. Violence is not measured by the amount of force used or the degree of coercion exercised. It is measured by its conformity to the law. It is virtue if it helps to prop up the

7. The proportion is for Britain in 1960. But it does not differ much either across western frontiers or across time. The concentration is even more striking when stockholding is analyzed.

established order, and a horrible vice when directed against it. Pick up your paper, switch on your television set, and you will find countless examples of such double standards. Only it is not easy to discard our distorted spectacles. As Bertolt Brecht put it:

> One blames the swift current for its violence,
> But no one speaks of any violence
> When the banks tighten the current between them.

Whatever its future performance, the new radical opposition has at least made public the secret of the game. It has done so by completing the Churchillian quip: Parliamentary democracy is better to perpetuate capitalist rule than "all those other forms that have been tried from time to time."

Even so qualified, the proposition is probably not universally valid and certainly not accepted by all. Gaullism, for instance, was initially greeted with enthusiasm in many quarters as a more up-to-date method for preserving a capitalist regime.

Servitudes of Gaullist Grandeur

Nothing fails like failure. Shattered by the May explosion, the discarded Gaullist model is now treated with such indifference or contempt that it is hard to remember that not so long ago it was being held up as an example. We are not referring here to Gaullist foreign policy, to General de Gaulle's abortive attempt to break the American hegemony, which had so mixed up his critics and his admirers that Gaullist or anti-Gaullist became outside France the most deceptive tests of political complexion. We are talking about Gaullism as an institution, as a method of political rule, which once excited the envy of many outsiders. If only we had our General, was a sigh often heard in Rome and even in London a few years ago.

This bout of Gaullist flu was obviously linked with the more general parliamentary disease, of which the Fourth Republic was not the only victim. Everywhere elected national assemblies are

increasingly inadequate to cope with the workings of a modern
state. Parliaments used to provide room for the settlement of
conflicting interests between the landed gentry and the growing
capitalist class, then between the upper and lower sections of the
bourgeoisie. They even managed to fit labor movements into the
system. Yet being suited to the needs of a more or less liberal
capitalism, they have not adapted themselves and look rather
obsolete in the era of monopolistic competition.

The big corporations, with their administered prices and very
heavy investments spread over a period of time, require a special
framework to function comfortably. They need guarantees of a
certain stability, insurances against serious labor unrest and
against big swings of the trade cycle. In order to go on making
its profits, big business requires a strong state. It is the role of this
state to provide the necessary education or to relieve dangerous
tensions through the social services. Its function is also to introduce a degree of coherence, of planning, into the economy with
the help of a huge budget boosted by high military expenditure.
State intervention in the economic and social life of the nation is
now incomparably greater than in the nineteenth century, but the
elected assemblies have not kept pace with this evolution. Whatever their legal competence, nowhere are they in effective control
of what is really determining the life of the country. For socialists,
who want to abolish capitalism, the inability of the assemblies to
keep it in check reduces parliament to a talking shop. For many
technocrats, concerned with the efficient functioning of the existing system, the highly inadequate parliament is still an interfering
nuisance. It is to them, to the ideologists of technocracy, that
Gaullism appeared for a while as a more up-to-date or superior
system of rule.

Unlike Napoleon III General de Gaulle needed no great-uncle.
He had a legend of his own. He had reconquered power despite
the opposition of the labor unions and the Communist party. He
had tamed the workers and exercised a Bonapartist attraction
over some of them. His system of plebiscitary democracy—with
occasional referenda legitimizing his claim as the only repository

of power—made it possible for him to appear as a national ruler above class or sectional interests. Since he was the only source of legitimate power, he could by-pass Parliament and contemptuously neglect all the intermediaries between the sovereign and his faithful subjects. While this elected monarch of divine right was ruling through direct communion with his people, his technocrats could get on with modernizing the country.

At least, this was the assumption behind the technocratic dream. In all the apologetic theories, the grand design of Gaullist foreign policy was coupled with a domestic counterpart. The regime was going to free the country from a good portion of dead weight—marginal farmers, superfluous tradesmen, inefficient small manufacturers—and build up the big French corporations so that they could take up the leadership in Europe. To describe General de Gaulle as the man of the trusts, *le représentant des grands monopoles,* was much too simple; he was less directly influenced by big business than his predecessors or his successor were. The connection was more complicated: His vision partly coincided with the broader interests of France's big corporations.

But the technocratic dream did not come true. Profits did handsomely, so that businessmen could not complain, but in France society, as we saw earlier, was not reshaped more rapidly during the decade of Gaullist rule than in its more orthodox neighbors. Some critics even maintain that French growth during this period was more distorted because money was spent on the highly advanced sectors, partly connected with the nuclear strike force, and on unproductive subsidies. The modern industrial branches of mass production were relatively neglected and were not sufficiently developed to benefit from the technological fallout from advanced research. The Gaullist economy was sometimes compared to a misshapen animal with a stunted body between a big head and a huge tail. The future will tell whether the investment in nuclear energy, electronics, computers, was wasted so badly because of lack of industrial support. For the sake of our argument it is enough to point out that authoritarian Gaullism achieved no more than the "political dwarfs" in the German Federal Republic or the Italians with their parliamentary *combina-zioni*.

  Direct democracy, rule by referendum, proved less ruthlessly efficient than both admirers and critics had assumed. True, each plebiscite enabled the President to ask his questions and then consider the positive answers a popular mandate for his reign. But he still had to get his vote from somewhere. Big business could provide the money, not the votes. The attempts to involve the labor movement in the system—through an incomes policy or through the corporatist schemes of participation—were half-hearted and never got very far. Some workers, and even more their wives, voted for the General, but their backing could only be an addition to his plebiscitary majority. A great deal of his support had to come from farmers, shopkeepers, small industrial-ists, from those traditionally conservative forces that the dynamic regime was supposed to uproot; and so, at least near election time, votes had to be bought with concessions. Herein lay the paradox and the weakness of Gaullism. For the technocratic scheme to work smoothly, even biased elections were too much.

  If Gaullism thus shared some of the drawbacks of electoral democracy, it added some weaknesses of its own. Because the whole system rested on one man, any conflict tended to be turned into a crisis of the regime. Because deputies and other interme-diaries mattered relatively little, they were not able to sound the alarm effectively. In May 1968 the regime headed straight for the collision with students and workers without any warning sig-nals. Henceforth it was doomed. General de Gaulle had become dispensable. Big business had tolerated him in spite of misgivings about his foreign policy because he had looked like the best ram-part against the forces of revolution. That no longer being true, it was preferable to switch to more orthodox conservative rule, more flexible and less openly authoritarian. The change-over was only a question of timing and opportunity.

  Those who had hailed Gaullism as a superior form of capitalist rule had mistaken for a model what was essentially a product of particularly awkward circumstances. Gaullism, so dependent on its legendary hero, was inevitably affected by his personality. Yet its main features also reflected the peculiarities of the French situation. General de Gaulle might never have returned to power but for the Algerian crisis. Heavy reliance on the state was the result of the relative weakness of French capitalism. The fragility of France's parliamentary democracy, and the need for a substitute, were connected with the weakness of its social-democratic party and the militant mood of its working class. Considering the circumstances, the current verdict on Gaullism is too harsh from a conservative point of view. General de Gaulle extricated French capitalism from its colonial adventure and granted it a respite of ten years. His successors still have to prove that they can cope with the explosive situation more adroitly.

The Gaullist experiment confirms the theory that capitalism resorts to more authoritarian forms of rule not out of strength but out of weakness. Constitutionally, Gaullism was a hybrid system, half-presidential and half-parliamentary. It was presidential without checks and balances. It was parliamentary though the national assembly was not even supreme in law. Basically, it was authoritarian because so much power was concentrated in the hands of one man and so many freedoms were dependent on his goodwill. But being more authoritarian, experience has shown, does not make a regime safer for capitalism. If France had a labor party bound to play according to the rules, the risks would probably have been fewer. For most European establishments the problem, at this stage, is how to obtain the collaboration of the working class through the absorption of its leaders—hence the recent outbreak of Swedish flu. The divisions within, say, the Italian establishment over whether the Communist party should also be brought within the system are symptoms of the same trend. Whether all these efforts will lead to the consolidation of European capitalism or simply to the utter bankruptcy of the social-democratic solution is another question, one which is likely to get a quick answer. The fact remains that if a less authoritarian regime, such as a parliamentary democracy, is preferable for capitalist survival, only a dwindling number of countries can still afford such a luxury.

In Gorki's *The Lower Depths* the illiterate Satin collects long-winded words in search of a formula that will bring the Redeemer back to earth. In Paris, in the 1960's, learned experts and politicians were seeking a constitutional formula that would bring democracy to France. They were not illiterates. They were professors, and should have known that a political system depends on social forces, economic relations, class conflicts, and not simply on the election of a President through universal suffrage. They were deceiving the public, and possibly themselves, when they pretended that they were seeking the most genuine method for the expression of the popular will. Socialist democracy has still to be invented and won: invented, because the best means for the producers to control their production and for the citizens effectively to control their city still have to be found; won, because at all levels, from the factory to the top of the state, obstacles of property, wealth, and privilege will have to be removed, and those who benefit from them will not give up without struggle.

The constitutional exercises serve quite a different purpose. Whether the French regime is more presidential or more parliamentary, whether Britain is governed by Cabinet rule or the Prime Minister's rule, whether federal powers in the United States are widened or not—these may be important questions. They are exercises in the management of existing society. Our learned professors, whether they know it or not, are seeking the best method for insuring the survival of capitalism or, to put it differently, for fooling most of the people all of the time.

A spade is best called a spade. What we have just described used to be called in plain Marxist language the dictatorship of the bourgeoisie. The idea need not necessarily conjure up the image of a tyrant or of a police state. It simply means a system designed to perpetuate the economic, political, and cultural supremacy of the propertied classes. The term has the advantage of avoiding confusion between the constitutional wrapping and the social content, though care must be taken to remember that it is a generic term covering a huge range from fascism to parliamentary democracy on the British model. Here, too, confusion is dangerous.

The area of freedom is shrinking. The number of countries where even elementary liberties are preserved is dwindling. The scope for arbitrary administrative decisions is growing. The modern state crushes the individual, and science places sinister weapons at its disposal. When wiretapping becomes a habit and the very words electronic surveillance summon the nightmarish prospect of a computer tyranny, it would be as absurd to lump together all forms of bourgeois rule as it was folly in the 1930's to draw no distinction between social democracy and Nazism. Gaullism is preferable to the Greek junta, and parliamentary democracy to Gaullism. (American rule in the United States is more bearable than its rule by proxy in the banana republics.) Socialists should fight in defense of even formal freedom at a time when its alleged liberal upholders turn a blind eye to all sorts of violations of it. They should never forget, however, that this is only a part of their struggle for socialism. Accurate terminology should help them to remember.

What is true of one concept is true of its opposite. The dictatorship of the proletariat need not necessarily conjure up an image of concentration camps. It means a system designed to assure the supremacy of the working people, a framework allowing the proletariat to eliminate all forms of exploitation. Here, too, the generic term covers a wide range of potential forms depending on a country's stage of development, its level of culture and civilization, its traditions, the nature and acuteness of its inner conflicts, and so on. If bourgeois dictatorship can be as ruthless as in Greece or as liberal as in Britain, it should be granted that in the advanced countries of western Europe proletarian dictatorship could assume a radically different shape than in barbarian and backward Mother Russia. Instead of a dictatorship over the proletariat, exercised by a man or a clique allegedly representing the working class, it could be a system of socialist democracy, offering the mass of the people not only greater freedoms but also a genuine opportunity to exercise them.

The new revolutionaries must make this case not in answer to their liberal or conservative critics; to them it is easy to retort that however pure their intentions, their action is always ultimately destined to preserve profit and privilege, because such are the rules of their game. The new revolutionaries must make their case in order to gain mass support, because with all due respect to Fidel Castro, freedom of expression is not a luxury for intellectuals or a question of long hair.[8] Ask Czech trade unionists about its importance. Ask the working people of Britain, France, or Italy. They may be bemused by the surrounding atmosphere and often fall victim to the ruling ideology. Yet they feel instinctively that without freedom of expression, freedom of thought, without freedom of assembly and debate, they cannot defend their interests, let alone impose their class interests as the interests of society as a whole. They also sense something deeper. Without the creative and active participation of the masses there can be no question of building socialism. To carry them along, the revolutionaries will have to convince them that in struggling for power they are—in the words quoted at the opening of this chapter— seeking "to create socialist democracy to replace bourgeois democracy—not to eliminate democracy altogether."

How convincing this slogan may be will depend on the strategy, the behavior, and the very nature of the revolutionary movement itself.

Spontaneity and Organization, or *Lenin and Luxemburg*

The French crisis was a refresher course on the theory of revolution. It was instructive both in what it did and in what it failed to achieve. Spontaneous is the recurring adjective in all the de-

8. See Fidel Castro's speech on the Czech affair, August 23, 1968.

scriptions of the movement. Spontaneity, however, has several meanings in class struggle. An explosion is partly the result of an elemental protest, the outcome of the revolt of the workers against their condition, the instinctive expression of popular discontent. But it is also the reflection of political consciousness, of the militant spirit acquired in previous conflicts, the delayed product of past theoretical work and past propaganda. The May Movement was visibly spontaneous in the sense that the official parties and unions never took the initiative, except in the negative sense that they wanted to arrest it. The masses were more militant, more "ripe," than their alleged leaders. The official vanguard was in the rear and only appeared in the front line to hold the movement back.

After years of talk about the backwardness and apathy of the masses, the French crisis, which laid bare the apathy and backwardness of bureaucratic leaderships, was a natural vindication of spontaneity. Yet although the crisis underlined the importance of spontaneity, it also pointed out its many limitations. First, the strikers who wished to go farther than their leaders had no clear idea of where they were heading. Their lack of purpose was a lack of political consciousness, which in turn reflected the failure of years of theoretical and practical education in socialism. Second, at each turning point in the crisis, like the Night of the Bourse and the day when the workers rejected the Grenelle Agreements, there was nobody to channel the forces, to give them a lead, to suggest a direction. The absence of such a co-ordinating organ would have been felt even more acutely if the May Movement had made a real bid to seize power, let alone to exercise it. Finally, the turn of the tide confirmed the limitations of an elemental force. The March 22 Movement, the most original development produced by the French crisis, was able to transcend sectarian differences among students while the tide was rising. It rapidly vanished when the ebb came. The action committees held out somewhat longer because they were more organized.

The French experience, though unsuccessful, or rather incomplete, has marked out the frontiers within which a revolutionary force will have to operate to stand a chance of success. It proved that a revolution cannot be accomplished through its own momentum, nor can it be carried to its conclusion by a neo-Stalinist bureaucracy; neither pure anarchism nor the PCF. The territory lying between these two frontiers is fairly large, and ever since, all the revolutionary groups throughout Europe have been debating about the indispensable share in it of spontaneity and organization, of autonomy and centralization; about the respective roles of the "masses" and the "vanguard." Since a revolutionary movement too must draw on its experience, the old debate between Lenin and Rosa Luxemburg has thus been revived and brought up to date. Even the briefest summary of the issues involved must be preceded by a few preliminary remarks, because the images and positions of the two protagonists in this controversy have been so distorted in the eyes of the general western public.

Stalin's falsification of history and ideas is well known. It is no secret that Soviet historians were forced to write to measure and to orders. For them the alternative was not silence but Siberia. The western powers do not have such drastic means at their disposal, but the tasks of propaganda are nevertheless carried out. The social need somehow prompts the necessary supply,[9] and the treatment of Leninism is an excellent illustration of this phenomenon. Until 1953, while Stalin was alive, the works of Marx, Trotsky, and Lenin were excellent ammunition in the cold war. It was quite useful, on top of everything else, to show the gap separating Soviet reality from socialist aspirations, the fulfillment

9. It is not being suggested either here or elsewhere in the book that the upholders of the established rule or its ideologists are bribed into their position. In most cases their convictions may be perfectly genuine. A society in which the dominant ideology ceases to rule is threatened with collapse. Nevertheless, the speed with which the social need is filled suggests that other groups may deserve a ditty similar to the well-known one about my own profession:

> There is no way to bribe or twist,
> Thank God, an honest English journalist,
> But if you knew what he can do
> Unbribed, there's no occasion to. . . .

from the promise. The picture changed completely with Stalin's death and his successors' pledge, however verbal, to "go back to Leninism." Just in case they really did, it was now necessary for the West to prove that the system was rotten from the start, and as if by a miracle, books were duly published painting Lenin as having been almost an agent of German imperialism. Two versions were rapidly elaborated. The cruder and more popular showed Lenin as a sly, ruthless, cynical leader interested only in power, the Stalin of his time, and completely blurred the line dividing the old Bolshevik party from its Stalinist successor. The more sophisticated one did not attempt to conceal the glaring differences between the two men and their regimes. It argued nevertheless that the roots of Stalinism were contained in Lenin's conception of the party.

The cruder version is pure propaganda. Anyone who has read Lenin, whether with sympathy or hostility, cannot genuinely maintain that the man was interested in power for its own sake. Anyone even vaguely acquainted with the life of the Bolshevik party before and during the first years after the October Revolution, the sweep, the theoretical level, and the frankness of its debates, cannot honestly equate it with the Byzantine adulation of the Stalin era or even the conformist mediocrity of, say, a French Communist congress today. The sophisticated version has the advantage of hindsight. Yet to argue that Lenin's party was bound to degenerate into Stalinism, one has at least to assume that the failure of revolution in western Europe and Soviet Russia's isolation were also inevitable, an assumption the Bolsheviks did not share. All that has happened had to happen. The fashionable, more sophisticated, version stands or falls with the fatalistic interpretation of history.

Rosa Luxemburg is made use of more sporadically, though no more honestly, in western propaganda. From time to time, as in January 1969, the fiftieth anniversary of her assassination, a few passages of her moving prose are taken out of context and presented adroitly to a wide public. Because she said that "freedom is always and exclusively freedom for the one who thinks differently," because she rebelled against the idea of a socialism "decreed from behind a few official desks by a dozen intellectuals," she can be dressed up as the scourge of the Bolsheviks and the defender of parliamentary democracy. How is the ordinary reader to know that Rosa Luxemburg hailed the Bolshevik revolution as "the salvation of the honor of international socialism"? How is he to guess that this Polish-born fighter for socialism struggled all her life in the international movement, particularly in Germany, against parliamentary illusions, against the preachers of a peaceful, painless transition to a socialist society? She even paid with her life in this struggle, and the unscrupulous exploitation of her writing was particularly shocking during the anniversary celebrations. Her sentences taken out of context were used to the advantage of latter-day social-democrats. When in January 1919 Rosa Luxemburg and Karl Liebknecht were murdered by military thugs, social-democratic ancestors—Ebert, Noske, and Scheideman—were at the head of the German government. It is a tribute to this great internationalist that half a century after her death her message still has to be distorted, whether in her native Poland, in Russia, or in the West. Undistorted, it has preserved its "subversive" power.

The important thing to remember is that Lenin and Luxemburg belonged to the same family: They were revolutionary Marxists. They had many differences, including a well-known debate over national self-determination. The two controversies pertinent to our subject, however, were concerned with the structure of the party and the use the Bolsheviks made of their victory. In the former, Rosa Luxemburg was not the only critic. The debate, in fact, takes us back to 1903 and the famous split between the Bolsheviks and the Mensheviks. In retrospect, the pretext for this historical division really looks minor. Lenin's draft required of a member "personal participation in one of the party organizations." Martov was satisfied with "regular personal assistance under the direction of one of its organizations." [10] If one remem-

10. In both versions of this clause a member had to accept the program of the party and to support it financially.

bers that socialists in czarist Russia were hunted by the police, the bitter quarrels over the admission or nonadmission of students selling party literature or sympathizers attending study courses are not very relevant to the western situation of today. The Bolsheviks, with twenty-three thousand members on the eve of revolution, were somewhere between a "grouplet" and a sprawling mass party.

Working conditions under czarist rule were so different from those today that the incidentals of this dispute have only a historical interest. But Lenin's central argument remains relevant. The gist of it is that left to their own devices, the workers can only wage a trade-unionist class struggle, a fight for the improvement of their lot within the system. Socialist consciousness is brought to them originally from outside, by intellectuals, and this is understandable since the elaboration of a scientific theory required a thorough knowledge of the functioning of society as a whole. The socialist consciousness is something that the workers acquire—but not all of them. The working class is not homogeneous. It has its advanced and its backward sections. The party, in Lenin's conception, is the organization of the advanced elements, expressing the interests of the class as a whole and attempting to mobilize as many of its members as possible.

Though the general level of culture and education has greatly changed since then and the conditions of work are different, the dilemma raised by Lenin has not vanished. One cannot, on the one hand, proclaim the existence of a dominant ideology (more subtle and more efficient than in the past) and, on the other, expect all the working people to be politically conscious socialists. Now as then the really controversial problem concerns the interaction of, and the relationship between, the vanguard and the mass. Lenin was in favor of a tight, closely knit and highly centralized organization. Loose doors, in his view, would open the way to opportunism: Instead of leading the workers to socialist consciousness and revolutionary struggle, the party would be dragged down to their spontaneous level, the level of trade-unionism. Rosa Luxemburg replied that the risks of opportunism varied according to the social and political conditions of the country, and so should the rules of organization. But the chief accusation against Lenin was that his conception of the party contained the germs of bureaucratic degeneration and would lead to a dictatorship over the proletariat by a clique. "The lion's head of Marx would be the first to roll under the blade of the guillotine," thundered young Trotsky,[11] who at that stage argued on the same lines as Rosa Luxemburg, and she herself concluded her indictment with a *cri de coeur:* "Historically, the errors committed by a truly revolutionary movement are infinitely more fruitful than the infallibility of the cleverest central committee."

The year 1917 apparently vindicated Lenin's thesis, since he alone forged the instrument of revolutionary success.[12] The Stalinist nightmare exceeded the worst fears of his critics. It would be wrong to imply that Lenin was not aware of the dangers. His subsequent writings, particularly in the early phase of the revolutionary upheaval, must make awkward reading for Communist officialdom now. They have a rather leftist ring, with their emphasis on all power to the soviets, on control from below. Sensing the danger of bureaucratic growth, he repeated Marx's remedies: not only the election of officials but their recall at any time, the fixing of their salaries at the level of the workers, and so on. Indeed, in *The State and Revolution,* from which these examples are drawn, Lenin devoted many pages to explain the long-term goal, the withering away of the state. But whatever his precautions, more than half a century later in the so-called land of the soviets the state towers over the nation and stifles the birth of a socialist society.

The issues of party organization and the exercise of power are so closely linked that we have drifted imperceptibly from split to revolution, from the first controversy to the second. In 1918,

11. Quoted in Isaac Deutscher, *The Prophet Armed* (New York, Oxford University Press, Inc., 1954).

12. Even here one may question how much the success was due to Lenin's genius and how much to the structure of the party, since so many of the leading Bolsheviks were bewildered by the course of events in 1917 until Lenin's return.

from her German prison, Rosa Luxemburg continued to plead along the same lines. She pleaded with Lenin and Trotsky—who now stood by his side—not to rely on ukases but as far as possible on the creative spirit, the imagination of the broadest popular forces; in short, not to forget that socialist democracy is the best form of proletarian dictatorship. If the quotations are not taken out of context, it is clear that she made a most friendly appeal, full of sympathy and admiration. Unlike her cowardly German colleagues, Lenin, Trotsky and their comrades had "dared." They had opened new vistas to mankind. She took great pains to stress that even what she considered to be their mistakes were partly imposed on them by atrocious circumstances, by Russia's isolation and, therefore, by the historical failure of the western proletariat. Ultimately, she had only one major fear: "The danger begins only when they make a virtue of necessity and want to freeze into a complete theoretical system all the tactics forced upon them by their fatal circumstances and want to recommend them to the international proletariat as a model of socialist tactics."

Whether the charge was fair to Lenin or not, it was prophetic about his successor. For thirty years this principle was the ruling dogma. The dogma is now crumbling, and the old debate has started afresh all over the world.

A party, whatever its leaders may think and do, is not an end in itself. It is an instrument. Its shape should be determined in accordance with the tasks it is destined to perform. The form to be taken by a party, a movement, an organization, in the western world today cannot be separated from its strategy designed for the neocapitalist environment. Still, this brief historical interlude was not a digression. Russia's unwithering state is a crucial factor in the international debate and in the search for new solutions.

TAKE YOUR DREAMS *for reality.*

IMAGINATION *seizes power.*
                            —On the walls of the Sorbonne

Without a Model

Between them these two slogans sum up the weakness and strength not just of the French revolt but of the whole western movement of protest. Quixotic or farsighted, Utopian or salutary? One is tempted to answer that it is both. The man who scribbles that he takes his dreams for reality because he believes in the reality of his dreams can be a wishful thinker contracting out of the struggle, or an idealist fighting his private battle with windmills. Imagination, however, can be quite a different matter. It can be the mind's eye perceiving the hidden horizon, the prospect purposely concealed by vested interests. With a labor movement so preoccupied with its daily struggle that it saw nothing beyond its capitalist environment, the West had a great need for such a seizure of power by the imagination.

The two tendencies often coexist. An excellent illustration is provided by *We Are on the March,* a vivid text published by the action committee of a Paris arts faculty.[1] As an example of the Utopian, one can quote its proposition that to abolish a concept it is enough to ignore it, not to pay any attention to it. No wonder that in another passage it is almost being suggested that the rulers might understand the meaning of the necessary change and bow to the inevitable, as the French landlords are alleged to have bowed during the Great Revolution on a memorable night in August 1789. While thus occasionally contributing to the creation of new myths, this manifesto also does a splendid job of exposing old ones with illuminating shorthand such as "The minority owns property, the majority has the feeling of ownership." It also goes farther and projects in many of its pages the deep, unsatisfied aspirations of our society. The thirty-hour week, it proclaims, is the maximum tolerated. The overtime will be reserved for "education, improvement, cultural and critical activities." This is linked with a long argument about permanent education, one consequence of which should be to enable everybody to exercise, in turn, "any post of responsibility." *We Are on the March* expresses some of the real needs of our time, yet it does so often in Utopian fashion as if in its impatience it were echoing Rimbaud's cry "Science is too slow, let prayer gallop."

A key to this duality is to be found in the book by the Cohn-Bendit brothers, or, to be more precise, in its original title.[2] As

1. The first version was published under the title *Amnesty for Blinded Eyes.*

2. Daniel Cohn-Bendit and Gabriel Cohn-Bendit, *Le Gauchisme, Remède à la Maladie Sénile du Communisme* (Paris, Éditions du Seuil, 1968). Published in the United States as *Obsolete Communism: The Left-Wing Alternative* (New York, McGraw-Hill Book Company, 1969).

the Communists were using for their propaganda highly selected passages from Lenin's pamphlet *"Left-wing" Communism, An Infantile Disorder,* the Cohn-Bendit brothers returned the charge, calling their book *Leftism, A Remedy for the Senile Disorder of Communism.* A remedy is not a prescription for a healthy patient. It is the cure for a disease, a counterpoison, an antidote. The working class, or rather the traditional parties claiming to represent it, having failed in their mission, other social forces and new groups are trying to fill the void. They are bringing their own limitations to this gigantic task, but equally the treatment they propose is inevitably affected by the state of the disease: no organization, no delegation of powers, no leaders, all in reaction against bureaucratic growth and degeneration. Everything must be here and now, because the traditional parties always put off any radical transformation till Doomsday.[3]

Socialism has always been faced with an awkward dilemma because of the duality of its fight. It is through everyday class struggle that workers must gain strength, acquire experience, and improve their lot within the system. Yet the real solutions to their problems lie outside the capitalist system. Indeed, they must smash it to achieve them. It was the task of theoretical work to preserve the link between these two aspects and the task of propaganda to spread this awareness. This connection has been lost by social-democratic parties for years now, and by their Communist successors for quite a time. The former have openly dropped all pretenses about the search for a way out of the capitalist environment. The latter still pay lip service to their revolutionary duty, but are increasingly discreet about the society they propose and the ways for reaching it.

Imagination was and still is needed in order to remake this vital connection. "Be realistic, ask for the impossible," the other famous slogan of May lends itself to two possible interpretations.

3. Communists, so fond of quoting Lenin's *"Left-wing" Communism, An Infantile Disorder,* would do well to ponder this sentence from the book: "Anarchism was often a sort of punishment for the opportunist sins of the working-class movement."

The meaning may be simply elegantly romantic, namely that one should always aim higher than necessary. It could also be revolutionary: The workers should be realistic once again and fight for their own objectives, not bothering about whether or not the capitalist system can absorb them. Which is it going to be? The striking feature about all the movements now gathering momentum throughout the western world is that if they do not lack a purpose, they have no model.

The American Nightmare

It should not surprise anybody that European revolutionaries are not inspired by the American dream. Nobody, after all, expected the fighters for national liberation in the post-Napoleonic era to cherish the name of Metternich, and the United States is now a much mightier pillar of the new Holy Alliance for the preservation of the status quo. They intervene, directly or by proxy, wherever the social order is threatened, from Taiwan to Greece to Guatemala. Wherever profit and privilege are under attack, they can rely on the forces of "freedom." In Vietnam the American bombers spell out for the local population the bloody message "Better dead than red." The Green Berets are ready to jump in order to rescue the ruling oligarchies of the banana and other republics of Latin America (though the profits of American companies are now better insured by training local troops for the struggle against "subversion"). Like a black knight in nuclear armor the United States Navy patrols the seas, proclaiming that no more social revolutions will be allowed, that China's in 1949 was the last to be tolerated, while the Cuban affair was simply a misunderstanding. And the world listens to its warning in awe. The Vietnamese resistance aroused enthusiasm far from Hanoi and Saigon because it challenged American presumption and proved that human courage still counted even in the world of nuclear balance. The Tet offensive in 1968 drove western students to action because it revealed that the enemy was not invincible. Che Guevara, alive or dead, was hailed as the symbol of solidarity, of the international nature of the anti-imperialist struggle.

The salesmen of the American dream, and they are legion in Europe, prefer to by-pass this role of international gendarme, or to justify it in terms of domestic achievement. They point to the democratic niceties, to the civil liberties the United States can still afford. They stress even more the economic achievement, the technological lead, the intellectual investment that vast accumulation has rendered possible, the level of research and management, the high productivity—in short, the superior wealth of the nation; and they turn to the young revolutionaries with the rhetorical question, Can you dismiss the American model in spite of all this? The answer is not in spite of it, but because of it. The most frightening prospect, the American nightmare, is that with so much wealth man should not be able to build a different kind of society. In fact, the Europeans are merely echoing the indictment of America's new left, which, instead of being dazzled by the moon, points to the dark side of American society: its inequality and racism, its collective poverty amid private plenty, its derelict health services, its belated discovery of pollution and urban chaos—and to the system responsible for it all.

To its admirers, the United States has discovered the secret of perpetual motion for capitalism. Advertising, as a new dynamic method of sales promotion, is a superior way of getting rid of industrial surpluses than was coffee-burning in agriculture. Above all, with military expenditures absorbing, even in official figures, about one tenth of the national product, the state has a powerful lever to direct the rhythm of output. Advanced capitalism differs from its predecessor. The vagaries of the cycle are less pronounced, unemployment is relatively smaller, growth comparatively more regular. This is not the place to discuss whether this post-Keynesian equilibrium, resting on a militarization of the economy unprecedented in peacetime, is stable and lasting. The painful discovery of America's rulers is that even while the going is good, the system runs into new contradictions. American expansion meets resistance at home as well as abroad. The outsiders rebel. The hitherto passive blacks refuse to continue being pariahs in the alleged land of plenty. The growing movement of protest among students and the radical part of the intelligentsia is a symptom of something deeper—the clash between the direction to which the expansion of productive forces is geared and the social needs of our age.

At the beginning of this century in backward Europe industrial workers were struggling for an eight-hour day. Soon after, the slogan was for a forty-hour week, which the French workers obtained, at least in principle, before the last war. In the highly advanced American economy, with its computers, automation, and time-and-motion studies, the average work week in manufacturing was still around forty-one hours in the late 1960's. The figure would not matter much if American capitalism had performed the vital feat of providing mechanized labor with a satisfactory substitute for the craftsman's pride and pleasure in a well-finished job. On the contrary, its natural tendency, as we saw, is to reduce all forms of work to the broken-down, atomized labor of industry. The evolution is perfectly in keeping with Marx's dialectical prognosis. In its search for profit, capitalism is driven to raise productivity and to reduce the hours of work needed to produce a commodity; it is also driven to invent profit-bearing jobs. Growth for its own sake is an unfair charge. Its motto is growth for the sake of profit.

The "consumer society" is a misnomer suggesting that at least as regards consumption the average citizen is the uncrowned king. Though his material conditions have in many ways improved beyond recognition, modern man is still an alienated producer and a highly conditioned buyer of goods, a dissatisfied purchaser of leisure and pleasure with very little control over his environment. A producer society, guided by industrial and commercial profit, would be a much more accurate description. That problems such as pollution and urban decay are only tackled when they become unbearable is in the logic of things. Modern capitalism has changed enough in method and manner to tackle the unprofitable under pressure. It has preserved its essence. Profit remains its ultimate driving force, and it is intrinsically unable to face the collective or individual problems of our society from any other angle. Consciously or unconsciously, this is what the protest is really about.

The similarity of some of its manifestations on both sides of the Atlantic is quite natural. The Englishman, the Frenchman or the German traveling in the United States is less struck by contrasts than by resemblances. He has the strange impression of making a journey through his own country's more or less distant future. For the most political among them, however impressed they may be by the technological progress, it is a journey to night's end. They know that this is their inevitable prospect unless Europe can forge a different kind of society. The bitter controversies between "Europeans" and "anti-Europeans," it will be argued later,[4] are really irrelevant in this context. The conflict that has begun cuts across continental as well as national frontiers. The European protesters looking ahead are joining hands with America's new left. In western Europe the real division is between those who seek socialism and those who opt for the American model. *"Et tout le reste est littérature."* It was no accident if during the French May crisis, after a spell of *schadenfreude,* the United States authorities trembled for the fate of Gaullism. They had sensed, quite rightly, that the forces then launching the assault against Gaullism are the same that are waging the struggle against Europe's American future.

The conflict is now intercontinental, and so is the solidarity. Revolutionary "grouplets" across western Europe used to look exclusively to the third world, to the Vietnamese or the Latin American guerrillas fighting against United States imperialism from without. They are now also looking to America's young radicals, who are beginning to carry on the same struggle from within. By the same token, they have discovered their own independent and intermediate role.

In mood at least, there are some parallels between the present

4. See the chapter "The International Dimension."

period and the middle of the nineteenth century in Europe. Then, too, solidarity was the order of the day, and during the so-called Spring of the People fighters for national liberation journeyed from country to country battling "for your freedom and ours." Now, whatever policemen may think, direct intervention is still rare. The community of purpose and struggle is nevertheless growing. Europe's young students and workers salute their fellows across the Atlantic with the new message: "Against your present and our future."

West wind, east wind . . . There is nothing new in the violent reaction of Europe's radicals against American interventionism nor in their hostile rejection of the American model. The real novelty is that the Soviet Union has practically vanished as a counterattraction. During the French crisis there were many references to the Bolshevik October, but none, apart from contemptuous dissociation, to the bureaucratic rule of Stalin's heirs. This antagonism or indifference to the Soviet model—revisionist for some, Stalinist for others, irrelevant for most—characteristic of the May Movement was one of the reasons why orthodox Communists viewed it from the start with deep mistrust. Yet even the orthodox in the West are by now highly discreet about citing Russia as an example. They are particularly reticent about dwelling on the prospects of the Soviet bloc since the invasion of Czechoslovakia.

Spring in 1968 flourished in unison in Paris and Prague, but hopes faded separately. The French crisis was over, at least temporarily, by the time Russian tanks rolled into Prague on August 21, and their invasion marked the beginning of the end of the unique experiment of Czech students and workers. The epilogue in Prague came after the French act, and therefore could not affect it. But it has affected the European horizon. The Czech tragedy throws a new light on the problem of the dismantlement of Stalinism in eastern Europe. It makes it necessary to reassess the hopes of a socialist revival within the Soviet bloc and, by the same token, the chances that inspiration in Europe may once again come from the east.

The Lessons from Prague

Should one bother about one's bedfellows? In the case of Czechoslovakia the company is particularly numerous and distasteful.
The tears shed over Czech freedom and independence by men
who deplored the Bay of Pigs expedition only because it failed,
who turned a blind eye on American intervention in, say, Guatemala or the Dominican Republic, applauded the massive ship-
ment of United States troops to Vietnam and the bombing of both
the North and South, and now cannot recognize torture in Greece
—their tears undoubtedly come straight from the heart. The sudden enthusiasm for the struggle of the Czech workers and students
by people who at home are always on the opposite side of the
fence, the sudden love for "socialism with a human face" by
faceless men whose very function is to fight against socialism of
any kind—all this simply provides confirmation that hypocrisy
can be an important ingredient of propaganda. It does not alter
the fact—quite the contrary—that the Soviet tanks that rolled
into Prague were said to be coming to the rescue of socialism in
danger. (No side has an exclusive right to hypocrisy.)

Let us not get carried away by moral indignation. Soviet practice provides plenty of immoral precedents. Vyshinsky's violent
abuse in the ghastly Moscow trials, Molotov's telegram to Von
Ribbentrop, and the handing over of German Communists to the
Nazis are equally sickening examples on moral grounds. The significance of the invasion of Czechoslovakia, however, is essentially political, and it is important to determine where it really lies.

The invasion does not mark a turning point in the policy of
coexistence. Contrary to some expectations,[5] it did not inaugurate a tougher Russian line toward the United States. Nor did it
bring about any basic changes in American conduct. Propaganda
is one thing, and policy another. The two superpowers confirmed,
at least for the time being, that each is the master in its sphere of

5. Fidel Castro's, for instance. See his speech of August 23, 1968.

influence. If anything, Washington may have concluded that the
Soviet Union, in difficulties on two fronts—the European and
the Chinese—would be even more cautious in the third world,
more conciliatory in such areas of conflict as Vietnam or the
Middle East. If there was a second victim of the Czech tragedy
—in addition to the Czech experiment itself—it was not peaceful
coexistence. It was the theory of peaceful transition from Stalinism, the hope or illusion that the dismantlement of the Stalinist
heritage in eastern Europe could be carried to its conclusion
gradually by a mixture of inner pressures and reforms from above
without the masses taking the affair into their own hands; in other
words, without a political revolution.

Such hopes were shattered by the Soviet tanks. The lessons
from Prague are plain. Any country in the bloc that in its inner
transformation gets sufficiently far ahead of Russia to threaten its
neo-Stalinist system of rule runs a strong risk of armed intervention. The pace of change within the bloc is set by Russia, or rather
by the action of its people. There, too, freedom will have to be
conquered. The frightened bureaucrats in the Kremlin who decided to send in troops when their rule was menaced by proxy
will not yield gracefully at home.

To grasp the meaning of this conclusion one must glance back
for a moment. That Stalinism could not survive as such is now a
truism. In 1953, when Stalin died, the proposition was almost
a heresy. But this minority opinion was based on strong grounds.
It rested on the premise that Stalinism was also the product of
surrounding conditions and had changed these conditions so much
in a quarter of a century that it had rendered itself obsolete as a
system. The reign of terror had lost its purpose. Fear of deporta-
tion could instill some labor discipline into peasants turned workers; it was a most inefficient way of improving the productivity
of their more skilled successors. The fast growing technical intelligentsia needed a certain amount of freedom of thought to
fulfill its tasks. The party bureaucracy itself wanted to get rid of
purges in order to enjoy its privileges. The Byzantine cult of the

leader designed for semi-illiterate *muzhiks* was anachronistic in a land of mass education.

At first, change proceeded at a faster pace than the most sanguine forecasters had dared to suggest. Millions were freed from concentration camps. Some semblance of the rule of law was restored. After years of exertion the Russian people were promised some immediate rewards. Quite visibly, life in Russian had become freer and brighter. The euphoria, however, did not last. The efforts of Stalin's heirs were inevitably half-hearted and inconsistent. They were trying to dismantle one system, but they had nothing to put in its place. They had inherited an autocracy, and they made no real attempt to revive some democratic life, either in the ruling party or in the country's economy. They could not even condemn the system properly without revealing their own role as accomplices, nor explain its mechanism without endangering their own position. Whenever a writer dipped too deeply into the past or raised awkward problems, there was a panic and a temporary relapse into stricter censorship. The Twentieth Congress, in 1956, shook not only Russia. The tremors spread throughout Stalin's former empire, first in Poland, then in Hungary. Alarmed, the new rulers called a hasty retreat.

Nevertheless, even after this first setback it was still perfectly reasonable to expect that Stalin's successors, driven by events rather than guiding them, would somehow muddle through the long and awkward transition. Two steps forward, one step back. The intellectuals, particularly the writers, acting once again in Russia as the spokesmen for the inarticulate opposition, were imperceptibly extending the frontiers of freedom despite the periodic counteroffensives of the conservative censors. Each year was tilting the demographic balance against the relatively backward countryside. Each year was increasing the proportion of men and women with secondary or higher education in Russia's population. To such social pressures for change was added an economic pull, the growing need to overhaul the methods of management of the country's economy.

In the years when the emphasis in the West was on the "Soviet menace," the accent used to be put on Russia's mighty industrial progress, the road from the wooden plough to the Sputnik, rather than on human and economic wastage. Now the accent has been reversed, and the talk is mostly of failure. The balanced judgment on the economic achievement of the Stalin era, on its stupendous transformations as well as the avoidable sacrifices, remains to be spelled out. The achievement, whatever its unnecessary social cost, cannot be denied. Isolated and therefore deprived not only of foreign aid but also of the advantages of the international division of labor, the Soviet Union managed to compress its industrial revolution into an exceptionally short space of time. National planning, however crude and experimental, has helped it to perform this feat. But by the middle of this century the planning instrument designed for "primitive accumulation" was no longer adequate. It was not flexible enough to cope with a complex economy, in which the customer began to count, quality mattered, and the spread of technological progress was paramount.

In theory the planners had two choices in tackling the new situation. They could preserve central planning, prop it up with the latest discoveries of cybernetics and consumer research, while seeking flexibility from below through new forms of industrial democracy. Such a "leftish" solution was really ruled out in advance. Economic democracy was bound to clash immediately with the authoritarian structure of post-Stalinist rule, and no leaders opt consciously for political suicide. The alternative was to rationalize the price mechanism, rely more on the pulls of the market, and allow greater powers to the managers in their quest for maximum profits. It is this second solution that the Soviet leaders picked. In the West it gained the name Libermanism, after Yevsyei Liberman, a Kharkov professor who was one of the advocates of this kind of reform.

Profit and the market—the combination of these two words allowed the Chinese and some western observers to speak of a restoration of capitalism. It was not difficult for Professor Liberman and for his more important fellow reformers to show that the project did not involve any revival of private ownership of the means of production. They could have added that many remnants of capitalist practice had not only survived but flourished during the Stalinist period. Wage differentiation had been tied to such a complicated scale of norms for piece rates that the new regime had to reduce the range and differentials if only for reasons of efficiency.

The socially significant—and potentially disruptive—feature of the new course was the decentralization from above and the widening scope given to managers. As long as Russian factory directors were essentially executives carrying out detailed orders handed down from the top, it was possible to argue that Soviet industry was collectively owned and centrally managed for the community and that the workers therefore had no need for any traditional organizations to defend their class interests. It was a highly specious argument, rendered even more so by the big discrepancies in remuneration, but it was at least tenable in the abstract. The moment individual managers are given more say in fixing the level of wages (say, through bonuses) and the level of employment—two inevitable steps in the logic of the reform—the proposition becomes untenable and the pressure for traditional trade-union activity starts building. The fear of thus unleashing social forces explains the caution with which the reform has been introduced and the conflicts it has aroused within the Soviet leadership, conflicts between conservatives and reformers that have resulted in successive and contradictory moves toward decentralization and away from it.

For the western public this conflict has been confused by fashionable theories of a Russian struggle between the party bureaucrats and the industrial managers. Almost everybody who matters in the Soviet Union is to be found among the thirteen million or so members of the Communist party. The conflict is being waged within the party, and the labels do not always fit. Kosygin, reputed to be the leader of the reformers, has a longer record in the highest ranks of the party hierarchy than any of his colleagues. A rough division can be drawn within the party between those responsible for ideology and order, who reflect the views of the *apparatchiks,* frightened that the machine will get out of hand, and the men more concerned with running the economy, who are more influenced by the views of the factory managers and the technical intelligentsia. The frontier, however, is not clearly drawn and can easily be crossed. The officers' corps, for instance, might in the end throw its weight on either side. Two points should be kept in mind: The balance is unstable, and the struggle takes place within the establishment.

Until the Czech crisis the odds were in favor of irregular but continued change. The combination of economic and social pressures was pushing the reluctant leaders toward some kind of reform, reintroducing an element of movement into the politically frozen country. Now the forecast must be reversed. The decision to invade was not just a move in foreign policy. Watching developments in Prague, the Soviet rulers saw one possible, even probable, version of their own future unfolding before their very eyes, and they opted against it.

Of all the countries in the Soviet bloc, Czechoslovakia was the best suited for a peaceful transition from Stalinism. Here was a country with a rather western past of economic and democratic development. Its working class had long traditions, and the Communist party once had genuine roots within it. Besides, the Czechs, unlike most of their neighbors, had never been either anti-Russian or anti-Soviet. Altogether, in eastern Europe they had a well-deserved reputation as an orderly people with a strong sense of social discipline, as realists rather than romantics. When the Poles and the Hungarians rebelled in 1956, the Czechs kept quiet. Not surprisingly, economic deadlock was at the root of the political unrest in the 1960's. More industrialized than the other members of the Soviet bloc, Czechoslovakia had initially derived some benefits from its postwar integration into a bloc of more backward countries, though it also suffered most, in the long run, from being cut off from the technologically more advanced West. With a more complex economy, Czechoslovakia was among the first in the bloc, too, to feel the need for a switch from quantitative to qualitative growth.

The remedies proposed by the Czechs were not of a nature to shock their Soviet colleagues. The economic reforms associated with the name of Professor Ota Sik moved in the same direction as their Russian counterparts, only they went farther. They were Libermanism plus. Similarly, the inner Czech conflict did not begin as a struggle between the rulers and the ruled. It started, as in Russia, as a tug-of-war between the conservative and reformist wings within the party establishment. It started as in Russia, but was allowed to go farther, so that it revealed where the political forces, once unleashed, were likely to lead. What must have struck the men in the Kremlin, and driven them to intervene, was not so much the incidentals of the Czech crisis as its inner logic, the dialectical process that pushed to the left a movement initiated on the right, that turned initiatives from above into popular action from below and the search for managerial reform into a struggle over socialist democracy.

How Novotny and his conservative supporters blundered in their repression of the students is a detail. The important factor is that once the students and the radical intelligentsia entered the battle, its very nature changed. The inner controversy over the management of the economy was broadened into a conflict over civil liberties, freedom of expression, assembly, and so on. The second, even more important, point is that in a country where private property has been abolished, this struggle for "bourgeois" freedoms rapidly switched into one over socialist democracy. The reformers in their confrontation with the diehards were driven to seek popular support. It was the merit of some Czech intellectuals to grasp that the outcome in this trial of strength depended on the choice made by the main social force, the working class. But to get the industrial workers involved on the side of change was not so simple as it might appear.

In all the countries in which they are supposed to be the masters, the workers have not only political chains. The regimes could not last for long if that was the case. The workers have also advantages. The central one is full employment, the guarantee of a job. Without fear of unemployment the managers have quite a problem in trying to increase the intensity of labor (which should not be confused with its productivity). In Czechoslovakia, in addition to this, the discrepancy between wages and salaries was small by western standards, and the range of wages was less extended than elsewhere in eastern Europe. As a class, Czech workers had fared comparatively well. All these gains were potentially threatened by the managerial reform. The only way to mobilize the workers was to offer them a genuine share in political rule and in the managment of their own affairs, to turn them from possible victims into the new architects of the Czech transformation. As the movement was gathering momentum throughout 1968, its most interesting aspects were the new alliance between progressive intellectuals and workers, the link between students and trade unionists. A revival of the workers' councils was on the agenda of the Czech Communist party congress, which was due to meet in September. One is almost tempted to suggest that the men in the Kremlin decided to send in their tanks when they saw the shadow of new soviets.

They did it in the name of Marx, Lenin, and socialist solidarity, as the Americans send theirs in the name of freedom. The confusion was easy to spread on this occasion. When political forces compressed for two decades are suddenly released, they tend to jump in all directions. There were elements in Czechoslovakia, consciously or unconsciously, driving toward a return of capitalism, and western as well as Soviet propaganda underlined this aspect of the crisis. It was not the most important. Since the drama was not allowed to be played to the end, it is impossible to prove that such elements were bound to lose. All that can be said is that the risks in the situation were less in Czechoslovakia than in any other country of the bloc (with the possible exception of Russia itself). It should be added that throughout the crisis the Soviet bureaucracy and its allies seemed more perturbed by the Dubček regime's experiments in socialist democracy than by any revival of capitalist practices.

One alleged sin of the Dubček experiment was that it was leading Czechoslovakia to change sides. In fact, the Rumanians had gone much farther with their flirtation with the West without major trouble. But then the Rumanians had only indulged in diplomatic independence. Domestically, their system was as rigid as the Russian. They could not infect their neighbors with the dangerous germs of freedom. The second charge in the Soviet indictment was that Alexander Dubček and his colleagues were endangering "socialist conquests." The Russians were not alone in invading Czechoslovakia. Among their henchmen on this occasion was the Polish leader Wladyslaw Gomulka, who twelve years earlier on his return to power had actually redistributed all collective land to the peasants. Imagine the outcry if the Dubček regime had made a similar move.

To accuse the men in the Kremlin and their east European allies of invading merely to save their skin may be too simple. Their argument rests on a strange confusion between socialism and their authoritarian bureaucracy. Stalinist or neo-Stalinist, their system of rule is incompatible with debate, with the initiative of the masses, with any real form of workers' participation in the management of the country. We now know that faced with the threat of socialist democracy they are ready to call on the tanks. Do they know for how long the tanks will prevail over the power of attraction of the soviets?

Power Without Soviets

The Czechs did not lose their humor along with their hopes. For a time after August, Prague was buzzing with bitter jokes as if *galgenhumor* was a defensive mechanism against occupation. "We have already reached socialism," runs one story, "we had electricity, we now have the power of the Soviets." It was a joke for the initiated, since it paraphrased Lenin's shorthand formula defining socialism as electrification of the country plus the power of the soviets. Yet never was a truer problem raised in a bitter jest. When

Lenin coined his rather simplified slogan, he may or may not have imagined that half a century later the Soviet Union would be producing over six hundred billion kilowatt-hours of electricity, some of it nuclear. It was more difficult to conceive that in that distant future the soviets would be a fiction, the authoritarian dictatorship a parody of socialist democracy, and the so-called workers' state a mighty organ of coercion. The unimaginable just after a victorious revolution was to think that the Russian people might one day be forced to do it again, or rather to complete it by smashing political institutions that stood in the way of their country's socialist development.

The Bolsheviks, as we saw, started their rule perfectly aware of their country's primitive conditions. They relied on successful western socialism to help them to extricate Russia from its backwardness. During the harsh times of civil war they used the shock tactics of "war Communism" to drag their country toward its egalitarian future. The revolution did not win in the West. They themselves got bogged down in the primitive countryside and called a retreat. Amid terrible scarcity they had to reintroduce price mechanisms, allow substantial differences in wages, abandon the dream of socialism. Yet the retreat was to be temporary, and the socialist objectives were in principle simply shelved. They were to crown the edifice of economic construction. The flaw in the reasoning can easily be perceived in retrospect. Not enough allowance was made for the influence of the means employed on the ends being sought, for the impossibility of building socialism by decree without the active participation of the masses. Who could have guessed that the temporary concessions, far from being withdrawn, would be widened as material conditions improved, that the radical upheaval of society would leave the socialist objectives on the shelf, that the Communist party, the main instrument of the transformation, would become a stumbling block on the road to socialism?

The process of substitution, brilliantly analyzed by Trotsky and Deutscher, is now well known. The party substituted itself for the working class, the Stalinist faction for the party, and finally its general-secretary for society at large. It is the reverse process that now needs defining. The omnipotent ruler inevitably gave way to the collective leadership of the Politburo. Since then on a few occasions decisions have been made by the somewhat larger body, the 360-strong Central Committee of the party. So far democracy has stopped there, and judging by the Russian behavior in the Czech crisis, it will not extend beyond the top layers of party bureaucracy unless the political powers are once again conquered from below.

The proletarian dictatorship was inaugurated in Russia without the proletariat because at the end of the civil war the survivors among the men who made the revolution were absorbed by political, administrative, and managerial jobs. The working class had to be created out of the surrounding peasant sea. By now the Soviet Union has some 130 million town-dwellers, around 90 million workers and employees outside collective farming, nearly two thirds of them proletarians. The *muzhiks*-turned-workers— the product of Stalin's industrialization and through their political passivity the foundation of his absolutist rule—no longer dominate the labor force. The younger men, who have started work since Stalin's death, are fast becoming its biggest component. Yet even these newcomers, less frightened and more educated, have no channels for independent action. They can cynically climb the party ladder, or equally cynically mind their own business. Marx's comment about his compatriots fits them perfectly: "Here where the worker's life is regulated from childhood on by bureaucracy and he himself believes in the authorities, in the bodies appointed over him, he must be taught before all else to walk by himself." [6] The task of the Soviet authorities is to prevent him from learning. Russia has no ruling class of hereditary owners of property. It has a bureaucratic caste, divided, illegitimate, unsure of itself, but with a stake in the existing system and, as it showed in the Czech affair, with enough energy to fight for its own preservation.

6. Letter to J. B. Schweitzer, October 13, 1868.

"The powerful have only their power,[7] let's take it way from them," chanted French students in May, and during that crisis, with the factories and offices occupied, there was a semblance of truth in the slogan. In normal times there is none. To take an extreme example, when Nelson Rockefeller loses an election, he may be out of office, not out of a job or out of power. Political power is only one aspect of capitalist domination in the West. Its influence rests on wealth and what it can buy, on property and a complex social system designed to protect it. This is the sense in which it can be argued that in the West the bourgeoisie is always in power either directly, when the conservatives are in office, or in the intervals by proxy. The May slogan, on the other hand, was made to measure for the Soviet rulers. Their only power is power, exorbitant, all-pervading because it is precarious. Defeated, they cannot fall back on property. They are not even certain of a good job. They have no solid ground on which to justify their position and privileges. Why should the working people not be the masters in a workers' state? Why in a country claiming to have reached socialism and being well on its way toward Communism should there be such a discrepancy between the bureaucrats with their *dachas* and ordinary people? The rulers have to cheat, to distort their Marxist heritage, to control every form of political and cultural activity in order to survive. No opposition can be tolerated, because if it were allowed room for action, it would sweep away the present masters with much greater ease than in the West. For Russia's new revolutionaries the most difficult thing is the beginning.

Until Stalin's death the political bureaucracy did not even have a feeling of security. Periodic purges prevented its cohesion. The tyrant gone, its first aspiration was to consolidate its position and enjoy its advantages. The Soviet establishment—in a broader sense, all those benefiting from privileges gathered on the nation's surplus—wished to enjoy its comforts in peace. After years of terrible exertion and horrible insecurity the whole nation undoubt-

7. *Le pouvoir n'a que le pouvoir.* Power, in French, has also the meaning of authority, the established power.

edly yearned for a better, brighter, and freer life. Since there was no question of entrusting the nation at large with the task of social transformation, the establishment tried to impose its own mood, methods, and values. Market, profits, incentives, were slogans greeted with sympathy and understanding in the West. Khrushchev's "goulash socialism" was a crude Soviet adaptation of François Guizot's "Enrich yourselves." Though there were differences of opinion between conservatives, frightened of upsetting the balance, and reformers, stressing the need for change, the latter seemed to have the logic of history on their side until the Czech crisis projected the likely consequences of a policy of movement: economic reform leading to a political revival and an innocuous beginning ending with the frightening echo of the birth-pangs of the regime—All Power to the Soviets.

We stated bluntly at the opening of this argument that the theory of a peaceful transition from Stalinism was buried in Prague. This assertion should not be taken to mean that the reign of Stalin's successors is anything but transitional. Unable to restore the mystique and terror on which their master's rule rested, and incapable of putting anything in its place, Stalin's heirs have all the appearance of provisional rulers: supported by half-truths, they take half-measures half-heartedly. They only showed their full strength and determination when their system of rule was threatened, even from a distance. Then they made it plain that power will not be diffused gradually, that it will not be handed down, that there too it will have to be taken. The Soviet tanks in Prague have put on the historical agenda the question of political revolution in Russia.

What form it will take, how violent it will be, and how soon it will come—these are problems for prophets. If one scans the political surface of Soviet society, the leaders look safe: a handful of writers daring to challenge authority, a dozen intellectuals brave enough to face prison in order to express the protest of an inarticulate opposition. The signs foreshadowing a revolutionary movement,[8] announcing the march of a conquering class, were incomparably stronger a century ago, and the new rebels have to face a system of censorship, control, and social coercion that czardom would have eyed with envy. If only the dissenting students and intellectuals can be isolated from the workers—the rulers must hope—unrest will not spread. But their prospects are not so bright when one looks below the surface. The intellectual ferment is deeper than it appears. The mood of the workers is the unknown, but the gap between the generations is undoubtedly more important in Russia than in the West. On top of it all, the regime must live with the contradiction that has been revealed by the Czech crisis. The leaders need rapid growth to consolidate their position. The economy must be overhauled so that it can spurt ahead. But the rulers now know what might happen once the social forces are let loose.

Historical opportunities are always unique in a sense, and 1968 provided two that were particularly exceptional. It is doubtful whether a Communist party will ever again be backed by a united nation like the Czech party was in August. It is highly improbable that any western regime will be taken as completely by surprise as Gaullism was that May. Yet the two crises do not mark the end of history. On the contrary, they are signs of its acceleration in the two halves of the European Continent. In eastern Europe the center of gravity now moves back from the periphery to Russia. It is up to the Russian people to do it again, to complete their task, to set up genuine soviets in conditions that are now more than ripe for socialist democracy. Until they do, inspiration will not come from the East. For the rising generation of western revolutionaries, a Russia squeezed in its bureaucratic strait jacket will be the other nightmare, even if it also manages to get "air conditioned."

8. The 1870's saw the rise of the *narodniki,* or populists.

Inspiration Rather Than Example

China, Vietnam, Cuba, si . . . Those three countries have been, to a greater or lesser extent, a source of inspiration for the action of the new left in the western world. China is the most important of the three, and not only because of its size. Alone it has made an open challenge to Moscow for the leadership of the international Communist movement, publicly questioning both Russia's conduct of foreign affairs and its model of socialist construction. Mao's China offered its own example as an alternative.

In foreign policy, at least, Stalin's successors can claim to be his true heirs. Their practice of Socialism in a Single Bloc is a continuation of his doctrine of Socialism in One Country. In spite of his reputation, Stalin was no fiery exporter of revolution. He was a practitioner of coexistence, a determined, if often clumsy upholder of the international status quo.[9] Naturally, he had to conceal his indifference to the spread of socialism and his contempt for foreign Communist parties, which he regarded only as his tools. He had to take into account the Bolshevik heritage and Russia's national interests. But the same is true of his successors. The difference is that Stalin got away with his revolutionary reputation unscathed, while his heirs are branded revisionist traitors.

Among the many reasons for this different treatment, three at least are worth mentioning. First, in Stalin's time millions still believed Russia to be the model for socialism; their numbers have dwindled since. Secondly, the Soviet Union really was isolated at the time, and its defense could be interpreted as an international duty; the "sacred egoism" of the only workers' state still had a halo. Now, Russia no longer stands alone, which leads us to the third point. Stalin's foreign critics—the domestic ones were in concentration camps—were isolated groups that could be attacked as imperialist agents or worse. Now the Soviet press can brand

9. Isaac Deutscher has made and proved this point in his biographies of Stalin and Trotsky. He sums it up in his *The Unfinished Revolution* (New York, Oxford University Press, 1967).

Mao Tse-tung as an American stooge, and it does. But it cannot really hope to carry conviction. (Soviet and Chinese policies are there for everybody to compare.)

In keeping with Mao's dictum of strategic boldness and tactical caution, Peking's foreign policy can hardly be described as reckless. It was Khrushchev, not Mao Tse-tung, who sent missiles to Cuba only to call them back. China, on the other hand, has a more dynamic conception of coexistence. It does not believe that co-operation between the nuclear superpowers is the supreme goal, nor does it consider that there is any need to subordinate the chances of revolution wherever they occur to the search for an understanding with the United States. Naturally Russia does not spell out its opposite interpretation publicly. It cannot even practice it at will. It is forced to supply arms to the Vietnamese fighters and guarantee the independence of Cuba. Yet the Kremlin hardly conceals its distaste for revolutionary "troubles" likely to increase its commitments and cause friction with Washington. Hence, political parties refusing to endorse the status quo tend to look to Peking rather than to Moscow. What was true for Asia and Latin America is beginning to happen in the advanced western countries, as new forces appear with political ambitions going beyond the management of capitalist society.

The roots of the clashing foreign policies of the two Communist giants can be traced to their domestic backgrounds, to the contrast between Mao's "uninterrupted revolution" and the Khrushchevian goulash socialism. China's cultural revolution has merely deepened the rift. In describing it, most western commentators have put the accent on its Stalinist side, on the antics of the cult of Mao.[10] It is a superficial emphasis. When Stalin wished to purge his opponents, he used the political police and the public prosecutor. He was not setting the masses into motion. If there is a period of Soviet history with which an analogy might be drawn, it is rather the brief spell of "war Communism," when the Bolsheviks were trying to storm their way to a socialist society.

10. For the Chinese attitude toward Stalin see K. S. Karol, *China: The Other Communism* (New York, Hill and Wang, 1967).

Mao's method is in many ways the very opposite of Stalin's. In his vision, socialism is not jam for tomorrow. It must be introduced step by step, side by side with the economic construction. Political change must in fact precede economic change and pave the way for it. Necessary evils cannot be turned into virtues. They must be extirpated whatever the risks. If big differences in standards of living and behavior between the rulers and the ruled are allowed to crystallize, if bureaucratic deviations are tolerated for long, China's "long march" will be pushed off course and will end up on a Russian trail. The Soviet Union is not Mao's model. It is his bogey.

Can it be done? Can socialism be built by painful political efforts in primitive surroundings? Classic Marxism did not foresee the question and cannot provide the answer. How gigantic the task is may be seen at every stage. One of the purposes of the cultural revolution was to uproot men with bureaucratic leanings, those who are divorced from the masses. Today in the United States, Britain, France, and even in Russia by now, if a man is kicked out of a job, he can be easily replaced by colleagues of roughly equal qualifications. Not so in China, where qualified people are terribly scarce. In most cases he will have to be "reclaimed." Such examples can be multiplied. The long march has barely begun, and the Chinese millions have still to prove that Mao's egalitarian dream can overcome the reality of China's backwardness.

A country cannot escape artificially from its mental climate and stage of development. However inspiring the Marxist project of "uninterrupted revolution," it has to be carried out in a backward and predominantly peasant country. The clash between the Marxist aims and the Chinese environment results not only in methods often jarring to the western mind; it also brings about inner tensions and contradictions. There is a conflict between the appeal to the rank and file and the need for reasserting central authority. Thus, the great cultural revolution that began in 1966 by unleashing popular forces and that involved an unprecedented attack on the Communist establishment ended in 1969 with the Ninth Party Congress held behind closed doors.

Similarly, the struggle for egalitarianism, the antiauthoritarian fight against hierarchical structures, against orders from above, is being waged in China in the name and on the authority of Chairman Mao. This is not the place to discuss whether such a reliance on a charismatic leader is an inevitable part of social transformation in a backward country. All that can be said is that western Maoists are not doing their cause a service when, instead of emphasizing the immense difficulties of China's revolutionary task, they raise the Chinese example as a model for the world at large, including the most industrialized countries.

The Vietnamese have inspired the whole world by their extraordinary struggle. Their historical service was to remind all people that even in the age of balance of terror the superpowers are not the only political actors, that their hand can be forced, their rules of coexistence twisted. Through their refusal to yield, the Vietnamese have revealed the ambiguity of Soviet policy, both Russia's reluctance to face the Americans and its inability to contract out. Above all, they have revealed the limits of American power and other have learned their lesson.

The case of Cuba is more complex. It has attracted sympathy not only as the small David defying the American Goliath. For a time, at least, its libertarian exuberance, its heterodox behavior, its attempts to exorcise the fetishism of money, caught the imagination of socialists in search of a different example. But it is not easy to build socialism in one tiny island surrounded by a mighty enemy and its satellites.[11] Far from presenting a model, Cuba required one for itself, though the Soviet bloc, to which it got linked, has little that is relevant to offer. Cuba's salvation lies in the Latin American revolution, but its distant supporter has no enthusiasm for such a risky solution. Whatever the intentions of both sides, their relations are bound to be tense. It is Cuba's zeal for revolution throughout the continent that attracted young radicals out-

11. For a study of these difficulties, see K. S. Karol, *Guerrillas in Power* (New York: Hill and Wang, 1970).

side its frontiers, and the symbol of this attraction is still Che Guevara, the Argentinian who fought in Guatemala, won in Cuba, and died in Bolivia, a living reminder that the revolution remains unfinished, not only until it has set up a classless society of plenty, but also until it has spread socialism across the globe.

The same vision but different stages of development; the same objectives but different means: The young socialists in the advanced western countries can draw inspiration from the struggle carried on by others, but they cannot rely on any model. They are doomed to be pioneers, entering an uncharted road. It is their role to prove that they can seize power, smash the state, put another one in its place, and start dismantling it at once.

BUT SOCIALIST DEMOCRACY is not something which begins only in the promised land after the foundations of socialist economy are created; it does not come as some sort of Christmas present for the worthy people who, in the interim, have loyally supported a handful of socialist dictators. Socialist democracy begins simultaneously with the beginnings of destruction of class rule and the construction of socialism.

—ROSA LUXEMBURG

The Unwithering State

It was the end of June or the beginning of July 1968, and Paris was not yet entirely recaptured. There were still a few oases to which the young were flocking in order to pick up leaflets and pamphlets, and to discuss what could be done next. At the faculty of sciences on the embankment they were showing pictures that evening, a film of the street battles of a few weeks earlier. While the forces of order were performing on the screen, a voice off summed it all up with the comment that this was a "police state."

349

From the back of the hall a man yelled *"Pléonasme."* The audience, suddenly relaxed, burst out laughing, dismissing the heckler
with good humor as an *anar,* an anarchist. The public may, though
need not, have been right. If there is a point on which socialists
and anarchists have always agreed, it is that any state is a form
of coercion and that society will not be free until it has got rid of
the state. Their bitter quarrel has been over the means by which
this desirable end can be achieved.

The great masters of socialist thought have not written much
about the future stateless society. Their main purpose has been
to analyze the contradictions of existing society—the fundamental
clash between labor and capital—and show how they should
drive the working class, the main productive force and the chief
victim of exploitation, to seize power and abolish the contradictions. To embroider the details of a distant society, the ultimate
result of permanent revolution, was from their scientific viewpoint Utopian. Even the broadest outlines of this full-fledged
Communist society were derived indirectly, projecting the trends
of development of productive forces and by contrast (negatively)
removing in this projection the social relations acting as a brake
on this development and, in the first place, private ownership of
the means of production.

The Communist society was by definition a society of plenty,
in which the satisfaction of material needs had ceased to be a
problem. The market had been replaced by distribution, each
man taking from the collective fund "according to his needs." It
was stateless because it had no need for an organ of repression
to defend the privileges of any ruling class. It was not only classless. Even the differences in productive skill had become irrelevant, since labor itself had been turned into "a prime necessity
of life." In any case, with the difference between mental and
physical work abolished and the socially necessary labor reduced
to a minimum by the harnessing of science, most of man's time in
this society could be used for his own fulfillment, which in turn
enriched society as a whole.

No attempt was made to foreshadow the dialectics of the new

society, to guess what would happen to other human instincts once the biggest source of oppression was removed. No efforts were wasted in finding out in advance what new literature, music, and art it would produce, to imagine to what intellectual or physical heights the new man would rise. This would have been socialist science-fiction.[1] The difference between now and then was simply summed up in the beautiful metaphor of Engels about mankind taking a leap from the "realm of necessity" to the "realm of freedom." [2]

Beautiful, yet misleading when taken in isolation. To the uninitiated the image conveys the idea of a sudden jump, whereas for Marx, Engels, and their followers it was obviously the culmination of a long historical process, the process of permanent revolution. There is no possibility of a misunderstanding when the metaphor is put back into its place. The full-fledged Communist society was described by Marx as a higher or second stage. The first or lower stage—which some also describe as the socialist one [3]—begins with the successful revolution as soon as the new order emerges from the womb of the old. The basic difference between the old and the new is that the exploiters have been expropriated. Otherwise, the infant still bears the marks and influence of its capitalist origins. Work is not yet a "necessity of life," and differences in skill must still be rewarded "to each according to his labor." Mankind has not yet been allowed to develop its productive capacities to the full and therefore cannot quite afford a system of free distribution. And man is still burdened with his

1. Trotsky allowed himself to write a few beautiful pages of such anticipation at the end of his *Literature and Revolution* (Ann Arbor, University of Michigan Press, 1960).

2. Friedrich Engels, *Herr Eugen Dühring's Revolution in Science* (*Anti-Dühring*) (London, Lawrence and Wishart Ltd., 1934), p. 312. In the same chapter Engels explains how the state is not abolished but "withers away."

3. In this book I have tried deliberately to stick to the terms of lower and higher stages of a socialist society. The division into socialist and Communist has been used and abused to promise paradise for a distant Communist future and, meanwhile, to degrade the name of socialism by applying it to all sorts of regimes and situations.

capitalist upbringing, not quite ready for the free association of collective producers. The passage from the first phase to the second, from budding socialism to full Communism, from necessity to freedom, cannot in this conception be a sudden leap. It is a drawn-out process of organic growth, the new order gradually getting rid of the vestiges of the old, and while the transition proceeds, the need for coercion progressively disappears. The state, to use again the eloquent expression of Engels, "withers away."

It is at this point, over the gradual disappearance of the state, that anarchists and revolutionary socialists move apart. They do agree that the victorious revolution cannot just take over the bourgeois state and use it for its own purposes, that the mechanisms and men designed for the maintenance of capitalist rule cannot simply be switched over to work for the construction of a classless society. In this view they both differ from social reformers, who see no need for a break at all. Starting from the concept of a peaceful conquest of the state from within, the revisionists were led quite logically to drop the idea of revolution and then the goal of socialism altogether; they were turned into reformers of the capitalist order. Anarchists and revolutionary Marxists cannot be bracketed with them. They are both convinced that the bourgeois state must be smashed. But for the anarchists, this is the end. The state at once vanishes from history. The Marxists retort that the victorious working class requires an instrument to consolidate its victory, to repel attacks, to direct the new society on the road to socialism and freedom. This instrument of power, the proletarian dictatorship, was never clearly defined. Marx mentioned the Paris Commune of 1871 as an example, and after 1905 the Russian soviets suggested a new pattern. In any case, it was going to be a peculiar sort of state, transitional by definition, since it was designed from the very start to carry out its own destruction—to build a stateless society.

In Marxist theory, until it was affected by Soviet practice, the more or less spontaneous and automatic dismantlement of the state after the revolution was taken for granted; it was also taken for granted that proletarian dictatorship was merely another expression for socialist democracy. The two convictions sprang from the same basic premise, from the fundamental assumption that a socialist revolution could only take place when conditions were "ripe"; that is, in a fairly advanced and industrially developed country where a large, politically conscious working class could lead the bulk of the exploited, that is to say the overwhelming majority of the nation. Force would have to be applied only against a tiny minority, the exploiters and some of their servants. The degree of violence and its duration would thus depend on the resistance provided by this minority and its foreign capitalist allies. In principle, this was not to affect proletarian democracy and could not delay for long the withering away of the state. The very idea of a socialist revolution taking place in a single backward country was so alien to socialist thought that the Bolsheviks, bred on classical Marxism, could not until 1917 envisage that it would happen in their country. Trotsky, who anticipated the event, could only square his vision with the general theory by describing the Russian upheaval as the starting point of world, or at least European, revolution.

In October 1917 the Bolsheviks proved that revolution could begin in a primitive country. They showed that a socialist revolution was in fact possible and thus opened a new era in the history of mankind. But the first chapter written by the Russians in half a century has shattered some of the established assumptions and hopes. It is no longer possible automatically to equate proletarian dictatorship with socialist democracy. It is no longer reasonable to assume that once private ownership of the means of production is eliminated the state will spontaneously begin to wither away. The Russian experience has shown that once the workers, the broad masses, have ceased to shape their destiny, once they are excluded from socialist construction, it is not easy to bring them back. The converse is equally true. Once a party, a leadership, has been allowed to rise above the class and society it is meant to represent, it is difficult to bring it down. The ruling bureaucracy acquires its own interests and a momentum of its own. The new society emerging from the capitalist womb is still heavily burdened by its origins. Its postcapitalist development is full of dangers. It can still be checked or fatally distorted. The creation of socialism is continuous. Permanent revolution must be permanent.

The Russian pathfinders have written this warning with their sweat and blood (a kind of collective What Ought Not To Be Done). The Chinese, embarking on a similar gigantic journey from primitive surroundings, have grasped the message. Maoism can be described as a tremendous effort to guide China on its long march toward socialism so that it will not get bogged down in bureaucratic marshes as Russia has done. Yet though the vagaries and distortions peculiar to Russia have a great deal to do with the primitive starting point of the Soviet experiment, the warning is also valid for the advanced West. If by a miracle revolution triumphed tomorrow in the United States, even there a classless and stateless society could not be set up overnight. The question of postcapitalist development, of the stages in the transition to socialism, can no longer be dismissed by the western labor movement as an abstract issue that will be solved in practice as it comes. It cannot be put off to the Greek calends, because the problem of the unwithering state is no longer abstract or distant. It hangs around our necks.

Man can walk on the moon and send rockets to Mars. Not only the frontiers of European midgets but those of the superpowers are much too narrow for the productive forces he has developed. The nation-state has long been rendered obsolete by the international division of labor. Nationally, too, the bourgeois state has outlasted its function. The progress of science has made it possible for modern technology to carry out a complete overhaul of economic management, of the process of production. "The theft of somebody else's labor, on which wealth now rests," is a ridiculously outworn criterion in this age of automation. The conditions are more than ripe for the abolition of a system of production resting on class exploitation and, therefore, requiring a capitalist state for the maintenance of this exploitation. Indeed, they are ripe for beginning to get rid of the state altogether. An anachronistic institution, however, does not necessarily die. On the contrary, in its effort to hang on, to survive beyond its appointed time, it may be forced to grow artificially. This is the impression given by the state in our times. We mentioned earlier the nightmarish vision of Europe's young generation: Whether it looks to the West or to the East, it perceives a leviathan, showing no apparent intention of ever withering away.

In the case of the United States the exasperating feeling is that this dismantlement is both so near and yet so far. So near, because technologically everything seems ready for the rapid transformation of man and society, of society and man. Within a couple of generations America's collective producers could lay the foundations of socialism, and the old project of a stateless society could be a reality there in the early years of the new millennium. So far, because the United States will never get there set on its present course. American capitalism can send man to the moon; it cannot turn him into the master of his social environment. It cannot radically alter the nature of his labor and leisure, or train the American producers to run their own factories, their offices, their economy. Without committing suicide, it is unable to uproot poverty amid plenty, to eradicate racial and social discrimination, to eliminate differences between rich and poor, between rulers and ruled.

It knows how to produce a different model of a car each year and how to persuade the customer that the slight modification of the chassis is an earthshaking innovation. It cannot think, until it is forced to do so by utter chaos, about the pollution the mass-produced car will cause, the traffic or urban problems it will create, and so on. It cannot because, as was argued earlier, the driving force of American capitalism, for all its metamorphoses, remains ultimately the private appropriation of surplus. It can see progress in terms of profit, and human needs in terms of demand backed by the almighty dollar. Its historical prospect, barring a catastrophic fall, is of a senseless and monstrous growth, paralleled by an expansion of the complex machinery of repression, because the movement of protest is only a first sign of the revolt against this monstrosity.

The Soviet Union is, in a sense, even more depressing. Here is a country that set out to abolish the contradiction between capital and labor by eliminating the private ownership of the means of production. Here, then, the state was to perform its progressive function and begin to vanish as it carried it out. Despite the most fantastic odds the first experiment in national planning enabled the Soviet Union to become the second industrial power in the world, to educate an illiterate country, to develop social services, and so on. But the past that was being uprooted took its revenge. When economic development had gone far enough to allow a natural transition to socialism, when Russia was no longer isolated, when the tyrant who had been determined to arrest political development was out of the way, a movement of reform began, only to come to a stop. The Soviet state is at once omnipresent and fragile. It has an ambiguous role as a defender of public property and as an instrument of class rule in an allegedly classless society. The bureaucracy exercising its dictatorship in the name and place of the working class cannot turn its rule into socialist democracy if it wishes to survive. It now stands in the way of the development of Soviet society and of its productive forces.

To complete the picture one should also mention the satellites in each system. The countries of eastern Europe, if Czechoslovakia is a guide, will not be allowed to seek their own breakthrough. The west European states, for their part, claim to respond to the "American challenge" by producing a poor man's model of the United States. Or to look just at the three biggest actors in the world drama: there is China, with a vision of a different society, but at the very beginning of a most difficult road; Russia, which has reached the halfway stage, but which in acquiring the means has apparently lost sight of the end; and, finally, the United States, which should be there but has no vision of the future, except its drive for capitalist survival through artificial growth and domination of the globe. A mad world, the pessimist will conclude, bound to blow up in a nuclear suicide. The optimist will retort that however strange it all may seem to the contemporary onlooker, mankind has its own ways of advancing and of recovering sanity on the edge of the abyss. The militant will go one step farther. He will perceive in the upheavals of Paris and Prague the first signs of coming change, a glimmer of hope, and a call to action.

In a world dominated by anachronistic nation-states vague forms of anarchist thought are enjoying a revival. There are valid, if partial, sociological explanations of this trend. The second, or scientific, stage of the industrial revolution repeats on a larger scale the movement of social transformation begun by its predecessor. Peasant farmers are threatened with extinction. Shopkeepers fear they will be reduced to the rank of shop assistants. Millions of employees are gradually finding themselves with working conditions resembling those of large-scale production. Large sections of the middle and lower middle classes are deeply perturbed and worried by the social consequences of technological change. In their apprehension, they react in a way that is not unlike that of their ancestors a century ago, and sometimes even borrow their ideas. In the French May Movement there were discernible antiauthoritarian echoes of Proudhon as well as of Bakunin.

The fashionable sociological explanation does not go far enough. The revival of the anarchist call for the immediate abolition of the state reflects something much deeper that affects the workers as well as the newly alienated sections of the population. The state is naturally regarded here as an instrument for the maintenance of an oppressive society of class rule, of a social division of labor that, even when providing more goods, does not make work, and hence life, more bearable.[4] Along with the depressing

4. This socialist criticism of the state as an instrument of class rule should not be confused with conservative criticism that purposely ignores this class nature of the state. For the bewildered small shopkeeper, the Poujadist, the state is the tax collector and capitalism the big store. The conservative approves the state as the defender of law, order, and property. He is not bothered by the aid and protection given to big business. He

feeling that man is the slave of the machine, that the authoritarian state is there forever to keep him under, the opposite idea is gaining ground, the idea that life could be different, that science instead of helping to keep man in bondage provides the means for his liberation, for throwing the state onto the scrapheap.

The old controversy between anarchists and socialists is now resurrected in a new form, as acute as ever, yet more ambivalent. The anarchist remedy, the abolition of the state overnight by a successful revolution, is probably less realistic than in the past. True, the French crisis showed the modern industrial state to be more vulnerable than it appeared. Yet it would be utter folly not to expect defeated capitalism to fight back with all the means at its disposal—political and ideological, economic and military— both from within and from without. The victorious revolution would need an instrument with which to defend its conquests and to consolidate them. It would also have to perform, for its own purposes and in a radically different fashion, all sorts of functions carried out in its own interests by the capitalist state. The freely associated collective producers would still require a central organ to run the highly complex economic machinery, to co-ordinate their aspirations into a coherent plan, to impose a pattern aiming at the gradual elimination of differences between regions, between country and town, between factories and offices, between skills. Until the "administration of things" can be entirely substituted for the "government of people," the community will need a strong instrument of class rule to reshape the social services, starting with education, so as to speed up the transition to a classless society. The abolition of private property is but a beginning, and it does not provide guarantees against setbacks or fatal distortions—this is the bitter lesson of the Russian experience.

Yet it is only one of its lessons. Another, pointing in the oppo-

---

only grumbles about redistribution: unemployment benefits, social insurance, subsidies for education, and so on. The enemy is the welfare state. What an egalitarian socialist society will have to do for education, health, and the social services in general will show the present "welfare" for what it really is—a miserable palliative designed to preserve basic injustice and inequality.

site direction, is that socialism cannot be built by proxy. If the party takes over from the class, the rulers from the ruled, the chances of distortion and then of a new conflict between social relations and productive forces are high. The victorious revolution must at the same time insure its temporary class rule against the capitalist counteroffensive and create everywhere new mass institutions for economic management and social administration. It must both invent a new state and begin the process of its disappearance. The anarchist slogans now find an echo because the achievements of modern science have rendered the withering away of the state topical. A stateless society, if not within grasp, is within reach in a relatively short historical period. For the technologically advanced countries, including by now the Soviet Union, the march to socialism should no longer be a very long march.

The revival of vague forms of anarchism among the intelligentsia and of anarchosyndicalism among the workers is thus a healthy reaction against the bureaucratic degeneration of the official labor movement. Under the combined influence of the Stalinist distortion of Marxism and of the dominant ideology of growth, the western labor movement seems to have forgotten both its revolutionary and its libertarian origins. The industrial workers, the crucial exploited class, were supposed to seize power in order to abolish exploitation and, by the same token, to set up a classless society. Socialism was destined to bring about the liberation of man, to lead him to the realm of freedom, where the oppressive state would merely be a bad memory. Social democracy does not even claim this heritage as its own. Communist officialdom still respects the message as long as it remains sealed in the holy books and kept locked up along with other family heirlooms. In 1968 Communist bureaucrats got a shock when they discovered that the message was still so very much alive. When the famous "ghost of Communism" made its reappearance in Paris, they were as frightened as all the capitalist rulers should have been.

We saw earlier that during the May uprising the young students and workers were eloquently described in their own journal as

"the grandchildren of Marx and the [Paris] Commune." We saw
also during the French general strike that contrary to the most
fashionable theories, the industrial workers still remain the chief
factor in the process of production and therefore the main force
in political struggle. It is not the object here to determine how
far Marx's analysis of the bourgeois society of his time fits the
detailed performance of advanced capitalism or how many of the
recent "discoveries" can be traced to his books.[5] It would be most
un-Marxist not to study thoroughly the impact on society of the
technological transformations introduced over a century, and
highly undialectical not to seek the contradictions resulting from
them. But for our purpose what is striking is the conscious and
unconscious resurrection of the Marxist message in the new crisis
that is beginning to shake the advanced countries of the world
and of which French May was only an episode.

The conscious use of Marxist analysis or terminology is not so
surprising. It would have been strange if the young militants of
Paris and Milan had not borrowed some slogans from the *Communist Manifesto*. It is quite natural that in the vast literature
published in recent years against the so-called consumer society,
the earlier writings of Marx, with their emphasis on alienation,
should have been one of the sources of inspiration. After all, many
pages need no more than minor verbal alterations to read like a
tract for our times. Marx's description of salesmanship, his analysis of the commercialization of bourgeois society, the reduction
of all values—and of man—into commodities, and the erection of
money into the only social link ("money is the other") have such
a contemporary ring that it is surprising they have not been exploited on an even larger scale.

What is more interesting is the unconscious or semiconscious
revival of the Marxist message. Whole passages from the *Grun-*

---

5. A good example is provided by the now fashionable theory about
the separation between managers and employers, which Marx analyzed
and foresaw when dealing with gross profit and interest, with the division
between industrial and financial capital.

drisse,[6] from which a large extract is quoted at the opening of this part, could be taken as the refrain for the protest movement spreading from San Francisco to Tokyo across Europe. The rejection of the "theft of other people's labor time" as the criterion of wealth; the revulsion against a world in which work is an "external compulsion," while freedom or happiness is its opposite, "nonlabor"; the search for a system in which labor and leisure are a form of social and individual self-fulfillment; the revulsion against capital, the "animated monster" that turns scientific thought into objects—these are only some of the themes that can be lifted from the book and put verbatim into the mouths of the protesters. On reflection, this trend is not surprising either. The scientific revolution, the growing shadow of the machine dominating man, have rendered the Marxist message more topical.

What does it contain for the new revolutionary generation? In the first place, it holds a warning against "eternal ideas" and the eternity of their own environment. Capitalism is neither the beginning nor the end of history, only an evolving phase. Secondly, Marxism provides a method of historical analysis. Marx's major work is a detailed description of a battlefield, a monumental history of an epic struggle between labor and capital, or, to be more accurate, between living, wage-earning labor and capital, its accumulated embodiment; a struggle waged within the framework of private property.

Capital, as it started gathering strength, seemed invincible. It swept away everything in its path, breaking down barriers, crossing frontiers, extending its mode of production everywhere. The growing division of labor made it possible to introduce increas-

6. *Grundrisse der Kritik der Politischen Ökonomie* (Berlin, Dietz Verlag, 1953). The book has not yet been translated into English. These manuscripts written in 1857–1858, include extraordinary pages anticipating the age of automation, the extent to which "knowledge has become an immediate productive force," and so on. They have inspired most of this chapter. The relevance of *Grundrisse* to the present crisis is mentioned by Tom Nairn in A. Quattrocchi and T. Nairn, *The Beginning of The End* (London, Panther Books, 1968). For a text in English on the *Grundrisse*, see Martin Nicolaus in *New Left Review*, March–April, 1968.

ingly more complex machinery, to harness science, all human knowledge, for the successful advance of capital. Gradually it began to look like an unequal struggle. *Le mort saisit le vif,* as the French legal saying has it. The dead hand of accumulated labor has been limiting the scope of the living workingman, reducing his job to a fraction, breaking him down to an automatic function until in the end life apparently changed sides, moving from man to the all-powerful machine. Yet in this hour of triumph capital reaches the point of potential defeat, a fall it has been preparing throughout its rise.

Marx does not look to the past for idyllic contrasts with the woes of the modern workingman. The ancient slave or the medieval serf are no model for resurrection. The free workingman, or, to put it differently, the wage slave, of the capitalist economy differs basically from his predecessors. While he was being deprived of all autonomy through increasingly automatic production, he was acquiring a thirst for universality, for "integral development as an individual." He was also being turned into a social producer entirely dependent on the community. Capital is thus creating its own gravediggers—the workers—and preparing conditions for their reign by cutting down physical work, turning simple tasks over to the realm of science, laying the foundations of a society in which productive labor will be a "collective activity mastering the forces of nature." If it could be described up to a point as "progressive," in the narrow sense of a system that allows the fullest development of productive forces, capitalism loses this quality. In its search for surplus, capital reduces labor "in its necessary form to increase it in a useless form." The relations based on private property are an obstacle to further development. Capital cannot preside over the advent of a society in which free time will be the yardstick, the complete fulfillment of the individual the objective, and the rapid growth of productive forces merely a by-product. This is the task of the "freely associated producers" who must take over. The dialectical analysis thus leads to a call to action, and the last point in the message is revolutionary.

It is quite understandable that this message should find a louder echo now. The educated philistines who, in the name of whatever was the latest theory in fashion, used to dismiss Marxism as antediluvian and its followers as flat-earthers would have been better advised to attack it as too modern. A century ago an analysis pointing to the invasion of all walks of life by mass production and to the transition of the machine age into the age of automation may well have looked visionary. Even today, because of uneven development, it is still prophetic for large parts of the globe and for many branches even of the American economy. But in the advanced countries of the world it all now sounds very relevant. With the expansion of electronics and the spread of the computer ours is to be the age of automation. The task of scientific management is to extend the capitalist search for surplus to sectors that have hitherto performed this duty inefficiently. Only now is the harnessing of science for the development of capital acquiring its full meaning. As to the mobilization of labor for the superfluous while essential human needs are neglected, and the transformation of the superfluous into what is apparently indispensable, as things go this may become the main task of our system, the mechanism for its survival.

The signs of the growing sickness of our society are to be seen everywhere. Look at the men rushing away from their jobs as if they were leaving some place of perdition, at the huge traffic jams every weekend as the frustrated city-dwellers line up for their breath of fresh air, at the manual workers inventing manual hobbies so as to produce a whole object. Can one be genuinely surprised by the mounting and often wanton destruction, by the violent reaction of man to the wholesale commercialization of all human relations? Despite its relative material wealth, our society has proved incapable of solving the problems of man's relations with his neighbors, with his social and natural environment, with himself. It cannot find an escape through growth, which will only increase the contradictions between productive capacities and social organization, between the aspirations of more educated man and the absurdity of his life.

The alienation of the more conscious producer brings with it the thirst for the "universal." Passages from the Parisian *Amnesty for Blinded Eyes,* mentioned earlier,[7] can be read as a call for an immediate leap into freedom where man should discover his unity. Protests against the separation between rulers and ruled, between teachers and taught, are linked with slogans demanding shifting jobs, a turnover in posts of responsibility. The search is really for the abolition of the social division of labor and, in the meantime, for its reorganization by the producers themselves. Behind it lies the revolutionary aspiration toward a society that will put the "fulfillment of man" at the heart of the process of production. The distorted progress of technology only strengthens this feeling. The students and the radical intelligentsia have simply been the first to express loudly this new mood. The rulers can no longer feel complacent as Marx's message begins to get a new hearing among the proletarians for whom it was destined. The young Frenchmen striking at Rhodiaceta and their fellow strikers in Turin were not only fighting for higher wages. They were resuming in a new form the old struggle against the reign of capital.

Most of the young protesters are still talking Marxist as Jourdain in Molière's play was talking prose, unaware of it. Only a small minority, for the moment, is fighting consciously for a new social order. The masses pick up their language, or some of it, in moments of political awakening such as the French May crisis. They then return to the routine, to the concepts imposed by the ruling ideology, limiting their horizon to the bourgeois state and to their betterment within it. And yet the "ghost of Communism" has been revived, and not only because a few young people have dared. It has been thrust into the center of the political stage by something deeper, by mighty productive forces, fed by scientific progress, clashing anew with social relations. And it will go on haunting the scene because the old struggle for mastery between man and the machine, between the living producer and the dead hand of capital, has now entered a new phase.

7. See page 323 above.

THE PROGRAM *is not to be given up but only postponed—for an indefinite period. One accepts it though not really for oneself or one's own lifetime but posthumously, as an heirloom to be handed down to one's children and grandchildren. In the meantime, one devotes one's whole strength and energy to all sorts of petty rubbish and the patching up of the capitalist order of society so as to produce the appearance of something happening without at the same time scaring the bourgeoisie.*
— KARL MARX AND FRIEDRICH ENGELS,
circular letter, September 17–18, 1879

Tests for a Strategy

"They don't know what they want" is the classical accusation against protesters; it invites the obvious retort that they know what they don't want. The upholders of the established order are on stronger ground with their second charge, "They don't know how to get there." The old socialist goal, a classless society of plenty, where labor is pleasure and leisure creative, is more attractive than ever. It is the road toward this goal that is still obscure, and the clouds looming on the Soviet horizon discourage millions from joining the march.

365

The questions about the difficulties on the journey are often put by men who are not in the least interested in any movement. They are rhetorical questions raised by professionals with a stake, material or ideological, in the maintenance of the status quo. Their crudest objections are well known and can be answered with ease. They claim that the road to socialism is dangerous since it leads through revolution, and revolution means violence, they claim, forgetting that the degree of violence required to establish a new order depends on the resistance of the old and on the hidden violence it contained. The other traditional objection is that socialism is Utopian, since man is essentially selfish, greedy, lazy, and asocial. This metaphysical definition of Homo sapiens is even more absurd than the opposite description of him as altruistic, generous, gregarious, a glutton for work. Social man is to a large extent the product of his social environment, and if the typical product of bourgeois society contains only a fraction of the vices that the panegyrists of that system attribute to him, this is itself one major reason for getting rid of it. Pressed hard, the conservatives of all countries will use their ultimate argument, echoing the reply of the Grand Inquisitor to Christ in Dostoevsky's *The Brothers Karamazov*—namely, that men do not wish to be free. In the mouths of the capitalists and their ideological servants such a proclamation sounds as sincere as the drug peddler's plea for the rights of the addict.

Polemical points scored against opponents do not remove the issue. The road to socialism is not clear. The problem of the unwithering state is topical, and all the questioners are not biased or hostile. True, all great revolutions have happened because the old order was getting unbearable, because the old ruling class was unable to provide answers to new questions springing from the depth of society. The same will be fundamentally true of the next one. But workers in the advanced countries, if they still have a world to win, have also discouraging examples before their eyes. They will not give power to a movement, let alone fight for its victory, unless they know how it intends to profit from the victory and use the power. To get the indispensable support of the masses, the socialist movement must at least outline its objectives, its policy and methods for the transitional period. It must show the direction in which it is heading and how it hopes to get there.

In drafting its plans and sorting out its ideas, western socialism can draw on the theoretical and practical heritage of the revolutionary movement. It can learn from past and present experience, successful or unsuccessful. It can draw its net wide from China to Cuba. It should study the rise and fall of the Russian soviets, the dialectics of the Czech crisis, the limitations of the Yugoslav experiments with workers' councils, and so on. Yet it must digest all these lessons, remembering their respective backgrounds and knowing it has to face a different stage in the development of capitalism. It can rely on no precedent in its historic task. In forging solutions for its own environment, it has the painful duty of restoring confidence in the two interconnected assumptions that, as we saw, used to be taken for granted, namely that the dictatorship of the proletariat is another name for socialist democracy and that revolution is the beginning of the withering away of the state.

Although the first obstacles are the biggest, the path does not become smooth once the initial hurdles have been removed. Problems have to be solved all along the way. How is the revolutionary violence to be limited to the struggle against the exploiters and how is it to be compensated for by mass participation in the struggle and in the shaping of new policies? The question does not vanish with the seizure of political power. Admittedly, a new democracy will take root more easily if the capitalists are rapidly deprived of the source of their social and political influence; that is, of their wealth. But the weight of the old system will not be entirely lifted with their expropriation. The revolution will not be made by socialist man, nor will it produce such a man overnight. It will have to be carried out and consolidated by working people born and bred in bourgeois surroundings and still partly conditioned by them while trying to bring them down. It will be up to them to put into practice new methods of industrial and political rule that will turn a dictatorship into a democracy.

The removal of capital from its position as the pillar of the regime will shift the burden to the community and to the new state. If the proletarian dictatorship is not to be a misnomer, as in Russia, it must be at least the dictatorship of a vast class, and since the capitalists are a minority, it should tend to be a system of mass rule. Government will have to be replaced by self-government at all levels, from factory floor to central planning office, from the smallest local council to the provisional executive in the capital. New forms of collective rule and permanent control, of rotation and recall for delegates and officials, will have to be invented so that a national network of popular power culminates in a central political and economic authority really representing the will of the masses and relying on their support to carry out its tasks, including the provisional task of preparing the ground for its own disappearance.

Though a revolution, which removes old barriers, is a great school of mass education, the difficulties appearing at every stage will be legion. They will reflect the uninterrupted struggle between the old and the new, between conditioned reflexes and changed conditions, between old habits and new tasks. Most of the answers may have to be improvised on the spur of the moment. It is the duty of a socialist movement, nevertheless, to study the probabilities in advance, to offer proposals for debate, to suggest draft solutions.

Lack of space or the limitations of an author are no valid excuse for skipping over such crucial, practical problems. Space can always be found, and the reader is entitled to pass his verdict on clumsy suggestions. If these issues are by-passed here so as to be looked at from a different angle, from the point of arrival rather than departure, it is for more fundamental reasons. No country, no party, and certainly no man can now claim to have a blueprint for the seizure of power and its successful exercise, let alone a detailed schedule applicable throughout the world. If the concept "different roads to socialism" has any meaning at all, it is in the limited sense that various countries will be joining the main road at a different stage in their economic development and, therefore, with dissimilar levels of civilization and culture, and varying political and social traditions, including the traditions of their respective labor movements. All these differences will have to be taken into account when elaborating the immediate program for action in individual cases. The infallible scheme sent down from international or even national headquarters would simply repeat the mistakes of yesterday, the errors and dangers of command from above. To be effective and flexible, a tactical plan must spring from the soil, be tested in local conditions, be worked out and approved by its future actors.

This may sound like a hymn to pure spontaneity, leaving to the socialist movement no other job than to endorse the healthy instincts of the working class. The spontaneity of the masses, is indeed, a vital ingredient of any revolutionary policy, yet left to itself it cannot bring lasting victory. The ruling ideology does not rule only because it has money and might on its side. It is also dominant because its corresponds to the logic of the ruling system. Left to develop "spontaneously" within a capitalist framework, the working class will either be organized into a reformist movement, or if the breaking point is reached, it will burst out in a rebellion that for lack of perspective is doomed to defeat. The role of the socialist movement is to provide it with an objective, a sense of direction, a strategy. The international movement will one day recover its cohesion only if it can rise above tactical discrepancies and reach agreement on the broad lines of a socialist strategy for the world as a whole.[1]

Strategy is understood here in a precise sense. If it were simply a decorative cloak in the shape of a program, a loose collection of pious hopes to be handed down to grandchildren, as in the ironical passage from the circular letter quoted above, the international movement could be reconciled at once. Chairman Mao, Secretary Brezhnev, Mollet, Nenni, and even Harold Wilson, so proud of his ignorance of Marxism, could all express their approval for a distant socialist paradise, just as any gathering of

1. An agreement obviously means consent, not dictation, and far from excluding, implies shades of opinion.

churchmen can reach agreement, in principle, that they are against sin. But strategy is understood here as something infinitely more binding. It is linked as intimately with tactics as the ends are interconnected with the means. Strategy and the long-term perspective are the spur or rather the instrument for transforming daily battles within the system into a struggle leading to the overthrow of the system and beyond. Each tactical concession, each retreat imposed by circumstances, must be admitted as such, explained, and justified.

Program and strategy must, if only for this reason, be open and public. Although secrecy is imperative at the stage of insurrection, a revolution is not a conspiracy. Empires, it has been suggested facetiously, can be acquired "in a fit of absent-mindedness." Socialism cannot be won or built in this way. The working people can only be bullied, foxed, or cheated into a parody of socialism. It is not a question of morals, but one of practical sense. They are to be the architects and the material of the new society. The solidity of its construction largely depends on their awareness, their political consciousness, and the strength of their convictions. To acquire the builders under duress or under false pretenses is, in the best of cases, to erect a new edifice with dangerous cracks.

Mobilizing for socialism is not the same thing as wooing voters in a parliamentary or a presidential election. While not yet quite so efficient as their conservative competitors at promising the moon and playing on prejudices, socialist and Communist parties have unfortunately learned their lesson about the votes that can be caught by playing on a variety of disparate discontents. A socialist strategy is not such a catalogue of grievances. It must present a coherent alternative to capitalism even at the risk of antagonizing, temporarily or not, some sections of the population. It must show the interests of the working class as "the superior interests of society as a whole." (Mass support is the long-term test of the validity of its theories; its variations are a less reliable yardstick of practical work.)

Once strategy is defined in this way, its contents are not far to seek. The objective of a socialist strategy is to set up a socialist society. Since the job is to reach a classless and stateless future, the strategic task is to remove the successive obstacles on the way. A few of the signposts are briefly resketched below, redrawn as they should be after the Russian experience.

The movement of protest spreading throughout the western world is being given added momentum in Europe by the strains of the economic transition. The capitalist establishment still hesitates whether to meet it head on or to try to absorb it. Some of its barely concealed spokesmen are "contesting" the old bourgeois order and trying to sell its American version in the guise of modernism. A socialist refresher, to borrow their metaphors, will send them running like the Devil at the sight of holy water. But many people more genuinely muddled by confused propaganda also need a plain reminder. Socialism is not capitalism with frills, private property and a dose of planning, a bourgeois order with a bit of social welfare thrown in. Socialism is the antithesis of capitalism, a radically different conception of man and society, and there is no use smuggling it under a false label. Men, after all, should not be expected to rise of their own free will, and die if necessary, for anything less than such a radical change.

The Abolition of Private Property

Property, every "modern" pundit will explain, is by now irrelevant. Technocrats, managers, are now the masters on both sides of the great divide. The capitalist is a curious specimen exhibited in the social museum in the section devoted to the nineteenth century. Yet venture to propose the suppression of private property and the howling cry *"Vive la petite différence"* coming from the same quarters will be so loud that its very echo will bring the Galbraithian technostructure down, showing the more complex reality lying behind it. It is obviously not for the sake of such intellectual fun that the abolition of private ownership of the means of production must figure at the top of any socialist program. We now know for certain that it is far from sufficient even to insure a march toward socialism. In Russia, it has so far ushered in a strange postcapitalist breed. In western Europe, nationalized industries have been the handmaidens of capitalist development. Insufficient but nevertheless indispensable: Without the abolition of private property there can be no question of eliminating the exploitation of man by man, no possibility of replacing a system ultimately based on the search for surplus value with a more rational method of social organization.

Peaceful coexistence may survive for a time on the world scale, imposed as it is by nuclear stalemate. Within a single state even such an uneasy coexistence is impossible. One system must gain the upper hand. Throughout western Europe capitalism is dominant, and references to a mixed economy are misleading. Nationalized industries, either through subsidies or through a monopoly position, may have prices not corresponding to their cost of production. They charge them, however, in order to prop up the structure of private property and not to upset it. Thus, deficit financing of basic production or transport by state monopolies helps their private customers to swell their profits. The state can provide risk capital where private investors are shy to venture. It can also simply compete on equal terms. The ownership of nationalized industries or banks helps a state to introduce an element of coherence into the modern capitalist economy of imperfect competition, but like other forms of state intervention this influence is designed to consolidate the existing system. Indeed, the modernists, with a certain degree of consistency, want the nationalized industries to be run on purely commercial lines, without subsidies, the state intervening in a sector only when private enterprise fails to fulfill its function or draws an excessive profit from a monopoly position. As a matter of fact, state firms do not differ substantially from private concerns, either in their organization or in their labor relations, and it was not really surprising that the French wave of strikes actually started in the nationalized aircraft and automobile industries.

One system must prevail, and if socialist planning is to impose its own pattern on a country's economy, it must occupy its "commanding heights," to use a classical expression. But by now, as a result of concentration, these heights are enormous, and, as a result of technological change, they are shifting. If the capitalists are allowed compensation for their assets, they will invade new territory, or providing the present freedom of capital movement remains, they will seek safety and profit abroad. A government trying gradually to introduce planning on noncapitalist lines would be rapidly driven by the logic of the resistance to socialize all key sectors of the economy and to overhaul the state machinery so that it could serve new interests and a new purpose. In other words, it would have to carry out a revolutionary transformation of both property relations and institutions. What class resistance it would meet is another matter, but socialism will not prevail without such a radical break. There can be a greater or lesser degree of violence and bloodshed; there can be no economy of revolution.

Yet revolution itself is but a prelude. In postcapitalist Russia all industry is state-owned. It would require a good dose of naïveté or cynicism to suggest that the collective producers in Russia are the masters of their social environment or even to claim that they participate actively in the shaping of economic policy. Most of the features once associated with the concept of a socialist society are absent in the Soviet Union, and, disquietingly, they show no sign of developing as the country grows richer. The revolution and the abolition of private property are but a beginning, yet without this start there can be no question of building a socialist society. This is why, despite the Soviet experience, the abolition of private property remains a dividing line between those who struggle for a socialist future and those who do not.

Through Planning to Distribution

Socialism does not emerge full-fledged from the capitalist womb. Its most serious problems are problems of transition, springing from the contrast between the long-term goal and the limitations of its postcapitalist setting. Thus, in the future socialist society there should be no money, gold in Lenin's colorful image being available to build public lavatories. In fact, there should be no need for money with the disappearance of commodity production, free distribution taking the place of the market. The snags lie in the interval. Free distribution presupposes plenty. Even in the advanced western countries relative scarcity would involve rationing for most goods and the risk of a black market. Rationing by the card rather than by the purse may have advantages in certain circumstances. In the present state of western development it would be neither the most efficient nor the most popular form of distributing consumer goods.

This does not mean that a socialist regime could not act against the prevailing rules from the very start. It could spell the "death of the salesman" and the beginning of genuine information about the use and quality of products. The cost of advertising goes well beyond the two to three per cent of the national product most western countries spend on it. The social cost of aggressive salesmanship lies in the distortions it brings to the pattern of consumption and the pattern of life. From the point of view of the capitalist firm, particularly the big corporation, the money is well spent. It provides outlets for the goods and by speeding up turnover increases the return on capital. From the point of view of society the benefit is not the same. The average consumer, the alleged hero of our age, has simply lost some more of his much vaunted freedom. He already has no say in the long-term investment decisions that determine the framework within which his choice will be exercised; these are made by the big corporations, by now in co-ordination with the state. As a producer he has no influence on the output nor on conditions of work. And by now his freedom of choice as a consumer is being twisted by the crafty advertiser. In any case, it should never be forgotten that this freedom depends on the size of his purse.

All this could be changed fairly rapidly by a socialist regime. One of its first tasks would be a drastic equalization of incomes, thus uprooting one of the major distortions of the present market. Advertising could be put under the supervision of public boards keeping a check on the truthfulness of claims, the level of expenditure, and so on. Consumer councils and co-operatives might help in this. Sociologists and other investigators would not be out of work in the period of transition to socialism. But their duties would be radically different. Instead of market research, aimed at finding out the preferences of various income groups, their job would be to help the planners to measure the real aspirations of the consumer. Instead of persuading potential buyers to buy, it would be necessary to explain to consumers the implications of their choice.

These and similar measures would mark a step forward so long as it was clear that they were half-measures, that the objective was not to improve the market but to get rid of it. At every step, when economic conditions would allow it, new sectors would have to be shifted to free distribution. (All western countries could probably begin their transitional period by taking over the full cost of the social services and by making public transport free of charge.) The socialist aim is not to revive the price mechanism and restore a perfect competition straight out of the textbook. It is to help the collective producers to become as rapidly as possible the masters of their economic and social life.

It may be objected that even in capitalist society the big corporations are not slaves of the costs of production in fixing their prices, that the capitalist state, too, provides welfare services and redistributes income through social transfers and taxation. Yet its purpose in doing so is diametrically opposed to that of socialism. The capitalist regime makes such concessions to preserve private property, social inequality, and injustice. The postcapitalist regime, having uprooted private ownership of the means of production, would have to attack all the remnants of inequality in order to pave the way for socialism. It could not do so with the same institutions.

New Institutions

Each society needs institutions that suit its own needs. Capitalist society, which rests on private property and profit, requires a framework to protect them. If the state has grown so mighty in most western countries it is because in the phase of monopolistic competition its interventions are indispensable to preserve the system. In the postcapitalist society, with collective producers seeking their way toward socialism, property and wealth will cease to be the mainstay of social organization. The tendency, in the early transitional period, will be for the state to grow in stature. The new institutions will thus have to perform several apparently contradictory functions. They will have to be strong enough to enable the state to carry out its provisional tasks; democratic enough to counter the dictatorship and prevent the state from becoming permanent; flexible enough to inherit its successive functions as it withers away.

In the initial phase the role of the state is bound to be important, particularly in the economic life of the country. The postcapitalist society will not be able to dispense with a central organ expressing and imposing collective decisions about the aggregates of economic activity, about the levels and pattern of production and consumption, about the degree of accumulation, the direction of long-term investments crucial for the future. How are these key decisions made now? They are not, if they ever were, made entirely haphazardly by a host of producers responding individually to the pulls of the market. But neither are they made rationally to satisfy social needs. They are determined essentially by a few big corporations, seeking to maximize their profits over a period in monopolistic competition, after a study of the market and of its prospects. They are taken in conjunction with the administration, which has means to influence them, the duty to co-ordinate the measures and to back them through its economic policy.[2] In

2. There are real conflicts between the two, but their contradictions are not antagonistic.

countries like France, where this co-operation is more articulate, the medium-term projection—a mixture of plan and a kind of weather forecast—is published and has to get parliamentary approval. The advocates of democratic planning in a capitalist economy would like the draft to be made up of several versions based on the hypothesis of differing rates of growth.

Socialist planning would be quite a different matter. Its main targets would be binding, imperative not indicative, which would make sense since at least all the big industrial firms would be collective property in a postcapitalist society. For the planning debate to be meaningful, all the answers that the computers can now provide, all the latest findings obtained through improvements in input-output analysis or consumer research, could no longer be kept in the darkness of the administrative boardrooms. They would have to be explained to the vast public to allow it to judge the consequences of the decisions.

It would not be enough to announce, say, that it was proposed to build x million cars of such and such models. In addition, it would have to be stated how many more could be produced—or how much could be saved—by temporarily reducing the number of models. The real cost would have to be explained not just in terms of steel, garages, and roads, but also by taking into account the necessary expenditure on the struggle against pollution, on city planning, and so on. Moving beyond a single item, the planners would have to spell out the link between variables, the opportunity cost, the alternative between additional labor and leisure, between health or education and more consumer goods. The citizen should be able to know what kind of future is being prepared for him through current investments and what social or human costs are involved in, say, shifting southern Italian peasants to Turin or in introducing new methods and rhythms of production.

No amount of open debate, of genuine popularization on television, radio, and in the press, can make the process of planning and counterplanning democratic if people do not have the feeling that they are really concerned and directly involved. Politically, this requires an entirely new framework of local self-government, based on what Americans call the community neighborhood and what the French once used to mean by the *commune*. Economically, the May slogan *autogestion* would fast come into its own. Here would lie the opportunity to move quickly from workers' control to a share of the management and then to full management by collective producers.

Full management by the workers should not be confused with a kind of free enterprise. Socialism is not a system of free competition between jointly owned co-operatives. This would not eliminate differences between rich and poor co-operatives or the elements of anarchy in the market. Socialism is an attempt by the collective owners of all productive capacity to rise above commodity production. In the transitional period the major danger, illustrated by the Soviet example, would be allowing the state to dwarf society and thus to perpetuate itself—hence the need for built-in safeguards in the form of democratic institutions. The other danger would lie in so weakening the central authority that it could not guide society toward socialism. Postcapitalist society will still be a system of class rule, but it must be the collective rule of the have-nots, eliminating the remnants of class differences and social inequalities, removing the vestiges of the bourgeois past so as to clear the road toward freedom. In this drive two interconnected elements—egalitarianism and education—are destined to play a more crucial role than was once assumed.

The New Levelers

Complete economic equality is another of the goals that, in principle, is to be reached only at the stage of full socialism. Indeed, equality is the natural companion of free distribution. Yet as we saw earlier, each is to pick from the common fund according to his needs only when social labor has become a prime necessity of life and the differences in skill have become irrelevant. In the meantime, the capitalist profit having been removed, each is to be rewarded according to his labor, and the existing differences in productive capacity will thus be reflected in wage differences. To level wages when economic conditions, and minds, have not been prepared for the change, the argument runs, is to destroy the incentive, break the economic link, create chaos, and put off the day when the switch will become possible. It is, nevertheless, taken for granted that the postrevolutionary society would move inexorably toward equality, another assumption that must be re-examined in the light of the Soviet experience.

When the chairman of the board of a nationalized industry in Britain earns twenty or thirty times more than the workers in his firm, the reason is obvious. In the so-called mixed economy, predominant capitalism imposes its habits. But when in Russia, half a century after the revolution, a huge gap separates the salaries of factory managers, party dignitaries, and academicians from the lowest income brackets, the explanation cannot be the same. True, the member of the Soviet establishment has no shares in the firm and cannot hand them over to his children. The logic of the privileged caste might have driven it to seek to re-establish private property. (Some critics of Soviet bureaucracy, like Trotsky, envisaged such a development.) It has not done so, at least not yet, and this is why the Chinese charge of a "restoration of capitalism" is inaccurate. Yet it has done the second best. It has managed to preserve a hierarchical society, consolidating its privileged position at the top.

Admittedly, the dramatic changes in Soviet society and the openings created by the revolution mean that even now social mobility is greater there than in the capitalist West. But it is still very much mobility up a ladder, and as time passes, it increasingly favors those born nearer the top. For the privileged, whose position rests on a hierarchical structure, it is quite natural, consciously or not, to opt always for solutions emphasizing differences and to resist leveling trends. But the Soviet rulers cannot proclaim, or even apply, their doctrine with complete consistency. On the one hand, egalitarianism has been branded as the heresy of heresies both in Stalin's time and since. On the other, the myth must be maintained that equality will fall from heaven in a future Communist paradise.

Not quite from heaven. In the Marxist interpretation, reduced here to a mechanical formula, equality will follow automatically in the wake of technological progress and spread of education. When automation has taken over all mechanical tasks and all has become scientific, productivity will become a by-product of human development, the difference between mental and physical work will vanish, and so will the problem of equality. One can imagine an intermediate stage, in which the socially necessary amount of manual labor and of the monotonous work of supervision have been so drastically reduced that everyone will gladly agree to carry out, say, three hours of this social work a day. In the meantime, the bosses are the bosses, and the subordinates should know their station.

It is argued here that the process is not at all automatic, that in the postcapitalist society the provisional can last and hinder development in a socialist direction. The drive toward equality must be aided and abetted. It must begin with the revolution itself and be sustained afterward by permanent social pressure. It is the job of the new socialist levelers to keep it up. But before this argument can be developed, one must look at one major ingredient of equality, or inequality, in our age.

School for Socialism

Education is vital in any project of social transformation because its role is so important both in production and social organization. The school, from kindergarten to adult education, provides training for work and is also an instrument of integration. It is both the main channel of social mobility and the pillar of the existing structure, the upholder of its stratification. It legitimizes privileges by giving them an air of achievement. The Bolsheviks were so conscious of the class bias of bourgeois education that to redress it they originally gave top priority in universities to sons of workers and peasants. In those early days, they toyed with the idea of going farther, of reshaping the contents and methods of education so as to prevent the creation of a new division between rulers and ruled. Absorbed by the gigantic tasks of mass education in an illiterate country, they soon gave up their experimental efforts. The educational system then became more hierarchical along with the whole of Soviet society.

"Do you expect a bourgeois state to run a Cuban university?" This rhetorical question put in May 1968, presumably meant that one could not expect any society to sponsor a system of education designed to bring down its institutions. Yet this is exactly what a postcapitalist society should do if it is to be a transitional stage on the road to socialism. It must prepare for the withering away of its state. The future socialist school may be able to afford to concentrate on teaching men to gain a collective mastery over nature. The school for socialism must also teach them to master their social environment. Cooks, as Lenin put it, must know how to run the affairs of the state. But administration and control, like cooking, have to be learned. If, on the one hand, the veil of secrecy surrounding the political and economic life of the country has to be lifted, if new institutions have to be created in order to bring power to the people, on the other hand, the subjects of yesterday will have to learn to run their own affairs, and the school will have to help them in this effort.

In developed socialist society differences of skill will be irrelevant. They will not disappear. This point is stressed on purpose. Socialism does not aim at a leveling of talents or a stifling of personality. On the contrary, its main ambition is to put man's fulfillment at the heart of social development. Many years will naturally elapse before economic expansion becomes a mere by-product of this fulfillment. In the meantime, education will have the dual job of strengthening the productive forces of the nation and of replacing the old conception of achievement at the expense of others, which is finally rewarded in financial terms. After centuries during which men's minds were fashioned by the "acquisitive society," this will require a revolutionary change in the whole process of education. The school will get nowhere in this respect if outside big differences in salary remain the reward of varying skills. The egalitarian school must go hand in hand with a rapidly narrowing range of remuneration. And for several reasons egalitarianism, spurned by Stalinist as well as bourgeois ideology, must recover pride of place in the socialist program.

The French crisis confirmed that the industrial workers, for all the changes in their inner makeup and living standards, remain the main force capable of paralyzing and overthrowing existing capitalist regimes. The workers have acquired durable consumer goods. They have not regained control over their tools. Indeed, the growing importance of education has added yet another handicap to their condition. If they now seize power in order to establish a classless society, the privileges they will have to abolish will include the privilege of education.

But simultaneously the frontiers separating the proletariat from its social neighbors have become less clear. Shop assistants, employees, office workers, are being reduced to similarly alienating labor conditions. There is only a thin line dividing skilled workers from technicians, researchers, and part of the professional intelligentsia. These new proletarians, it was argued earlier, have to accept their educational advantage as a temporary windfall if they opt for a socialist rather than a managerial revolution. Egalitarianism will thus be a good first test of the cohesion of the new socialist movement.

Nobody suggests that all salary and wage differentials should be canceled with one stroke of a pen. It can be readily granted that such a switch, if unprepared, would have catastrophic effects. The snag is that in the East as well as in the West, the leveling lags far behind the technological possibilities. Wage differences are maintained in order to divide, to render the working class less homogeneous. What is more important, the very preservation of the hierarchical order as a system of rule prevents technological progress from performing its leveling function. Only a conscious effort, a method of planning that puts man's leisure, his fulfillment, at the center of economic activity, will spur on science to speed up the process of automation and open the way for a society in which broken-up, mechanical labor is gradually reduced to a minimum.

Here lies the answer to the awkward question of whether a given country is "ripe" for socialism. The advanced western nations are so ripe for transition that they are rotting. The last long stretch, however, will not be covered automatically. The American example shows that capitalism is still able to invent by-passes. The Russian example proves that even a successful revolution does not insure a subsequent "inevitability of gradualism." Equality, like socialism, will only be reached by continuous effort, by permanent struggle backed all along by mass support.

Masses in Motion

This is where the biggest difficulty lies for a socialist movement. It is not enough to mobilize for one great, heroic heave and then leave the leadership to an elite that directs things from above. The masses must intervene directly at all stages from beginning to end.

First change the nature of man—priests, preachers, and moralists have been repeating this for centuries. Since our commercial soil is not particularly propitious for the mass production of saints, their plea, whatever their intentions, continues to serve the interests of the rulers. Change society in order to change man —this is the socialist reply. The slogan remains profoundly true, although, like the one about the leap into freedom, it can be misleading if interpreted mechanically.

Even before the Soviet experiment nobody seriously thought that with the signing of a decree proclaiming the abolition of private property and the establishment of a workers' state men would wake up on the morrow magically turned into socialists. There was, however, a certain illusion that they would inevitably develop in that direction. But the idea contained in the slogan is different. It suggests continuous interaction; man changing society, altering himself in the process, then being affected by his new environment, and so on. The seizure of power by the workers and the abolition of private property are only a vital and privileged moment in the organic process of permanent revolution, in the uninterrupted struggle that can only end in the "realm of freedom."

A march, or better still a climb, the masses conquering the mountain layer by layer, conveys this idea more accurately than the image of a "leap to the realm of freedom." But it will be a peculiar climb, getting easier and easier as man progressively struggles out of the realm of necessity. Unless we blow our planet to pieces before he can get there, free socialist man will one day look down from his height, puzzled by the timidity of what are now described as our boldest and most "Utopian" projections. He will study them with amusement but also with sympathy, as we look on the Promethean efforts of prehistoric man.

Having glanced at the direction in which the climb or march may be heading, it is possible to get back to the marchers, to return to the question, purposely left unanswered earlier in the book, about the nature of the movement, organization, or party most suited for the tasks ahead. Ideally, it should be the whole changing proletariat and its growing potential allies. If all the exploited, if all those who stand to gain, if the overwhelming majority of the nation, were conscious of their broader political interests, there would be no gap between movement and organization, and the problem of a party would be by-passed. Yet even short of such an unrealistic ideal, the duties of a revolutionary organization are still enormous. They spring from the tasks that were described above.

To start with, the organization must provide a strategy based on a scientific appreciation of the balance of forces national and international. It must widen its analysis and supply the link between daily struggle within the system and the solutions lying beyond. This "collective intellectual" must also be disciplined and organized enough to co-ordinate the movement in its trials of strength. But its role does not end with the first victory. It must be the party of permanent revolution, placing itself at the head of the masses when they advance and in the rear, sustaining them when, temporarily wearied and exhausted, they feel like retreating. Yet we also saw that the organization, by its own behavior, must guarantee that the proletarian dictatorship will spell socialist democracy and the revolution will mark the beginning of the withering away of the state.

The central point is the relationship with the masses. The party's duty is to do theoretical work and carry out propaganda so as to counter the ruling ideology. This domination, nevertheless, must be taken into account. The party cannot just pander to the majority. It must stick to its principles, to its socialist goal, and try to conquer "majority through action." But the organization, or its leadership, should never stand in for the working class. To express the profound aspirations of the people and guide them in a socialist direction, the organization should reflect them in its own ranks. It must educate itself while educating the movement. For this it requires inner democracy, open debate, the breaking of barriers between leaders and led. After so many bitter experiences both its statutes and practice will have to give proofs that they are genuine.

New times, new tasks, call for a new instrument. We are concerned here not with paragraphs in the party statutes, but with the underlying conception, the conception of the organization best suited to carry the socialist movement to a successful conclusion in the advanced western countries. Conditions are different here from what they were in czarist Russia. The scope for open political action is incomparably greater, the repression being more subtle. The stage of economic development has its consequences. The workers are more numerous, more skilled, more educated. They have potential allies who can help them in the rapid transformation of society, and they are not drowned in a peasant sea. The productive forces have a potential that makes the transition to socialism a concrete prospect, not a goal requiring a superhuman effort. All this and Russia's post-Bolshevik vargaries, despite the precautions taken by Lenin, seem to militate in favor of an organization pinning its hopes on "a series of great creative acts of the often spontaneous class struggle seeking its way forward," on "the active, untrammeled, energetic political life of the broadest mass of the people"; in other words, in favor of the conception of Rosa Luxemburg, from whom these lines are taken, rather than in favor of Lenin's model of a tightly knit vanguard.

"All theory, dear friend is gray, but the golden tree of life springs ever green"—this was Lenin's favorite quotation from Goethe. Between the theoretical need and the immediate practical possibilities the distance is great, and the theoretical model itself could be altered by circumstances. If France and Italy were to be victims tomorrow of a coup by their brand of colonels, the organizational recipe would not be the same. In more general terms, if the authoritarian forces gain the upper hand in the western world and by more direct forms of repression drive the revolutionary movement underground or into a semiclandestineness, the best methods of struggle for that movement will be different. The shape taken by the Bolshevik party, after all, was largely the result of illegality and czarist terror.

An even bigger qualification must be made when one shifts from abstract requirement to concrete possibility. The new organization would not be created *ex nihilo*. It would have to reckon with the local traditions of the labor movement and the existing structures. In the United States it will have little competition but must meet the resistance of a hitherto hostile working class. In western Europe, where the soil is more propitious, most of the territory is occupied by social-democratic parties completely integrated into the system or by Communist parties moving the same way. The young revolutionary workers, students, and intellectuals may find scope for action in labor unions. With the highly doubtful exception of Italy, they can achieve next to nothing in the existing political parties.

If they were to start on their own, they could at most form a loose association, a somewhat more organized version of the French March 22 Movement described earlier in this story. The members would have to agree on some basic principles and let action to be determined by joint decisions. The various groups to be found throughout the western world reflect different strands of the revolutionary tradition: Trotskyist, Maoist, anarchosyndicalist, and so on. The danger for such a loose movement would be centrifugal rather than the threat of overcentralism. In order to survive, it would have to allow the component groups to confront their ideas in open debate, leaving it to the test of time and history to settle the conflicts.

Can the sects be merged and transformed by the movement? Can they provide the theoretical link, elaborate a strategy, give a sense of direction to the masses or, more modestly, exercise enough influence to break the restraining control exercised by the traditional parties and unions? On the answers to such questions depends the reply to the central issue of this book: Will Europe's age of conflict turn into an age of revolution? There can be no clear answer. Against the weakness of divided "grouplets" one must set the building pressure and the rather optimistic assumption underlying much socialist thought and action; namely, that when the need is strong, history forges the necessary instrument—history with the help of man.

Even if the revolution were to triumph somewhere and set up a socialist democracy, could such a society function and its economy prosper? A new pioneer, it would certainly advance learning through trial and error. Yet the doubters who know no other productivity than the one expressed in the yield columns of *The Wall Street Journal* or *The Financial Times* can be easily silenced. Let them look at their own model, at the degree of organization it has been compelled to introduce, at the ersatz planning it was forced to absorb. Let them look at the efforts their society makes to integrate the workers into the firm, at the zeal with which it jumps on all ideas of partnership or participation. This is not only "vice paying homage to virtue." [3] It is the past trying to borrow fragments of the future in order to survive.

More serious is the final objection that if revolution triumphed in one country, it would still have to face a hostile world.

3. The celebrated sentence from Vauvenargues was aptly quoted in this context by E. Mandel in *Traité de l'Économie Marxiste*.

THE NEW FRENCH REVOLUTION *will at once be forced to leave its national soil and to conquer the European terrain.*
—KARL MARX, *Civil War in France*

WE DON'T GIVE A DAMN *about frontiers.*
—*May slogan*

The International Dimension

French workers and students could not have seized power in May because Europe would not have liked it, and who would make a revolution that involved taking the risk of a deficit in the balance of payments? It will not surprise anybody that the very men who put up such strange arguments to defend Communist strategy during the May crisis can only conceive a socialist victory if it has established law on its side. They are ex-Communists who fell a second time in love with their party when they found it so

389

sweetly reasonable.[1] If one understands them correctly, they are in favor of socialism, of a seizure of power, even of a kind of revolution, provided these can be achieved with the blessing of the domestic bourgeoisie and a green light from European capitalism. It is to be hoped they are patient men, because they may have to wait a long time for such a graceful takeover.

However ridiculously, the self-appointed defenders of the Communist party have raised serious and important issues. The revolution is national to start with, and socialism is international in its very essence. The division of labor has now reached such proportions that no country, particularly no medium-sized state, can extricate itself from it without heavy cost. This general rule has a particular relevance for the Common Market because the economies of the member countries are growing progressively integrated.

Europe will never like it, or, to be more accurate, the European capitalist establishment could not welcome a genuinely socialist government in its midst even if it should arrive clad in the full majesty of the law. Whatever its legal birth certificate, it is the nature of the regime that matters, and capitalist rulers must fight their socialist rival tooth and nail, with all the means at their disposal.[2] The socialist movement should, therefore, prepare for this struggle, seek allies beyond its frontiers, and fit its strategy into an international context. Even a nationalist regime daring to rebel against the Euratlantic setup dominated by the United States is rapidly shown the limits of its freedom of action. The Gaullist

1. See Jean Dru in *Le Nouvel Observateur*, No. 189, June 26, 1968.
2. In dealing with the French May crisis we did not discuss the risks of American intervention simply because we found no trace that it was contemplated at the time. It must be remembered, however, that circumstances were particularly favorable: (1) The events took everybody by surprise; (2) there were no American troops on French soil; (3) France was outside NATO and it was difficult for General de Gaulle to turn to America for support; (4) the Russians had not yet invaded Czechoslovakia. What would happen now in, say, the case of an Italian crisis is another matter. Would the Americans intervene directly? Would they take the risk of a "European Vietnam"? Such questions are a subject in themselves, and they are on the agenda of the revolutionary movement both in Europe and in the United States.

experience, with its successes and shortcomings, is not only interesting in itself. It is also instructive for its potential successors.

It is for his foreign policy that General de Gaulle will probably be best remembered. To say this is not the same as to endorse the view of his admirers that the General was a visionary consistently following a single course. In fact, he was more masterly as tactician than as strategist, and the only consistency in his policy was his striving for a role as one of the big three, on a par with the rulers of America and Russia.[3] Since France, to his chagrin, was no longer powerful enough to lift him there, he had to turn to Europe. Violently opposed to the Rome treaty when it was being negotiated, he nevertheless brought France into the Common Market on his return to power. The European mass was a price worth paying for the leadership of little Europe, of the countries bordering on the Rhine, the Alps, and the Pyrenees. This was the grand design, resting on the Paris-Bonn axis, that he tried to erect during the first half of his second reign. Not until 1962–1963, when it was too obvious Germany could not be a junior partner, particularly for a policy designed to question the American leadership, did he switch with brilliant skill to the line now associated with his name. Challenging the United States on all fronts, leaning toward Russia in order to redress the European balance, he also gathered laurels throughout the third world as the new champion of independence.

Gaullist policy is best defined as one of anachronistic realism, both aspects resulting from the same cause, from the role played by the nation-state in our times. General de Gaulle was realistic enough to grasp that far from having vanished, the modern nation-state was much mightier than in the age of nationalities. And he used effectively the weapon at his disposal. A man of military upbringing for whom "the sword is the world's axis," he understood from the start that France could not have an independent policy while its troops were integrated in NATO under

3. For a left-wing criticism of Gaullist foreign policy see Daniel Martin in *International Socialist Journal*, No. 22, August 1967.

American command. Ruler of a country where the industrial giants are smaller than their German or British competitors, but where the power of the state is greater, he was naturally opposed to supranationality; that is, to the transfer of state power from a national to a European capital, from Paris to Brussels. Although no economist, he nevertheless sensed that the economic recovery of European nations had given them more scope for action. He dared to venture and oppose when others still stood at attention. He took France out of NATO, slowed down the process of Europe's supranational integration, challenged the mighty dollar, openly criticized American policy in Vietnam and Latin America. He did all this and got away with it.

The anachronism sprang from the same source. The bourgeois state did not allow him to compensate for the limitations of scale by the socialization of production. Indeed, he was not even able to prevent the penetration of American capital.[4] When a European firm was ready to be swallowed, it usually chose to be eaten by the giant with the greatest technological and financial power, which as a rule happened to be American. In the name of what principles and what kind of society were the Gaullists to reverse this trend? Also, the national state is obsolete. France genuinely could not provide General de Gaulle with the means for his policy. He was driven beyond its frontiers. There, however, he was not strong enough to impose his will, nor did he offer an alternative that could attract. He was able to prevent and perform. Playing the same game as the Americans, he was bound to lose. Even before the May crisis put the nail in its coffin, it was possible to write an epitaph on Gaullist foreign policy: a magnificent struggle that a conservative General was not equipped to win.

The controversy over Gaullism in foreign policy was not exclusively French, nor did it close with the end of General de Gaulle's rule. It reflects the contradictions of west European capitalism, torn between its natural tendency to move in the American orbit and the equally natural resistances, national or other-

4. The takeover of Machines Bull by General Electric and of Simca by Chrysler created the biggest stir.

wise, to this attraction. The quarrels between the Gaullists and the "Europeans" of the Monnet variety,[5] between the nationalist advocates of co-operation among states, of a Europe of Fatherlands, and the champions of a rapid advance toward a west European federation, will go on bitterly for some time to come. They remind the outsider of the dispute between the blind and the paralytic, in which each side sounds right when it enumerates the vices of the other.

You are men of the past, the Europeans charge the Gaullists, still living in the time of Louis XIV. The present is the era of great continental units. A country the size of France does not carry enough weight. Its *force de frappe* impresses nobody. Its firms cannot have the size or financial power to stand up to their American competitors. Separately, the west European countries can only be colonized by the United States. Their chance lies in unity, which can only be sponsored by common institutions. You Gaullists pretend to fight against the American hegemony, the indictment concludes, but in practice, by preventing unity you facilitate the American invasion.

You Europeans, the Gaullists retort, are either fools or knaves. States are the only concrete reality. A stateless Europe would inevitably lead to an Atlantic community under American leadership. To have a federation, you need a federator. No west European country can be one. The concealed federator is an outsider, the United States. All forms of European integration, whether military, political, or economic, are at this stage a disguise for consolidating the American domination of Europe. Dressed in Euratlantic colors, thunder the Gaullists, you are the American party.

A socialist listening in is forced to nod and elaborate. Gaullism, for all its useful negative actions, could offer no positive alternative. For lack of a socialist content, its gestures of independence were doomed in the final analysis to remain empty gestures. As for the European phrasemongers, they were masters of a verbal

5. Their American sympathizers, particularly prominent in the State Department, were known as "the theologians."

smokescreen. Their fashionable "responses" to the American "challenge" are a recipe for surrender and a disguise for their only preoccupation—how to preserve capitalism in Europe. The quarrel, for all its bitterness, is a family quarrel and has no bearing on the main issue. Neither of the protagonists offers the prospect of a society radically different from the American and hence cannot propose any serious means of resistance to the United States. Both are basically irrelevant, because the real choice lies between the United Socialist States of Europe and the Europe of the United States.

It would be highly inaccurate to report that the European left has treated the partners in this dispute with such a contemptuous "A plague on both your houses." Most of the leaders of European social democracy have actually been among the most vociferous spokesmen for the Euratlantic side, showing underneath their verbiage that "western" is for them synonymous with "capitalist." The Communists, especially in France, had to take up a more complicated position. Opposed to General de Gaulle for domestic reasons, they were forced to approve the "positive aspects" of the General's foreign policy. Yet both their criticisms and praise were couched in terms of national sovereignty, not of a socialist alternative for Europe. Against this background of social-democratic submission and Communist narrow-mindedness, a nationalist General could appear for five years or so as the "progressive" figure on the European horizon.

The Gaullist precedent should help the socialist movement to work out a strategy suited to the present stage of European development. Capitalist supranationality is not yet the rule in the Common Market. The big financial and industrial firms still seek aid and protection from their national capitals rather than from an embryonic central authority in Brussels. The tendency for supranational firms to rule bourgeois Europe collectively through a European proxy rather than through national states has not yet prevailed. Indeed, during the first decade of the Common Market, concentration was essentially a national phenomenon, and the few big mergers that cut across frontiers more often than not involved American firms. On the other hand, the disappearance of inner tariff barriers within the EEC, the interpenetration of business activity and of its swings as well as the recent speeding up of supranational mergers, make it absurd for the labor movement in any of the six countries to elaborate its policies in splendid isolation. Co-ordination of trade-union activity, still in its infancy, is fast becoming an imperative. It could lead to a revival of solidarity, which will be badly needed by the first of the members to make its bid for socialism.

Member countries of the Common Market can still make their bid one by one. By now, it is impossible to imagine a revolution triumphant in, say, one region of France or one province of Italy; it either spreads immediately to the rest of the country or is bound to collapse. But it is still possible to imagine a socialist victory in, say, France or Italy, with the resulting regime holding on for a time. State power is not yet to be conquered in Brussels,[6] nor are the various socialist forces in Europe ready for a frontal, simultaneous assault. This time lag, this different degree of preparedness of the individual battalions, and not any national nonsense, should be at the root of socialist oppostion to European supranationality. Each international project, each institutional change or transfer of power to Brussels, must be examined in the light of the effect it is likely to have on the first socialist pioneer: How far does it reduce its scope for planning, its room for maneuver, its chances of survival?

With such immediate proposals as a withdrawal from the Atlantic alliance and a close, critical scrutiny of all projects of European integration, the socialist program might have a rather ultra-Gaullist ring. To avoid the demoralizing effect of the nationalist perversion, it would have to spell out its quite different reasons. It would have to stress that it does not fight supranationality in the name of jingoist national grandeur or the patriotic defense of profit margins. It would have to say that it does not

6. Except for the Belgians.

give a damn about national sovereignty and keeps it only in trust
for socialist Europe. It would have to repeat time and again that
a deal with Krupp, Fiat, Philips, or Rhône-Poulenc is not the
same thing as an agreement with their workers' councils.

What the movement should preach in opposition, a socialist
government would have to practice in power, by whatever means
it used to get there. A genuine socialist government, carried forward by popular support, will be at one and the same time in a
more difficult and much stronger position than Gaullism to cope
with its Euratlantic environment. It will be in greater trouble,
because under heavier fire. This will not be a phony war, with
studied skirmishes, marathons in Brussels, and diplomatic niceties.
It will be a struggle for survival, the capitalist powers trying to
strangle the socialist intruder before its example can prove contagious. The newcomer would be doomed if it relied on a scrap
of paper, a certificate of constitutional legitimacy. To defend its
revolutionary birthright, it will have to count on its own forces,
on popular support and international solidarity.

But a socialist regime in France or Italy will be in a better
position to fight back than would be a Gaullist equivalent. Its
advantage will lie in the superiority of the postcapitalist state. It
will propose a different society and new means for defending it.
With its control of the "commanding heights" and with planning
on a national scale, it will be better placed to defend vital sectors
of the economy or to make up through a proper direction of investment some of the disadvantages of size. Admittedly, it will not
be able to overcome fully the limitations of a nation-state, but its
struggle should be essentially a holding operation. A socialist
government will not only bargain with hostile partners. It will
appeal above their heads to the workers of Europe, and pin its
hopes on their action.

For once, such hopes have a fair chance of not being disappointed. A successful revolution in France is now likely to precipitate an upheaval in Italy, and vice versa. It might spread to
Spain and Belgium. Of the Common Market countries, the Dutch
and, essentially, the Germans would be on the other side. The

balance of forces would then be different. We would be faced with the highly exceptional situation of two aggressively hostile systems coexisting within the same framework. Provisional by its very nature, the confrontation would be full of explosive and complicated unknowns. Thus, the German government might be tempted to squeeze its rivals with American support, but it would be afraid lest they turn to Russia in retaliation. With each side fighting for its life, there might be plenty of maneuvers, yet the main stake in the battle would finally be clear: Who is to have the mastery in western Europe, capitalism or socialism? Behind the verbal fog this is what it has always been about.[7]

Let us go farther and imagine that socialism emerges victorious from this trial of strength. Even this would not mark the end of external problems for socialist western Europe. American productivity is roughly twice the European level. To avoid being dominated by a hostile social system still enjoying a technological superiority, Europe would have to preserve a protective wall and keep control of foreign exchanges so as to limit the admission of American goods. It would thereby still deprive itself of some of the advantages of the international division of labor. But socialist Europe would have many compensations. It would also possess the human, social, and political resources to make up the ground. However, its motto could not be a repetition of the celebrated Russian slogan about catching up and overtaking America. Its objective would have to be to by-pass America and create a radically different society. Advanced Europe freely forging its socialist future could exercise a tremendous attraction on the rest of the world. The neo-Stalinist system, if it were still the rule in the Soviet bloc, would be its first victim. The United States, the last isolated bastion of capitalism, would in turn be shaken to its foundations. . . .

But let us not dream aloud. We are not there yet, and national-

7. It would then be impossible for nationalist Tories and left-wing Labourites to stand together, as they now seem to do, united against the Common Market, in the confused European debate that divides British parties across curious lines.

ism, apparently stronger than ever, stands triumphantly in the path of possible socialist development.

Nationalism versus socialism: In projecting such a contest one must define the limits of the antagonism. The community of language and culture, of customs and habits, presents no problem in itself. Nor does the struggle for freedom of an oppressed nation. Socialism standing for the elimination of all oppressions and the fulfillment of man can only gain strength from such movements. But nationalism is also something different. Playing on atavistic fears and on the irrational dislike of the strange, the alien, it proclaims the supremacy of the bond uniting the citizens of the same nation. In this it clashes with the class analysis, the international solidarity, and the universal destiny of socialism.

It took workers a long time to grasp that though they were competing to sell their labor, they were united in their struggle against the employer. It took longer still for this class solidarity to cross the borders of craft and region. But the most difficult task has always been the crossing of national frontiers. At none of these three levels is the unity of the working class obvious. It requires a rising degree of political consciousness, and this awareness of class interests must overcome the daily resistance of divisive tactics and ideology. International solidarity has been the most precarious of the three conquests. In the irrationality of nationalism world capitalism still has a powerful weapon at its disposal.

This century was born with great hopes in the international brotherhood of the working man. These were shattered in 1914. The workers were supposed to turn their weapons against their rulers. They used them to butcher each other for four terrible years. But from the blood and ashes hope re-emerged in the form of the first workers' state, heralding a classless society and a new age in which socialism and fraternity would triumph throughout the world. The pull of this ideal, the potential internationalism of the masses, may be gathered from the fact that for decades to come, millions of people all over the globe did strive for it, rising above their narrow interests, making all sorts of sacrifices big and small. But the mood gradually changed. Conscious devotion was replaced by discipline, inspiration by orders. The alleged Russian champions of internationalism put on the uniform of their czarist ancestors, borrowed their nationalist vocabulary and then showed that they, too, could indulge in national oppression. The ambiguity never disappeared, since it is contained in the Soviet system, but the progressive perversion of the original hope has once again led to disenchantment.

The bill international socialism has to pay, and will go on paying, not so much for the shortcomings of the Russian regime as for the identification of the Soviet Union with socialism, is so huge that one can only mention a few of its items. Belief is one. Socialism was supposed to eliminate national and racial discrimination along with economic and social inequality. In vain will it be objected that none of this has been achieved in Russia. Since Russia stands for socialism and nationalism flourishes there, then socialism is helpless against national prejudices. Disillusion breeds despondency and cynicism. The second victim is the international movement itself. After decades of ruthless Soviet dictation it is only too natural for other parties to stress noninterference in each other's affairs. The meaning is obvious. Yet an International cannot be run like the General Assembly of the United Nations. Many years and great changes will be needed before confidence is sufficiently restored to invest the international movement with a new momentum.

The highest price will have to be paid by the Soviet Union and its bloc. The extent to which its alleged Communist elite has been infected with the nationalist bug was shown again recently in the controversy with China. The language used on this occasion by the Russians, in private even more than in public, could not have been improved on by czarist chauvinists or American hawks. Their east European colleagues have also been infected. Here the record is held by the Polish rulers, who have managed to launch a major campaign against the vanishing remnants of a race and to revive official anti-Semitism in a country where there are virtually no Jews left.[8]

Nationalist propaganda brings its own penalties. The sponsoring of Russian nationalism has reinforced similar trends among the other nationalities of the Soviet Union. The expansion of Soviet domination has stimulated counternationalism in eastern Europe. Atavistic forces, far from being uprooted, have been strengthened either directly or through compression. Here again, more than time will be needed to repair the damage, particularly the harm done by the identification of socialism with Russia. To cite but a recent example, a Czech worker would need a good deal of political wisdom not to confuse socialism with the invading tank.

If the damage is likely to be less lasting in the western world, this is due to circumstances rather than to any antidote administered by the official left. The social-democratic parties have long lost any ambition to play a role other than a national one. The Stalinist and neo-Stalinist contortions have not helped. On the official level "labor solidarity" is an empty phrase in Europe. Capitalists can give workers lessons in class consciousness and in the understanding of international issues. The Common Market provides a perfect illustration. Run by officials, it is the Europe of business with a side seat for union leaders. Indeed, the contrast between the need for a labor strategy on the European scale and its utter absence is such that it cannot last. As multinational companies develop and mergers spread, as more and more often centers of decision are to be found beyond national frontiers, for

8. "No society can tolerate excessive participation of a national minority in the elite of power, particularly in the organs of national defense, security, propaganda, and representation abroad. . . ." Jews are the target of this remark, but this is no extract from some anti-Semitic rag. The words were printed in the June 1968 issue of *Miesiecznik Literacki,* and their author, Andrezej Werblan, was then head of the cultural section in the central committee of the Polish Communist party. That party claims Rosa Luxemburg as one of its intellectual ancestors. Rosa the internationalist would not only have been kicked out of it as a "deviationist." She could have been removed in the process of "correction of the irregular ethnic composition in the central institutions . . ."—to quote Werblan once again.

labor to carry on its struggle along purely national lines is literally self-defeating. The younger generation seems to sense this new mood. The labor leaders may have virtue imposed on them by necessity. If in the very near future the union leaders do not work out a strategy on the European scale as a start, they might as well pack up and officially take jobs as the public- and labor-relations officers of international capital. European labor is now condemned to internationalism.

The failure so far of the socialist movement to come to grips with national and racial discrimination raises fundamental questions that can only be touched upon here. The explanation is not the same in the East and in the West. In Russia the problem is yet another aspect of the way in which the regime has tackled its task of "primitive accumulation." In the West the dominant ideology has a great deal to do with it. It is in the West that this inability of the socialist movement to handle national and racial discrimination raises the broader question of its capacity to gain power. For a Marxist, the victory of socialism is to be the combined result of the class contradictions of capitalism and of workers' action spurred on by these contradictions. The socialist movement has a big arsenal, but its ultimate weapon is political consciousness, the masses' awareness of their real interests. This is why when socialism stoops to the established rules of the game, when it panders to prevailing prejudice, it is doomed. Nowhere is this better illustrated than in its handling of national and racial prejudices.

What a labor movement entirely subservient to the bourgeois ideology is capable of doing is shown by the shameful discrimination against blacks in American labor unions. The European official left, however, is hardly in a position to preach, because of its own cowardice rather than its prejudices. Not fighting against anti-Arab feelings among French workers for a start means that they cannot be mobilized fully afterwards against the Algerian war. Sweeping the issue of prejudice against colored immigrants under the carpet so as not to lose by-elections gradually prepares the ground for Powellism. Let sleeping dogs lie and pay when they are awakened.

Wog, wop, yid, frog, nigger, and whitey . . . How deep-seated, or superficial, such ancestral feelings are will not be known until their causes are analyzed and exposed, until they are attacked at the grassroots. Other parties can live with fetishism, prejudices, irrationality, and prosper. A socialist movement cannot if it genuinely intends to reach its goal. It will not recover its capacity for victory until, rising above immediate electoral gains, it summons the courage to remember that "truth is revolutionary."

Meanwhile, our shortsighted squabbles and selfish maneuvers must look shocking to the fighters of the third world. The gap in preoccupations may sometimes hinder the necessary dialogue. Earlier in the book, we referred to Fidel Castro's speech about the invasion of Czechoslovakia, deploring his apparently contemptuous dismissal of the problem of intellectual freedom.[9] The same speech contained some bitter truths: ". . . Those who fight for Communism in any country cannot forget for an instant the rest of the world and the situation of misery, of underdevelopment, of poverty, ignorance, and exploitation of that world, the amount of misery and poverty that has accumulated there. . . ."

There was a lot more in the same vein. The message was addressed to the leaders of the Soviet bloc. Its lesson was equally valid for western socialists. It was a timely reminder that revolution will not be complete until socialism has conquered the globe, that the advanced countries will have to provide not only aid and technicians but also an example. It was a timely reminder of the length of the road ahead, on which the socialist movement occasionally gives the impression of advancing backward.

Real or apparent setbacks seen against the immensity of the task may breed despondency and doubt. True, there are explanations for the setbacks, but man gets tired of explaining defeats. Doubts creep in. What if there were always to be an explanation

9. See p. 314.

for failure? What if capitalism had discovered in the irrational recesses of the human mind a lasting nationalist response to the universalist challenge of socialism? In such moments of despondency the intellectual of the tired generation, which has lived through such "times of contempt," may well be tempted, not to change sides as so many have done, but just to stop explaining and to cultivate his own garden. Yet what is that noise in the distance? What are the young students and workers shouting? Bred on national grandeur, on *Allez France,* in a country where nationalism is so rampant that even the Communist party wraps itself in a tricolor, what jingoist slogans may they well be chanting?

We don't give a damn about frontiers. We are all aliens. We are all German Jews. Ho, Ho, Ho Chi Minh and Che Guevara. National interest is the interest of big business. . . . Who said this was the age of contempt?

Internationalist and egalitarian, spontaneous and libertarian, the May Movement suddenly recalled what socialism once stood for and showed what it could mean again in our times. It accomplished next to nothing, yet holds a promise for the future. It was clearly but a prelude. A prelude to what?

AND IN THE NEXT REVOLUTION, *which is perhaps nearer than it appears* . . .

—KARL MARX *to* FRIEDRICH ENGELS,
September 11, 1867

Age of Conflict
or Age of Revolution?

With its French and Czech crises, 1968 undoubtedly marks a turning point in postwar history. It is important, however, to define the nature of the turning. It is not a turn or twist in the policy of coexistence. Since the Caribbean crisis of 1962 this policy has been shaped by two conflicting trends. One the one hand, in 1962 the United States had clearly gained the initiative. It was intervening all over the world, visibly determined to dictate its terms. The Russians, while keeping control of their bloc, were only responding outside it and even then rather passively. On the other hand, the world refused to stand still. The heroic resistance of the Vietnamese revealed both the limitations of American power and the limits beyond which Russia could not, or not yet, retreat. The invasion of Czechoslovakia did not upset this unstable equilibrium.

Nor did the two crises of 1968 inaugurate an era of inner conflict between the members of the two blocs. This, quite logically, had begun much earlier, in the late 1950's, as soon as the leaders of the two blocs started groping toward a much closer understanding. The Sino-Soviet dispute was a dramatic illustration of the new trend, and Gaullism a less significant example. What the tremors of Paris and Prague announce are new upheavals inside countries belonging to one or another of the blocs. The way in which the Soviet rulers have stifled the Czech experiment puts the revolutionary burden on the Russian people themselves. In the west, France and Italy remain the most likely places for a new explosion. To view these inner threats as more important than the confrontation between blocs or to assume that the center of revolutionary gravity is now shifting away from the third world might be going too far. All conflicts are by now interconnected. It is not exaggerated, however, to suggest that it might be Europe's turn to go through a period when history moves at a faster pace.

Russia's role in the present phase of coexistence is complicated and ambiguous. In Manichean terms it plays Satan to the American God, or vice versa. But it is also an indispensable element of the system. Soviet nuclear weapons balance, at least in principle, the power of the United States. Russian arms are to be found in the hands of Cuban and Vietnamese soldiers. Russia can thus be described as the protector of revolution. Yet it is also the joint upholder of the status quo, barely concealing its distaste for revolutionary upheavals, particularly from below. To complete the picture, the Soviet Union is also a useful bogey for western use because of some of its most repulsive features and acts. This duality and ambiguity of the Russian posture complicates the analysis of international alignments.

The struggle against imperialism, against the United States, the mighty capitalist Metternich defending everywhere the old order against the new, remains naturally inseparable from the struggle for socialism. But the link between the two is not always apparent, not even to the participants. The unity between the Vietnamese fighter in the jungle, the Cuban keeping guard along the coast, the Latin American guerrilla, is obvious. Less obvious, though no less real, is their unity with Czech students and trade unionists searching for a socialist democracy, with Jacek Kuron and Karol Modzelewski [1] sitting in a Polish jail because of their belief in socialism, with nameless young Russian workers dreaming up new soviets for their land. It is into this dispersed yet common struggle that some of the American protesters have been drawn. It is into this struggle that Europe's young workers and students have now entered with a bang. From spectators they have been turned into actors; from distant supporters they might yet grow into crucial pioneers.

At the end, as at the opening, of this book, this bold prediction must be qualified in order to avoid illusions. Even the place where Europe's next revolutionary confrontation may occur cannot be foretold with any degree of certainty. Revolutionary battles cannot be pinpointed as in *kriegspiel*. Che Guevara died heroically in Bolivia, yet the next serious Latin American upheaval may take place in, say, Mexico or Venezuela. Similarly, one can only say that France and Italy appear at the moment the most likely European contenders. Both countries are in the throes of a deep social transformation, old conflicts merging with the new; in both, militant workers can rely on the support of students and a growing radical intelligentsia; in both, there is a belief in the historic role of the working class. But if they do not seize their revolu-

1. Two young intellectuals sentenced to three years in jail back in 1965 because they had dared to circulate a critical open letter to party members. No sooner had they been released than they were rearrested in the spring of 1968 as the alleged inspirers of the Warsaw student demonstration in March of that year.

tionary opportunity in the next few years, the two countries may well be overtaken later. Who knows when and how Germany will emerge from its postwar conformity to the American pattern, or Britain awaken from its postimperial slumber? As things stand, the odds are only against the United States taking the revolutionary lead that, because of its technological superiority, would have greatly simplified matters. But, then, in historic practice a new social order does not take over from the economically most advanced representative of the old.

There is uncertainty about the place of the next confrontation and even more about its outcome. The young students and workers have revealed the unsuspected depth of their pent-up discontent. Neither they nor anybody else so far has provided the vision, the strategy, the instruments, to channel this discontent toward a successful revolutionary conclusion. The conflict that has begun is in this sense spontaneous. Liberals waste their time urging protesters to keep quiet for fear of the backlash. Protest and backlash are themselves symptoms of something deeper. They are signs of the sickness concealed by the commercial glitter of capitalist society; of mass yearning for a different life; of a clash between the productive forces, driven by the progress of science, that could usher in a different life, and the social relations, the political system, the institutions, that stand in the way.

If the young revolutionaries cannot promise success, what do they offer? A glimpse of the future, the resurrected belief in radical change, the end of what we have called marginalism by analogy with the economic doctrine that studies changes "at the margin," taking the socio-economic framework as given. Economics was not the only field in which the basic foundations were thus unquestioned. Property relations and the distribution of wealth as well as the institutions, the political rules of the game, the assumptions of the ruling ideology, were also taken for granted. Marginal minds had to seek marginal solutions. Anything more drastic was Utopian, out of this world. The discontented had their choice of escapism, from pot to religion. The radical transformation of society was practically ruled out.

This is the state of mind that recent events have disturbed. Breaking the rules of the game, the young revolutionaries have shaken the confidence in the permanence of existing structures and suggested that the modern state might not be as impregnable as it looks. They have put new life into such old notions as the power of the workers, class conflict, political commitment. If one may elaborate on the celebrated May slogan, they have told the people to be realistic enough to ask for the *apparently* impossible. If the old system cannot provide the life for which men are yearning, there is something wrong with it. Bring it down and put a new one in its place.

In some intellectual circles in Paris there is a tendency to reduce vast social movements to quarrels between schools of thought. The revival of commitment was hailed as the revenge of existentialism, influential after the last war, over structuralism, which has gained ground since. Such a conclusion is in fact unwarranted. The May Movement did not prove that man can rise above social structures and jump over historical periods, that Hottentots can leap straight into socialist freedom. The advanced western countries, it was argued earlier, are more than ripe for a transition to socialism. If the current crisis shows anything in this respect, it is the conservatism of the human mind, the time lag between the sweeping technological, and hence social, changes of the last thirty years and the beginning of their political expression.

Neither the earthly embodiment of the free will nor a robot; conditioned by social structures, yet not their helpless prisoner, man has always struggled with his environment. In reviving such concepts as class struggle, the intervention of the masses in the historical process, and revolution from below, the young students and workers of France have given a new impetus to man's unending, if sometimes slow and subterranean, struggle for mastery over his fate. And this was enough to frighten rulers from Paris to Moscow, from Warsaw to Washington. The ghost is walking abroad again.

If there is an intellectual victim of the current crisis, it is the fatalistic interpretation of history, the belief that what is must be so and that if it is to be swept away, the upheaval will come on its own. Man counts, the Vietnamese reminded the world, even in the nuclear age. This is why, once the description and analysis is over, there can be no clear answer to the question running through this book—whether the age of conflict, which has already begun, will see the victory of authoritarian rule or the triumph of revolution. The future will be what you will make it. What we shall make it.

Don't run, young comrades. Don't climb onto exposed barricades just to be shot at. Watch your step, because the ground is full of pitfalls. For you, workers in industry, some traps will be dressed up as "truly revolutionary." For you, students, technicians, intellectual workers, not all the traps will be so obvious as "participation." Watch out and learn. But go on advancing together, in a fighting formation, because your generation can take us on the road to socialism and freedom. And the alternative is still a relapse into barbarism, with or without nuclear doom.

THE SUN WAS SHINING *over Montparnasse as, red flags flying, the demonstration got on the move. There were some thirty thousand marchers, most of them young, the students outnumbering the workers. They were chanting together in a fearless mood. Amid the slogans old and new, one was again predominant, the slogan forever associated with the French May Movement, the jerky, confident, infectious "Ce n'est . . . qu'un début. . . . Continuons le . . . combat."*

'Tis but a beginning. A skeptic, listening in, was entitled to doubt. It was June 1, 1968. The shaken Gaullists had regained their poise. General de Gaulle, "the royal captain of this ruin'd band," had just recovered his voice and authority to proclaim that he was soldiering on. Georges Séguy, the Communist leader of the biggest trade union, had just called on his troops to make an orderly retreat. The police, their confidence restored, were not going to put up with any more mass demonstrations. It

looked like the turn of the tide, the beginning of the end.

And yet the young students and workers were in the right mood. This was no funeral procession. They had not come to mourn the past. They could proudly look toward the future. Beaten, betrayed, yet undefeated, they had just shown Europe the way. They had brought hope again, prefacing a new chapter in revolutionary history.

Abbreviations

AFP	Agence France-Presse (French News Agency)
CAL	Comités d'Action Lycéens (School Action Committees)
CAP	Certificat d'Aptitude Professionelle (Certificate of Professional Aptitude)
CEA	Commissariat à l'Énergie Atomique (Atomic Energy Commissariat)

411

CFDT   Confédération Française Démocratique du Travail
        (French Democratic Workers Confederation)

CFTC   Confédération Française des Travailleurs Chrétiens
        (French Confederation of Christian Workers)

CGC   Confédération Générale des Cadres
        (General Confederation of Scientific, Technical,
        and Managerial Workers)

CGT   Confédération Générale du Travail
        (General Confederation of Labor)

CNJA   Centre National des Jeunes Agriculteurs
        (National Center of Young Farmers)

CNPF   Conseil National du Patronat Français
        (National Council of French Employers)

CNRS   Centre National de la Recherche Scientifique
        (National Scientific Research Center)

CRS   Compagnies Républicaines de Sécurité
        (National Security Guards)

CVB   Comités Vietnam de Base
        (Basic Committees on Vietnam)

CVN   Comité Vietnam National
        (National Committee on Vietnam)

EEC   European Economic Community

ESU   Étudiants Socialistes Unifiés
        (Unified Socialist Students)

FEN   Fédération de l'Éducation Nationale
        (Federation of National Education)

FER   Fédération des Étudiants Révolutionnaires
        (Federation of Revolutionary Students)

FGDS   Fédération de la Gauche Démocrate et Socialiste
        (Federation of the Democratic and Socialist Left)

Abbreviations

FLN	Front de Libération Nationale (National Liberation Front)
FO	Force Ouvrière (Workers' Force)
IUT	Institut Universitaire de Technologie (University Technology Institute)
JCR	Jeunesse Communiste Révolutionnaire (Revolutionary Communist Youth)
MAU	Mouvement d'Action Universitaire (University Action Movement)
OAS	Organisation de l'Armée Secrète (Secret Army Organization)
ORTF	Office de Radiodiffusion-Télévision Française (French Radio and Television Broadcasting Office)
PCF	Parti Communiste Français (French Communist Party)
PCI	Partito Comunista Italiano (Italian Communist Party)
PSU	Parti Socialiste Unifié (Unified Socialist Party)
RPF	Rassemblement du Peuple Français (Rally of the French People)
SDS	Sozialistischer Deutscher Studentenbund (Socialist German Student Federation)
SFIO	Section Française de l'Internationale Ouvrière (French Section of the International Workers' Association)
SNCS	Syndicat National des Chercheurs Scientifiques (National Union of Scientific Researchers)
SNES	Syndicat National de l'Enseignement Secondaire (National Union of Secondary Education)

SNESup	Syndicat National de l'Enseignement Supérieur (National Union of Higher Education)
SNI	Syndicat National des Instituteurs (National Union of Elementary School Teachers)
SPD	Sozialdemokratische Partei Deutschlands (Social-Democratic Party of Germany)
UEC	Union des Étudiants Communistes (Union of Communist Students)
UJCML	Union des Jeunesses Communistes Marxistes-Léninistes (Union of Marxist-Leninist Communist Youth)
UNEF	Union Nationale des Étudiants de France (National Union of French Students)

INDEX